GODLY FEAR
The Epistle to Hebrews and Greco-Roman Critiques of Superstition

Patrick Gray

Society of Biblical Literature
Atlanta

GODLY FEAR

Copyright © 2003 by the Society of Biblical Literature

Library of Congress Cataloging-in-Publication Data

Gray, Patrick, 1970-
  Godly fear : the Epistle to the Hebrews and Greco-Roman critiques of superstition / by Patrick Gray.
      p. cm. — (Academia Biblica ; no. 16)
  Includes bibliographical references and index.
  ISBN 1-58983-100-4 (alk. paper)
  1. Bible. N.T. Hebrews—Criticism, interpretation, etc. 2. Superstition. 3. Fear. 4. Philosophy, Ancient. I. Society of Biblical Literature. II. Title. III. Series: Academia Biblica (Series) (Society of Biblical Literature) ; no. 16.
  BS2775.52 .G72 2003b
  227'.8706—dc22
                                        2003014812

07 06 05 04   5 4 3 2 1

Printed in the United States of America
on acid-free paper

GODLY FEAR

Society of Biblical Literature

Academia Biblica

Saul M. Olyan,
Old Testament Editor

Mark Allan Powell,
New Testament Editor

Number 16

GODLY FEAR
The Epistle to Hebrews and
Greco-Roman Critiques of Superstition

Table of Contents

Acknowledgements   ix

Note on Texts and Translations   x

Chapter One

Introduction   1

The Question: "Superstition" or "Godly Fear"?   1

Self-Definition in the Early Church: Christianity as Superstition   6

Plutarch and the Epistle to the Hebrews: A Common Milieu   12

New Testament Studies and the History-of-Religions School   16

Contextualization, Comparison, and "Parallelomania"   16

Plutarch and the New Testament   21

The Greco-Roman Background of Hebrews: The State of
the Question   24

Approach   30

Chapter Two

Plutarch and Superstition   33

Introduction   33

Terminology   36

Latin   36

Greek   42

Plutarch on Superstition in the *Moralia* and the *Lives*: Typical
or Atypical?   52

The Role of Fear in Plutarch's Religious Thought   54

Hellenistic Analyses of the Emotions   55

Platonic Antecedents   57

Aristotle   60

Stoicism   65

Epicureanism   75

Summary   82

Plutarch on Superstition as Inappropriate Fear   84

The Question of Authenticity   84

Plutarch's Argument: Summary and Analysis   88

Superstition and the Emotions   89

Positive and Negative Fear	93
Fear of Death	95
Atheism and Superstition Compared: Theological and Practical Aspects	98
Piety as a Mean	104
Conclusion	106

Chapter Three
Freedom from Fear as a Christian Ideal in Hebrews — **109**
Introduction — 109
Fear of Death (Heb 2:15) — 111
  Sources of Fear of Death — 112
  Subjective Quality of Fear of Death — 114
  Scope: Whom Does Fear of Death Affect? — 115
  Assessment: Is Fear of Death Morally Culpable? — 118
  Prescription: How to Be Free From Fear of Death — 123
    "Help in Time of Need": Jesus the Great High Priest — 123
    Priesthood as Fraternity: Brotherly Love and "The Order of Melchizedek" — 125
"Confidence" before God: ΠΑΡΡΗΣΙΑ in Hebrews — 138
  Confidence as Members of God's Household (Heb 3:6) — 139
  Confidence Before the Throne of Grace (Heb 4:16) — 143
  Confidence in the Heavenly Sanctuary (Heb 10:19–31) — 145
    The Clean Conscience (Heb 10:19–25) — 145
    Apostasy and the Forfeiture of Confidence (Heb 10:26–31) — 148
  The Reward of Confidence (Heb 10:35) — 154
Fearlessness in the Face of Earthly Dangers — 155
  Withstanding Persecution — 156
    Heb 10:32–39 — 156
    Heb 11:32–38 — 161
    Heb 13:6 — 163
  Defiance of Human Authorities: Moses' Fearlessness (Heb 11:23–28) — 166
  Reinterpreting Adversity as God's Education (Heb 12:5–11) — 167
Conclusion — 185

Chapter Four
Reverence and Awe: Fear as an Appropriate Response to God in Hebrews — **187**
Introduction — 187
Jesus' "Godly Fear" (Heb 5:7) — 188
  What Does Jesus Pray For and How Is He "Heard"? — 189
  The Exemplary Function of Jesus' Submission — 198

Fear as a Concomitant of Revelation and Worship (Heb 12:18–29)   206
   Moses' "Fear and Trembling" at Sinai (Heb 12:21)   206
   Worship in the Last Days: "Reverence and Awe" (Heb 12:28–29)   209
Conclusion   214

Chapter Five
Conclusions   **215**

Bibliography   229
Index of Modern Authors   253
Index of Ancient Authors   258
Index of Biblical Texts   261

Acknowledgements

A number of people deserve recognition for the assistance they have provided in the course of completing this dissertation. Alice Hickcox of the Woodruff Library at Emory University taught me how to use the TLG database. Dale B. Martin of Yale University and Robert Hodgson, Jr., of the American Bible Society each allowed me to consult their unpublished manuscripts dealing with superstition in antiquity. As members of my dissertation committee, Cynthia B. Patterson of the Department of History, Walter T. Wilson, and Gail R. O'Day have all made critical contributions at various points and in sundry ways. Most of all, I want to thank my advisor Carl R. Holladay, who provided invaluable advice and encouragement at every step. It has been a privilege to study with these scholars as well as the other members of the New Testament faculty in the Graduate Division of Religion—Robert Kysar, Michael J. Brown, Vernon K. Robbins, and especially Luke T. Johnson.

I also want to thank Leigh Andersen of the Society of Biblical Literature and Mark Allan Powell of Trinity Lutheran Seminary for their help in preparing the manuscript for publication in the Academia Biblica series.

Most deserving of my gratitude are my parents and my wife Alex, without whose love and support I would not have completed this project.

Note on Texts and Translations

Unless otherwise noted, translations of biblical texts are my own. Quotations of classical texts are taken from the Loeb edition. Where an author is not included in the Loeb Classical Library, the text consulted is the standard edition listed in the *Thesaurus Linguae Graecae: Canon of Greek Authors and Works* (ed. L. Berkowitz and K. Squitier; 3rd ed.; New York: Oxford University Press, 1990). All abbreviations follow the list in *The SBL Handbook of Style* (Peabody, Mass.: Hendrickson, 1999).

Chapter One

Introduction

The Question: "Superstition" or "Godly Fear"?

When Plutarch concludes his essay on δεισιδαιμονία (*De superstitione* [*Moralia* 164E–171F]) by stating that "true religion" (εὐσέβεια) lies between superstition and "rough and hardened atheism," he voices a sentiment to which most readers in most times and places would give ready assent.[1] Even David Hume, though no friend of traditional theism in any form, nonetheless refers to

---

[1] Cicero: "The destruction of superstition does not mean the destruction of religion" (*De divinatione* 2.72.148). Francis Bacon, who quotes Plutarch, decries superstition but warns against discarding true religion along with it: "There is a superstition in avoiding superstition" ("Of Superstition," in *The Essays, Or Counsels Civil and Moral* [ed. B. Vickers; Oxford: Oxford University Press, 1999], 40). Later in the seventeenth century, see also Spinoza: "How blest would our age be if it could witness a religion freed also from all the trammels of superstition!" (*A Theologico-Political Treatise* [trans. R. Elwes; New York: Dover, 1951], 164); and the Cambridge Platonist Henry More, who bemoans the human tendency to go "out of one dark prison into another, out of superstition into Atheism itself" (*An Antidote Against Atheism* (3rd ed.; London: James Flesher, 1662), §1.1.1.1; in the eighteenth century, Edmund Burke: "Religion, and not atheism, is the true remedy for superstition" (*Report of Speech of Edmund Burke, Esq., on moving His Resolutions for Conciliation with the Colonies, March 22, 1775* [London: Dodsley, 1775], 67); Swami Vivekananda, at the 1893 Parliament of Religions in Chicago: "Every system, therefore, which . . . makes one superstitious, makes one mope, makes one desire all sorts of wild impossibilities, mysteries, and superstitions, I do not like, because its effect is dangerous" ("The Freedom of the Soul," in *The Complete Works of Swami Vivekananda* [ed. S. Swananda; 8 vols.; Calcutta: Advaita Ashram, 1989], 2:201); and Ren Jiyu, of the Academy of Social Science of the People's Republic of China, who says that while "some people mistakenly believe that feudal superstition and normal religious activity are the same thing, . . . to wipe out superstition ought not to unduly affect religious freedom" ("Religion and Superstition," *Ching Feng* 26 [1983]: 159).

superstition as a corruption of true religion.[2] Similar views of the relationship of "religion" and "superstition" are so common across cultures because neither term is content-specific. The term "superstition" and its equivalents are connotative rather than denotative. In modern languages, it is almost always used in a pejorative sense. One man's religion is another man's superstition. As Voltaire notes, "It is therefore plain that what is fundamental to one sect's religion passes for superstition with another sect."[3] Almost no one claims to be superstitious, and the English term never appears as a term of self-designation for a given religious group. It possesses relative instead of absolute meaning because it is always defined in terms of deviation from the norms of some dominant culture. Consequently, most people in most times and places have a quick, intuitive grasp of what a speaker means when he or she refers to a superstition. As a judge once said when discussing the legal definition of hard-core pornography, "I know it when I see it."[4] Because of the nature of the concept, anything stigmatized as a superstition is, in effect, a superstition, however much the particulars may change from one context to another.[5]

---

[2] D. Hume, "Of Superstition and Enthusiasm," in *Writings on Religion* (ed. A. Flew; La Salle, Ill.: Open Court, 1992), 3–9.

[3] *Philosophical Dictionary* (2 vols.; trans. P. Gay; New York: Basic, 1962), 2:476. The statements of Lactantius (*Div. Inst.* 4.28.11) that "religion is the worship of the true, superstition is that of the false," and of John Calvin (*Institutes* 1.12.1) that superstition differs from true religion on the same grounds also illustrate the inherent subjectivity of the concept. Absent any elaboration, proponents of diametrically opposed perspectives could nonetheless agree in principle with this dual definition. On the use of the concept in inter-religious polemic, see the discussion of Burkhard Gladigow, "Aberglaube," *Handbuch religionswissenschaftlicher Grundbegriffe* 1:387–88.

[4] Cf. Supreme Court Justice Potter Stewart's concurring opinion in *Jacobellis v. Ohio* (378 U.S. 184).

[5] Its essence is captured in the title of Michael Shermer's recent book about superstition: *Why People Believe Weird Things* (New York: W. H. Freeman, 1997). Shermer, like many other writers, has faith that the spread of a scientific world view and universal access to education will eradicate superstition by cultivating the capacity "to discern the character of evidence." This phrase is Alice Gardner's, in her 1922 entry on superstition in the *Encyclopedia of Religion and Ethics* (12:121). Her readers are assured that, if great intellects in the past have sometimes exhibited superstitious tendencies, "these exceptions would seem due to a want of mental balance." This is typical of the post-Enlightenment shift in the sense of superstition from "bad religion" to "bad science" (Mary R. O'Neil, "Superstition," *ER* 14:165–66). Much social scientific research, however, has shown that there is almost no statistically significant data demonstrating a hard correlation between the presence of superstitious beliefs and lower educational, social, or economic status (F. Askevis-Leherpeux, "Les corrélats de la superstition," *ASSR* 45 [1978]: 165–76). On the difficulty of defining superstition and an acknowledgement of the inevitable arbitrariness of all such definitions, see Gustave Jahoda, *The Psychology of Superstition* (London:

To say that the concept of superstition is not content-specific is not to say that it has no content in the eyes of the one using the term. Specific behaviors and attitudes provide the occasion for Plutarch's comments. For Plutarch, the quintessential element of δεισιδαιμονία is fear.[6] Believing the gods to be wrathful rather than beneficent, the superstitious man is gripped by a paralyzing fear contrary to reason: "Of all kinds of fear the most impotent and helpless is superstitious fear" (*Superst.* 165D). Invoking God's fearsomeness has a long history in Christian tradition, though the intent—as in Jonathan Edwards's 1741 sermon, "Sinners in the Hands of an Angry God"—is typically not to foster feelings of impotence. Usually the intended effect is just the opposite, to encourage or discourage certain kinds of behaviors that are under the audience's control. Kierkegaard has a different view of the role of fear for the Christian. He describes fear of punishment as one of the barriers to "willing one thing."[7] A person who only wills the Good out of fear of punishment is double-minded and therefore does not truly know God, the One. Some things are certainly to be feared—namely, doing wrong—but when punishment aims to assist the

---

Allen Lane; Baltimore: Penguin, 1969), 1–10; and Peter Jarvis, "Towards a Sociological Understanding of Superstition," *Social Compass* 27 (1980): 285–88.

[6] As it also is for Bertrand Russell: "Fear is the main source of superstition" ("An Outline of Intellectual Rubbish," in *Unpopular Essays* [New York: Simon and Schuster, 1950], 106); Spinoza: "Superstition, then, is engendered, preserved, and fostered by fear" (*A Theologico-Political Treatise*, 4); and the apostate French priest, Jean Meslier, whose fuming diatribe against *Superstition in All Ages* (New York: Arno, 1972) was published posthumously by Voltaire: "Ignorance and fear are the two pivots of all religion" (51). Note that Meslier sees no distinction between religion and "the most sombre and servile superstition" (92–93). Ludwig Wittgenstein, in contrast, sees the two as quite distinct: "One of them results from fear and is a sort of false science. The other is a trusting" (*Culture and Value* [trans. P. Winch; London: Blackwell, 1976], 72). From a sixteenth-century Anglican perspective, Richard Hooker states that fear, "if it [has] not the light of true understanding concerning God, wherewith to be moderated, breedeth superstition" (*The Works of that Learned and Judicious Divine Mr. Richard Hooker, containing Eight Books of the laws of Ecclesiastical Polity* [3 vols.; Oxford: Clarendon, 1807], §5.3.2); and in the following century, Jeremy Taylor: "A great fear, when it is ill-managed, is the parent of superstition; but a discreet and well-guided fear produces religion (*The Rule and Exercises of Holy Living* [29th ed.; London: Longmans, 1815], 317). In his discussion of belief in demons, Geraardus van der Leeuw sees fear and superstition as closely related but nonetheless distinct. What they have in common is incongruity with rationality: "Neither fear nor superstition, however, is ever the outcome of reflection" (*Religion in Essence and Manifestation: A Study in Phenomenology* [trans. J. E. Turner; 2 vols.; New York: Harper & Row, 1963], 1:134).

[7] S. Kierkegaard, *Purity of Heart Is to Will One Thing* (trans. D. V. Steere; New York: Harper & Row, 1956), 79–98. Like Plutarch, Kierkegaard cites unbelief and superstition as two possible misguided reactions to fear (83).

individual in willing the Good, it is to be welcomed and not feared.[8] John Newton, in the second verse of his well-known hymn "Amazing Grace," has a similar notion of the instrumental yet ancillary role which fear may temporarily play in the divine plan: "'Twas grace that taught my heart to fear, and grace my fears relieved." For Agobard, ninth-century archbishop of Lyons, fear and hope were essential Christian qualities, the one as a check on presumption and the other as a safeguard against despair.[9]

The topic of fear and the hortatory strategy of invoking God's fearfulness have roots in the NT, notably in the Epistle to the Hebrews. According to the author, God is "a consuming fire" who must be approached "with reverence and godly fear" (12:28–29). He[10] reminds his readers that their god is a vengeful god who will punish apostates (10:29–30). The day of judgment is a source of hope for the faithful but a "fearful prospect" for those who fall away (10:27). Thus "it is a fearful thing to fall into the hands of the living God" (10:31). Twice the author alludes to Numbers 14:21–23 (Heb 3:11; 4:3) and emphasizes God's wrath. So that the audience does not miss the point, he spells out the consequences in 4:1. "Therefore, while the promise of entering his rest remains," he writes, "let us fear lest any of you be judged to have failed to reach it." No one can hide from God; everything is "open and laid bare to the eyes of

---

[8] Cf. the Bampton Lectures delivered by Kierkegaard's contemporary, Joseph E. Riddle (*The Natural History of Infidelity and Superstition in Contrast with Christian Faith* [London: Parker, 1852], 166–70). Faith results in a conscience aroused to be delivered from sin, while superstition is characterized by a "disordered conscience and a perverted moral sense" that is traceable to a "spirit of bondage and guilty fear" (170).

[9] See his brief treatise *De Spe et Timore* (PL 104:323–26). The relationship between hope and fear described by Agobard is in many respects close to that described by Rudolf Bultmann (*Theology of the New Testament* [trans. K. Grobel; 2 vols.; New York: Scribner's, 1951–55], 1:320–22). Much of Agobard's literary energy was devoted to combating the superstitions of his day, but unlike Plutarch, fear is not for him the defining aspect of *superstitio*. Agobard's treatise *Contra eorum superstitionem qui picturis et imaginibus sanctorum adorationis obsequium deferendum putant* (PL 104:199–228), written near the end of the Iconoclastic controversy, deals mainly with undue veneration for images. His younger Byzantine contemporary George the Monk, in the course of attacking iconoclasm, also employs the category of δεισιδαιμονία in his *Chronicon Syntomon* (PG 110:101, 668, 1025).

[10] With apologies to those who have proposed the Virgin Mary (J. M. Ford, "The Mother of Jesus and the Authorship of the Epistle to the Hebrews," *The University of Dayton Review* 11 [1975]: 267–81) or Priscilla (A. v. Harnack, "Probabilia über die Adresse und den Verfasser des Hebräerbriefes," *ZNW* 1 [1900]: 16–41) as the author, masculine pronouns will be used here when referring to the author. The use of the masculine singular participle διηγούμενον in 11:32—one of the few personal references made by the author in the epistle—creates difficulties for theories positing female authorship, especially in the absence of more substantive grounds for doing so (cf. H. W. Attridge, *The Epistle to the Hebrews* [Hermeneia; Philadelphia: Fortress, 1989], 347).

the one with whom we have to do" (4:13). Jesus' own prayers, according to 5:7, are answered only on account of his "godly fear" (εὐλάβεια).

If fear is the hallmark of δεισιδαιμονία, one might reasonably conjecture that Plutarch would count the author of Hebrews among the superstitious. Being a Christian, according to Hebrews, means believing in a certain kind of deity who acts in certain ways and has peculiar qualities of character. Foremost among these qualities is objective existence: "For whoever would draw near to God must believe that he exists and that he rewards those who seek him" (11:6). Hebrews, then, would appear to disagree with Plutarch's proposition that—everything else being equal—atheism is preferable to superstition.[11] On the other hand, Hebrews' efforts at reinterpreting various aspects of the Israelite cult in chapters 8–10 recall Plutarch's critique of δεισιδαιμονία on the grounds that it encourages excessive and absurd ritualism. Also in line with Plutarch is the characterization of Jesus' death in 2:14–16, where it is said to effect liberation from life-long fear of death inspired by the devil. The resulting situation for the readers is compared favorably with that of Moses, who is terrified by what he sees at Sinai and says, "I tremble with fear" (12:18–24). At another point, when the author recounts the circumstances surrounding Moses' birth and subsequent flight from Egypt to Midian (11:23–28) he refers to his parents' and his own fearlessness—a detail missing from the biblical account of the former (Exod 2:1–4) and directly contradicting the account of the latter (Exod 2:11–15). The intended result of the moral instruction listed in 13:1–5 is that the audience may say with confidence (quoting LXX Ps 117:6), "The Lord is my helper; I will not be afraid" (13:6). Finally Plutarch is generally positive toward the religious attitude indicated by the term εὐλάβεια, which is predicated of Jesus in Heb 5:7 and of proper Christian worship in 12:28, thus it is not perfectly clear that the two authors are so very far apart at every point.[12]

With its seemingly mixed messages as to the propriety of fear, does Hebrews, when it describes the appropriate human disposition towards God, represent a species of the religious genus that Plutarch labels δεισιδαιμονία? Did members of the church think of themselves as having converted to a

---

[11] Nor does the most recent edition of the *Catechism of the Catholic Church* (The Vatican: Libreria Editrice Vaticana, 1994), which lists both as violations of the first commandment (§§2110–11; cf. §2138). Superstition represents "a perverse excess of religion" and is defined as "the deviation of religious feeling and of the practices this feeling imposes." For the general equation of superstition and idolatry in the patristic period, see Clement of Alexandria, *Protr.* 4.52.1; *Strom.* 7.1.4.3.

[12] *Is. Os.* 354D, 382E; *Def. orac.* 420F, 432F; *Sera* 549E, 551C; *Gen. Socr.* 586F. According to P. J. Koets (*Δεισιδαιμονία: A Contribution to the Knowledge of the Religious Terminology in Greek* [Purmerend: Muusses, 1929], 68–69), εὐλάβεια and εὐσέβεια are practically synonymous and are listed as the positive alternative to δεισιδαιμονία for Plutarch.

superstitious cult? To appreciate how Christians came to understand who they were and what they had become in entering the new faith, one must first appreciate how others—outsiders—understood who Christians were. Because superstition was such a pervasive category for describing debased religion in general and Christianity in particular, one must grasp what this label connoted for those who used it. Because different observers may emphasize different aspects of the pattern of religion denoted by the term "superstition" (δεισιδαιμονία in Greek, *superstitio* in Latin), it is necessary not only to sketch the broadly held views and assumptions about superstition in Mediterranean antiquity, but also to concentrate narrowly on particular instantiations of this common critique. Furthermore, it is necessary to focus on specific, historically attested manifestations of Christianity if one is to avoid the high level of abstraction characteristic of many comparative studies attempting to situate the NT in its Hellenistic context. Accordingly, this dissertation isolates one fundamental component of one substantial critique of superstition, on the assumption that it will shed significant light on a contemporaneous articulation of Christian faith. Fear is the defining element of superstition according to Plutarch, whose essay on the topic is the most detailed treatment surviving from antiquity. Fear is likewise a recurring motif in the Epistle to the Hebrews, whose author holds up confidence as a Christian ideal yet also on occasion employs language which evokes fear in the starkest of terms. The question posed here is this: to what extent and on what basis would the form of Christianity found in Hebrews qualify as a superstition in the eyes of an outsider like Plutarch? This question suggests the following thesis: The articulation of Christian faith in Hebrews may be understood in the context of debates about appropriate and inappropriate fear such as that seen in Plutarch's essay on superstition. Insofar as the author has an apologetic interest in addressing the perception that Christianity is a superstition, he works from the inside out, that is to say, by considering the biblical testimony about the human condition vis-à-vis God, making sense of it all in light of God's new revelation, and then drawing conclusions about the propriety of fear that intersect at key points with analogous concerns commanding the attention of contemporaneous Hellenistic students of philosophy and religion.

Self-Definition in the Early Church: Christianity as Superstition

The delimitation to superstition as a point of entry should first be justified. Superstition is of explicit interest to Plutarch, but δεισιδαιμονία does not occur in Hebrews and it occurs only once in the NT (Acts 25:19, and the cognate form δεισιδαίμων once [Acts 17:22]). Later Christian apologists turn Plutarch's critiques of superstition against contemporary paganism, and it is not at all inconceivable that the earliest Christians also would have had their own ideas of what constituted δεισιδαιμονία.[13] The lingering desire to combat superstition in the following centuries demonstrates how deeply entrenched this category was in the ancient Mediterranean. Eusebius, for example, describes the spread of the gospel as a liberation from idolatrous superstition and depicts the newly converted Constantine delivering sermons debunking the superstitions of his pagan subjects.[14] Increasingly, anything at odds with orthodox Christian religion is deemed superstitious.[15]

The significance of superstition for understanding the early church resides primarily in the fact that it is under this heading that the earliest pagan references to Christianity appear. Tacitus, describing the events surrounding the fire at Rome during Nero's reign, speaks of Christianity as a "pernicious superstition" (exitiabilis superstitio) breaking out after being temporarily checked by the death of Jesus.[16] Recounting Nero's punishment of the Christians, whom the emperor blamed for the fire, Suetonius calls them "a class of men given over to a new and mischievous superstition" (superstitio novae ac maleficae).[17] Also Pliny the Younger, in a letter to Trajan, describes the Christians of Bithynia as adherents of "a degenerate sort of cult carried to extravagant lengths" (superstitionem pravam et immodicam).[18] Christians would

---

[13] Cf. Justin, 1 Apol. 2.5; Origen, Cels. 7.69; Tertullian, Pall. 4.10; Nat. 2.8.8. Augustine quotes from Seneca's lost work on superstition (Civ. 6.10–11). He goes beyond Seneca when he acknowledges the existence of demons and describes superstition as worship illegitimately offered to them (Ep. 102.16; cf. Doctr. chr. 2.20–23).

[14] Eusebius, Hist. eccl. 2.3 (cf. Clement of Alexandria, Protr. 10); Vit. Const. 4.29. He also describes Abraham, the forerunner of future Christians, as forsaking superstition when called by God (Hist. eccl. 1.4).

[15] Eusebius, Dem. ev. 1.2.14; 1.5.4. The meaning and evolution of superstitio and δεισιδαιμονία are examined by Koets, Δεισιδαιμονία; S. Calderone, "Superstitio," ANRW 1.2:377–96; D. Grodzynski, "Superstitio," REA 76 (1974): 36–60; L. Janssen, "Die Bedeutungsentwicklung von superstitio/superstes," Mnemosyne 28 (1975): 135–89; and M. Smith, "Superstitio," SBL Seminar Papers, 1981 (SBLSP 20; Chico, Calif.: Scholars Press, 1981), 349–55.

[16] Tacitus, Ann. 15.44.

[17] Suetonius, Nero 16.2. Cf. J. Beaujue, "L'incendie de Rome en 64 et les Chrétiens," Latomus 19 (1960): 65–80, 291–311.

[18] Pliny, Ep. 10.96. Tacitus knew Pliny and may have had access to his letters (Harald Fuchs, "Tacitus über die Christen," VC 4 [1950]: 72). At least five of Plutarch's friends mentioned in his writings—Fundanus, Philopappus, Sosius Senecio, Avidius Nigrinus, and Quietus—were also friends of Pliny (C. P. Jones, Plutarch and Rome [Oxford: Clarendon, 1971], 51–59). According to later traditions, Trajan, the recipient of Pliny's letter about the Christians, was also acquainted with Plutarch. The dedication of the spurious work Regum et imperatorum apophthegmata consists of a letter purporting to be from Plutarch to the emperor (Cf. R. H. Barrow, Plutarch and His Times [Bloomington and London: Indiana University Press, 1967], 43–49; Jones, Plutarch and Rome, 29–34).

naturally take exception to such characterizations of their faith, so it is clear that, with respect to the particulars, they would not define δεισιδαιμονία or *superstitio* in the same terms as would their pagan neighbors. There is no guarantee, furthermore, that all of their pagan neighbors would have shared precisely the same notion of superstition or the belief that Christianity was in fact a superstition. Accordingly, not all pagans had the same reaction to the gospel when it was preached to them. Many scoffed, some suspended judgment, and a few became believers (Acts 17:32–34). Because local conditions were a crucial variable, each case must be adjudicated on an individual basis to determine the degree of correspondence between rhetoric and reality. Is it simply upper-class Roman bias or popular suspicion of the new and the foreign that explains the common opinion that Christianity is a superstition? It is necessary to focus upon particular manifestations of Christianity so as to avoid painting the entire movement with the same broad brush, as many did then and many scholars still do. Would the church addressed by Hebrews have made the impression of *superstitio* on the likes of Tacitus, Pliny, and Suetonius? Answering these questions requires the refinement of one's definition of superstition and a focus upon a specific strand of Christianity.

To ask whether and in what ways the phenomenon described by Plutarch under the rubric of δεισιδαιμονία corresponds to the religious sensibilities represented by Hebrews is one way to approach this task. The presence of converts in the audience makes this an appropriate question to raise. Converts, by definition, were at one time outsiders and, as Ramsay Macmullen notes, they were not washed completely clean of their pagan ways of thinking by the waters of baptism.[19] This does not mean that converts would retain their view of Christianity as a superstition once they had become Christians since "superstition" is always a term of denigration. Yet it can be illuminating to examine the degree to which such outsider perceptions coincide with the self-understanding of the insiders.[20] The perception of Christianity by outsiders, as with almost any minority group unable to control the attitudes of the dominant

---

[19] R. Macmullen, "Conversion: A Historian's View," *SecCent* 5 (1985–86): 68.

[20] On pagan perceptions of Christianity during this period, see W. Nestle, "Die Haupteinwände des antiken Denkens gegen das Christentum," *AR* 37 (1941–42): 51–100; P. de Labriolle, *La réaction paienne: Étude sur la polémique antichrétienne du Ier au VIe siècle* (2nd ed.; Paris: L'Artisan du livre, 1948), 19–54; W. Speyer, "Zu den Vorwürfen der Heiden gegen die Christen," *JAC* 6 (1963): 129–35; R. L. Wilken, "Roman Criticism of Christianity: Greek Religion and Christian Faith," in *Early Christian Literature and the Classical Intellectual Tradition: In Honorem Robert M. Grant* (ed. W. R. Schedel and R. L. Wilken; Paris: Editions Beauchesne, 1979), 117–34; S. Benko, "Pagan Criticism of Christianity during the First Two Centuries A.D.," *ANRW* 23.2:1054–1118, esp. 1056–78; idem, *Pagan Rome and the Early Christians* (Bloomington: Indiana University Press, 1984), 1–29.

culture toward itself, shaped the world in which Christian identity was itself shaped.[21] This is especially the case with Christianity because, when Hebrews is written, it is still a new religion and, hence, composed of a disproportionate percentage of converts (that is, recent outsiders). Only during the early stages in the historical development of a religion may neophytes exercise so much power in shaping that religion.

Early Christians like the author and audience of Hebrews were engaged in the crucial process of creating Christian identity. But it was not creation *ex nihilo*. Although novel claims about Jesus were the leaven in the lump, so to speak, Christian identity was formed from preexisting Jewish and Gentile elements in the cultural contexts of the converts. The preponderant influence of converts (owing to Christianity's newness) on the development of the faith is an important factor in considering which elements taken over by the church from its environment were key in forming Christian identity. Is the idea of δεισιδαιμονία, with its special emphasis on fear, one of these "foreign" elements that have been assimilated into the nascent *sensus ecclesiae*, if only by negation?[22] That is to say, are there indications in a document like Hebrews that Christian self-understanding is articulated, consciously or not, so as to neutralize the potential charge of *superstitio*?[23] Or, conversely, do those elements which outsiders would regard as nonsense actually receive special emphasis, as when Paul describes the gospel as a form of power and wisdom in light of Jewish and Gentile perceptions that it was weak and foolish (1 Cor 1:21–25; cf. 2 Cor 11:23). Another possibility is that between parallel motifs and concepts there exists no direct genealogical relationship; their function and relative significance

---

[21] Robert L. Wilken, "The Christians as the Romans (and Greeks) Saw Them," in *Jewish and Christian Self-Definition: The Shaping of Christianity in the Second and Third Centuries* (ed. E. P. Sanders; vol. 1 of *Jewish and Christian Self-Definition*, ed. B. F. Meyer and E. P. Sanders; Philadelphia: Fortress, 1980), 100. See also Roger Hodgson, Jr., "Superstition and Submission: A Study in Roman Social History and Early Christian Ethics" (Unpublished Paper, Dept. of Religious Studies, Southwest Missouri State University, 1990), 21–33, for the application of labeling theory and symbolic interactionism to the study of the NT and early Christianity.

[22] On the *sensus ecclesiae*, see Luke T. Johnson, *The Writings of the New Testament* (Philadelphia: Fortress, 1986), 541–43.

[23] In his study of Rom 14–15, Mark Reasoner concludes that the "strong" regard the "weak" as superstitious, and that Paul is concerned to prevent this stigma from attaching to the church at Rome (*The Strong and the Weak: Romans 14:1–15:13 in Context* [SNTSMS 103; Cambridge: Cambridge University Press, 1999], 159–74). Along with asceticism in dietary matters and overly scrupulous observance of special days, the general stereotype of the superstitious person fits with the "weak" position and suggests that Paul's argument reflects an actual situation in first-century Rome. See also Robert Hodgson, Jr., "Superstition," *ABD* 6:241; and Hans Dieter Betz, "Christianity as Religion: Paul's Attempt at Definition in Romans," *JR* 71 (1991): 316–17.

may in fact vary so widely that "parallel" may be the wrong term to describe the correspondence. That there should be some measure of cultural continuity across religious lines is not surprising. But a thicker description of early Christianity requires greater specificity: which elements from the wider milieu were "baptized," by which Christians, and at what time? If the borrowing is only apparent but not historically verifiable, how does one understand the conflict or confluence of shared religious language? To answer this question, more narrowly focused investigations must precede broader statements about the pagan assessment of Christianity.

Hebrews provides a very suitable focus for such a study. The delicate process of resocializing converts into the church while Christianity (as well as the concept of "church") was still very much a work in progress must have been complicated, and the community represented by the author and audience of Hebrews is no exception.[24] Since superstition was a prevalent label placed upon Christian groups by the dominant culture, it is highly probable that the audience of Hebrews was familiar with this perception. Widespread pagan assessments of Judaism as a superstition increase this likelihood.[25] Jewish Christianity, of which the brand of Christianity seen in Hebrews is likely an example, probably inherited the aspersions that pagan observers sometimes cast upon Judaism. The author of Hebrews is nurturing Christian identity over against rival construals of what it means to be in authentic continuity with the faith traditions of Israel.[26] But Jewish identity, especially but not exclusively in a diasporic setting, is articulated in part as a response to what Gentiles believe a Jew to be. Because Judaism is seen as a superstition by many first-century observers, the differentiation of Christianity as a distinctive form of Judaism very likely involves coming to terms with the charge of superstition. Hebrews has been largely neglected by those seeking to understand this process of differentiation and self-definition in the early church.[27]

---

[24] Wayne A. Meeks, *The Origins of Christian Morality* (New Haven and London: Yale University Press, 1993), 26–36.

[25] Strabo, *Geogr.* 16.2.37; Cicero, *Flac.* 2.67; Valerius Maximus 1.3.3; Horace, *Sat.* 1.9.69–71; 2.3.281–95; Josephus, *C. Ap.* 1.208–211; Juvenal, *Sat.* 14.99; Persius, *Sat.* 5.179–84; Tacitus, *Ann.* 2.85; Quintilian, *Inst.* 3.7.21.

[26] Historical and political developments make it difficult to untangle this process. The Jewish revolt of 66–70 is a watershed event. Whereas non-Christian Jews under the Julio-Claudian emperors were anxious to distance themselves from the messianists, Christians in the Flavian period had as many, if not more, compelling reasons to distinguish themselves from the Jews (James C. Walters, "Romans, Jews, and Christians: The Impact of the Romans on Jewish/Christian Relations in First-Century Rome," in *Judaism and Christianity in First-Century Rome* [ed. K. Donfried and P. Richardson; Grand Rapids: Eerdmans, 1998], 183–89).

[27] One exception is S. G. Wilson, who devotes part of a chapter on supersessionist thinking in early Christianity to Hebrews (*Related Strangers: Jews and Christians,*

The second-century *Epistle to Diognetus* is one text which invokes the specific language of δεισιδαιμονία in delineating the differences between Christianity, Judaism, and paganism.[28] In the greeting the author states that his letter is a response to Diognetus's questions about Christian belief and practice. The letter describes the life of Christian discipleship and the benefits it offers to converts, those who are "exceedingly zealous to learn the religion of the Christians" (*Diogn.* 1). Diognetus has noticed that "the god in whom they believe, and how they worship him" differ from Greek thought and practice (1; cf. 2.1–8).[29] Nor do Christians, it is noted, "keep the δεισιδαιμονία of the Jews." The author goes on to ridicule Jewish "scruples about food and δεισιδαιμονία about the Sabbath" (4.1), on which Plutarch also comments.[30] *Diognetus* 1–4 offers a polemical critique of Judaism that in many respects resembles standard pagan attacks on Judaism and Christianity. Parts of this critique, especially in *Diogn.* 3, overlap with Hebrews' statements about the obsolescence of the Israelite cult in light of Christ's high priesthood.[31]

70–170 C.E. [Minneapolis: Augsburg Fortress, 1995], 110–27). The major monograph of Iutisone Salevao (*Legitimation in the Letter to the Hebrews: The Construction and Maintenance of a Symbolic World* [JSNTSup 219; Sheffield: Sheffield Academic, 2002]) appeared after this study was completed.

[28] Due to the paucity of Jewish literature written in Greek after the rise of Christianity, it is not clear if Jews returned the favor by calling Christianity a δεισιδαιμονία.

[29] It is in these two areas—conception of the divine and mode of worship—where writers like Cicero and Plutarch find the defects that are indicative of superstition.

[30] *Superst.* 169C. Agobard (*De judaicis superstitionibus* [PL 104:77–100]) expresses the same idea. Much later, Calvin (*Institutes* 2.8.33) and Heinrich Bullinger (in the 1562 *Second Helvetic Confession* [5.225]) also refer to Jewish celebration of the Sabbath as a superstition from which the early church distanced itself by worshipping on Sunday. Throughout his writings, Martin Luther refers to the judaizing tendencies of non-Pauline Christianity as *Aberglaube* (cf. *Luther's Works* [ed. J. Pelikan et al.; 55 vols.; St. Louis: Concordia; Philadelphia: Fortress, 1958–86], 16:33; 27:161 et al.).

[31] Heb 8:13. While Jews are superior to pagans by virtue of their monotheism (*Diogn.* 3.2), their continual offering of sacrifices is foolish instead of reverent since God has no need of them (3.3–5; cf. Heb 7:27; 9:11–14, 25–28; 10:1–18). For the attitude of Hebrews towards priesthood in the context of Jewish attitudes in the Second Temple period, see W. Horbury, "The Aaronic Priesthood and the Epistle to the Hebrews," *JSNT* 19 (1983): 43–71. By this time, the parting of the ways between church and synagogue is a *fait accompli*. When Hebrews is written, the split, if it has in fact already occurred, is a much more recent event. The church could not break entirely with Israel's faith traditions without denaturing itself (as the anti-Marcionite strand of Christian orthodoxy asserted) yet the retention of "superstitious" elements had somehow to be rationalized to Christian converts. Hebrews' articulation of Christian self-understanding may be part of an attempt to pre-empt accusations of superstition with respect to its view of God and its religious practices without abandoning its Jewish roots.

Given the currency of the charge of superstition against Christianity and Judaism, as well as against other religious groups, it is reasonable to ask whether and why specific groups (like the one represented by the Epistle to the Hebrews) fostered the impression of Christianity as δεισιδαιμονία, or if certain ones did so more than others. The evidence of Pliny suggests that this is the case. Some groups may have been more sensitive to such accusations than others, and some writers may have felt that this perception was an especially pressing problem to address. How would the author's approach to the problem of fear factor into this equation? To rule out this common topic of discussion in the early empire as a possible context for understanding the language of Hebrews is to accept the limitation of the letter's cultural matrix—implicitly imposed by the majority of commentators—to the non-Hellenized Jewish side.[32] Studying Hebrews alongside Plutarch's critique of δεισιδαιμονία is one way to overcome this artificial dichotomy.

Plutarch and the Epistle to the Hebrews: A Common Milieu

Though it has been neglected in previous research, there is much to commend the decision to view Plutarch and the Epistle to the Hebrews as part of a common milieu.[33] Though only half of his literary output is extant, Plutarch

---

[32] Sometimes this bias is more explicit, as when Ronald Williamson suggests that the presence of Greek philosophical categories—which some believe to have been mediated to Hebrews via Philo—would place the author outside the Jewish-Christian theological mainstream of the early church (*Philo and the Epistle to the Hebrews* [ALGHJ 4; Leiden: Brill, 1970], 579–80). Jonathan Z. Smith documents the bias in nineteenth-century scholarship that posited a radical opposition between "Platonic Christianity" and "authentic" Christianity (*Drudgery Divine: On the Comparison of Early Christianities and the Religions of Late Antiquity* [Chicago: University of Chicago Press, 1990], 1–35). Augustine calls it madness to claim that Jesus might have learned anything from Plato, therefore this bias is not peculiar to Protestant apologetics (*Doctr. chr.* 2.28.43).

[33] So far as his extant writings indicate, Plutarch, though he is acquainted with Judaism, has no knowledge of Christianity; cf. *Superst.* 169C; [*Reg. imp. apophth.*] 184E–F; *Is. Os.* 363D; and *Quaest. conv.* 669C–672C, where he discusses the reasons Jews abstain from pork and shows some familiarity with Jewish holidays. Intriguing but inconclusive is the suggestion of Barry S. Mackay that Plutarch makes veiled allusions to the virgin birth and ascension of Jesus, both recounted in the gospel of Luke, who spent his old age in Plutarch's Boeotia according to the so-called anti-Marcionite prologue written in the second century ("Plutarch and the Miraculous," in *Miracles: Cambridge Studies in their Philosophy and History* [ed. C. F. D. Moule; London: Mowbray, 1965], 109–111). Theodoret and other Greek patristic authors thought that Plutarch had converted to Christianity, had read the OT and the NT, and may even have written a biography of Jesus (cf. John Oakesmith, *The Religion of Plutarch: A Pagan Creed of Apostolic Times* [London: Longmans, Green, and Co., 1902], 45).

remains the most comprehensive witness to the religious and philosophical atmosphere of the Roman Empire in the first century C.E.[34] This alone makes his writings of relevance for Hebrews. The author and audience of Hebrews are a part of this environment. A Platonist who studied at the Academy in Athens and wrote several philosophical treatises on technical subjects, Plutarch also served as one of the two priests at Delphi for over twenty years and thus had a deep interest in "popular" religion as well. His *Quaestiones Romanae* is a collection of questions and answers on topics of antiquarian interest pertaining to Roman religion. There was no sharp distinction between religion and philosophy in the spiritual life of Plutarch's time, as his own writings and career demonstrate.

The erosion of distinctions between religion and philosophy weakens one possible objection to the use of Plutarch to illuminate a document like Hebrews. Often only a fine line separates traditional σοφία from the φιλοσοφία practiced in the schools of the period. As A. D. Nock and many others have noted, in antiquity the phenomenon closest to Jewish and Christian conversion was conversion to philosophy.[35] According to David Sedley, the cohesion and identity of philosophical movements is less the result of "a disinterested common quest for the truth than a virtually religious commitment to the authority of a founder figure."[36] Many of the pervasive concerns of philosophers contemporary with the NT, such as the nature of the transcendent world and the role of *daimones* in connecting humans with it, modern observers would regard as "religious" rather than "philosophical." This remains the case in spite of the attacks on superstition made by a number of philosophers like Plutarch during this period.[37]

Apart from this general cultural milieu and the similar educational level suggested by the author's rhetorical sophistication, at least three other specific factors support the decision to read Plutarch with an eye to understanding Hebrews and the symbolic world in which it participates. The first is chronological. Hebrews and Plutarch are contemporaries. Plutarch the biographer left behind no autobiography, but it is possible to establish his dates

---

[34] A description of the cultural world shared by Plutarch and the NT authors is given by Helge Almqvist, *Plutarch und das Neue Testament: Ein Beitrag zum Corpus Hellenisticum Novi Testamenti* (ASNU 15; Uppsala: Appelbergs, 1946), 4–17.

[35] A. D. Nock, *Conversion: The Old and New in Religion from Alexander the Great to Augustine of Hippo* (Oxford: Clarendon, 1933), 14, 164–86; Gustave Bardy, *La Conversion au Christianisme durant les premiers siècles* (Paris: Aubier, 1949), 46–89; Thomas M. Finn, *From Death to Rebirth: Ritual and Conversion in Antiquity* (New York: Paulist, 1997), 78–89.

[36] David Sedley, "Philosophical Allegiance in the Greco-Roman World," in *Philosophia Togata: Essays on Philosophy and Roman Society* (ed. M. Griffin and J. Barnes; 2 vols.; Oxford: Clarendon, 1989–97), 1:97.

[37] Cf. H. W. Attridge, "The Philosophical Critique of Religion under the Early Empire," *ANRW* 2.16:45–78.

with some certainty using clues from his writings.[38] He was born no later than 45 CE and died some time around the year 120. Establishing a chronology for his writings is notoriously difficult, but his literary activity likely stretches from 70 into the early part of the second century.[39] Dating Hebrews is likewise no simple matter. A *terminus ad quem* of 95 C.E. is generally recognized on the basis of *1 Clement*'s use of Hebrews near the end of Domitian's reign.[40] Some allow that *1 Clem.* may have been written as late as 120.[41] Many attempts to determine a date have focused on Hebrews' preoccupation with the Jewish cult and its possible relation to the destruction of the Jewish temple in 70. Neither a pre- nor a post-70 date of composition enjoys a clear majority opinion.[42] The earliest date to be suggested, by Hugh Montefiore, is between 52 and 54.[43] Thus the possibilities almost perfectly overlap with Plutarch's lifetime, with the most likely dates of composition coinciding with Plutarch's most prolific period.

A second reason for viewing Plutarch and Hebrews as part of the same milieu is geographical. Plutarch was from the Greek mainland but traveled widely and spent considerable time in Rome and Italy.[44] While in Rome on business, he also delivered lectures, dispensed advice in post-lecture discussions, consulted libraries for material for his *Lives*, and carried on friendships with members of Rome's cultured elite. He was in Rome during Vespasian's reign and again close to the time when Domitian expelled all philosophers from the city in 89 and from all Italy in 95.[45]

The closing greeting from "those from Italy" (Heb 13:24) strongly suggests that Hebrews was written either to or from Italy. The emerging consensus of modern scholars is that Rome is the most likely destination of the letter.[46]

---

[38] On Plutarch's life, the most comprehensive guide is Konrat Ziegler, "Plutarchos von Chaironeia," PW 22.1:639–96.

[39] Cf. C. P. Jones, "Towards a Chronology of Plutarch's Works," *JRS* 56 (1966): 51–74.

[40] 1 Clem. 17:1=Heb 11:37; 17:5=Heb 3:5; 36:2–5=Heb 1:3–13. If, however, *1 Clem.* is later than 95 or relies upon a shared Christian tradition and is not directly dependent upon Hebrews, this evidence is of less use in dating the epistle. See Laurence L. Welborn, "On the Date of First Clement," *BR* 29 (1985): 35–54; Gerd Theissen, *Untersuchungen zum Hebräerbrief* (SNT 2; Gutersöh: Mohn, 1969), 35–37.

[41] Attridge, *Hebrews*,7–8.

[42] Attridge (*Hebrews*, 8–9) and J. C. McCullough ("Hebrews in Recent Scholarship," *IBS* 16 [1994]: 118–19) provide a review of the positions.

[43] Hugh Montefiore, *A Commentary on the Epistle to the Hebrews* (New York: Harper; London: Black, 1964), 12.

[44] Cf. Barrow, *Plutarch and His Times*, 36–42; and Simon Swain, "Plutarch, Plato, Athens and Rome," in Griffin and Barnes, *Philosophia Togata*, 2:165–87.

[45] Jones, *Plutarch and Rome*, 21–27.

[46] For example, see H.-F. Weiss, *Der Brief an die Hebräer* (KEK 13; Göttingen: Vandenhoeck & Ruprecht, 1991), 76; M. Rissi, *Die Theologie des Hebräerbriefes*

Internal and external evidence are seen to point in this direction. The first external attestation of Hebrews is in Rome, where *1 Clement* likely quotes it.[47] "Those from Italy," then, would be those who had been separated from the church in Rome and are with the author as he writes to their former neighbors. It is also possible that the author is writing from Rome to some other destination, though this is less probable.[48] Furthermore, the reluctance in the west to recognize Hebrews as canonical may be based on knowledge in Rome of the letter's non-Pauline authorship. The expulsion of Jews (and possibly of Christians) from Rome in 49 "at the instigation of Chrestus" (*impulsore Chresto*: Suetonius, *Claud.* 25.4) and the persecution of Christians under Nero in 64, while not conclusive, would also accord with the allusions to persecution in 10:32–34.[49] The term for the community's leaders (ἡγούμενοι, 13:7, 17, 24) was a popular one in documents of Roman Christianity.[50] Finally, the numerous similarities between Hebrews and 1 Peter also support a common destination in Rome.[51]

The third reason for reading Plutarch and Hebrews together has to do with the matter of the epistle's putative Platonism.[52] It is frequently assumed by NT scholars that if the Platonic tradition has influenced the author of Hebrews, it has done so by means of the Middle Platonism represented by Philo of Alexandria. But Philo is not the only first-century Platonist. Plutarch is also a prominent Platonist and, as has already been shown, he stands chronologically and geographically closer to Hebrews than does Philo. While it is not an aim of the present investigation, consideration of Plutarch is an indispensable complement to Philo in the reconstruction of the Middle Platonism that may have exerted a formative influence on Hebrews.[53]

(WUNT 44; Tübingen: Mohr-Siebeck, 1987), 11; and W. L. Lane, *Hebrews* (2 vols.; WBC 47A–B; Dallas: Word, 1991), 1:lviii–lx.

[47] D. A. Hagner, *The Use of the Old and New Testaments in Clement of Rome* (Leiden: Brill, 1973), 179–95; Paul Ellingworth, "Hebrews and 1 Clement: Literary Dependence or Common Tradition?" *BZ* 23 (1979): 262–69.

[48] Raymond E. Brown and John P. Meier, *Antioch and Rome* (London: Geoffrey Chapman, 1983), 147. If the author is writing from Rome, one would expect him to refer to "those from Rome" instead of "from Italy."

[49] The generosity for which the author commends the audience (6:10) also fits with what is known about the church in Rome. Cf. F. F. Bruce, "'To the Hebrews': A Document of Roman Christianity?" *ANRW* 2.25:3517–18; and P. Lampe, *Die stadtrömischen Christen in den ersten beiden Jahrhunderte: Untersuchung zu Sozialgeschichte* (Tübingen: Mohr-Siebeck, 1987), 53–78.

[50] *1 Clem.* 1:3; 12:26; Herm. *Vis.* 2.2.6; 3.9.7.

[51] Attridge, *Hebrews*, 30–31.

[52] See the discussion below, pp. 26–27.

[53] John Dillon considers Plutarch in the context of contemporary Platonism in *The Middle Platonists* (Ithaca: Cornell University Press, 1977), 184–230. He bemoans the general

New Testament Studies and the History-of-Religions School

Within the larger context of NT studies, then, this study seeks to attain some of the objectives of the *religionsgeschichtliche Schule* by situating Hebrews more firmly and more precisely in its Hellenistic context. As an auxiliary or subordinate aim, it simultaneously seeks to reconsider some of the ways the history-of-religions program has pursued its objectives in three separate but related areas of immediate relevance to the topic at hand: (1) comparative method, (2) the relationship of Plutarch to the NT, and (3) the religious and cultural matrix of the Epistle to the Hebrews.

Contextualization, Comparison, and "Parallelomania"

Integrating Hebrews with its Hellenistic context, by putting its author into dialogue with Plutarch on superstition and the propriety of fear involves more than the collection of disparate lexical and conceptual parallels between the two authors. Such a task is perhaps a preliminary and even a necessary one as a mode of entry into the material, but it is not sufficient by itself. The study of ancient texts—due to the absence of contemporary lexicons—requires an inductive approach simply to decipher the languages in which they are written. In the seventeenth and eighteenth centuries, the *Observationes* and *Annotationes* literature aimed at providing just such a service.[54] J. J. Wettstein's *Novum Testamentum Graecum*, published in 1751–52, is the prime example of this genre. The modern successor to Wettstein's work is the Corpus Hellenisticum Novi Testamenti (CHNT).[55] Its aim is to provide "a collection of all parallels and antiparallels in expression and contents that exist between the Greek and Roman world and the NT."[56] The approach is typically microscopic, focusing on specific words or motifs found in both the NT and in classical texts.

---

neglect of Middle Platonism by classicists, who treat writers like Plutarch as "dimly seen milestones on the way to Neoplatonism" and as "precursors to Plotinus" in particular (xiii). Heinrich Dörrie differs from Dillon, regarding Plutarch's thought as a departure from standard Academic interpretations of the Platonic tradition ("Die Stellung Plutarchs im Platonismus seiner Zeit," in *Philomathes: Studies and Essays in the Humanities in Memory of Philip Merlan* [ed. R. B. Palmer and R. Hamerton-Kelly; The Hague: Martinus Nijhoff, 1971], 36–56).

[54] G. Delling, "Zum Corpus Hellenisticum Novi Testamenti," *ZNW* 54 (1963): 1–3.

[55] For an overview and extensive bibliography on the project by one of its chief contributors, see P. W. van der Horst, "Corpus Hellenisticum Novi Testamenti," *ABD* 1:1157–61.

[56] W. C. van Unnik, "Words Come to Life: The Work for the 'Corpus Hellenisticum Novi Testamenti'," *NovT* 13 (1971): 204.

Two difficulties attend this daunting task. One is the basic step of identifying parallels. A hypersensitivity to generalization and a hesitance on the part of scholars to make broader, synthetic statements has led to the more modest "empiric-positivistic interest in amassing 'hard facts' which . . . 'speak for themselves'," a trend which, according to C. R. Phillips, ignores the role of human subjectivity in studying ancient religion.[57] What constitutes a parallel is simply not self-evident, but the ambitious scope of individual contributions to the CHNT project leaves little room for systematic reflection on this fundamental methodological question. A second difficulty is related to the first and has to do with assessing the significance of parallels. Neither the NT nor the non-Christian literary output of Greco-Roman antiquity is monolithic with regard to purpose, form, perspective, or emphasis. Within each body of literature as well as between the two, identical motifs may function in completely different ways. To take just one example, the meaning of παρρησία, due to its different senses in Acts and Hebrews, cannot be homogenized so as to produce a single NT concept which may then be compared with its sense in non-Christian texts.[58] Nor is every occurrence of παρρησία in pagan texts automatically of assistance in understanding its meaning in specific NT passages. Failure to address these and related issues are symptomatic of the syndrome Samuel Sandmel calls "parallelomania."[59]

Here a consideration of the term "parallel" helps to highlight the conceptual issue. In Euclidean geometry, the term "parallel" describes lines or planes that do not intersect. Points, by themselves, cannot be parallel to one another. Only when two or more points are joined to form a line can the parallelism of that line with other lines be determined. Single points cannot be compared using the category of parallelism. "Parallel" does not mean "similar," as it usually does in non-mathematical contexts. Rather, it describes a relationship between one set of points (a line) and another series of points (another line). Likewise, in the study of ancient texts, the discovery of similar terms or motifs in two bodies of literature is not in itself a demonstration of "parallelism." Only when similar elements in two separate texts are first understood in their respective contexts

---

[57] C. R. Phillips, "The Sociology of Religious Knowledge in the Roman Empire to A.D. 284," *ANRW* 2.16:2680.

[58] This topic will be discussed below in chapter three. For a preliminary review and interpretation of the data, see W. C. van Unnik, "The Christian's Freedom of Speech in the New Testament," *BJRL* 44 (1962): 466–88.

[59] S. Sandmel, "Parallelomania," *JBL* 181 (1962): 1–13. Updated presentations of Sandmel's argument may be found in Shemaryahu Talmon, "The 'Comparative Method' in Biblical Interpretation—Principles and Problems," in *Congress Volume: Göttingen 1977* (ed. J. A. Emerton et al.; VTSup 29; Leiden: Brill, 1978), 320–56; and Meir Malul, *The Comparative Method in Ancient Near Eastern and Biblical Legal Studies* (AOAT 227; Kevelaer: Butzon & Bercker, 1990).

can the analogy of parallelism be appropriated. Does a series of elements in one text cohere according to an internal logic that also seems to govern the relationship between a series of similar elements in a second text? This line of questioning allows for a degree of depth (if not breadth) that is lacking in many comparative studies of the NT and its Greco-Roman environment.

Whereas the misuse of technical terms from other fields can unintentionally lead to conceptual confusion, as it has in the appropriation of the category of parallelism in NT studies, sometimes comparative strategies are less innocent. This is the thesis of separate studies by E. P. Sanders and Jonathan Z. Smith addressing methodological issues in the study of religion.[60] Sanders wants to compare "patterns of religion," as his subtitle indicates. He emphatically does not want to treat Palestinian Judaism from 200 B.C.E. to 200 C.E. simply as "background" for understanding Paul; rather, his goal is "to compare an entire religion, parts and all, with an entire religion, parts and all."[61] The "backgrounds" approach is the methodological mistake made by the nineteenth- and twentieth-century authors he surveys in his opening chapter. Most studies of Paul and his relationship to Judaism consist of comparison of their reduced "essences" (e.g., a religion of faith versus a religion of works) or of individual motifs present in both bodies of literature, neither of which constitutes an adequate category of comparison according to Sanders. One approach often misrepresents the entities being compared and the other overlooks the differences in function and significance of the shared motifs. The resulting portraits, drawn largely by Christian authors, regularly distort rabbinic Judaism and depict Paul as offering a far superior version of the Jewish faith. At times this is simply a consequence of the naïve acceptance of Paul's polemical presentation of Judaism as an accurate and objective one. On other occasions this tendency coincides with the antisemitic biases of the scholar. Sanders, then, wants to repudiate prevailing understandings of Palestinian Judaism and to substitute a version more faithful to the sources, which may then be compared with Paul.

The patterns of religion that are to serve as the basis of comparison are in some ways easier to define negatively than positively. They are not entire historical religions. A pattern of religion does not include every theological proposition or concept within a religion, nor does it detail all that an adherent does on a daily basis. Positively defined, a pattern of religion is "the description of how a religion is perceived by its adherents to function."[62] It addresses the

---

[60] E. P. Sanders, *Paul and Palestinian Judaism: A Comparison of Patterns of Religion* (Minneapolis: Fortress, 1977); Smith, *Drudgery Divine: On the Comparison of Early Christianities and the Religions of Late Antiquity.* The bulk of this comparative research, in Smith's estimation, is "an enterprise undertaken in bad faith" (143).

[61] Sanders, *Paul and Palestinian Judaism*, 16.

[62] Ibid., 17.

questions of "how one moves from the logical starting point to the logical conclusion of the religion" and *"how getting in and staying in are understood."*[63] Many of Sanders's critics are generally positive towards his methodological objectives and principles but find problems in the execution. Among the difficulties is a definition of "pattern of religion" that skews his investigation by overemphasizing soteriological questions. His project is an ambitious one; comparison of "whole" to "whole" is difficult when "wholes" are generally not available from the extant sources. He does not quite accomplish his objectives, though this may not have been such a problem had his desire not been to present whole patterns of religion.

Sanders focuses on a specific sector of Judaism in his investigation. J. Z. Smith, on the other hand, considers the Gentile milieu. Much of the comparative study of Christianity and its early competitors, Smith contends, has been embedded in covert attempts to demonstrate Christianity's uniqueness. A characteristic tendency of the scholars he surveys is that they identify and compare motifs common to Christianity and pre-existing Mediterranean mystery cults yet deny any genealogical relationship between the two. An exception is made when the pagan evidence post-dates the rise of the church. There is less hesitation to see a genealogical link in these later cases, where the habit is to see pagan borrowing of Christian concepts or motifs. Conceptual dependence, when it is ascertained, rarely works in the opposite direction. "True" Christianity is "original" Christianity, that which existed before later (that is, pagan) accretions. Any departure from this pristine version of the faith is taken to be decline instead of positive development. This line of reasoning serves a dual purpose, of preserving Christianity's uniqueness by insulating it from its environment and of undermining the Catholic Church's claims to legitimacy by equating non-biblical tradition or development in doctrine with pagan contamination.[64] The mass of evidence Smith marshals effectively shifts the burden of proof onto anyone who would dispute this part of his argument.

Whereas Smith's deconstructive aim is to uncover the presuppositions driving much post-Reformation scholarship, the constructive aim is to formulate a better method for pursuing the comparative study of religions. Here he favors

---

[63] Ibid., 17 (emphasis in original).

[64] Smith, *Drudgery Divine*, 143. Smith earlier discusses this construction of "pagano-papism" in "The Temple and the Magician" (in *Map is Not Territory* [SJLA 23; Leiden: Brill, 1978], 172–89). Similar strategies play a part in nineteenth-century definitions of superstition, as when Riddle identifies "the principle of acknowledging human Tradition of coordinate authority with the word of God" as the most productive root of superstition (*The Natural History of Infidelity and Superstition*, 166). An equally subtle attack on Catholicism is seen in his claim that the increase in superstition among Christians over the first four centuries was a chief cause of Rome's decline and fall (201).

the language of analogy over that of genealogy.[65] Focus on local manifestations of a religion serves to aid in the discovery of broader religious and cultural patterns which are analogous.[66] Smith seems to regard the drawing of analogies and the tracing of possible genealogical relationships as mutually exclusive tasks. As a historian of religion, he is interested in phenomena that are in some kind of geographical and temporal proximity, and so it is not clear why, to take Smith's example, Christianity and the mysteries must be kept hermetically sealed off from one another when they come together in the scholar's study. When analogous religious developments appear at roughly the same time and in the same general neighborhood, how does one explain their concomitance?[67] Some type of influence is a natural possibility to explore, as is the mutual but independent reliance upon some common, prior source or tradition. An alternative explanation for analogous but historically unrelated occurrences is to posit some type of inherent human religious sensibility transcending cultural boundaries, an option Smith is not likely to favor. Difficulties in securing certain results and potential for misapplying the results for theological purposes are not sufficient rationales for eschewing the study of sources and influences operating in a given geographical and cultural milieu. The position Smith takes here undercuts his own stance as a historian of religion. History, after all, has to do with the relation of events in time and space. Sanders, by contrast, allows for both the comparative task and for cautious generalizations about "the horizontal context of religious thought" obtaining in a specific milieu.[68]

While the aim of the present study is certainly not to prove that specific historical sources such as Plutarch's writings provide the only appropriate context for understanding the language and thought of Hebrews because it is in some way dependent on them, neither is it to rule out a priori the possibility that these two authors writing at the same time, in the same language, and about similar subjects may be mutual participants in a historically and culturally

---

[65] This terminology goes back to Adolf Deissmann, *Light from the Ancient East* (trans. L. R. M. Strachan; New York: Doran, 1927), 265.

[66] Smith, *Drudgery Divine*, 43, 112–13. Local description, however, is also a convenient tool whereby Smith may deny the existence of a single, monolithic Christianity. Soteriology in Pauline Christianity is, in his mapping of early Christian theological terrain, "utopian" due to the centrality of the resurrection while other traditions are thoroughly "locative" in that they do not emphasize the need to conquer death (121–42).

[67] Hans Kippenberg asks much the same question in his review ("Comparing Ancient Religions: A Discussion of J. Z. Smith's 'Drudgery Divine'," *Numen* 39 [1992]: 220–25); cf. also John Ashton, *The Religion of Paul the Apostle* (New Haven: Yale University Press, 2000), 15, whose discussion of Smith and Sanders dovetails at several points with the comments offered here.

[68] Sanders, *Paul and Palestinian Judaism*, 24. It is possible to ask, however, whether Palestinian Judaism over a period of four centuries is sufficiently homogeneous to permit the generalizations Sanders puts forward.

contiguous realm of religious discourse. Smith's repeated assertion that the basis for comparing two entities is a third idea born in the scholar's mind is to the point, but only partly so. Hebrews and Plutarch were not engaged in an actual conversation, therefore any such comparison is of course initiated by the scholar. [69] But not all ideas generated by scholars for comparative purposes constitute equally arbitrary points of departure, notwithstanding Smith's intimations to the contrary. Some are better than others by virtue of their grounding in the sources and currency in their original context. The constellation of ideas—present in both Hebrews and Plutarch—associated with superstition in the milieu of which both were a part supports the *prima facie* validity of the investigation proposed here.

Plutarch and the New Testament

The most ambitious attempts to identify the parallels to the NT found in Plutarch are two volumes edited by Hans Dieter Betz.[70] In the preface to the first volume, Betz notes that care must be taken so that Plutarch's writings do not become simply "quarries" from which "material" can be extracted.[71] Largely absent is ideological bias of the kind observed by Smith. While each author attempts to respect the integrity of Plutarch by following his text, it is clear that the emphasis is upon identifying as many NT parallels as possible rather than upon providing a continuous commentary on the essay under consideration. As a result, each contribution contains a staggering amount of information.

The chapter on *De superstitione* in the first of these volumes is an extremely dense one by Morton Smith.[72] It is difficult to summarize since it consists largely of citations to ancient sources accompanied by very brief comment. Smith is keenly aware of the complexities in relating this treatise to Plutarch's others, so much so that, in a major departure from the mainstream of Plutarchan scholarship, he concludes that the attribution of authorship to Plutarch is a

---

[69] To juxtapose the treatments of fear in Hebrews and Plutarch may thus be regarded as an attempt to carry out what Smith calls "a disciplined exaggeration in the service of knowledge" (*Drudgery Divine*, 52).

[70] H. D. Betz, ed., *Plutarch's Theological Writings and Early Christian Literature* (SCHNT 3; Leiden: Brill, 1975); *Plutarch's Ethical Writings and Early Christian Literature* (SCHNT 5; Leiden: Brill, 1978). For an assessment, see A. J. Malherbe's review (*JBL* 100 [1981]: 140–42). In spite of any shortcomings, the contributions to these volumes far surpass the earlier work of Almqvist, *Plutarch und das Neue Testament*, which lists only eight parallels with Hebrews.

[71] Betz, *Plutarch's Theological Writings*, ix.

[72] M. Smith, "De Superstitione (Moralia 164E–171F)," in Betz, *Plutarch's Theological Writings*, 1–35.

mistake.[73] His comments on specific motifs are generally on target, one exception being the reference to *Superst.* 167F–168C and Heb 12:4–11 as parallel expressions of the idea that misfortunes are signs of divine displeasure.[74] (Surely the author is trying to make precisely the opposite point in Heb 12.) He makes an important distinction when he notes that Plutarch's concern is not so much superstition in general as it is superstitious practices as manifestations of fear, hence "scrupulosity" or "fear of the gods" is a better translation equivalent for δεισιδαιμονία. On a methodological level, Smith makes the astute observation that there are two kinds of content-parallels between Plutarch and the NT. One set includes Christian fear of God and its issuance in the types of belief and practices attacked by Plutarch. The other includes correspondences between Christian attacks on inappropriate ways of relating to the divine prevalent among pagans and Plutarch's critique of similar practices. Elements of each may be found among the parallels with Hebrews. It is impossible, however, to assess the relative significance of each set of parallels in such short compass. Consequently, neither Plutarch nor the NT receives the attention it deserves.

A more compelling comparison is one that envisions the transformations of a given motif when it crosses the boundaries separating different religious perspectives. One of the few attempts at such a comparison to take this dynamic interplay into account is a brief essay by Herbert Braun.[75] Braun aims to uncover the compatibilities and incompatibilities between the gods Plutarch describes and the God of the NT. He also sees Plutarch as addressing the same symptoms of spiritual agitation as John the Baptist, Jesus, and Paul (Matt 3:7; 23:33; Rom 7; Gal 3:1; 4:3). His analysis goes far beyond the superficial citation of parallel motifs and tries to get at the "decoded subject matter" underlying the mythical descriptions in both bodies of literature.[76] At a few points, Braun relates the differences to the differences in their respective world views, most notably Plutarch's faith in the natural goodness of humans versus the Christian conviction of human sinfulness. He regards Plutarch and the NT authors as inhabitants of the same environment but he construes this environment in existentialist terms, where the continuities between the ancient and modern

[73] Ibid., 1–7. Frederick E. Brenk surveys the issues involved in determining the essay's authenticity and sides with those who see Plutarch as the author (*In Mist Apparelled: Religious Themes in Plutarch's* Moralia *and* Lives [Leiden: Brill, 1977], 9–15).

[74] Smith, "De Superstitione," 25.

[75] H. Braun, *Plutarch's Critique of Superstition in Light of the New Testament* (trans. H. D. Betz and E. W. Smith, Jr.; Institute for Antiquity and Christianity Occasional Papers 5. Claremont, 1972).

[76] The affinities with Bultmann are not accidental. Braun was a student of Bultmann and this essay was first published in German in 1948, not long after Bultmann's popularizing of demythologization in NT studies (*Plutarchs Kritik am Aberglauben im Lichte des Neuen Testamentes* [Der Anfang 9; Berlin: Verlag Haus und Schule, 1948]).

readers—by virtue of their common nature as fallen human beings—override the discontinuities that result from different historical and cultural contexts.

As a consequence of Braun's prescriptive theological aim to determine whether Plutarch's or the NT's is "the deeper and more real myth," the essay is flawed on a number of points. First, the ancient context for Plutarch's views remains undeveloped and the place of *De superstitione* in his larger corpus is not even mentioned. Second, the NT witness through which he interprets Plutarch's critique of superstition is a composite based largely on Paul.[77] Whatever theological insights it offers, Braun's approach is problematic on historical grounds since it does not proceed inductively, adducing the distinctive witness of each document on its own terms before correlating it with the rest of the NT. And third, while he demonstrates his assertion that Plutarch and the NT offer similar diagnoses of the condition of the superstitious, his argument that the NT offers the "more adequate myth" is accompanied by no specific textual support.

Like Braun, Hans-Josef Klauck has a theological objective in his study of Plutarch and the NT, namely, to show that fearfulness is not an authentically Christian mode of discipleship.[78] After a rhetorical analysis of *De superstitione* in which he summarizes its main points, Klauck criticizes Plutarch for failing to recognize the positive value of the myths he finds outrageous. Yet Klauck sides with Plutarch on the essential incompatibility between fearfulness and a godly life. He adduces two NT texts as illustrations. In Rom 8:15, Paul describes life in the Spirit as a life of freedom: "For you did not receive the spirit of slavery to fall back into fear, but you have received the spirit of sonship." The adopted child of God must realize that the fearsome perils described in Rom 8:35–36 cannot separate one from God's love. Fear and love are also antithetical in 1 John 4:17–18: "In this is love perfected with us, that we may have confidence for the day of judgment . . . . There is no fear in love, but perfect fear casts out fear. For fear has to do with punishment, and he who fears is not perfected in love." Klauck points out the connection between φόβος on the one hand and παρρησία at the eschaton on the other, but his analysis does not extend beyond these two verses. His approach, then, is too closely tied to a very narrow range of texts, while Braun's is too broadly conceived.

Though the scope of their studies when surveying the NT is problematic—too narrow at some points and too general at others—Braun and Klauck both recognize that it is the element of fear in δεισιδαιμονία that constitutes the most natural point of contact between Plutarch and early Christian thought. The focus of the present study upon a single topic in two

---

[77] Over half of the citations are from Romans or Galatians.

[78] Hans-Josef Klauck, "Religion Without Fear: Plutarch on Superstition and Early Christianity," *SK* 18 (1997): 111–26. Many of the same ideas are found in Klauck's *Alte Welt und neuer Glaube: Beiträge zur Religionsgeschichte, Forschungsgeschichte und Theologie des Neuen Testaments* (Göttingen: Vandenhoeck & Ruprecht, 1994), 61–66.

discrete *corpora*—Plutarch and Hebrews—represents an attempt to avoid the
two extremes characteristic of many treatments of similar material: excessively
narrow concentration on specific terms on the one hand, and broad
generalizations about "the" NT, early Christian, or Greco-Roman view on a
given question on the other.

The Greco-Roman Background of Hebrews:
The State of the Question

The nearly universal acknowledgement that early Christianity did not
develop in a vacuum is the chief legacy of the history-of-religions school.
Reacting against the turn-of-the-century tendency to regard early Christianity as
a syncretistic mystery religion similar to others flooding into the early Roman
Empire from the east, however, Johannes Weiss, Albert Schweitzer, and others
vigorously reasserted the Jewishness of Jesus and Paul to the virtual exclusion of
any possible Hellenistic influence.[79] Contemporary scholars are less likely to
posit Jewish and Gentile influences as mutually exclusive alternatives.
Nevertheless, many still assume that if a certain concept appearing in the NT
may be explained on the basis of the Jewish background, without recourse to
pagan sources, then it must be explained without any recourse to pagan sources.
Such is the case in much research on the religious and cultural context of the
Epistle to the Hebrews. Given the Jewish roots of early Christianity and of the
religious terminology in Hebrews in particular, this attention to the Semitic
context is entirely appropriate. However, a narrow focus upon the Jewish
background of Hebrews carries with it the unfounded assumption that pre-
Christian Judaism or Jewish Christianity developed in a cultural ghetto. The
burden of proof ought to rest with those who hold that Hebrews is totally free of
shared cultural assumptions that transcend distinctions between Jew and Gentile
or that nothing is to be gained by fleshing out the larger symbolic world in
which it participates. A common occurrence in this world is the slur of
"superstition." A description of the cultural context in which Hebrews was
written and first read involves an attempt to understand how its author, through
his approach to the problem of fear, may be equipped to counter this and similar
criticisms leveled at religious groups in the first century.

In contrast to the legion of studies focusing upon the Jewish context,
relatively few studies have focused upon the broader Gentile background against
which the thought and language of Hebrews may be brought into sharper relief.

---

[79] J. Weiss, *Die Predigt Jesu vom Reiche Gottes* (Göttingen: Vandenhoeck & Ruprecht,
1892); A. Schweitzer, *Die Mystik des Apostels Paulus* (Tübingen: J. C. B. Mohr, 1930).
For a discussion, see W. G. Kümmel, *The New Testament: The History of the
Investigation of its Problems* (trans. S. Maclean Gilmour and H. C. Kee: Nashville and
New York: Abingdon, 1972), 226–44.

The most influential attempt to understand Hebrews in terms of a non-Jewish conceptual framework is that of Ernst Käsemann.[80] His reading of Hebrews, which presents Jesus as a type of Gnostic "redeemed redeemer" and the addressees as travelers on a pilgrimage from the oppressive world of matter to a heavenly homeland of spirit, has come under considerable criticism as subsequent research has shown that Käsemann's version of Gnosticism is incomplete and unlikely to have exerted any direct influence upon the epistle.[81] Since Käsemann, a relatively small number of shorter essays and monographs have appealed to non-Jewish materials to explain isolated elements in Hebrews.[82] The literary features of Hebrews have also been the subject of a number of studies which evaluate the epistle with reference to the standards of Greco-Roman rhetoric.[83]

---

[80] E. Käsemann, *The Wandering People of God: An Investigation of the Letter to the Hebrews* (trans. R. A. Harrisville and I. L. Sandberg; Minneapolis: Augsburg, 1984); trans. of *Das wandernde Gottesvolk* (FRLANT 55; Göttingen: Vandenhoeck & Ruprecht, 1939). Cf. also O. Hofius, *Katapausis: Die Vorstellung vom endzeitlichen Ruheort im Hebräerbrief* (WUNT 11; Tübingen: Mohr-Siebeck, 1970), 5–21.

[81] Among the main problems with Käsemann's thesis is the absence of firm evidence for the variety of Gnosticism he describes that pre-dates Hebrews. Most of the texts he cites are late. Cf. L. D. Hurst, *The Epistle to the Hebrews: Its Background of Thought* (SNTSMS 65; Cambridge: Cambridge University Press, 1990), 67–75; and Floyd Filson, "The Epistle to the Hebrews," *JBR* 22 (1954): 20–26.

[82] David E. Aune, "Heracles and Christ: Heracles Imagery in the Christology of Early Christianity," in *Greeks, Romans, and Christians: Essays in Honor of Abraham J. Malherbe* (ed. D. L. Balch, E. Ferguson, and W. A. Meeks: Minneapolis: Fortress, 1990), esp. 13–19; in the same volume, see P. W. van der Horst, "Sarah's Seminal Emission: Hebrews 11:11 in the Light of Ancient Embryology," 287–302; J. H. Neyrey, "'Without Beginning of Days or End of Life' (Hebrews 7:3): Topos for a True Deity," *CBQ* 53 (1991): 439–55; Michael E. Gudorf, "Through a Classical Lens: Hebrews 2:16," *JBL* 119 (2000): 105–8. Cf. also the earlier study of E. Riggenbach, ("Der Begriff der ΤΕΛΕΙΩΣΙΣ im Hebräerbrief: Ein Beitrag zur Frage nach der Einwirkung der Mysterienreligion auf Sprache und Gedankenwelt des Neuen Testaments," *NKZ* 34 [1923]: 184–95). Recent dissertations on Hebrews in its Greco-Roman context include David A. deSilva, *Despising Shame: Honor Discourse and Community Maintenance in the Epistle to the Hebrews* (SBLDS 152; Atlanta: Scholars Press, 1995); and N. Clayton Croy, *Endurance in Suffering: Hebrews 12:1–13 in Its Rhetorical, Religious, and Philosophical Context* (SNTSMS 98; Cambridge: Cambridge University Press, 1998).

[83] The subject of genre has been examined by H. Thyen, *Der Stil der jüdisch-hellenistischen Homilie* (FRLANT 47; Göttingen: Vandenhoeck & Ruprecht, 1955), esp. 16–18; and C. C. Black II, "The Rhetorical Form of the Hellenistic Jewish and Early Christian Sermon: A Response to Lawrence Wills," *HTR* 81 (1988): 1–18. Michael R. Cosby examines one sub-unit in *The Rhetorical Composition and Function of Hebrews 11 in the Light of Example Lists in Antiquity* (Macon: Mercer University Press, 1988). Several scholars have dealt with more specific rhetorical devices employed by the author.

It is the alleged Platonism of the author that, in terms of the Greco-Roman context, has received the most attention.[84] Language reminiscent of Plato's Forms (in such passages as 8:1–5; 9:11, 23–24; 10:1) leads many interpreters to agree with James Moffatt's judgment that "the philosophical element in [the author's] view is fundamentally Platonic."[85] Few go so far as to call the author a Platonist but rather focus on Philo or the Alexandrian Judaism of which he is a product as the conduit through which Platonic influence came to bear on Hebrews.[86] Though few would follow Ceslaus Spicq in seeing signs of direct literary dependence upon Philo or in claiming that its author is "un philonien converti au Christianisme," investigation of Hebrews' putative Platonism remains subject to a Philonian captivity.[87]

The inadequacies of this approach to the Greco-Roman background of Hebrews becomes apparent when one recalls that there is much more to the

---

Cf. T. Haering, "Gedankengang und Grundgedanken des Hebräerbriefs," *ZNW* 18 (1917–18): 145–64; Keijo Nissilä, *Das Hohenpriestermotiv im Hebräerbrief: Eine exegetische Untersuchung* (Helsinki: Oy Liiton Kirjapaino, 1979); Barnabas Lindars, "The Rhetorical Structure of Hebrews," *NTS* 35 (1989): 382–406; and W. G. Übelacker, *Der Hebräerbrief als Appell: Untersuchungen zu* exordium, narratio *und* postscriptum *(Hebr 1–2 und 13,22–25)* (Stockholm: Almqvist & Wiksell, 1989); A. C. Mitchell, "The Use of πρέπειν and Rhetorical Propriety in Hebrews 2:10," *CBQ* 54 (1992): 681–701.

[84] J. Héring, "Eschatologie biblique et idéalisme platonicien," in *The Background of the New Testament and Its Eschatology* (ed. W. D. Davies and D. Daube; Cambridge: Cambridge University Press, 1954), 444–63; J. H. Burtness, "Plato, Philo and the Author of Hebrews," *LQ* 10 (1958): 54–64; A. M. Fairhurst, "Hellenistic Influence in the Epistle to the Hebrews," *TynBul* 7–8 (1961): 17–27; R. Williamson, "Platonism and Hebrews," *SJT* 16 (1963): 415–24; L. D. Hurst, "Eschatology and 'Platonism' in the Epistle to the Hebrews," *SBL Seminar Papers, 1984* (SBLSP 23; Chico, Calif.: Scholars Press, 1984), 41–74. For an overview, see Hurst, *The Epistle to the Hebrews*, 7–11; and J. W. Thompson, *The Beginnings of Christian Philosophy: The Epistle to the Hebrews* (CBQMS 13; Washington, DC: The Catholic Biblical Association of America, 1981), 15–16, 152–62.

[85] James Moffatt, *A Critical and Exegetical Commentary on the Epistle to the Hebrews* (ICC; Edinburgh: T & T Clark, 1924), xxxi. Cf. also Barrett's remark, at the end of an essay in which he argues against the Platonic interpretation, that the author of Hebrews "may well have read Plato and other philosophers, and must have known that his images and terminology were akin to theirs" ("The Eschatology of the Epistle to the Hebrews," in Davies and Daube, *The Background of the New Testament and Its Eschatology*, 393).

[86] A. R. Eagar, "Hellenistic Elements in the Epistle to the Hebrews," *Herm* 11 (1901): 263–87; J. Gamble, "Symbol and Reality in the Epistle to the Hebrews," *JBL* 45 (1926): 162–70; C. Spicq, "Alexandrismes dans l'Épître aux Hébreux," *RB* 58 (1951): 481–502; L. K. K. Dey, *The Intermediary World and Patterns of Perfection in the Epistle to the Hebrews* (SBLDS 25; Missoula, MT: Scholars Press, 1975).

[87] The quotation is from C. Spicq's commentary (*L'Épître aux Hébreux* [2 vols.; Paris: Gabalda, 1952–53], 1:91).

Platonic tradition than those elements taken over by Philo. Even the work of James W. Thompson, the foremost advocate of a Middle Platonic background for Hebrews, concentrates too narrowly upon the author's metaphysical and cosmological assumptions which may be traced back through Philo to the Platonic distinction between the noumenal and the phenomenal.[88] No one has yet responded to Abraham J. Malherbe's call for a thorough examination of Hebrews in the light of contemporary Platonism.[89] In fact, aside from research on Philo, very little has been done in the way of relating Hebrews to any aspect of the contemporary philosophical environment. References to philosophical literature and to Plutarch in particular in the major commentaries is typically limited to the occasional citation of lexical parallels.

Neglect of the non-Jewish milieu is especially surprising in those commentaries positing a Gentile readership for Hebrews.[90] The consensus view is that Hebrews is addressed to a Jewish-Christian or perhaps a mixed audience. A number of major commentators, however, believe that a Gentile audience is more likely in light of certain clues the author drops about the readers and their relationship with God.[91] Theories of a Jewish-Christian readership, say Weiss

---

[88] J. W. Thompson, "'That Which Abides': Some Metaphysical Assumptions in the Epistle to the Hebrews" (Ph.D. Diss., Vanderbilt University, 1974).

[89] A. J. Malherbe, "Greco-Roman Religion and Philosophy and the New Testament," in *The New Testament and Its Modern Interpreters* (ed. E. J. Epp and G. W. MacRae; Atlanta: Scholars Press, 1989), 15. See, however, Peter Busch's foray into this territory in "Der mitleidende Hohepriester: Zur Rezeption der mittelplatonischen Dämonologie in Hebr 4,14f.," in *Religionsgeschichte des Neuen Testaments: Festschrift für Klaus Berger zum 60. Geburtstag* (ed. A. von Dobbeler et al.; Tübingen: Francke, 2000), 19–30.

[90] An overview of the issues involved may be found in W. Manson, *The Epistle to the Hebrews: An Historical and Theological Reconsideration* (London: Hodder & Stoughton, 1951), 16–18; E. Grässer, "Der Hebräerbrief 1938–1963," *TRu* 30 (1964): 147–51; and Helmut Feld, *Der Hebräerbrief* (EdF 228; Dardstadt: Wissenschaftliche Buchgesellschaft, 1985), 6–12.

[91] Most proponents of this view are German, though a few are English-speaking. The first appears to have been E. M. Roeth, *Epistolam vulgo "ad Hebraeos" inscriptam non ad Hebraeos, id est Christianos genere Judaeos sed ad Christianos genere gentiles et quidem ad Ephesios datam esse demonstrare conatur* (Frankfurt am Main: Schmerber, 1836). Among the other proponents are Adolf Jülicher, *An Introduction to the New Testament* (trans. J. P. Ward; New York: Putnam's; London: Smith, Elder, and Co., 1904), 163–67; Hermann von Soden, *Books of the New Testament* (ed. W. D. Morrison; trans. J. R. Wilkinson; London: Williams and Norgate, 1907), 266–67; E. F. Scott, *The Epistle to the Hebrews: Its Doctrine and Significance* (Edinburgh: Clark, 1923), 14–21; Moffatt, *Hebrews*, ix; Herbert Braun, *An die Hebräer* (HNT 14; Tübingen: Mohr-Siebeck, 1984), 2; Franz Laub, *Hebräerbrief* (SKKNT 14; Stuttgart: Verlag Katholisches Bibelwerk, 1988), 18; H. Hegermann, *Der Brief an Die Hebräer* (THKNT 16; Berlin: Evangelische Verlagsanstalt, 1988), 18; Claus-Peter März, *Hebräerbrief* (NEchtB 16; Würzburg: Echter, 1989), 18–19; Weiss, *Hebräer*, 70–72; E. Grässer, *An die Hebräer*

and others, place too much credence in the late second-century superscript πρὸς
Ἑβραίους. Moffatt puts it very succinctly in his preface: the situation
prompting the letter "had nothing to do with any movement in contemporary
Judaism," "[t]he writer of πρὸς Ἑβραίους knew no Hebrew, and his readers
are in no sense Ἑβραῖοι."[92] There is never any specific warning against
reverting to Judaism, only of forsaking Christ.[93] Christianity is the highest and
truest religion, and the author demonstrates its superiority through a sustained
comparison with its closest competitor, Judaism.[94] The pressing Jew-Gentile
question which runs through Acts and Paul's letters is entirely absent, thus
Hebrews belongs to a stage in Christian history when Paul's position had won
the day and the Christian movement was predominantly Gentile.[95] That the
alternative to progress in faith is described as apostasy "from the living God"
and a return to the performance of "dead works" (3:12; 6:1; 9:14) is taken as
further proof that the author is not describing their former life in Judaism but in
paganism.[96] In support of this reading, a number of commentators have appealed
to the similarities between Heb 6:1–2 and the missionary preaching aimed at
pagans in Acts and 1 Thessalonians, as well as to the resonance between the
elements included by the author as foundational and the content of the
catechumenate for Gentile proselytes to Judaism in the Second Temple period.[97]
The thoroughly scriptural character of Hebrews' argument is not seen as a
difficulty by proponents of a non-Jewish audience since the Gentile church
adopted the LXX (as has Hebrews) as its scripture at a very early stage. One

---

(EKKNT 17.1–3; 3 vols.; Braunschweig: Benzinger, 1990–97), 1:24. W. G. Kümmel
believes a Gentile audience is most probable and lists a number of earlier German
scholars unconvinced by the evidence put forward in support of a Jewish-Christian
audience (*Introduction to the New Testament* [rev. ed.; trans. H. C. Kee; Nashville and
New York: Abingdon, 1975], 399 n. 49). The most recent advocate is Bart D. Ehrman
(*The New Testament: A Historical Introduction to the Early Christian Writings* [New
York and Oxford: Oxford University Press, 1997], 354–59).

[92] Moffatt, *Hebrews*, ix.

[93] Von Soden, *Books of the New Testament*, 266–67; Braun, *Hebräer*, 2.

[94] Scott, *Hebrews*, 16–17; Moffatt, *Hebrews*, xvi, xxvi.

[95] Jülicher, *Introduction*, 163–66; Grässer, *Hebräer*, 1:24; Scott, *Hebrews*, 18–19.
Contrary to many interpreters for whom Gentile elements put a given document outside
the Jewish-Christian mainstream, Scott emphasizes the letter's appeal to Gentiles as
evidence that it belongs within the mainstream of early Christianity.

[96] Hegermann, *Hebräer*, 10; Braun, *Hebräer*, 94; Weiss, *Hebräer*, 71–72. Would the
hortatory strategy of 5:12–6:1 be suitable for a Jewish audience? Grässer's answer
(*Hebräer*, 1:24) is emphatic: "Kaum!"

[97] Braun, *Hebräer*, 157–60; Grässer, *Hebräer*, 1:24, 333–45; Weiss, *Hebräer*, 71,
337–39. Cf. also W. Thüsing, "'Milch' und 'feste Speise' (1 Kor 3,1 und Hebr 5,11–6,3):
Elementarkatachese und theologische Vertiefung in neutestamentlicher Sicht," *TTZ* 76
(1967): 242.

need only look to Paul's letters to Galatia and Corinth, *1 Clement*, or Justin
Martyr for examples of equal or greater appropriation of Hebrew scripture in
addressing a Gentile audience. As a result of this reliance on the LXX, the
author's discussion of Judaism has almost a bookish feel about it. Rather than
discussing contemporary Judaism and railing against the still-standing Jerusalem
temple as one sees in the Dead Sea Scrolls, Hebrews is concerned with the
tabernacle and its priestly ordinances as set out in the Pentateuch.

The case for a Gentile audience is based partly on positive internal
evidence, partly on negative evidence against a Jewish audience, and partly on
arguments from silence. Largely missing is extratextual evidence from the
Hellenistic milieu that would shed light on the matter. A very plausible case
could be made for the relevance of Greco-Roman sources for understanding the
religious sensibilities of Hebrews, but they are noticeably absent where one
might expect to find reference to them, namely, in the commentaries positing a
Gentile readership. Gnosticism is typically the only non-Jewish aspect
mentioned in surveys of the epistle's religious-historical background.[98] This is
odd given the view that the author of Hebrews "is a child of the Hellenistic
culture, and employs the conceptions which were native to it in his presentation
of the gospel."[99] Moffatt, who sees the author's concern as the presentation of
Christianity as the fullest embodiment of "real religion," does very little to place
Hebrews' notion of religion in the context where (on Moffatt's own terms) it
would make the most sense.[100] Braun is the exception. Of the major
commentaries on Hebrews of previous generations, his perhaps makes the most
extensive use of Greco-Roman sources.[101] On account of the commentary
format, however, he is not able to pursue the discussion of individual motifs at
any great length.[102] Given the recurring motif of fear and of Jesus' priestly

---

[98] Cf. Weiss, *Hebräer*, 96–114; Hegermann, *Hebräer*, 11–14; Grässer, "Der Hebräerbrief
1938–1963," 177–86; Scott, *Hebrews*, 69–84. Moffatt (*Hebrews*, xxx–xxxiv) briefly
mentions Plato but does not make reference to the Gnostic literature.

[99] Scott, *Hebrews*, 48. For similar statements, see 50, 53, 69.

[100] Moffatt, *Hebrews*, xxvi. He does make passing reference, however, to Seneca,
Epictetus, and Plato in his discussion of Hebrews' rejection of atheism at 11:6 (166–67).

[101] In connection with the reference to "the living God" in 3:12, he draws a parallel with
Plutarch (*Superst.* 165B) (*Hebräer*, 94). God's fearsomeness in 10:31 is related to
Plutarch's discussion of superstition (325). Braun also states that Heb 11:6 belongs in the
general context of ancient discussions of practical atheism carried on by Plutarch,
Epicurus, and Epictetus (348).

[102] The same is true of Craig R. Koester's new commentary (*Hebrews* [AB 36; New
York: Doubleday, 2001]), which includes extensive references to Greek and Roman
sources. David deSilva's recently published commentary (*Perseverance in Gratitude: A
Socio-Rhetorical Commentary on the Epistle "to the Hebrews"* [Grand Rapids:
Eerdmans, 2000]), likewise provides extensive analysis at several points of the author's
engagement with Greco-Roman culture and society.

accomplishments as the ground for confidence in the approach to God, the neglect of Greco-Roman discussions of the propriety of fear in the religious realm that lay behind Plutarch's treatment of superstition is regrettable.

Approach

To determine the extent to which the form of Christianity one finds in Hebrews would qualify as δεισιδαιμονία in Plutarch's eyes, one must begin by setting out Plutarch's construal of what it means to be superstitious. This is the task taken up in chapter two after the scholarly frame of reference within which the topic is to be pursued has been established. A survey of the lexical data in Latin will show the areas of confluence with and divergence from the Greek vocabulary employed by Plutarch to describe superstition. A brief but comprehensive review of the use of cognates of δεισιδαιμονία in Greek will reveal the range of traits and dispositions covered by this term used by Plutarch in his treatise. His usage fits relatively comfortably within the tradition of philosophical critique of religion and touches on all the recurring indicators of superstition current in the Hellenistic period. By far the most pervasive in this depiction of the superstitious shared by Plutarch and his contemporaries is the element of fear. Because Plutarch locates the core of δεισιδαιμονία in the emotions, his work will be examined in the context of the analyses of the emotions in the philosophical traditions with which he is in dialogue. After this excursus on the main schools of thought, attention will turn back to Plutarch and *De superstitione*. This final section of the chapter summarizes and provides detailed commentary on the essay, with special attention to the way he views fear (especially fear of the gods), how these views cohere with those found elsewhere in his immense corpus, and what basic assumptions compel him to pass such harsh judgment on superstition.

Because fear is the core component of superstition according to Plutarch and other Hellenistic authors, who regard the emotion as a fundamental human problem arising in both sacred and secular contexts, chapters three and four look in detail at the various occurrences of this motif in Hebrews. Chapter three examines passages in Hebrews which advocate freedom from fear as a desirable and attainable ideal for the Christian. Of particular concern to the author is fear of death, a theme of recurring interest to the moral philosophers whose ideas inform Plutarch's characterization of superstitious fear. The causes of and remedy for fear of death according to Hebrews will be interpreted as an integral component of the author's christological presentation, as will the way in which he puts forward "confidence" (παρρησία) as the obverse of fear in the believer's approach to God. Once the nature of this "vertical" relationship between God and the individual is established, those passages will be examined which seek to inculcate a posture of fearlessness on the horizontal plane, that is, in circumstances where earthly circumstances and other humans appear to pose a threat to the well-being and emotional equilibrium of the believer. The nexus of belief, feeling, and action, familiar from Hellenistic analyses of the emotions, also underlies the author's mode of argument and helps to clarify his views on the place of fear in the life of faith.

Chapter four concentrates primarily on two passages (Heb 5:7; 12:18–29) where apparent manifestations of fear signify a disposition the author regards in a quite positive light, and by that token may make him and his readers susceptible to a charge of superstition. One passage celebrates the "godly fear" (εὐλάβεια) of the human Jesus, while the other speaks approvingly of this same quality of "reverent awe" as a fitting accompaniment of thanksgiving and worship offered to God under the new covenant inaugurated by Jesus' sacrifice.

A final chapter draws together the key insights of the preceding chapters, returns to the question posed at the outset of the study, and reflects briefly on the complexities involved in formulating an answer.

Chapter Two

Plutarch and Superstition

Introduction

The concept of "superstition" functions sometimes not like a delicate instrument suited to comparative study but rather like a blunt object with which to bludgeon one's opponents.[1] Between 1550 and 1700, for example, nearly four thousand cases of *supersticion* were tried by the Spanish Inquisition, all without the benefit of a careful, scholarly definition of the offense in question.[2] The Inquisition's implicit definition differs in some respects from Plutarch's over a millennium earlier. Plutarch's definition in turn may or may not differ from those of his contemporaries, hence the need for focus and caution in making generalizations about "the" (singular) ancient understanding of superstition. Plutarch naturally shares much with those living at the same time and observing the same kinds of activities like Tacitus and Pliny, but this overlap should be shown and not simply assumed. Part of the present chapter is taken up with this task. There is also much common ground between the mentality that generally passes for superstitiousness today in the West and δεισιδαιμονία or *superstitio* in ancient Greece or Rome. It is not the objective of this chapter to formulate a

---

[1] The same can be said of the German *Aberglaube*. As Gladigow ("Aberglaube," 1:388) and Walter Sparn ("Aberglaube: II. Kirchengeschichtliche und dogmatisch," *RGG* 1:58–59) both note, its descriptive usefulness is limited because it functions primarily as a normative concept, whether in inter-religious or intra-religious dialogue; cf. the similar discussion of the Spanish concept in Carlos Alonso del Real, *Superstición y Supersticiones* (Madrid: Espasa-Calpe, 1971), 73–86. Not every attempt to distinguish religion and superstition, however, is undertaken in a polemical context. Note the serious discussion among linguistic philosophers (R. J. Ray, "Crossed Fingers and Praying Hands: Remarks on Religious Belief and Superstition," *RelS* 26 [1990]: 471–82; D. Z. Phillips, *Religion without Explanation* [London: Blackwell, 1976], 100–121; Wittgenstein, *Culture and Value*, 5, 72, 83).
[2] William Monter, *Ritual, Myth and Magic in Early Modern Europe* (Athens, Ohio: Ohio University Press, 1984), 63.

universal definition or some abstract, all-embracing notion capable of covering every conceivable manifestation of superstition. Rather, the aim here is to trace the "logic"—if there is one—not only of those illogical actions and attitudes labeled δεισιδαιμονία by the Greeks, but of Plutarch's impassioned brief against them as well.[3]

The approach of the present chapter, in focusing upon the specific language of δεισιδαιμονία used by Plutarch and other Greek writers, is in the first place an inductive one. What do they explicitly refer to as δεισιδαιμονία? It is of little use to proceed from a posture of false ignorance; that is, to pretend that modern observers are totally in the dark as to his meaning when Plutarch refers to a person as δεισιδαίμων. The family resemblance with superstition is in fact quite impressive. While recognizing this area of agreement, it is imperative to keep in mind that the fit between ancient and modern ways of construing superstition is not a perfect one. This study of Plutarch's understanding of δεισιδαιμονία is an inductive process of discovery, where the delimitation is imposed by the language he uses. The ideas expressed by the language of δεισιδαιμονία are by no means limited to those passages where that term appears, but to broaden the search prematurely to other areas begs the question by introducing evidence prejudged to be relevant. Given the basic datum that Plutarch uses δεισιδαιμονία in the same broadly pejorative way that an English speaker would use "superstition," what can be discerned about its deeper structure? What unites the variegated phenomena that go by this name? Why, for example, is one type of divination deemed superstitious, while Plutarch's priestly service at Delphi is eminently respectable in the eyes of first-century Greeks?

Dale Martin quite properly maintains that it is anachronistic to construe ancient superstition either in terms of a natural/supernatural or a rational/irrational dichotomy.[4] To begin with the first false criterion, perceptions of supernatural intrusion into the natural world are often identified as instances

---

[3] Nicole Belmont has in view a similar goal in her attempt to bring to light the "submerged" system of popular religion. She employs structuralist and Freudian categories and sees the religion/superstition opposition as one between internalization and externalization ("Superstition and Popular Religion in Western Societies," in *Between Belief and Transgression: Structuralist Essays in Religion, History, and Myth* [ed. M. Izard and P. Smith; Chicago: University of Chicago Press, 1982], 9, 20). The difference between her approach and the present one is that here the attempt is to clarify the logic of superstition in terms of the native categories employed by first-century Greeks.

[4] Dale B. Martin, "Hellenistic Superstition: The Problems of Defining a Vice," in *Conventional Values of the Hellenistic Greeks* (ed. P. Bilde et al.; Aarhus: Aarhus University Press, 1997), 110–27. Jan Opsomer, "Divination and Academic 'Scepticism' according to Plutarch," *Studia Hellenistica* 32 (1996): 166–67, makes a similar point about the trend among historians after Eduard Zeller to interpret all post-Aristotelian philosophy in terms of dogmatic versus sceptical tendencies.

of superstition in the ancient world, but the metaphysical claims about the origin of these phenomena are frequently incidental to their classification as δεισιδαιμονία. Medical writers such as Hippocrates do indeed reject as superstitious many explanations of disease that attribute it to demons, but even more common is a belief in the providential role of the gods in health maintenance. Very few scientists or philosophers in antiquity—pre-Socratics like Thales, Anaximander, Anaximenes, and Democritus are major exceptions—reject across the board the idea that non-material or spiritual entities like gods or demons might impinge upon the physical world as would a modern materialist.[5] Martin goes so far as to say that it is illegitimate to attribute the category of the supernatural to the Greeks—it was invented by Descartes—since the concept depends upon a modern understanding of "nature" as a closed, mechanistic system that is alien to ancient thinkers.[6]

As to the second criterion, recent theorists of various stripes have drawn attention to the inadequacy of the concept of "rationality" as a descriptive category.[7] Neither the Enlightenment *philosophes* nor their modern successors

---

[5] Philosophical materialism is the doctrine that physical matter is all that truly exists. Minds and all other apparently non-material entities or events are in this view merely the epiphenomena of physical processes. Naturalism and physicalism are other names for the same general view of reality.

[6] Martin, "Hellenistic Superstition," 113. This assessment of the Cartesian legacy is not peculiar to Martin. Leszek Kolakowski also argues that Descartes and others, by positing a universe totally in accordance with all-explanatory laws of mechanics, reduced God to the status of a logically necessary support for the continued existence of the cosmos—a support that, because it is constant, is devoid of significance in explaining any particular event (*Modernity on Endless Trial* [Chicago: University of Chicago Press, 1990], 96–98). Plutarch recognizes the difficulty of comprehending God's providential oversight of the cosmos when he says that "those who make the god responsible for nothing at all and those who make him responsible for all things alike go wide of moderation and propriety" (*Def. orac.* 414F). Henri de Lubac (*Surnaturel: études historiques* [Paris: Aubier, 1946]) says that it is only in the last two centuries that there has arisen the idea that "pure" nature and supernature are two completely heteronomous realities. For a historical survey of the use of the term "supernatural," see Larry L. Rose, "Toward a New Supernaturalism" (Ph.D. diss., The Claremont Graduate School, 1967), 47–106. Adjudicating Martin's controversial claim about the origin of the category of "the supernatural" is too large a task for this chapter. It is true that the ancients included within "nature" much that moderns would consider outside the realm of ordinary nature, but this is not the same as saying that, for example, Plato did not conceive of a plane of existence completely independent of the world of appearances. For the present, he is correct to note that simple acknowledgement of the interpenetration of the natural and the supernatural is not the primary criterion by which ancient Greeks would recognize instances of δεισιδαιμονία.

[7] See, for example, Barbara Herrnstein Smith, *Contingencies of Value* (Cambridge: Harvard University Press, 1988); Paul K. Feyerabend, *Against Method* (3rd ed.; London:

have been able to agree upon exactly which principles are absolutely undeniable by any rational person. Consequently, all attempts to invoke irrationality as a criterion for recognizing superstition will inevitably degenerate into circular reasoning. Determinations of "rationality" are themselves conditioned by such non-rational considerations as the concrete contexts in which they take place.

More attainable than a universal epistemological criterion are answers to more narrowly circumscribed historical questions:[8] Superstitious to whom? Informed by what assumptions? Supported by what kinds of rhetoric? These questions will guide the investigation in this chapter. Martin speaks in terms of sketching the grammar of ancient rationality and superstition.[9] The focus on Plutarch is in part a strategy to make the task a manageable one. This focus also guards against the danger of constructing a composite understanding of superstition to which no particular Greek at any particular time can be shown to have subscribed on all points.

Fear of the gods is a concern of many Hellenistic thinkers, both professional philosophers and "popular" writers like Plutarch. However helpful, it is only a temporary solution to say that δεισιδαιμονία is bad in Plutarch's eyes because it involves fear. Why is fear to be avoided, particularly in one's dealings with the gods? A survey of the lexical data will make it possible to ascertain the degree to which Plutarch's understanding of superstition is typical for his day. Because Plutarch locates the core of δεισιδαιμονία in the emotions, it is best understood not just against the background of other "superstitious" activities but against other treatments of fear in his corpus and in the wider milieu as well. After a review of the representative analyses of the emotions among the Hellenistic philosophical schools, Plutarch's argument in *De superstitione* will be examined with special attention to the way in which it is in conversation with these other traditions and coheres with the ideas expressed in his larger corpus.

Terminology

Latin

In *Studies in Words*, C. S. Lewis describes a process wherein specific words shift in meaning over time.[10] This process, which he calls "verbicide," occurs

---

Verso, 1993); and Alasdair MacIntyre, *Whose Justice? Which Rationality?* (Notre Dame: University of Notre Dame Press, 1988), esp. 1–11. The problematic antithesis of myth and reason as modes of Greek thought is the subject of a volume edited by Richard Buxton (*From Myth to Reason?* [Oxford: Oxford University Press, 1999], esp. 6–13).
[8] Martin, "Hellenistic Superstition," 112.
[9] Ibid., 112, 124.
[10] C. S. Lewis, *Studies in Words* (2nd ed.; Cambridge: Cambridge University Press, 1967), 6–8.

when a word like "natural," "liberal," or "demonic," gradually becomes less descriptive and more evaluative. Whereas these terms originally denoted more or less precise qualities or entities, by the end of this historical-linguistic process they function almost solely as expressions of approval or disapproval. As virtual synonyms for "good" and "bad," they become of little use to the historian interested in determining the nature of the phenomena they modify. The speaker may have an idea of what a given term represents, but the historian must take into account the context in order to discover the referents and connotations of that term when it was first used.

Something very much like this occurs with *superstitio* between Plautus in the third century B.C.E. and the rise of Christianity.[11] By the time of Trajan, when Tacitus (*Ann.* 15.44), Pliny (*Ep.* 10.96), and Suetonius (*Nero* 16.2) each use *superstitio* explicitly in the earliest pagan references to Christianity, the standard Latin term for superstition is no longer a narrow, denotative one. Nor is it an ambivalent one. The neutral, descriptive sense with which it appears in the earliest stages disappears in the first century and *superstitio* becomes almost purely a term of opprobrium. Virgil is perhaps the last author to use it in a neutral sense, though the pejorative usage appears earlier.[12] Cicero calls it "worthless" (*inanis*), associates it with fraud, and blames it for all manner of "false beliefs, crazy errors and . . . old wives' tales" driven by inappropriate fears regarding the gods.[13] It is opposed to ancestral custom and "the purest, holiest and most pious way of worshipping the gods."[14] Horace associates it with melancholia, and though there is variation as to the particulars, *superstitio* is a generic quality that plagues all peoples without distinction.[15] As it is feeble-minded (*imbecillus*) and characteristic of old women (*anilis*), it is inconsistent with the philosophical life.[16] These associations undermine the stereotypical notion of Roman religion as concerned exclusively with what one does instead

---

[11] The nominal form first appears in Cicero but the adjective *superstitiosus* appears in Plautus over a century earlier (*Amph.* 323; *Curc.* 397; *Rud.* 1139). On these early occurrences and the possible derivation of *superstitio* from *superstes*, see Otto, "Religio und Superstitio," 550–54; Grodzynski, "Superstitio," 37–38; and Janssen, "Die Bedeutungsentwicklung von *superstitio/superstes*," 135–88. Cf. also A. S. Pease, ed., *M. Tulli Ciceronis De Divinatione, Libri Duo* (Darmstadt: Wissenschaftliche Buchgesellschaft, 1963), 580–81.

[12] Virgil, *Aen.* 12.817. Cf. Smith, "Superstitio," 352–53, though see Tacitus, *Agr.* 11.

[13] *Nat. d.* 1.42.117; 2.28.70; 3.39.92; *Div.* 2.41.85; 2.72.148; *Verr.* 2.4.51.113.

[14] *Nat. d.* 2.28.71. Because it is not "pure," it is therefore *contaminata* (Cicero, *Clu.* 68.194). Its danger is in how closely it borders on the virtue of *religio* (*Leg.* 2.54.165).

[15] Horace, *Sat.* 2.3.79. Cicero likewise regards it as incompatible with emotional tranquility: superstition "poisons and destroys all peace of mind" (*Fin.* 1.18.60; cf. *Div.* 2.72.149; *Nat. d.* 1.20.56; *Leg.* 1.11.32).

[16] Cicero, *Div.* 1.4.7; 2.6.19; 2.39.81; 2.60.125; 2.63.129; *Dom.* 40.105; *Tusc.* 3.29.72; *Nat. d.* 1.20.55.

of how one thinks or what one believes. Neither *superstitio* nor *pietas* "exist in mere outward show and pretense" (Cicero, *Nat. d.* 1.2.3–4).

From the imperial period forward, this sense of *superstitio* as a debased form of *religio* is the predominant one. Most of the negative connotations from the previous period persist and are intensified. Columella, for example, regards it as a womanly vice and he groups it together with drunkenness, greed, sloth, and promiscuity.[17] According to Livy, *superstitio* is contrary to human wisdom and trust in the beneficence of the gods.[18] Sometimes *superstitio* is a matter of form rather than of substance, as when Quintilian (*Inst.* 3.1.22) associates it with slavish, unthinking adherence to a school of thought. For Silius Italicus, *superstitio* is an "empty" (*vana*) emotion.[19] Somewhat in contrast to this idea of emptiness is the idea of superstition as religiosity run to excess.[20] Seneca has much to say about superstition, his personal experience with Nero no doubt providing him with a wealth of anecdotal evidence to illustrate the theme. He describes it variously as an improper form of fear, an outrage, and "the misguided idea of a lunatic."[21] Unfortunately, many of Seneca's views have been lost because his essay on superstition has been preserved only in selective quotations in Augustine, Lactantius, and Minucius Felix, who make use of his philosophical critiques of popular religion when they turn the tables on the Romans and attack pagan beliefs and practices.[22]

It is thus fairly simple to establish the thoroughly negative connotations carried by the Latin *superstitio* when Roman observers label Christianity a superstition. But what specific behaviors and dispositions fall under this category, and why are they deemed to be inappropriate from a Roman perspective? Latin *superstitio* included magic and "unofficial" divination and could cover a wide array of unseemly behaviors generally (but not exclusively) associated with the unlettered masses and with foreign cults. The most heinous

---

[17] Columella, *De re rustica* 12.1.3; Pliny, *Nat.* 7.1.5; Juvenal, *Sat.* 6.511.

[18] Livy 7.2.3. Cf. Seneca (*Clem.* 2.5.1): "Religion does honour to the gods, while superstition wrongs them."

[19] Silius Italicus, *Punica* 5.125. Cf. Seneca, *Nat.* 7.1.2; Tacitus, *Hist.* 4.54.

[20] Quintilian, *Inst.* 8.3.55; Aulus Gellius, *Noct. att.* 4.9.2.

[21] Seneca, *Ep.* 121.4; 123.16. On *superstitio* as one form of dementia, see Quintilian, *Inst.* 4.2.85; Q. Curtius Rufus, *Hist. Alex.* 7.7.8. The element of fear is emphasized by Livy (6.5.6) and Varro (apud Augustine, *Civ.* 6.9).

[22] For the Latin text and discussion, see Marion Lausberg. *Untersuchungen zu Senecas Fragmenten* (Untersuchungen zur antiken Literatur und Geschichte 7; Berlin: de Gruyter, 1970), 197–227; idem, "Senecae operum fragmenta: Überblick und Forschungsbericht," *ANRW* 36.3:1879–1961; and Léon Hermann, "Sénèque et la superstition," *Latomus* 29 (1970): 389–96. On the changed situation after the Christianization of the empire, see Michele R. Salzman, "'Superstitio' in the *Codex Theodosianus* and the Persecution of Pagans," *VC* 41 (1987): 172–88.

of these was human sacrifice.[23] At best, *superstitio* was to be avoided because it was undignified. At worst—and this is the common element among those activities considered *superstitiosus*—it was socially and politically subversive and, on that account, grounds for prosecution. The proconsul Statilius Taurus, for example, took his own life before the Senate could pass down a death sentence on trumped up charges of "addiction to magical superstitions."[24]

While the subversive nature of superstition in the early empire was in part a function of its association with foreign cults, Roman citizens, even at the highest levels, were not immune to this accusation. This critique could come from a foreigner, as when Posidonius describes Romans as exceedingly superstitious (σφόδρα δεισιδαιμονοῦσι [frg. 200, line 20]), or from within the imperial elite. Tacitus (*Hist.* 2.78) reports that Vespasian kept a court astrologer and had a keen interest in omens. One of Nero's superstitions had him urinating on the image of a Syrian goddess while another had him trusting in the image of a little girl in order to protect him from conspiracies (Suetonius, *Nero* 56). Many soldiers were "pliable to superstitions," and on one occasion a senatorial decision to alter the course of the Tiber is reversed due in part to *superstitio* (Tacitus, *Ann.* 1.28; 1.79). It would also be incorrect to conclude that all non-Roman cults were automatically deemed superstitious. On occasion, the stigma of superstition could be mitigated by a cult's antiquity.[25] This frequently worked in Judaism's favor—before the revolts, at least—and against Christianity, hence the efforts of some Christian writers to present the faith in such a way that emphasized its continuity with Judaism and downplayed any social disruptions caused by conversion.

During the first and second centuries discussion of superstition in Roman sources is increasingly concerned with foreign cults at the edges of the empire.[26] The size of the empire finally peaked under Trajan, after which Hadrian began to pull back strategically from trouble spots that proved to be too much of a drain on imperial resources. As the empire expanded leading up to the early second century, more foreign cults fell within its boundaries and entered the consciousness of Roman observers. Egypt was a well-known source of these exotic cults. Cicero (*Leg.* 1.11.32) had earlier ridiculed the Egyptian practice of worshipping cats and dogs. Seemingly innocuous rites of this sort, however, could pose a threat to Rome's social and cultural fabric. Cicero declares that his purpose in writing *De divinatione* is to fulfill a patriotic duty (*Div.* 2.72.148):

---

[23] Cicero, *Clu.* 68.194; *Font.* 31; Q. Curtius Rufus, *Hist. Alex.* 4.3.23; Livy 33.57.6; Pliny, *Nat.* 30.12–13; Tacitus, *Ann.* 14.30; *Germ.* 39.4.

[24] Tacitus, *Ann.* 12.59. Cf. also the accusation against Laebo of "inspiring a baseless fear" in Tiberius's wife through "magical arts" performed in secrecy (Tacitus, *Ann.* 6.29).

[25] Tacitus, *Germ.* 43.4; Pliny, *Pan.* 49.8; Suetonius, *Aug.* 93.

[26] Grodzynski, "Superstitio," 47–48. This remains constant in the late imperial period (Salzman, "'Superstitio' in the *Codex Theodosianus*," 173).

"For I thought that I should be rendering a great service both to myself and to my countrymen if I could tear this superstition up by the roots." Wisdom, he goes on to explain, partly consists in the commitment "to preserve the institutions of our forefathers by retaining their sacred rites and ceremonies." This connection between superstition and un-Roman activity is even more marked a century later. A number of writers make the link with foreign cults explicit.[27] Livy does so with the Samnites, who are defeated while "busy with superstitious rites" in a secret council, thus their superstitiousness led to their own downfall, a lesson not lost on Livy's readers (10.39.2). Both Suetonius and Tacitus associate *superstitio* with the Druids, whose religion Claudius outlaws because of their habit of prophesying Rome's downfall and of encouraging the fulfillment of this prophecy.[28] Though they do not perform propitiatory rites to avert events portended by omens as do other foreigners, the Jews also are nonetheless "prone to superstition."[29] Virtually any religious deviation could be regarded as *superstitio*. Dio Cassius has Agrippa advise the young Augustus to punish anyone who distorts Roman rites through innovations because new deities lead to foreign practices, "from which spring up conspiracies, factions, and cabals."[30]

Such an equation of the foreign with the superstitious is to be explained as much by Rome's understanding of its own rise to pre-eminence in the Mediterranean as by the particulars of the individual peoples and cults falling under its dominion. Rome's greatness was regularly attributed to the patronage of the traditional gods. So long as the Roman people rendered *pietas* to the gods, their city would thrive. " 'Tis by holding thyself the servant of the gods," Horace writes, "that thou dost rule."[31] This perceived symbiosis of political strength and religious propriety stretched back to the city's founding. According to tradition, Romulus and especially Numa Pompilius, Rome's second king, had made a covenant to honor the gods in exchange for divine protection. This national self-understanding is especially prevalent during the Augustan period but is

[27] Pliny the Elder, *Nat.* 30.2.7; Pliny the Younger, *Pan.* 49.8; Tacitus, *Hist.* 4.61, 81; *Germ.* 45; *Ann.* 13.32; Statius, *Theb.* 6.11; Suetonius, *Tib.* 36; for a long list of texts, see Hodgson, "Superstition and Submission," 182–83.

[28] Suetonius, *Claud.* 25.5; Tacitus, *Hist.* 4.54; *Ann.* 14.30.

[29] Tacitus, *Hist.* 5.13; Cicero, *Flac.* 67. See Peter Schäfer, *Judeophobia: Attitudes toward the Jews in the Ancient World* (Cambridge: Harvard University Press, 1997), 180–95.

[30] Dio Cassius 52.36. The proclivity of magicians and philosophers for fomenting rebellion agrees with Seneca's association of *superstitio* with treachery (*perfidia*; *Ep.* 22.15). On the intractability of these groups, see Ramsay MacMullen, *Enemies of the Roman Order* (Cambridge: Harvard University Press, 1966), 46–127.

[31] Horace, *Odes* 3.6.5; cf. Cicero, *Har. resp.* 9.18; Livy 5.51.4; Dionysius of Halicarnassus, *Ant. rom.* 1.4.2; 1.5.3; Pliny, *Pan.* 74.5; Valerius Maximus, *Factorum ac dictorum memorabilium* 1.3.3.

anticipated prior to the founding of the principate.[32] Cicero has Cotta declare that "Romulus by his auspices and Numa by his establishment of our ritual laid the foundations of our state, which assuredly could never have been as great as it had not the fullest measure of divine favour been obtained for it" (*Nat. d.* 3.5.2). Three centuries later, the Decian persecution, with its requirement of sacrifice to Roman gods, was motivated in no small part by the perception that the instability of the age had resulted when Rome violated the terms of this contract.[33] Christians, by advocating the abandonment of traditional Roman religion, were thereby guilty of treason. Jewish contempt for the deities of the Roman pantheon meant that their *superstitio* was also a form of practical atheism and therefore potentially disloyal to the state.[34] This political aspect of *superstitio* is accentuated by the frequent use of its antonym *pietas* to refer to loyalty in patron-client relationships.[35]

Disloyalty to the state as an aspect of superstition could take active or passive forms. Abstinence from meat could even be an indicator of superstitious inclinations, as the case of Seneca illustrates. Under the influence of a Pythagorean teacher, the young Seneca had been practicing vegetarianism for a year before giving it up as a concession to his politically sensitive father (*Ep.* 108.17–22). Vegetarianism was associated with foreign cults and philosophies with anti-imperial tendencies, and therefore was regarded with suspicion by

---

[32] On Augustus as a new Romulus as part of the propaganda of the early principate, see Paul Zanker, *The Power of Images in the Age of Augustus* (trans. A. Shapiro; Ann Arbor: University of Michigan Press, 1988), 201–10. Livy describes Numa's role in establishing the city's most important priesthoods and religious festivals (1.19.6–1.20.7), though not without considerable cynicism. Numa, he says, sought to instill fear of the gods as a means of social control over the rabble, now in a dangerous state of idleness due to the absence of a foreign threat. Tertullian later classifies Numa's religious initiatives as superstition and attributes their form to the devil's imitation of Jewish laws (*Praescr.* 40.6; *Apol.* 21.29). He also goes against conventional wisdom which attributed Roman power to Roman piety by crediting the undeniable success of the empire to the prayers of faithful Christians (*Apol.* 30.4).

[33] Cf. William H. C. Frend, *Martyrdom and Persecution in the Early Church* (Oxford: Blackwell, 1965), 404–21.

[34] Pliny, *Nat.* 13.9.46; Tacitus, *Hist.* 5.5. Cf. N. Brox, "Zum Vorwurf des Atheismus gegen die alte Kirche," *TTZ* 75 (1966): 274–82. Similarly contradictory are the twin charges of atheism and introducing strange gods leveled against Socrates by the Athenians. When Quintilian (*Inst.* 4.4.5) relates these charges, he says that Socrates has corrupted the youth and introduced *nova superstitiones*. That this view was not peculiar to Quintilian is inferred from the entry on Socrates in Suidas (Σ829), where δεισιδαιμονία is mentioned as the grounds for his prosecution by Anytus. Seneca (*Ep.* 123.16) and Cicero (*Nat. d.* 1.42.117) are closer to the Greek philosophical view that superstition is the polar opposite of atheism.

[35] Cicero, *Fam.* 10.23.7; Ovid, *Pont.* 2.2.21; Velleius 2.16.3; 2.71.1.

loyal Romans. The eagerness of the Gauls, stirred up by Druid prophecies, to rebel against Rome is a more active and egregious instance of *superstitio*. Their practice of human sacrifice was evidence of their *immanitas*, the antithesis of *humanitas*. Along with *pietas*, *fides*, *clementia*, and *iustitia*, *humanitas* had its roots in a *religio* that, in Roman eyes, was utterly inconsistent with *superstitio*.[36] L. F. Janssen finds in the derivation of *superstitio* from *superstes* another reason for its perceived incompatibility with the Roman order.[37] *Superstes* denotes survival, particularly of one's own family, friends, and patrons. Through prophecy and other magical arts, those who sought to become *superstes* through their children were seen as sinning against the state, to which every citizen's primary allegiance was due. In texts from both the late republican and early imperial periods this is again paralleled by instances in which *pietas* is said to be due to one's country even before one's family.[38] To be superstitious, then, is to allow one's private survival instincts to override the patriotic virtues of a model citizen.[39] The evil of *superstitio* in this view was thus in the potential threat it posed to the public order more than in the implausibility of the beliefs it involved.

Greek

Like its corresponding Latin term, the basic Greek word group for superstition (δεισιδαιμονεῖν/δεισιδαιμονία/δεισιδαίμων) saw significant development, from the neutral or even positive sense with which it first appears to the quite pejorative connotation it has for Plutarch and most writers after him. To appreciate any special meaning it might possess for Plutarch, it is necessary to place him within the context of this development. There is considerable

---

[36] Richard Gordon, "Religion in the Roman Empire: The Civic Compromise and its Limits," in *Pagan Priests* (ed. M. Beard and J. North; London: Duckworth, 1990), 235–38; W. Schadewalt, "Humanitas Romana," *ANRW* 1.4:43–62; and L. F. Janssen, "'Superstitio' and the Persecution of the Christians," *VC* 33 (1979): 146–54. See Tacitus' concomitant charges of *superstitio* and *odium humani generis* against the Christians (*Ann.* 15.44).

[37] Janssen, "'Superstitio' and the Persecution of the Christians," 139–43; and idem, "Die Bedeutungsentwicklung von *superstitio/superstes*," 161, 187.

[38] Cicero, *Resp.* 616; Livy 8.10. Gaius Gracchus is reproached for honoring the memory of his brother above his country (Cicero, *Brut.* 126) while Aeneas is praised for putting the interests of the state before the welfare of his father (Seneca, *Ben.* 6.36.1). The demands of *pietas* could at times be tragically conflicted, as when Agamemnon, out of a feeling of public duty, sacrifices his daughter Iphigenia, though human sacrifice is one of the practices commonly labeled *superstitio* (Ovid, *Metam.* 12.29). It is completely possible, however, for *pietas* simultaneously to include service to both kin and country (Cicero, *Inv.* 2.161; Ovid, *Fasti* 3.709–710).

[39] Janssen, "'Superstitio' and the Persecution of the Christians," 150.

overlap between the semantic range covered by the respective Greek and Latin vocabulary, but they differ slightly in that *superstitio* has more overtly political overtones and somewhat less emphasis on the element of fear than does δεισιδαιμονία.[40] Similar phenomena fall under the headings of *superstitio* and δεισιδαιμονία, but the equivalence is not an exact one. Because of his relative lack of facility with the Latin language, one must be cautious about transferring the nuances of *superstitio* to Plutarch when he uses δεισιδαιμονία.[41] Treating the two separately helps to specify more precisely what Plutarch means when he talks about superstition.

The overwhelming majority of instances where δεισιδαιμονία is used in a neutral or favorable sense occur prior to Plutarch.[42] Xenophon uses the adjective twice (*Ages.* 11.8; *Cyr.* 3.3.58) to characterize piety and the positive effects it has in the arena of human affairs. The passage in the *Cyropaedia* is noteworthy because he directly addresses the concept of fear and asserts that fear of the gods does not translate into fearfulness of humans; rather, οἱ δεισιδαίμονες are even less fearful, for example, in times of battle. Aristotle's use of the adjective is more complicated but also reflects popular approval of the quality the term represents. In an analysis later echoed in Machiavelli he says that, in addition to the other qualities he must possess, the successful tyrant must maintain the appearance of being δεισιδαίμων (*Pol.* 1315A). Here it reflects deference to religious tradition. A ruler regarded as δεισιδαίμων, it is thought, has the gods on his side, but care must be taken lest one fall into extreme δεισιδαιμονία, which gives the impression not of fastidiousness but of foolishness. Diodorus Siculus regularly uses this terminology, and while it is not always clear whether

---

[40] Cf. H. S. Versnel, "Deisidaimonia," *OCD* 441; Robert Muth, "Vom Wesen römischen 'religio'," *ANRW* 16.1:351–52. Dieter Lührmann ("Superstitio—die Beurteilung des frühen Christentums durch die Römer," *TZ* 42 [1986]: 206) says that, while not technically a criminal offense, *superstitio* implies a negative moral-political value judgment. Emphasis on the psychological aspect over the moral-political aspect as is found, for example, in Seneca's lost work on superstition is atypical for a Roman source.

[41] Plutarch states that he had little time for study while in Rome and was not able to pick up on the subtle nuances of the Latin language (*Dem.* 2.2). Cf. Jones, *Plutarch and Rome*, 81–87.

[42] For other surveys of the data, see Koets, Δεισιδαιμονία, 5–31; C. Spicq, "δεισιδαίμων, δεισιδαιμονία," *TLNT* 1:305–8; Julio Caro Baroja, *De la Supersticion al Ateismo* (Madrid: Taurus, 1974), 151–61; and H. Armin Moellering, *Plutarch on Superstition* (rev. ed.; Boston: Christopher, 1963), 42–52. Moellering's overview of Plutarch's predecessors, like the older treatments of Ernst Riess ("Aberglaube," PW 1.1:29–93) and Samuel Dill (*Roman Society from Nero to Marcus Aurelius* [2nd ed.; London: Macmillan, 1905], 443–83), includes Latin authors as well as Greek texts in which δεισιδαιμονία does not occur because he is interested in phenomena generally recognized as "superstition" from a post-Enlightenment perspective rather than in those activities and dispositions actually denoted by this term in the primary texts.

or not he is taking it over from a source, the generally positive or neutral connotation it carries in his writings shows that Theophrastus's caricature of the superstitious man did not singlehandedly transform δεισιδαιμονία into a univocal term of reproach.[43] In the centuries preceding Plutarch it could refer generally to piety, reverence, or a proclivity to see the active presence of the divine in auspicious events or at certain locations. More broadly it could serve as a generic term for religion, as it often does in Josephus.[44] In the NT, roughly contemporary with Plutarch, cognates appear only twice, in Acts 17:22 and 25:19. It is a generic term in the latter, but Luke seems to play upon the ambivalent ideas suggested by the adjective in the former passage, where Paul speaks before the Areopagus.[45] The favorable or neutral sense is attested after this but is much less common.[46] Its use by Christian authors from the second century onward is almost universally negative.[47]

Even in the classical period, however, there are antecedents of the derogatory sense that becomes the norm in the following centuries. The negative sense appears to have coexisted alongside the positive sense as early as the fifth century. Fragmentary texts from this early period show that it was used in

---

[43] Diodorus Siculus 1.62.4; 1.70.8; 1.79.1; 1.83.8; 4.51.1, 3; 5.27.4; 5.63.3; 11.89.6, 8; 14.76.4; 14.77.4; 17.41.6; 18.61.3; 19.108.2; 27.4.3; 27.5.4; 32.12.1; 34/35.10.1; 36.13.2; 38/39.17.1; Strabo, *Geogr.* 4.1.13; 12.7.3. Cf. also the anonymous *Alexandri historia* (*FGH* 151, frg. 1, line 55). As Martin also notes, the rare negative occurrence of δεισιδαιμονία in Diodorus Siculus usually appears to come from a source portraying philosophy as liberation from the false beliefs of the masses ("Hellenistic Superstition," 122–24).

[44] *Ant.* 14.228, 232, 234, 237, 240; 19.290. The positive sense of piety or zeal is seen in *Ant.* 10.42; *B.J.* 2.230. More ambiguous are the occurrences in *B.J.* 1.113; 2.174; *Ant.* 15.277. Josephus's Samaritan source in *Ant.* 12.259 uses δεισιδαιμονία as a negative term, as does the fragment from Agatharchides he quotes in *Ant.* 12.5–6; *C. Ap.* 1.208. The occurrence in the *Letter of Aristeas* 129 may also be seen as neutral, thought the context hints at an underlying Greek bewilderment at the purity requirements of Jewish law.

[45] H. Armin Moellering, "Deisidaimonia: A Footnote to Acts 17:22," *CTQ* 34 (1963): 466–71.

[46] Aelian, *Var. hist.* 5.17; Lucian, *Pro imag.* 7; Athenaeus, *Deipn.* 13.590E; Heliodorus, *Aeth.* 10.9; *IG* 14.1683.

[47] Koets, Δεισιδαιμονία, 84–103. Along with atheism, superstition is an extreme form of ignorance or delusion (Clement of Alexandria, *Protr.* 2.25.1; cf. 2.13.3; *Strom.* 7.4.22; Origen, *Cels.* 2.2; Eusebius, *Dem. Ev.* 1.6.63; *Praep. ev.* 2.5.2), it is opposed to θεοσέβεια (Clement, *Protr.* 4.58.4; cf. 10.108.3; Eusebius, *Praep. ev.* 4.4.2; Theodoret, *Hist. eccl.* 3.14.2), and, most frequently, it is related to idolatry (Clement, *Prot.* 1.7.5; 4.52.1; 10.96.4; *Strom.* 7.1.43; Origen, *Cels.* 6.17; Eusebius, *Praep. ev.* 3.14.2; *Hist. eccl.* 2.13.6; 9.4.3; *Dem. ev.* 1.5.4; 9.1.7; Athanasius, *C. Gent.* 8.4; 18.1; 22.1; 23.1; *Inc.* 46.4; 50.1; 51.2, 5; John Chrysostom, *Hom. Act.* 42.2; Hesychius, *Lexicon,* Δ544) or polytheism (Eusebius, *Dem. ev.* 1.2.5; 4.10.14; *Praep. ev.* 1.6.5; 3.6.1; 5.2.2).

medical writings, astrological discussions, and critiques of popular piety.[48] Menander makes fun of the δεισιδαίμων in a fourth-century comedy surviving only in fragments, and many of the same motifs recur in Athenian New Comedy.[49] Timaeus of Tauromenium (*FGH* 566, frg. 19, line 57) refers to those who are captivated by their dreams and by incredible myths as examples of lowbrow superstitiousness (δεισιδαιμονία ἀγεννής). Among philosophers, Democritus of Abdera integrates his views on ethics and religion with his atomic theory and holds that fear, δεισιδαιμονία, and other passions are impediments to the good life.[50] The Cyrenaic school founded by Aristippus reflected on the incompatibility of superstition and the life of the sage, holding that the sage will not yield to superstition because it is a function of uninformed opinion. Having learned to distinguish good and evil, he will be able to escape from δεισιδαιμονία as well as from the fear of death.[51]

The earliest treatment of the negative aspect of δεισιδαιμονία surviving in its entirety, however, is that of Theophrastus (*Char.* 16) which begins with a definition of superstition as "a sort of cowardice (δειλία) with respect to the divine." It manifests itself in an all-consuming concern for the performance of arcane rituals with, at best, a vestigial connection to respectable religious custom. This sketch also shares a number of points of contact with his caricature of the coward (*Char.* 25). Especially ridiculous in Theophrastus's eyes is the tendency of the superstitious man to see omens in every event and the obsessive-compulsive observance of apotropaic rites, especially those related to purification.[52] He describes in great detail examples of appropriate and

---

[48] Medicine: Hippocrates, *Decent.* 5. Astrology: Eudoxus, frg. 141. Plutarch's comment in *Is. Os.* 377A makes it clear that Eudoxus tended towards scepticism in such matters. Popular piety: Hecataeus, *FGH* 264, frg. 25, lines 784, 1022, 1234, 1342, though his use of the term with respect to Egyptian customs is generally neutral.

[49] Menander, frg. 104. Alciphron describes Athenian audiences going to see Menander's plays to hear about various stock characters, and δεισιδαιμονία is among the many vices they represent (Bk. 4 [*Letters of Courtesans*], Ep.19.6).

[50] Democritus, frg. 1, line 109 (Diels-Kranz 2:84). Plutarch later fixes on another aspect of Democritus's atomism that, he says, engenders a decidedly unphilosophical superstitiousness. Probably intended as a tongue-in-cheek remark, Democritus recommended praying that one encounters and inhales only good spirits in the surrounding atmosphere, presumably because he believed that anything good or bad that can happen to a person is the result of physical events like breathing (*Aem. Paul.* 1.5).

[51] Recounted by Diogenes Laertius (2.91–92); cf. also Strabo, *Geogr.* 1.2.8; 5.4.5; 16.2.37.

[52] Theophrastus alludes to ritual purity at several points in this short passage (*Char.* 16.2, 7, 9, 14 [three times]). Cf. also the anecdote about Menedemus recorded by Diogenes Laertius (2.132). Commentary on the details of this character sketch is provided by R. G. Ussher, *The Characters of Theophrastus* (rev. ed.; London: Bristol Classical, 1993), 135–57; and Hendrik Bolkestein, *Theophrastos' Charakter der Deisidaimonia als*

inappropriate sacrificial practices in ancient Greece in another work, *De pietate*, in which δεισιδαιμονία is used twice.[53] One is in reference to attempts at bribing (δεκάζειν) the gods, and the other refers generally to the impropriety of extravagant offerings to the gods. In connection with Plutarch, it is intriguing that in this essay Theophrastus explains the historical origins of atheism and also of false notions about the gods as two related reactions to the inappropriate developments of sacrificial practices in archaic times. Both atheism and superstition result indirectly from the perception that the gods are subject to the base human emotions these practices reflect. This way of framing the problem follows the general ethical principles of his teacher Aristotle and anticipates later Hellenistic definitions of piety as a mean (μεσότης).[54]

Like Latin *superstitio*, δεισιδαιμονία degenerates into a term of reproach in most authors after Theophrastus. It involves both defective beliefs about the nature of the gods and about their scope of activity, as well as issuing in behaviors looked down upon by the aristocracy.[55] The wide range of targets is an indication of how subjective the concept could be. Instances which at first glance appear positive turn out to be negative on closer inspection. Such is the case with Polybius (6.56.6), whose remarks are reminiscent of Aristotle's political analysis. Δεισιδαιμονία, he says, is partly responsible for Rome's greatness.[56] But this is not the positive evaluation it may at first seem because Polybius, like Livy (1.19) and Marx after him, contends cynically that the ancients introduced bizarre notions regarding the gods in order to keep the masses under control by means of their fear of supernatural punishment.[57]

Religionsgeschichtliche Urkunde (Religionsgeschichtliche Versuche und Vorarbeiten 21.2; Giessen: Töpelmann, 1929).

[53] Frg. 8, lines 9, 12 (Pötscher). Portions of this treatise are preserved only in Porphyry and Eusebius, and some scholars question whether the language is that of Theophrastus or of Porphyry (Dirk Obbink, "The Origin of Greek Sacrifice: Theophrastus on Religion and Cultural History," in *Theophrastean Studies* [ed. W. W. Fortenbaugh and R. W. Sharples; Rutgers University Studies in Classical Humanities 3; New Brunswick, N.J.: Transaction, 1988], 273).

[54] Martin, "Hellenistic Superstition," 115–19, demonstrates that an emphasis on balance runs through much of Theophrastus's thought, both in the area of ethics and in science.

[55] Ramsay MacMullen, *Paganism in the Roman Empire* (New Haven: Yale University Press, 1981), 70–76.

[56] In contrast to Lycurgus who, Polybius writes, did not draw up the Spartan constitution with δεισιδαιμονία in mind (10.2.9).

[57] Similar claims are made about the seventh-century lawgiver Zaleucus of Locri (Stobaeus, *Flor.* 4.2.19) and by Critias of Athens about the ancient lawgivers in general (Sextus Empiricus, *Math.* 9.54). Cf. also Diodorus Siculus 34/35.2.37; and the pseudepigraphical *Epistle of Phalaris* (93.2). Karl Marx's famous remark that religion is the opium or opiate of the people is found in the introduction to his "Contribution to the Critique of Hegel's *Philosophy of Right*" and is echoed by Ren Jiyu, who says that

Implicit in these observations is a cultural elitism. The tone of condescension could be in response to lower class Greek behavior or to that of the barbarians, who are superstitious "by nature."[58] But one need not encounter the barbarian to witness δεισιδαιμονία since women, whatever their nation, are "pioneers of superstition."[59] Tendencies such as an unhealthy interest in astrology or magic are often denigrated as "womanish" (Polybius 12.24.5), but according to Soranus, a physician and younger contemporary of Plutarch, not all women are prone to such superstitions. The best midwives are free of them (*Gynaecology* 1.4). By contrast, superstitious wet nurses, he says, are susceptible to ecstatic states and have very poor reasoning powers and so should be avoided because character was thought to be passed on to children through the breast milk (*Gyn.* 1.19; 2.80, 85).

To the modern observer, many of the specific topics discussed under the rubric of δεισιδαιμονία come as no surprise. An inordinate preoccupation with omens, oracles, oaths, prophecies, and prodigies is the regular object of derision in ancient Greek texts.[60] Times of war commonly see an increase in superstitious behavior, probably because the consequences of displeasing the gods, even inadvertently, are most extreme.[61] Nicias, the cautious Athenian general during the Peloponnesian War, is the most notorious case. His decision to delay his fleet's departure from Syracuse by twenty-seven days on account of a lunar eclipse leads to their slaughter and to the ultimate failure of the Sicilian expedition.[62] Obsessive concern for purity and activities related to the proper

---

"religion and superstition are both in opposition to the Marxist view" ("Religion and Superstition," 158–59). The former is an effective "tool of the exploiting classes" while the latter "disrupts the good order of society" when it 'is used to challenge party leadership in the socialist system.

[58] Xenophon of Ephesus, *Ephesiaca* 3.11.4; Athenaeus, *Deipn.* 15.672E; Heraclitus, *De incredibilibus* 23. In a spurious text attributed to Plutarch, the author uses cognates of δεισιδαιμονία when relating traditions behind the names of various rivers and mountains. The context is usually a reference to the religious customs of the foreign regions through which a river flows and the sense is almost always pejorative (*De fluviis* 7.5; 9.1; 17.1). On a few occasions the case involves a form a human sacrifice of virgins or children and is described as an irrational and fearful response to a bad omen (23.3; 25.1, 4).

[59] Strabo, *Geogr.* 7.3.4; Timaeus, *FGH* 566, frg. 19, line 57; Lucian, *Philops.* 37; Origen, *Cels.* 3.56–57. The regular term of derision is γυναικεῖος.

[60] Epimenides, *FGH* 457, frg. 4c, line 12; Hyperides, frg. 178, line 6; Polybius 9.19.1; Diodorus Siculus 20.43.1; 32.12.2; Titus Statilius Crito, *FGH* 200, frg. 2; Lucian, *Philops.* 38; *Alex.* 9; [*Am.*] 15; Diogenes Laertius 6.48.

[61] Dio Chrysostom, *Or.* 61.9; cf. Polybius, frg. 123; Diodorus Siculus 12.59.1; 15.54.4.

[62] Thucydides 7.50. Allusions to this instance of δεισιδαιμονία are common in antiquity (Diodorus Siculus 13.12.2; *Scholia in Thucydidem* 7.50.4; Marcellinus, *Vita Thucydidis* 51).

performance of sacrifices fall under this same category.[63] Frequently this brand of δεισιδαιμονία appears in the form of voluntary abstinence from certain foods. Temporary or long-term vegetarianism practiced on religious grounds is one such form of scrupulosity.[64] It is this custom that leads several writers to look down on Judaism, but non-Jews could also be the source of amusement on this count. Athenaeus (*Deipn.* 8.346C–E) quotes a story from Antipater of Tarsus to this effect about a Syrian queen who forbids the eating of fish among her subjects.

Common to nearly all of these characterizations of superstition is the element of extremism. Taking note of an omen or consulting a soothsayer for the interpretation of a dream is not inherently objectionable. Indeed, many of those activities derided as superstitious are actually necessary for a life that pleases the gods. Only when they become exaggerated or immoderate do they earn the label of δεισιδαιμονία. The basic element of excessive religiosity is seen in the second-century *Onomasticon* of Pollux, which defines the δεισιδαίμων as anyone who reveres the gods over and above (ὁ ὑπερτιμῶν) that which is appropriate (1.20–21). By overstepping the bounds of propriety and committing the sin of extravagance in matters of religion, one enters the realm of superstition, often indicated simply in terms of its deviation from εὐσέβεια or θεοσέβεια.[65] Marcus Aurelius says that freedom from superstition was one of the things he learned from his father Antoninus Pius (1.16.3), who was god-fearing yet not superstitious (θεοσεβὴς χωρὶς δεισιδαιμονίας; cf. 6.30). If δεισιδαιμονία consists largely in the ridiculous lengths to which it goes in the desire to fulfill the perceived requirements of εὐσέβεια, it could be avoided by

---

[63] Sopater, *Scholia ad Hermogenis* (Walz 5:135); *Scholia in Iliadem* 6.116A; 9.219C; 10.568A; Timolaus, *FGH* 798, frg. 1, line 12; Diodorus Siculus 13.86.1, 3; 38/39.7.1; Heraclitus, *All.* 1.4; Porphyry, *Quaestionum homericarum ad Iliadem* 6.116.

[64] Posidonius, *FGH* 87, frg. 70, lines 36–37; Diogenes Laertius 2.132; Iamblichus, *De vita pythagorica* 3.14. Cf. Riess, "Aberglaube," 1.1:36–37. More generally on vegetarianism and matters pertaining to cultic purity, see Theodor Wächter, *Reinheitsvorschriften im griechischen Kult* (Religionsgeschichtliche Versuche und Vorarbeiten 9.1; Giessen: Töpelmann, 1910), 76–115. It is possible that the attitudes underlying voluntary abstinence may have dovetailed in the minds of ancient observers with the greater propensity for asceticism among foreigners, seen in the fourth book of Porphyry's *De abstinentia*.

[65] E.g., Philodemus, *Piet.* frg. 40, lines 1135–1138; Appian, *Samnitica* 12.1; Clement of Alexandria, *Strom.* 7.4.22.2; Hephaestion, *Apotelesmatica* 2.15.9; Cf. Walter Burkert, *Greek Religion* (trans. J. Raffan; Cambridge: Harvard University Press, 1985), 273–74. Medieval lexica, however, occasionally retain the positive sense along with the negative by offering θεοσεβής as a possible synonym for δεισιδαίμων (*Suda* Δ369; *Etymologicum magnum*, s.v. δεισιδαίμων; Photius Δ142). Pseudo-Zonaras, citing only Paul's use of the superlative in Acts 17:22, simply equates it with εὐσεβής.

means of moderation. Thus one finds definitions of piety as a golden mean between the extremes of δεισιδαιμονία and impiety or atheism.[66] Deviance from this mean is regularly taken as evidence of some form of dementia. Superstition is recognized by the irrationality or emotional debility of the one plagued by it. Medical writers continue to take an interest in it and prescribe various measures—including music—as cures.[67] A generous diagnosis sees the superstitious merely as a good-hearted simpleton (εὐήθης) but just as common are terms indicating a more serious case of madness (νόσος/νόσημα).[68] Not infrequently, this disordered mental state also predisposes the sufferer to a variety of other vices condemned by moral philosophers. Whereas the pious man is the friend of God, Maximus of Tyre (*Lecture* 14.6) says that the superstitious man is the flatterer of God (κόλαξ θεοῦ). Related to flattery, which often has as its intent dishonest gain, is avarice (φιλαργυρία), a vice that a number of writers mention as a companion to δεισιδαιμονία.[69]

The root of these problems more often than not has to do with the emotion of fear, and this is by far the most pervasive motif in ancient discussions of δεισιδαιμονία.[70] In part this is simply a reflection of its etymology; literally, δεισιδαιμονία means "fear of demons." Dread and anxiety are standard components of the entries found in ancient and medieval lexicons, which define it using terms such as φόβος, δεδοίκω, δείδω, δειλός, δειλία, δεισίθεος, φοβοθεία, and θεόπλαγκτος.[71] Different aspects of this fear intersect with the complementary motifs which appear in other treatments of δεισιδαιμονία such as irrationality, emotional disturbance, and amazement before omens.[72] In his

---

[66] Arius Didymus, *Liber de philosophorum sectis* (apud Stobaeus, *Ecl.* 2.7.25); Gregory of Nyssa, *De virginitate* 8.2.

[67] Anonymus Londonensis 1.31; Aretaeus, *De causa et signis acutorum morborum* 1.5.3; Hephaestion, *Apotelesmatica* 2.15.8–9 (the δεισιδαίμων is also μανιώδης). Aristides Quintilianus (*De musica* 2.5) stresses the therapeutic value of music.

[68] Cf. Erotian, frg. 33, lines 1–27.

[69] Posidonius, *FGH* 87, frg. 33, lines 18–21; frg. 116, lines 55–57; Galen, *In Hippocratis librum vi epidemiarum commentarii vi* (=Kuhn, vol. 17b, p. 256). Teles the Cynic (4A.95, 135) posits a different causal relationship: superstition is the result of wealth, presumably a strategy for maintaining one's riches by placating the gods who have granted them.

[70] Chrysippus, *SVF* 3.394, 408, 409, 411; Polybius 6.56.6; Diodorus Siculus 4.51.1; 12.59.1; 13.86.1–3; 17.41.8; 20.14.5; 27.4.8; Anonymus Londonensis 1.31; *Scholia in Odysseam* 6.121; Lucian, *Philops.* 37; *Pro imag.* 7; Clement of Alexandria, *Strom.* 2.8.40; Diogenes Laertius 6.37, 48.

[71] *Lexica Segueriana* (s.v. δεισιδαίμων); *Etymologicum parvum* Δ20; *Etymologicum magnum*, s.v. δείδω, δεισιδαιμονία; *Etymologicum Gudianum*, s.v. δεισιδαιμονία; Hesychius, *Lexicon*, Δ544–545; Δ1966; Θ289; *Suda* Δ368–369; Photius Δ142.

[72] Aristides Quintilianus, *De musica* 2.5; Dionysius Scytobrachion, *FGH* 32, frg. 14, lines

discussion of the passions, Pseudo-Andronicus (*De passionibus* 1.3.1) regards fear as its defining aspect and groups it together with ὄκνος (hesitation), δεῖμα (horror), δέος (alarm), ἔκπληξις (terror), κατάπληξις (amazement), δειλία (cowardice), ψοφοδέεια (timidity), μέλλησις (procrastination), ὀρρωδία (fright), and θόρυβος (tumult).[73] In freeing one from superstition, according to the Cyrenaic school, proper philosophical training also frees one from the fear of death (Diogenes Laertius 2.92). This last example points to the prevailing idea in philosophical critiques, namely, that a solid understanding of reality ought to produce emotional stability.

It is also possible for a minority group like the Jews to appropriate the category of δεισιδαιμονία for evaluating its own special forms of religiosity and those of the dominant culture. Hebrew has no real equivalent of "superstition" but many of the same motifs are reflected, for instance, in the writings of Philo of Alexandria. He calls δεισιδαιμονία the heaviest of burdens and a great hindrance to holiness that causes the truth to appear as falsehood.[74] He is careful to distinguish Moses' concern in Exod 3:14 from the superstitious regard some have for the divine name, probably reflecting some of the concerns with magical practices behind prohibitions in the Decalogue of misusing the name of Yahweh (*Somn.* 1.230). Like the Stoics, Philo considers superstitious those who insist upon understanding all of Torah literally and have no tolerance for allegorical interpretation.[75] He furthermore sees the passions as a disease, of which fear is a major symptom.[76] Nurses and tutors encourage these destructive states of mind by their practices, thereby driving out piety and introducing δεισιδαιμονία, which is akin to impiety (*Sacr.* 15). True piety (εὐσέβεια) is a *via media* between δεισιδαιμονία and ἀσέβεια, and deviating too far from this mean is dangerous.[77] In commenting upon Deut 4:2, where Moses proscribes additions to or subtractions from the law, Philo states that additions to piety lead to δεισιδαιμονία while subtractions lead to impiety.[78] Although Philo is by no means a typical Jew, his views on religion may be taken as representative of a thoroughly hellenized segment of Judaism whose self-

---

284, 290; Diogenes Laertius 9.45; Pseudo-Plutarch, *De fluv.* 23.3; 25.1, 4.

[73] A very similar catalogue appears in Arius Didymus, *Liber de philosophorum sectis* (apud Stobaeus, *Ecl.* 2.7.10b–c).

[74] *Gig.* 16; *Deus* 102–3. In *Mut.* 138 he suggests that superstition adversely affects the faculty of spiritual discernment by drowning out God's voice.

[75] *Cher.* 42; cf. Cornutus, *Nat. d.* 27.50.16–18.

[76] *Sacr.* 15. The unceasing agitation caused by superstition is the soul's greatest evil. Cf. *Spec.* 4.145–146 on the relation of courage and cowardice to δεισιδαιμονία.

[77] *Deus* 161–165; *Plant.* 107. Both ends and means are important in the pursuit of piety. One cannot become pious through superstitious practices (*Det.* 18, 24; *Plant.* 107).

[78] *Spec.* 4.147. Philo concedes, however, that received wisdom about God's existence tinged with superstition, though inferior to true and complete knowledge of God, is to be preferred to atheism or scepticism (*Praem.* 40).

description is formulated in response to the entrenched notions of debased spirituality that obtain in the wider non-Jewish milieu of first-century Egypt, which also, coincidentally, produced Ammonius, Plutarch's mentor at the Academy in Athens.

To sum up, both *superstitio* and δεισιδαιμονία cover a broad range of dispositions, practices, and associations. The superstitious adhere to extreme forms of piety and are overly prone to account for perplexing phenomena by appealing to divine intervention. They tend to be preoccupied with prophecies, omens, and oracles, and are unusually scrupulous with regard to ritual and matters of purity. Women, barbarians, and the uneducated are three groups thought to be especially given to superstition. It is sometimes described as a form of dementia predisposing a person to vice, the most abominable of which is the practice of human sacrifice. A major difference between the Latin and Greek terminology, however, is seen in the heightened Roman sensitivity to the morally and politically subversive character of *superstitio*. In place of this political emphasis, Greeks worry over the psychological problems involved in δεισιδαιμονία, particularly in the debilitating influence of fear and the threat it poses to the well-being of the individual. These differences and similarities may be seen in microcosm in Plutarch's critique of superstition.

Plutarch on Superstition in the *Moralia* and the *Lives*: Typical or Atypical?

In most respects, Plutarch is at home within the semantic territory mapped above for δεισιδαιμονία. Occurrences in which it carries a positive connotation are difficult, if not impossible, to find.[79] He is typical in his impression of barbarians and the unsophisticated rabble as groups particularly prone to superstition.[80] Perhaps even more than his contemporaries and

---

[79] Koets, Δεισιδαιμονία, 78. According to Moellering (*Plutarch on Superstition*, 75–77), on the other hand, Plutarch sees it as performing a valuable function in rousing the afflicted person from complacency in a life of vice (*Virt. vic*. 100F). A similar case can be made for *Quaest. conv.* 703C. Here Plutarch defends certain "extreme observances" that in the opinion of many incline a person to δεισιδαιμονία on the grounds that they have a positive social side-effect; in this instance, certain scruples pertaining to different species of trees are seen as fostering the habit of expressing gratitude. Plutarch's argument actually reinforces the conventional notion that δεισιδαιμονία is to be avoided but he is contesting the criterion for including specific practices in this category.

[80] For superstition as βαρβάρος, see *Quaest. rom.* 272B; *Amat.* 756C; *Sert.* 11.3. The political necessity of introducing fear of the gods vis-à-vis the masses is recognized in *Gen. Socr.* 579F–580A; *Numa* 8.4; and *Cor.* 24.1. At least one reference shows that the upper classes are not immune. A newly acquired slave is advised to inquire not whether the new master is superstitious but whether he has a bad temper (*De calumnia*, frg. 153

sometimes in veiled language, Plutarch regards it as an "effeminate" shortcoming.[81] His letter to his wife comforting her on the death of their daughter (*Cons. ux.* 608B) opens with an admonition to keep her mourning within the proper bounds so as not to lapse into δεισιδαιμονία, and the tone indicates that he is confident in her capacity—rare for a woman—to maintain her customary sense of dignity in this situation. Mourning is not itself superstitious unless it is overdone. In this regard the rule is the same for almost any act of piety—nothing in excess.[82]

What garners the label of δεισιδαιμονία from Plutarch? Again, the catalogue of offenses will sound familiar. Heading the list is obsession with omens, prophecies, augury, dream interpretation, prodigies, and the like.[83] Wars witness a heightened awareness of the perceived intrusion of the supernatural into human affairs. Crises such as those arising in preparation for or during a battle are ideal literary occasions for the presentation of character, whether noble or ignoble, and Plutarch regularly employs the motif of δεισιδαιμονία to this effect in the *Lives*.[84] Signs from heaven are routinely taken as proof of some form of moral or physical pollution, thus requiring purification by means of a superstitious concern for proper modes of ritual sacrifice.[85] Whereas Roman sources indict foreigners as superstitious because of their practice of human sacrifice, Plutarch points out that Rome also was guilty of this pernicious form of δεισιδαιμονία.[86] A bit less prevalent in his writings is the association with purity concerns mandating abstinence from special foods. Not even the Jews receive the label—at least not on account of their prohibition of pork

---

[=*Cohib. ira* 462A]). This suggests that an owner's superstitiousness was regarded by some slaves as one key factor in assessing his or her new circumstances.

[81] *Conj. praec.* 140D; *Is. Os.* 355D; *Tranq. an.* 465D; *Num.* 22.7; *Dion* 2.3; *Caes.* 63.7; *Ag. Cleom.* 39.2. That this motif is not exhaustive of his views on women, however, is seen in the positive role models he holds up in *Mulierum virtutes*. Only at *Quaest. rom.* 264C does he discuss a superstition practiced exclusively by men.

[82] *Adul. amic.* 66C; *Num.* 22.7; *Cam.* 6.4; 19.8.

[83] *Quaest. rom.* 269E–F; [*Parallela graeca et romana*] 314D; *Gen. Socr.* 579F–580A; *Rom.* 24.1; *Pub.* 21.1; *Per.* 6.1 (cf. 35.2); *Nic.* 23.1, 5; *Cor.* 24.1; *Dion* 38.1; *Brut.* 39.3; *Tim.* 26.2; *Alex.* 75.2; *Caes.* 63.7; *Eum.* 13.3.

[84] *Sol.* 12.3; *Pub.* 21.1; *Fab.* 4.4; *Nic.* 23.1, 5; *Crass.* 16.6; *Marc.* 6.6; *Dion* 38.1; *Brut.* 39.3; *Tim.* 26.2; cf. *Superst.* 169C; [*Reg. imp. apophth.*] 201B; *Gen. Socr.* 581F. On the literary function of omens and portents in the *Lives*, see Brenk, *In Mist Apparelled*, 184–213.

[85] *Quaest. rom.* 264F; *Rom.* 11.3; *Sol.* 12.3; *Ag. Cleom.* 39.2; *Arat.* 53.2. For taboos related to burial practices as δεισιδαιμονία, see [*Apoph. lac.*] 238D; *Lyc.* 27.1; *Sulla* 35.2.

[86] *Quaest. rom.* 287F; [*Parallela graeca et romana*] 314D. Plutarch does not use the term in recounting cases where Greeks practice human sacrifice (*Arist.* 9.2; *Them.* 13.2; *Marc.* 3.6).

consumption (*Quaest. conv.* 669C–672C)—and he exculpates Egyptian priests from the charge of δεισιδαιμονία on the grounds that their abstinence from foods like onions, legumes, mutton, pork, wine, and seafood is of practical value (*Is. Os.* 353E). Plutarch's charitable stance when it comes to scruples about food probably has something to do with his own strict vegetarianism, grounded in the philosophical and ethical convictions about the moral status of animals voiced in *De sollertia animalium, Bruta animalia ratione uti,* and *De esu carnium.*

By definition, δεισιδαιμονία is in fundamental conflict with εὐσέβεια, though the severity of the rebuke may on occasion be mitigated if the practices in question do not constitute a departure from tradition.[87] One might conclude from Plutarch's characterization of superstition as a kind of disease or mental illness that the individual is not to blame for the condition, if, that is, such maladies are a consequence of external forces or unchangeable nature rather than of nurture.[88] But because superstition is implicated in or grouped with so many other vices, it is difficult to see Plutarch as exempting the individual from responsibility. Envy, licentiousness, anger, covetousness, distrust, harshness, and pettiness are all natural complements to δεισιδαιμονία.[89]

While it is not the case with every vice, the necessary (though not sufficient) cause of superstition is ignorance. In Plutarch's view, those who are addicted to divination may simply lack instruction in the rudiments of science. An understanding of natural cause and effect ought to dispel bizarre ideas about the way the world operates. Pericles had Anaxagoras to explain those phenomena that mystified the masses, but not everyone was so fortunate.[90] On this point Plutarch's thought sounds quite modern: education is the key to eradicating superstition. It would be anachronistic, however, to impute to Plutarch a doctrinaire materialism in the philosophical sense of the term. *Quaestiones naturales* consists solely of proposed explanations of odd natural phenomena based on materialist reasoning, but he makes no comments about the illegitimacy of nonmaterial explanations involving the supernatural. As his discussion of Socrates' sign indicates, he allows for the agency of the divine even in such mundane forms as a sneeze (*Gen. Socr.* 581F–582C). Natural

---

[87] *Num.* 22.7; *Per.* 6.1; *Fab.* 4.4; *Marc.* 5.4.

[88] Described as an "attack" (προσβολή): *Rect. rat. aud.* 43D; as an affliction (νόσημα): *Adol. poet. aud.* 34E; compared to a fever (πυρετός), inflammation of the brain (φρενῖτις), pestilence (ὄλεθρος) and throbbing (σφυγμός): *Lat. viv.* 1128D. Here superstition is a symptom that should not be concealed to avoid attracting the attention of the doctor, who alone can prescribe a cure. Cf. also *Tranq. an.* 465D; *Num.* 22.7; *Cor.* 24.1; *Dion* 2.3.

[89] *Adol. poet. aud.* 34E; *Adul. amic.* 53E; 54C–F; *Alex. fort.* 337C; *An vit.* 500A; *Sera* 555A, 556B; *Eum.* 13.3.

[90] *Per.* 6.1; cf. also *Gen. Socr.* 579F; *Aem. Paul.* 1.5; 17.5–6; *Ag. Cleom.* 39.2.

causes should be sought first, but "scientific" and "unscientific" explanations are in no way mutually exclusive in his view of the world.

More important than scientific ignorance in Plutarch's articulation of the concept of δεισιδαιμονία is ignorance concerning the gods. Ignorance by itself is unfortunate since right belief in the gods (ἀληθής δόξα περὶ θεῶν) is superior to any sacrifice (*Is. Os.* 355D). On matters touching on the gods, the human mind cannot stand a vacuum for very long, therefore a person who lacks right belief does not simply become a blank slate. Rather, other notions soon rush in to take the place of previously held beliefs. Animals enjoy a more blessed existence than humans on this count because they do not need to be stripped of any superstitious ideas about the gods (*Suav. viv.* 1092C). The question for Plutarch, then, is not whether to hold any beliefs about the gods but which beliefs to hold. Disbelief in the gods is still a form of belief, an extreme one which Plutarch says should be avoided. Atheism is a form of ignorance that stands at the opposite end of the religious spectrum from δεισιδαιμονία.[91] For an agnostic like Protagoras, ignorance poses no theoretical problem; indeed, ignorance is the fundamental human reality around which agnosticism is organized. But Plutarch is not an agnostic. He believes in the traditional pantheon and the traditional stories told about them, so long as they are read ὁσίως καὶ φιλοσόφως. His writings are filled with warnings about ridiculous, fabulous, misguided, or otherwise improper notions about the gods and this is perhaps a reflection of his own Academic training. Middle Platonists tended towards a negative theology, that is to say, the habit of describing the deity in terms of the qualities it does not possess rather than those positive qualities it might possess.[92] Even this cautious approach to thinking about the gods carries with it implicit assumptions, and this is also the case with Plutarch. Recognizing this is critical for understanding his approach to superstition. Again, because ignorance concerning the gods never means the absence of ideas but rather the presence of the wrong ideas, one must discover which ideas are defective in Plutarch's mind. In so doing, his positive ideas about the gods will come into clearer focus.[93]

The Role of Fear in Plutarch's Religious Thought

The clearest indication of what Plutarch regards as the salient element of δεισιδαιμονία is seen in the symptoms he describes. As it is with the majority of Hellenistic authors, the most common symptom is fearfulness. While this

---

[91] *Adul. amic.* 66C; *Is. Os.* 355D, 360A, 378A, 379D; *Suav. viv.* 1100C, 1101B–C; cf. *Alex. fort.* 330F; *Amat.* 757B; *Adv. Col.* 1125A.

[92] Dillon, *The Middle Platonists*, 284–85.

[93] A brief, lucid summary of Plutarch's remarks about the gods is found in Moses Hadas, "The Religion of Plutarch," *RR* 6 (1941–42): 270–82.

timid disposition on occasion appears as a non-specific personality trait, it is usually linked explicitly to misconceptions about the gods.[94] Simply stated, the chief misconception about the gods is that they are to be feared for what they may do to humans. Poets and philosophers are both among those whom he reproaches for imputing vengeful motives to the gods in their dealings with humans.[95] This implies that Plutarch's most basic theological axiom is that the gods are by their very nature beneficent and never malevolent. The relationship between defective theology and its doleful psychological consequences is developed most fully in his treatise devoted to δεισιδαιμονία. Plutarch's analysis of this relationship is steeped in the language and reasoning used by Hellenistic philosophical schools in their analyses of the emotions. Etymologically and phenomenologically, superstition is a special form of fear, which in turn receives great attention from these schools as one of the basic human πάθη. In order to appreciate fully the texture of Plutarch's views, it is instructive to survey these traditions in detail before proceeding to take a closer look at *De superstitione*.

Hellenistic Analyses of the Emotions

Morton Smith, who believes that Plutarch did not write *De superstitione*, correctly observes that any careful study of the essay "will have to seek the source of this serious concern about the fear of the gods as a major factor in human unhappiness."[96] The most natural place to look is the Hellenistic philosophical schools. As will become clear below, Plutarch uses much of the same language in his vivid depiction of the δεισιδαίμων as do the Epicureans and Stoics in their writings on the emotions. There can be no doubt that he is in substantive dialogue with these groups. No less than five of his surviving works aim explicitly to respond to Epicurean or Stoic teachings, several more mentioned in the Lamprian catalogue but not extant belong in this same class, and he frequently quotes Stoics like Antipater, Aratus, and Chrysippus, and Epicureans like Metrodorus and Idomeneus.[97] This conversation continues in the

---

[94] *Adol. poet. aud.* 34E; *Virt. vit.* 100F–101B; *Sera* 556B; *Suav. viv.* 1092C, 1100F, 1101C–E, 1102C, 1104B; *Lyc.* 27.1; *Num.* 8.4; *Sol.* 12.3; *Pub.* 21.1; *Nic.* 23.1; *Lys.* 25.2; *Sull.* 12.5; *Dion* 2.3; *Brut.* 39.3; *Alex.* 75.2; *Caes.* 63.7.

[95] *Adol. poet. aud.* 26B; *Sera* 555A; *Stoic. rep.* 1050E–1051E.

[96] Smith, "De Superstitione," 7.

[97] Cf. *De Stoicorum repugnantiis* (1033A–1057B), *Stoicos absurdiora poetis dicere* (1057C–1058D), *De communibus notitiis contra stoicos* (1058E–1086B), *Non posse suaviter vivi secundum Epicurum* (1086C–1107C), and *Adversus Colotem* (1107D–1127F). Discussion of the issues surrounding Plutarch's relationship with these two schools may be found in two articles by Jackson P. Hershbell, "Plutarch and Stoicism," and "Plutarch and Epicureanism," both in *ANRW* 36.5 (3336–52, 3353–83).

essay on superstition as well. The reference in the opening lines to an atomistic view of the universe is almost certainly a swipe at Epicurus, leading later editors of the Plutarchan corpus to add πρὸς ἐπίκουρον to the title.[98] In the following lines Plutarch makes veiled reference to the teachings of the Stoics on virtue and vice. The concluding endorsement of the mean is also a sign of the influence, perhaps indirect, of Aristotle's doctrine of the mean (μετριοπαθεία). Each of these traditions is important for understanding the treatment of fear that is integral to Plutarch's critique of δεισιδαιμονία. He says as much at the beginning of *De virtute morali* (440E)—another of his anti-Stoic treatises—when he announces his intention "to run summarily through the opinions of the philosophers holding opposing views, not so much for the sake of inquiring into them as that my own opinions may become clearer and more firmly established." The Peripatetic, Epicurean, and Stoic teachings on fear, however, are not easily detachable from their larger construals of the emotions and the role they play in the good life. To put their respective appraisals of fear in the proper context, it will be helpful to review the ways in which these schools understand the structure of an emotion (along with the role played by beliefs), how they classify the emotions, why they regard them as essentially positive or negative, and what they prescribe for coping with them.[99]

---

[98] Ziegler, "Plutarchos von Chaironeia," 700.

[99] The Sceptics will not receive separate treatment. Sextus Empiricus, the best source for their teachings, is a late source of questionable value in determining what sources may have been available to Plutarch. Earlier Sceptics such as Arcesilaus and Carneades left little or nothing from their own hand, and reconstructing their theories of the emotions is a speculative enterprise beyond the scope of this study. Though their main philosophical rivals were the dogmatic Stoics, in fact the Sceptics shared some of the same basic views of emotions, namely, that they introduce unnecessary elements into a life that would otherwise be free from disturbance, and that they are the result of one's beliefs about the world (cf. Richard Bett, "The Sceptics and the Emotions," in *The Emotions in Hellenistic Philosophy* [ed. J. Sihvola and T. Engberg-Pederson; New Synthese Historical Library 46; Dordrecht: Kluwer, 1998], 206–12). On the first point, it is plausible to construe the Sceptic ideal as one close to the Stoic ideal of ἀπάθεια and also to the Epicurean goal of ἀταραξία. Likewise, all three schools are in essential agreement that the heart of the problem of the passions is one of belief. Unlike the Stoics and Epicureans, however, the Sceptic solution is not to find the correct beliefs by which to gauge the truth or healthiness of an emotion. Instead, belief itself is the problem (cf. Martha C. Nussbaum, *The Therapy of Desire* [Princeton: Princeton University Press, 1994], 280–85). Many emotions will be unavoidable; the secret is to avoid making matters worse by clinging to the beliefs that are responsible for them. Sceptics, then, claim to do a better job of realizing the end of Epicurean and Stoic therapies than either school can, only by different means. Because beliefs are themselves the problem, the best strategy is one of ἐποχή, suspension of judgment. By refraining from strong commitment to any belief about the purpose of life—with the implicit exception of the belief that ἀταραξία is to be desired—one avoids the disappointment that goes along with missing the mark. In

Platonic Antecedents

Unlike Aristotle and the Hellenistic schools, Plato engages in relatively little systematic analysis of singular emotions like fear. He is interested in more abstract questions raised by experiences of pain and pleasure. To form an adequate understanding of Plutarch's approach to fear, brief attention to Plato's assessment of the emotions is nevertheless advisable on two counts. First, Plutarch's primary philosophical training takes place at the Academy in Athens and he regards himself as a faithful interpreter of the Platonic tradition. Especially in several of the lost works, Plutarch is deeply concerned with transmission of Plato's teachings on many different topics.[100] This is not to say that he is always the most accurate, consistent, or sophisticated interpreter of the tradition, but it is wise to try to see Plutarch as he sees himself. Second, Plato's discussion of pleasure and pain in the *Philebus* is the source of Aristotle's terminology in the *Rhetoric*, books one and two of which represent the first extended analysis of singular emotions in ancient philosophy.[101] Aristotle differed from his teacher on a number of points and provided a point of departure for the subsequent discussion among Stoics and Epicureans with which Plutarch is familiar.

---

keeping with their standard epistemological pessimism that it is not possible to know how things are in themselves by nature, they engage in the analysis of emotions only insofar as it is necessary to debunk the claims of rival schools. Their arguments thus duplicate some of the polemical ones employed by other schools in their debates with one another, but provide an uncertain basis for articulating any positive theory of the emotions to which the Sceptics would assent.

[100] Dillon, *The Middle Platonists*, 184–89; C. Froidefond, "Plutarque et la platonisme," *ANRW* 36.1:185–89, 230–33; and Swain, "Plutarch, Plato, Athens and Rome," 175–87. Lost works listed in the catalogue of Lamprias of interest on this point include nos. 63 (*On the Unity of the Academy since the time of Plato*), 64 (*On the Differences between the Pyrrhonians and the Academics*), 66 (*On the Fact that in Plato's View the Universe had a Beginning*), 67 (*Where are the Forms?*), 71 (*That the Academic Philosophy allows for the Reality of Prophecy*), and 221 (*What in Plato's View is the End of Life?*). On the basis of these and other lost titles (e.g., nos. 146 [*That Understanding is Impossible*] and 210 [*Whether He Who Reserves Judgment on Everything is Involved in Inaction*], Dillon surmises that Plutarch would minimize the apostasy of the more sceptical New Academy under Arcesilaus and Carneades. Jones, *The Platonism of Plutarch*, 17–19, points out that these titles stand alongside others which attribute decidedly unsceptical views to the Academics and concludes that whatever Scepticism can be sensed in his works generally takes the form of suspension of judgment on certain scientific questions. He does not approach the emotions from a Sceptic's perspective.

[101] Simo Knuuttila and Juha Sihvola, "How the Philosophical Analysis of Emotions was Introduced," in Sihvola and Engberg-Pederson, *The Emotions in Hellenistic Philosophy*, 8–9.

With Plato, as it is with most later thinkers, it is critical to remember that the emotions (πάθη) are distinct from purely physical urges and sensations, be they pleasant or painful ones. The latter are to a great extent unavoidable and uncontrollable reactions to stimuli, while the former are more complex phenomena.[102] First clearly visible in Plato's later dialogues, the debate in the Academy is over the degree to which cognition is involved in occurrent emotions.[103] Plato's tendency in the earlier dialogues (e.g., *Phaed.* 65E–67B, 83B) is to regard emotions such as love and fear as having their exclusive source in the body and are therefore to be extirpated as much as humanly possible.[104] Much of his thought in this area occurs in working out the implications of his notion of the soul as a tripartite entity.[105] Plato's distrust of the emotions is also connected to his general devaluation of the phenomenal realm. The internal source as well as the external object of the emotions are rooted in the mutable world, thus they are not a product of the rational, deliberative part of the soul which aspires to true knowledge.

In the *Philebus* Plato begins to apply his insights on physical pains and pleasure to the more complicated emotions and the role played by cognition. After distinguishing between sensations experienced on the purely physical level from pleasant and painful feelings of anticipation (προσδόκημα) experienced in the soul (32A–D), Plato argues that one may also make a distinction between true and false sensations (36C–39C). Socrates' interlocutor Protarchus is at first dubious but eventually agrees that, just as with opinions, pleasures and pains may also be either true or false. The truth or falsity of the judgments or opinions upon which they are based determines the truth or falsity of a given pleasure or pain.

Plato's discussion of so-called "mixed" (σύμμικτον) sensations brings the link between cognition and the emotions into sharper focus (44A–50E). He identifies three classes of mixed pleasures and pains (46B–C): those pertaining

---

[102] The common English rendering "passion," though etymologically closer to the Greek, often gives the inadvertent impression that πάθος is necessarily an exceptionally strong or irresistible feeling. On the difficulty of rendering πάθος in a consistent and accurate fashion, see Julia Annas, *Hellenistic Philosophy of Mind* (Berkeley: University of California Press, 1992), 103–5; and Nussbaum, *The Therapy of Desire*, 319 n. 4. The modern debates over what falls under the heading of "emotion" are reviewed by W. P. Alston, "Emotion and Feeling," *Encyclopedia of Philosophy* 2:479–86.

[103] W. W. Fortenbaugh, *Aristotle on Emotion* (London: Duckworth, 1975), 9–12.

[104] Focusing on the *Republic*, usually counted among the middle dialogues, Richard Patterson discusses "rational" desires as intellectual virtues and the need for the cardinal virtues of wisdom, courage, self-control, and justice lest these desires be led astray ("Plato on Philosophic Character," *Journal of the History of Philosophy* 25 [1987]: 325–50; cf. 345–49 on philosophers' fears).

[105] Fortenbaugh, *Aristotle on Emotion*, 23–44; Knuuttila and Sihvola, "How the Philosophical Analysis of Emotions was Introduced," 1–5.

to and involving the body (46D–47B); those pertaining to and involving both body and soul (47C–D); and those pertaining to and involving only the soul (47D–50E).[106] These last two classes contain examples in which Plato clearly assigns a role to cognition in explaining complex emotional responses. Emotions like anger, fear, longing, and lament, which he places in the third group (47E, 50D), are not merely modes or states of awareness pertaining to physical changes in the condition of the body. They are in fact the result of judgments about what will cause pleasure or pain and for this very reason may be deemed true or false; that is to say, accurate judgments concerning the cause or likelihood of distress, for instance, lead to a true sensation, in this case fear. One's beliefs, judgments, and opinions are so closely related to pleasure and pain that they are said to infect them with their own character (42A–B). Thus in many cases of emotional response, the genesis is to be found on the spiritual level and not the physical.

A different classification appears in two other late works, the *Timaeus* and the *Laws*.[107] Fear (φόβος), along with pleasure, pain, rashness, anger, and hope, is one of the basic affections implanted in the mortal soul by the creator (*Tim.* 68C–D). Plato later divides hope (ἐλπίς) into rashness (θάρρος) and fear (*Leg.* 1.644C–D). The one is the expectation of pleasure and the other is the expectation of pain. "Calculation" (λογισμός), he says, is present to discern which is the proper response.[108] There follows a brief exchange between Clinias and the Athenian on the two main kinds of fear: the fear of impending evil which leads to cowardice and the fear for one's reputation commonly designated as shame (*Leg.* 1.646E–649C; cf. 3.699C; *Resp.* 5.465A–B). Each, and especially the latter, has an appropriate part to play in the formation of model citizens and entails deliberation on the part of the individual. This construal of the emotions as—at least in part—cognitive events is even present in earlier dialogues. In the *Laches* (198B–C) and the *Protagoras* (358D, 360C–D) one sees fear and cowardice defined respectively as the expectation of evil and ignorance of what is appropriate to fear, while courage is defined as the knowledge of what is appropriate to fear.

The primary aim here is not to systematize all of Plato's statements regarding the emotions. Nor is it to construct a pattern of development in his

---

[106] By "mixed" (*Phileb.* 46A) Plato means states in which one is subject simultaneously to two opposite feelings. Among the examples he gives are, for the body, becoming warm by means of shivering; for the body and soul, the physical pain of hunger alongside the pleasant anticipation of replenishment; and for the soul, the enjoyment of a tragedy at which one is moved to tears.

[107] Cf. Fortenbaugh, *Aristotle on Emotion*, 23–25, 41–44.

[108] A little later, Plato says that true education (παιδεία) instills in children's souls the appropriate likes and dislikes through which these expectations take on their essential character as either fear or rashness (*Leg.* 2.653B–C).

thought, but to show how certain insights present in his writings pave the way
for Aristotle to treat the emotions as something other than uncontrollable
physiological reactions exempt from assessments of praise or blame. Aristotle
and later thinkers view the emotions as amenable to persuasion and modification
by various means and for sundry purposes. If they are essentially involuntary
physical reactions, this kind of reflection has no practical or theoretical
foundation and Plutarch's critique of superstition on the grounds that it involves
emotion makes little sense.

Aristotle

Plato's evaluation of the emotions and his prescriptions for handling them
are not as clear nor as consistent as one would wish in large part because such
questions are not central ones in most of his dialogues. Aristotle addresses the
topic in a more thorough fashion. This is perhaps the outgrowth of debates
within the Academy over the wisdom of eradicating the emotions, as later
championed by the Stoics, or simply moderating them.[109] Aristotle's picture of
the good life, with its emphasis on ordinary human attachments and the range of
possible emotions these entail, illustrates how he adopts the latter ideal.

Among the prime considerations that compel Aristotle to devote attention to
the emotions are the practical ones of the orator.[110] The orator seeks to persuade
an audience to see things in a certain way so that it will render a desired decision
(*Rhet.* 2.1.1–7). Because the decisions or judgments one renders are bound up
with the way one feels about a case, knowledge of the emotions is of obvious
value to an orator seeking to persuade. By arousing (or subduing) the proper
emotions, the orator increases the probability that the audience will see things in
a   sympathetic   light   and   will   decide   accordingly.[111]   These   practical

---

[109] Richard Sorabji, *Emotion and Peace of Mind* (Oxford: Oxford University Press, 2000),
194–96.
[110] Cf. Alan Brinton, "Pathos and the 'Appeal to Emotion': An Aristotelian Analysis,"
History of Philosophy Quarterly 5 (1988): 207–19; John M. Cooper, "An Aristotelian
Theory of the Emotions," in *Essays on Aristotle's Rhetoric* (ed. A. O. Rorty; Berkeley:
University of California Press, 1996), 241–42. Aristotle also discusses πάθη in highly
theoretical terms in the *Metaphysics* and the *Categories*, where one sees the important
distinction between those that one suffers passively (like a headache or a beating) and
those that approximate what in English are designated as "emotions." He spends little
time analyzing the former (cf. Amélie Oksenberg Rorty, "Aristotle on the Metaphysical
Status of *Pathe*," *Review of Metaphysics* 38 [1984]: 521–46).
[111] It is sometimes objected that Aristotle is not giving his own views in this part of the
Rhetoric but only reporting commonly held opinions (cf. Fortenbaugh, *Aristotle on
Emotion*, 40 n. 2, for a list of older proponents of this reading). Since he aims to give real
advice to orators about manipulating the emotions, however, it makes much more sense
to read this section of the *Rhetoric* as Aristotle's own idea of the truth of the matter.

considerations provide the immediate context for his definition of πάθη in *Rhet.* 2.1.8:

> Emotions are those things on account of which the ones altered differ with respect to their judgments and which are accompanied by pain and pleasure, such as anger, pity, fear, and all that are similar to these and their opposites.

Judgment (κρίσις) is the object of rhetoric (2.1.2), as the opening section of book two preceding this definition makes clear, and changes in emotions effect changes in judgment.[112]

Taking into account this immediate context rectifies a possible misunderstanding of Aristotle's theory of emotions. Read out of context, the definition in the *Rhetoric* leaves the misleading impression that πάθος is primarily responsible for the content of one's thoughts and opinions. Aristotle here uses κρίσις as a quasi-technical term for the desired result of deliberative, forensic, and epideictic rhetoric. Were he stating that emotions give rise to all "judgments" across the board, he would leave unexplained the genesis of the emotion, and this is precisely what he is trying to explain in this section of the *Rhetoric*. Since the subsequent discussion of particular emotions deals with the cause, structure, and constituent beliefs of emotional responses, it cannot be the case that Aristotle only means to say that emotions determine one's beliefs as a general rule and not the other way around. An orator works with the preexisting convictions of the audience in order to stir up specific emotions that are in turn likely to lead to the verdict he seeks. There is the risk of circularity at this point: which comes first, the emotion or the belief associated with that emotion? Aristotle emphasizes the latter, for to leave the root cause of the emotion unexplained is essentially to assign it a physical—and therefore non-cognitive and non-rational—basis. If this were the case, they would not be potentially open to rational persuasion by the orator.[113] The cognition involved in emotional

---

Knowledge of how emotions actually work is useful in a way that mere familiarity with what most people think about the emotions is not (cf. Gisela Striker, "Emotions in Context: Aristotle's Treatment of the Passions in the *Rhetoric* and His Moral Psychology," in Rorty, *Essays on Aristotle's Rhetoric*, 286–88; and W. W. Fortenbaugh, "Aristotle's *Rhetoric* on Emotions," *Archiv für Geschichte der Philosophie* 52 [1970]: 43–53). Likewise in the *Poetics* (6.1–4), the poet must first arouse pity and fear in the audience in order to purge them, thus a knowledge of the plots that tend to produce these emotions is essential and not just a familiarity with what, in the view of the masses, ought to elicit these feelings. The Stanislavsky method extends this principle from the poet to the actor on stage.

[112] Cf. S. R. Leighton, "Aristotle and the Emotions," in Rorty, *Essays on Aristotle's Rhetoric*, esp. 206–17, for a detailed examination of the processes by which such changes may take place.

[113] Fortenbaugh, "Aristotle's *Rhetoric* on Emotions," 54–61.

response is not merely concurrent but is its essential cause. This does not imply, of course, that all cognitions will be "rational" in some normative sense, but it does mean that Aristotle rejects the notion, alluded to by Plato (*Phaedr.* 267C–D) and affirmed by Gorgias (*Hel.* 10 et al.), that πάθη are like a disease (νοσήμα) or a spell cast by a sorcerer.[114]

Although one's emotions do predispose one to make certain judgments of fact—for example, a man is likely to give the benefit of the doubt to an accused woman for whom he feels deep affection—the arrow of causality usually points in the opposite direction. That is to say, prior beliefs, judgments (in the non-judicial sense), and convictions about the state of things loom larger in Aristotle's analysis of emotional response than do emotions when he explains the formation of beliefs. His discussions of fear are illustrative. Fear is not a physical disturbance disconnected from cognition. Some physical disturbance is involved—sweaty palms or nervous twitches—but the cognitive component of fear or any other emotion is not limited to the perception of that disturbance.[115] He includes a cognitive component in his essential definition of fear (*Rhet.* 2.5.1): "Let fear be defined as a painful (λύπη) or troubled feeling (ταραχή) caused by the impression of an imminent evil that causes destruction or pain." Following this definition is a detailed list of the types of persons towards whom and conditions under which it is customary to experience fear. Aristotle consistently lays stress on what the individual believes will happen. "It follows therefore that fear is felt by those who believe something to be likely to happen to them, at the hands of particular persons, in a particular form, and at a particular time," thus to believe oneself invincible is to be totally immune to fear (2.5.13).

This characterization is also in line with the definition of fear in the *Nicomachean Ethics* (3.6.2) as the expectation of evil (προσδοκία κακοῦ), a description which focuses on the propositional content and not on the sensation. Preceding the physical disturbance is a mental operation responsible for the distress. Absent this mental operation, which Aristotle denies to animals because they lack reason and the capacity to form beliefs (πίστις) and opinions (δόξα), the emotion does not come to fruition.[116] The cognitive aspect of emotion is

---

[114] Ibid., 62–63. William Lyons traces the historical development of this Aristotelian cognitive theory in Aquinas, Spinoza, and twentieth-century psychology and philosophy (*Emotion* [Cambridge: Cambridge University Press, 1980], 33–52.

[115] Cf. *De an.* 403a16–24 for the way in which emotions issue in physiological symptoms. In *Rhet.* 2.13.7, the cowardly inclination of the elderly is described in both its physical and mental aspects: they are apt to expect the worst (προφοβητικοί) and are not hot-blooded like the young. Old age predisposes one to cowardice because fear is a certain kind of chill (κατάψυξις).

[116] *De an.* 428a19–24. He specifically mentions fear as an emotion requiring cognition and the forming of opinions (427b21). On Aristotle's denial of rationality to animals and

further demonstrated by the distinction he draws (in *De an.* 432b30–31) between fear and surprise or fright. When startled by a sudden noise, for instance, the heart may skip a beat but one does not automatically experience fear. Why not? On the basis of his other comments, this is presumably the case because the experience of fear requires the expectation of harm in order to be complete. Aristotle does not individuate particular emotions with reference to the particular pains or pleasures attending them. Only by attaching a sensation to its characteristic belief can one mark off fear from anger, pity, or some other adverse sensation.[117] The belief, then, is not only a necessary precondition for an emotion but a constituent part of the emotion as well.

Keeping in mind the general structure of the emotions, one may ask, what can be said of their propriety? Aristotle begins the *Rhetoric* on a note of apprehension. Those orators who concentrate on arousing the emotions devote too much attention to matters that, properly speaking, lie outside the main subject (1.1.4–6). Appeals to the jury's emotions too often pervert those faculties whose purpose is to ascertain the truth. His writings in ethics, however, demonstrate that Aristotle is generally positive about the contribution made by the emotions to the virtuous life. Though they may, and often do, run to extremes, he is not of the view that the emotions necessarily miss the mark by excess. In fact, they are built into his basic theory of moral virtue, defined in various passages as a state of character concerned with choice and achieved by

---

the apparent inconsistencies in his position when he discusses their inner life, see Richard Sorabji, *Animal Minds and Human Morals* (London: Duckworth, 1993), esp. 12–16, 55–58; and Juha Sihvola, "Emotional Animals: Do Aristotelian Emotions Require Beliefs?" *Apeiron* 29 (1996): 105–44. These strong challenges to the consensus "belief-based" view (exemplified by Fortenbaugh, *Aristotle on Emotion*; Nussbaum, *The Therapy of Desire*; Thomas Conley, "*Pathe* and *Pisteis*: Aristotle, *Rhet* II 1–11," *Hermes* 110 [1982]: 300–15; and others) coincide with attempts to problematize Aristotle's qualitative distinction between humans and animals. Much of the debate centers on the role of "appearances" (φαντασία) in the structure of occurrent emotions (cf. Sihvola, "Emotional Animals," 116–21; Dorothea Frede, "The Cognitive Role of *Phantasia* in Aristotle," in *Essays on Aristotle's de Anima* [ed. M. C. Nussbaum and A. O. Rorty; Oxford: Clarendon, 1992], 279–96). Do emotions entail reactions to mere appearances or must they involve full-fledged beliefs? Proponents of an analysis in terms of φαντασία concede that the concept may admit propositional content, and so the difference is perhaps a technical one of degree rather than of kind. By pressing Aristotle on points where he is less than comprehensive or systematic, Sihvola is perhaps committing the same error for which he faults Nussbaum, namely, interpreting Aristotle too much in terms of the later Hellenistic debate carried on by Stoics and Epicureans ("Emotional Animals," 110–13, 114).

[117] Nussbaum, *The Therapy of Desire*, 88. See also the critique of Nussbaum by Sihvola, "Emotional Animals," 134–42.

observance of the mean with respect to both actions and feelings.[118] Certain emotions, such as shamelessness, envy, and pleasure at another's misfortune (German *Schadenfreude*), are by their very nature never appropriate and consequently have no mean state. That most emotions may lead to vice not only by excess but also by deficiency, however, suggests that they play a positive role in a life of virtue.[119] To err by feeling too little of an emotion is no less a vice than feeling it too strongly.

Aristotle's remarks on fear in discussing the virtue of courage show that he recognizes its value. Courage (ἀνδρεία) is observance of the mean with respect to fear and confidence (θάρρος); excessive confidence together with insufficient fearfulness is rashness (θρασύς), while excessive fearfulness is cowardice (δειλία).[120] This initial definition in *Eth. nic.* 2.7.2–3 is elaborated in 3.6–9 and in a similar discussion in *Eth. eud.* 3.1.1–33. There are some things that are noble to fear and base not to fear—for example, disgrace and acting viciously (*Eth. nic.* 3.6.3–4). Aristotle explicitly raises the question of whether there is anything that the truly brave man should fear, and his answer is affirmative if somewhat unspecific (*Eth. eud.* 3.1.12–14). The brave man feels fear and confidence only when it is reasonable to do so. Fearlessness not in accordance with reason is not courage but rashness. But those occasions when it is appropriate to be afraid occur rarely and only in response to matters of great magnitude, and even then the courageous are less violently affected by those things that are objectively fearful (3.1.5–11). Reason does not demand one to endure that which is extremely painful or destructive, Aristotle says, unless it is good (καλός).

This last caveat is a critical one because it calls attention to the all-important capacity for discrimination. The ability to recognize the good becomes a requisite condition for the exercise of courage. Aristotle offers a detailed review of various approximations of courage frequently mistaken for the real thing in which it becomes apparent that it is not the action alone that constitutes courage but rather right action joined with the right motives (*Eth. eud.* 3.1.15–19; *Eth. nic.* 3.8.17). Like all virtues, courage is purposive and intentional (προαιρετική). Since its exercise requires correct judgment as to the good, it does not face fearful things through ignorance (*Eth. eud.* 3.1.32). He puts it a

---

[118] *Eth. nic.* 2.6.10, 15–16; *Eth. eud.* 2.10.30. See also L. A. Kosman, "Being Properly Affected: Virtues and Feelings in Aristotle's Ethics," in *Essays on Aristotle's Ethics* (ed. A. O. Rorty; Berkeley: University of California Press, 1980), 103–16.

[119] Virtues and emotions are not coextensive, however, in part because emotions are not purely voluntary (*Eth. nic.* 2.5.2–6), but the virtuous do possess a state of character that, as a result of chosen practice, disposes them to do the right thing and to feel the right way about it (3.8.14–15).

[120] For commentary, see David Pears, "Courage as a Mean," in Rorty, *Essays on Aristotle's Ethics*, 171–87.

slightly different way in the *Nicomachean Ethics*, once with special reference to fear (2.6.10–11) and once with reference to the virtue whose function it is to moderate such emotions (3.7.5): a person possessing the virtue of courage is not utterly fearless but rather "faces and fears the right things and from the right motive, in the right way, at the right time." Aristotle's prescription for coping with emotions, then, is not their eradication—this is neither possible nor desirable. Moderation is the goal, and this requires training (παιδεία), especially for the young who live and act primarily at the level of their passions.[121] Moral education necessarily involves sympathetic education; in other words, learning to be good and cultivating the appropriate emotional responses go hand in hand.

By no means does this brief review do justice to all the complexities of Aristotle's theory of the emotions, but it is hoped that it brings into view the main outlines of the debate over extirpation and moderation carried on among philosophers in the Hellenistic period.

Stoicism

Early and late sources both identify the position of the Stoa with respect to the emotions as a vital area of disagreement with the Peripatetic tradition. To moderate or to eradicate? On this question Aristotle and the Stoics give quite different answers. Their differing evaluations of and advice regarding the emotions reveal deeper differences between the two schools as to the dynamics of emotional response. For Aristotle, πάθος is in accordance with nature (κατὰ τήν φυσίν) and to be ἀπαθής is as much a vice as it is to be unrestrainedly passionate (*Eth. eud.* 2.3.6). After describing the two opposing stances—moderate affection versus absence of affection—Seneca the Stoic says he cannot at all comprehend how a moderate form of any·disease could be healthy or beneficial (*Ep.* 116.1). In this remark the basic Stoic view of the emotions becomes clear. They are, with little or no qualification, a blight on the soul. For this position the Stoics were infamous in antiquity, incurring the charge that they lacked *humanitas* because they were moved neither by their own πάθη nor those of others.[122] This is the aspect of their philosophy that survives in the English adjective "stoic," which denotes austere indifference to pleasure or pain and carries a slightly less negative connotation than the word "apathy," derived from ἀπάθεια, the Stoic technical term for freedom from emotion.

---

[121] *Eth. nic.* 1.3.5–8. Cf. Nussbaum, *The Therapy of Desire*, 93–99.

[122] For this criticism, see Lactantius, *Inst.* 6.10.11; 6.15.2. T. H. Irwin offers a defense of Stoicism against its ancient and modern critics ("Stoic Inhumanity," in Sihvola and Engberg-Pederson, *The Emotions in Hellenistic Philosophy*, 218–41).

The Stoics did not coin this term, nor were they the first or the only school to advocate some form of detachment as a precondition for a happy life.[123] But their theory of the emotions plays a more crucial role relative to the other components of their comprehensive philosophical system than is the case with any other ancient school with the possible exception of the Epicureans. Not surprisingly, the subtlety of their treatment and the degree to which it is integrated with their cosmological, physical, and ethical views is impressive. Adequately representing the Stoic theory is a challenging task for at least two reasons. First of all, Stoicism is a movement with a very long history, beginning with Zeno of Citium near the end of the fourth century and flourishing for over five centuries, its last famous adherent being the emperor Marcus Aurelius but its effects felt even later due to its influence on many patristic authors. Development and diversity are naturally to be expected in such a far-flung movement. Later writers modify, qualify, and restate the vision of the founders, sometimes introducing innovations that are hard to square with the original insights, all the while claiming an allegiance to the Stoa. This appears to be the case, for instance, with Posidonius. At this point a second difficulty comes to the fore—the nature of the sources for reconstructing Stoic thought. Much of the evidence for the views of the early Stoics comes down in fragmentary form. Does Chrysippus distort the teachings of Zeno and Cleanthes on the role of judgment in the emotions? Is Posidonius unorthodox in his aetiology of the emotions and the view of the soul it presupposes? Do Roman writers like Cicero and Seneca grasp the essence of the original doctrine when they translate it into the Latin tongue? So much depends on how one interprets the sources.[124]

---

[123] Michel Spanneut, "*Apatheia* ancienne, *apatheia* chrétienne," *ANRW* 2.36:4644–51.

[124] The most influential proponent of the view that Chrysippus departs from his predecessors' teachings is Max Pohlenz, *Die Stoa* (2nd ed.; 2 vols.; Göttingen: Vandenhoeck & Ruprecht, 1959), esp. 1:141–53. Galen's *De placitis Hippocratis et Platonis*, books 4–5, is the chief source for the views of Chrysippus, Posidonius, and their relation to each other and to the older Stoics, but the evidence he presents is tainted by his desire to conform Posidonius's views to an orthodox Platonic picture of the soul; cf. Christopher Gill, "Did Galen Understand Platonic and Stoic Thinking on Emotons?" in Sihvola and Engberg-Pederson, *The Emotions in Hellenistic Philosophy*, 113–48, who recognizes this while at the same time pointing out the real similarities between the Platonic and Stoic theories. Much scholarly effort has been exerted in untangling Galen's misunderstandings and polemical exaggerations from his accurate portrayals of Chrysippus's thought. The consensus view is that Chrysippus faithfully transmits the broad outlines and most of the particulars of Zeno's theory of the emotions (cf. Annas, *Hellenistic Philosophy of Mind*, 108; Brad Inwood, *Ethics and Human Action in Early Stoicism* [Oxford: Clarendon, 1985], 140–43; and John Cooper, "Posidonius on Emotions," in Sihvola and Engberg-Pederson, *The Emotions in Hellenistic Philosophy*, 71–111, who also argues that Posidonius accepts the traditional Stoic notion that the emotions are grounded in the judgments of the rational faculty). On the problems created

This review will emphasize the views of Chrysippus (ca. 280–206 B.C.E.), without whom, it is said, there would have been no Stoa (*SVF* 2.6). Notwithstanding the qualifications made by Posidonius, Chrysippus's views on the emotions remain the orthodox Stoic position for most of antiquity. It may be argued that a writer closer to Plutarch's time would provide a more suitable focus. His relative lack of facility with the Latin language, however, made most of contemporary Roman Stoicism inaccessible. Plutarch never cites Seneca and refers to Cicero almost exclusively as an indirect source for the *Lives*. Contemporary Greeks like Epictetus and Musonius Rufus are quoted either rarely or not at all. Like the author of Hebrews with respect to Jewish worship, Plutarch seems more interested in older, classic expressions of Stoic doctrine than in contemporary thought and practice. He is certainly acquainted with contemporary Stoics, yet Chrysippus provides him with his main literary source. The number of citations is far more than the number for Zeno, Ariston, Cleanthes, and Posidonius combined.[125] To understand the view of the emotions underlying Plutarch's critique of δεισιδαιμονία, Chrysippus is a good place to start.

What is an emotion? "Passion" is an equally appropriate rendering of πάθος for the Stoics given their basic view of emotional response. The connotation of the English "passion" as an excessive, unruly, even uncontrollable state corresponds closely with the characteristics the Stoics ascribe to the πάθη. Indeed, the passions are, by Stoic definition, excessive and unruly, though not strictly uncontrollable. The standard definitions found in Stoic literature lay bare the structure of emotional response and explain why the sage is able to control them. The simplest definition, attributed to Chrysippus, is that passions are judgments (κρίσεις).[126] Nothing could be further from the idea that emotions are primarily physiological reactions to stimuli. Insofar as there is a connection between the bodily and the spiritual aspects of emotion, it is the opposite of that supposed by the physical explanation.[127] Chrysippus compares the passionate soul to the body of one who is prone to sickness (νόσημα). This

---

by Latin translations of Stoic terminology, see Spanneut, "*Apatheia* ancienne," *ANRW* 2.36:4677–79.

[125] William C. Helmbold and Edward N. O'Neil list nearly four hundred quotations of Chrysippus (*Plutarch's Quotations* [Baltimore: American Philological Association, 1959]). This number would be even larger if the two lost works mentioning Chrysippus in the title (nos. 59 and 152) had survived; cf. Daniel Babut, *Plutarque et le Stoïcisme* (Paris: Presses Universitaires de France, 1969), 225–38.

[126] Diogenes Laertius 7.110–11; cf. *SVF* 456, 463.

[127] Galen the physician, however, attributes to Posidonius the view that men and animals with wide hips and low body temperatures are more cowardly, and more generally that the passionate dispositions of the soul are determined by the body's disposition (*Plac. Hipp. Plat.* 5.5.9–10).

sickness, he says, consists in "an enticing opinion (δόξαν ἐπιθυμίας) that has developed into a disposition (ἕξις) and hardened, according to which one assumes that which is not worthwhile to be exceedingly worthwhile" (*SVF* 3.421). The heavily cognitive terms of this definition are a sign that "passion" has a special meaning for the Stoics that it does not have for most people today. Nevertheless, they do not neglect the felt experience with which most people associate emotional response. Rather, they define it in terms of its ultimate causes, which they take to be mistaken value judgments (*SVF* 3.459, 461).

Their acknowledgement of the familiar affective aspect comes as a part of their delineation of the dynamic structure of a passion. It is not simply a disembodied, detached judgment of fact; as Arius Didymus reports, it is an impulse (ὁρμή), one which is excessive and disobedient to the dictates of reason, or, put another way, an irrational (ἄλογον) movement of the soul contrary to nature.[128] One experiences these impulses variously as contraction, "shrinking," elation, or expansion. Plato and Aristotle do not regard these impulses as voluntary, but the Stoics regard them as the psychosomatic result of the freely given assent of the individual. The concept of "preliminary passions" or "first movements" (προπάθεια), seems to have been a way of confronting the undeniable fact that humans do have affective reactions which precede any mental reflection and are not voluntary in any reasonable sense.[129] Sudden reactions such as flinching at an unexpected noise do not qualify as παθή in Stoic psychology for it is the mental judgment that is key. When Chrysippus emphasizes the irrational character of the passions, he does not mean to say that they are the result of non-cognitive operations. A person always acts or feels for some reason or other, and so the emotions are in this descriptive sense "rational;" that is, there is always a rationale. But because passions are contrary to nature, they cannot be rational in a normative sense; in other words, the impulses of which they speak are not based on good reasons or, in the Stoic phrase, right reason (ὀρθὸς λόγος).[130]

---

[128] *SVF* 3.378. William James also stresses the embodied character of emotions but emphasizes the role of the physical in causation more than the Stoics (*The Principles of Psychology* [3 vols.; Cambridge: Harvard University Press, 1981], 2:1067–68). "A purely disembodied emotion is a nonentity," he writes after explaining that it is more accurate to say that humans are afraid because they tremble instead of that they tremble because they are afraid.

[129] Cicero, *Tusc.* 3.83; Seneca, *Ira* 2.1–2; *Ep.* 74.31–32. Plutarch claims that they are merely renaming what are actually full-fledged passions so as to avoid an inconsistency in their thought (*Virt. mor.* 449A). See the discussion of Inwood, *Ethics and Human Action in Early Stoicism*, 175–81.

[130] Annas, *Hellenistic Philosophy of Mind*, 105–6; cf. also J. M. Rist, *Stoic Philosophy* (Cambridge: Cambridge University Press, 1969), 25–36.

Like Plato, Chrysippus appears to distinguish "true" emotions, which are grounded in the accurate beliefs generated by right reason, from "false" ones. A crucial difference is that Chrysippus does not apply these predicates to the passion itself since, by definition, any πάθος is necessarily false, resting as it does on two false judgments.[131] The first, already mentioned, is that something external to the individual is good or bad. This judgment includes both broad assumptions about the objective, ultimate good as well as determinations about the goodness or badness of the particular circumstances giving rise to the impulse to which one is subjected.[132] A second judgment is that, given the circumstances, a specific behavioral response is fitting—for example, weeping when sad, shaking when scared, and so forth. Chrysippus refers to this judgment as a "fresh belief" (πρόσφατος δόξα) that may weaken over time, which explains why a man will not continue to tremble with rage every time he recalls an injustice done to him in the distant past. The injustice remains an evil but it is no longer proper to react to it in the same way.[133] It remains within the power of the wise man to give or to withhold his assent to the immediate impression with which these judgments are concerned.[134] Assent (συγκατάθεσις) is tantamount to a judgment that the impression is true to reality.

As the passions play a central role in their ethical and psychological theory, the Stoics consequently have a great interest in how they are classified. Cicero in fact complains that Chrysippus and the older Stoics, in contrast to the Peripatetics, are more concerned with categorizing the passions than with healing them (*Tusc.* 4.5.9). There are four generic passions under which all others may be grouped: delight (ἡδονή), desire (ἐπιθυμία), distress (λύπη), and fear (φόβος).[135] Delight is a belief that some present circumstance is good

---

[131] For analysis, see A. C. Lloyd, "Emotion and Decision in Stoic Psychology," in *The Stoics* (ed. J. M. Rist; Berkeley: University of California Press, 1978), 233–46; Annas, *Hellenistic Philosophy of Mind*, 106–110; Nussbaum, *The Therapy of Desire*, 366–78; and Sorabji, *Emotion and Peace of Mind*, 29–33.

[132] *SVF* 3.169, 391, 480; Seneca, *Ira* 2.3.1; *Ep.* 75.11. Epictetus makes the point very clearly: "It is not the things themselves that disturb men, but their judgments about these things. For example, death is nothing dreadful . . . but the judgment that death is dreadful, this is the dreadful thing" (*Ench.* 5).

[133] On "fresh beliefs," see again Arius Didymus (apud Stobaeus, *Ecl.* 2.89–90=*SVF* 3.378); Ps.-Andronicus, *De passionibus* 1 (=*SVF* 3.391); Galen, *Plac. Hipp. Plat.* 4.2.1 (=*SVF* 3.463); 4.7.12 (=*SVF* 3.466); Cicero, *Tusc.* 3.74–75. Inwood, *Ethics and Human Action in Early Stoicism*, 147–50, provides insightful analysis.

[134] Epictetus, frg. 9 (=Aulus Gellius, *Noct. att.* 19.1.17–18); cf. *SVF* 2.974; 3.77.

[135] This taxonomy may be found in *SVF* 3.378, 391, 394, 463. Lists where the sub-species of each generic πάθος are defined are seen in *SVF* 3.397, 401, 409, 419; Diogenes Laertius 7.110–114. "Delight" and "distress" are better translations than "pleasure" and "pain" since the latter pair gives the mistaken impression that Stoics see them as primarily physical reactions (cf. Nussbaum, *The Therapy of Desire*, 386 n. 64).

and cause for elation. Desire is a belief that something in the future is to be pursued because it is good. Distress is a belief that some present circumstance is an evil about which one ought to feel dejected. Fear is the belief that something in the future is an objective evil of the sort that one should avoid it. It is under the category of fear that δεισιδαιμονία appears (*SVF* 3.394, 408, 409, 411).

From these definitions, considered in their larger philosophical framework, it should be clear that the Stoic evaluation of the passions is a negative one. They are excessive and therefore—in violation of the cardinal tenet that one should live κατὰ φύσιν—contrary to nature.[136] Its irrationality also marks πάθος as an unnatural condition of the soul. It is excessive and irrational to have attachments that give rise to the sort of disturbances characteristic of the passions. All externals, including health, wealth, fame, family, and even life itself (*SVF* 3.117; cf. Epictetus, *Diatr.* 3.22.21; 3.26.38–39; frg. 32), are indifferent (ἀδιάφορα) and thus not to be desired for themselves (cf. Diogenes Laertius 7.102–110). To desire these things as worthy in themselves is to have the wrong attachments, which are in turn based on false judgments (*SVF* 3.256). Complete detachment enables the wise to realize the Stoic ideal of self-sufficiency (αὐτάρκεια).[137] Virtue alone is a good worth striving after as an end in itself (*SVF* 3.30, 40, 92, 237; Epictetus, *Diatr.* 3.3.14–19; 3.10.18–19; Diogenes Laertius 7.101, 127). And because the soul is a unity in Stoic thought, the passions that obscure this knowledge of virtue as the only good cannot be blamed on some irrational part of the soul as with Plato. Everything is a function of the rational faculty, perverted though it may be, and so each individual is responsible for his or her emotions and the havoc they wreak.

It is important to keep in mind the special sense in which the Stoics use πάθος and their underlying reasoning lest one conclude on the wrong basis that they advocate an unattainable or undesirable ideal when they assert that emotions must be completely eradicated. Do they really mean it when they claim that those who are truly wise are utterly free of emotion? Yes and no. Yes, if one means by "emotion" the affective state described and analyzed by Zeno and Chrysippus. Vice and virtue are all that matters, and the misguided commitments to any other apparent good that emotional responses reflect are not neutral but instead detrimental. But the answer is no if one understands the Stoics to say that any and all affective states resembling "emotions" are inappropriate. Indeed, it is difficult to imagine human life devoid of all feeling. What, then, do the wise feel? Stoic teaching allows three so-called "good feelings" (εὐπαθείαι) parallel to the four generic πάθη in the standard

---

[136] Excess: *SVF* 3.378, 384, 462; cf. Seneca, *Ira* 1.7.4. Contrary to nature: *SVF* 1.58; 3.378, 394. The best analysis of the excessive character of Stoic πάθη is that of Inwood, *Ethics and Human Action in Early Stoicism*, 155–73.

[137] *SVF*. 3.67; cf. Nussbaum, *The Therapy of Desire*, 359–65; and J. B. Gould, *The Philosophy of Chrysippus* (Albany: SUNY Press, 1970), 168–81.

taxonomy: joy (χαρά), volition (βούλησις), and caution (εὐλάβεια), which correspond respectively to delight, desire, and fear.[138] Technically, these are distinct from the passions because they are accurate judgments about the good in accord with right reason which do not ascribe more value to ἀδιάφορα than they actually possess (*SVF* 3.175, 264, 275, 480). Joy is rational (εὐλόγον) elation grounded in true knowledge (not imperfect opinion) about some present good. Voliton is rational reaching out grounded in true knowledge that some future good is worth pursuing. Caution is rational apprehensiveness grounded in true knowledge that some future circumstance is an evil rightly avoided. Eupathic affections are true judgments and therefore cannot be deemed excessive.

For the present study it is worth noting that εὐλάβεια has two, and only two, species listed in the standard taxonomies (*SVF* 3.431–2). While these are likely not the only two envisioned by Chrysippus, they may be seen as perhaps the two most important ones. The first, αἰδώς (respectfulness or shame), occurs only here and at *SVF* 3.416 and is defined as εὐλάβεια ὀρθοῦ ψόγου (caution regarding proper blame or censure). The other, ἀγνεία (purity), occurs only here in the fragments collected by von Arnim and is defined as εὐλάβεια τῶν περὶ θεοὺς ἁμαρτημάτων (caution with respect to sins or shortcomings concerning the gods). Though it is identified as the best form fear may take, the earlier discussion of αἰδώς is not part of a discussion of εὐπάθεια. Its definition here is basically the same—the desire to avoid shamefulness (ἀδοξία). But this definition of αἰδώς is too vague to be of much practical help especially since ἀδοξία is categorized as ἀδιάφορα in *SVF* 3.70, 117, 127, and so ought not to be among those things properly feared by the Stoic sage. Attempts to specify what the Stoics mean precisely by αἰδώς break down when one finds αἰσχύνη defined in *SVF* 3.407 as disapproved fear of ἀδοξία because αἰδώς is also defined approvingly as fear of falling into ἀδοξία when it is distinguished from αἰσχύνη in *SVF* 3.416. From this it would appear that the Stoic analysis of the sub-species of the eupathic affections has not reached the degree of systematization as has their ethical evaluation and their analysis of the structure of the passions. It is easier to say what is bad about them than what may be good. Absent any elaboration of the concept of αἰδώς, it is advisable to understand it according to its common sense as a mode of living that is

---

[138] Diogenes Laertius 7.115–116 (=*SVF* 3.431); Ps.-Andronicus, *De passionibus* 6 (=*SVF* 3.432); Cicero, *Tusc.* 4.6.14, translates εὐπάθεια as *constantia*. No affective state corresonds to distress, that is, to the apperception of a present evil. Because vice is the only true evil and the sage is, by definition, free of vice, there can never be true knowledge of a present evil without the condition becoming one of genuine distress. Cf. Tad Brennan, "The Old Stoic Theory of Emotions," in Sihvola and Engberg-Pederson, *The Emotions in Hellenistic Philosophy*, 34–35.

appropriate or befitting (τὸ καθῆκον) for one's given social nexus.[139] Respect for family, friends, and country are binding duties that following from life according to nature (*SVF* 3.491–500, 611–36; Epictetus, *Ench.* 30). Neglect of these puts one in the realm of αἰδώς. This aspect of appropriate fear is perfectly in line with the condemnation of superstition by Stoics like Cicero on the grounds that it is socially disruptive and destroys patriotism.

The definition of ἁγνεία appears to be the only reference to one's posture vis-à-vis the gods in the fragments dealing with the Stoic theory of the emotions. What does it mean for a Stoic to sin against the gods? It depends in no small part upon what they believe about the nature of the divine. This is no small subject, but for the present the report of Diogenes Laertius giving the main outlines of their theology is instructive (7.147). The deity is

> a living being, immortal, rational, perfect or intelligent in happiness, admitting nothing evil [into him], taking providential care of the world . . . but he is not of human shape. He is, however, the artificer of the universe and, as it were, the father of all, both in general and in that particular part of him which is all-pervading, and which is called many names according to its various powers.

Cicero's summary of Chrysippus's pantheistic view of the divine is basically the same (*Nat. d.* 1.15.39): God is rational, providential, the active force behind all that occurs. Such jargon-filled characterizations, though they are more typical than is the worshipful tone of Cleanthes's *Hymn to Zeus* (*SVF* 1.537), should not lead one to conclude that the Stoics reject the traditional Greek pantheon. They uphold popular religion with the proviso that it be interpreted allegorically. Thus, the object of the eupathic disposition labeled ἁγνεία may simply have to do with satisfying the ritual purity requirements of the popular religion. But this seems out of step with the overarching concerns of Stoic ethics since popular religion has so little explicit relationship to the practice of virtue as understood by the philosophers.

Perhaps it is closer to the spirit of Stoic thought to interpret the phrase εὐλάβεια τῶν περὶ θεοὺς ἁμαρτημάτων with a primary emphasis on ἁμάρτημα as it is used in their ethical writings, especially since their views on

---

[139] In Plato, *Prot.* 322B–D, there is the story that Zeus has sent αἰδώς, along with justice, to humans to bring order to the city-state and to save the race from total destruction. Rudolf Bultmann notes that the term becomes rare in the Hellenistic period but is revived in late Stoicism ("αἰδώς," *TDNT* 1:169). Douglas L. Cairns' excellent study does not cover the Stoics, but his review of Homer, the tragedians, Plato, and Aristotle shows that sensitivity to one's social responsibilities is at the core of this emotion while one's relationship to the gods is largely peripheral to it (*Aidōs: The Psychology and Ethics of Honour and Shame in Ancient Greek Literature* [Oxford: Clarendon, 1993], 135, 197–98, 208).

the emotions are so closely connected to ethical imperatives. If God is perfectly rational and has providentially ordained that the universe operate as it does, then to live in accord with the divine will is to live κατὰ φύσιν. This is the same as following right reason in one's thoughts and actions.[140] Another passage from Diogenes Laertius combines these different strands of thought in short compass (7.87–88):

> Again, living virtuously is equivalent to living in accordance with experience of the actual course of nature . . . for our individual natures are parts of the nature of the whole universe. And this is why the end may be defined as life in accordance with nature . . . And this very thing constitutes the virtue of the happy man and the smooth current of life, when all actions promote the harmony of the spirit dwelling in the individual man with the will of him who orders the universe.

All that happens is a result of the will of Zeus, thus to be upset at some circumstance or to wish irrationally for something that is contrary to the natural order of things is to show oneself at odds with the divine will.[141] It is the duty of humans to assimilate themselves to the will of Zeus as it is manifested in the world as it is (*SVF* 3.661). Passions are not the only ἁμαρτήματα, but they are the most pernicious. And since the passions are grounded in and issue from one's beliefs about the nature of things, perhaps it is in this area that one may be at fault regarding the gods, by entertaining distorted notions of their nature and of the nature of the universe. Epictetus says that the chief element of piety towards the gods is to have the right opinions about them, namely, that they exist and that they preside over the universe in a just manner (*Ench.* 31.1). False notions are responsible for the passions, which are in turn an impediment to a virtuous life.[142] Thus it is Stoic theology—in the narrow sense of beliefs

---

[140] *SVF* 3.499–500. The same point is made about ἁμάρτημα in *SVF* 445, 501, specifically in connection with the four generic πάθη.

[141] Cf. Inwood, *Ethics and Human Action in Early Stoicism*, 160.

[142] Cf. *SVF* 3.28, where it is said that most ἁμάρτημα begin with false assumptions about the proper end of life. Stoic approval of a limited number of eupathic dispositions like εὐλάβεια and its sub-species αἰδώς and ἁγνεία is logically connnected to their teachings on virtue. Vice is the only true evil. From this it follows that vice alone is to be feared and that such fear is not excessive because it is rational fear. The Stoic sage may feel this type of fear, which qualifies as εὐλάβεια but not φόβος. If Cleanthes is correct that the true wise man—an ideal type generally acknowledged as such—can never fall into vice after achieving sagehood due to the certainty of his understanding (διὰ βεβαίους καταλήψεις), then such fear would appear to be unfounded (Diogenes Laertius 7.127). Chrysippus believes that virtue can indeed be lost, namely, through drunkenness or melancholy. The internal Stoic debate about the theoretical possibility of

regarding the gods and in the broader sense of what they believe about the
nature of reality—that determines the Stoic view of the emotions and not the
other way around. They have not constructed so impressive a cosmology simply
by extrapolating from their own aversion to sentimentality, though it must be
said that the emphasis in their analysis is on the practical effect of their
cosmological views upon the individual. Viewed from this wider perspective,
ἁγνεία may be understood as an intellectual virtue, purity of mind, requisite for
virtuous action and consisting in the proper way of thinking about the divine.[143]

Although early Stoics make almost no explicit reference to the divine in
their discussions of the emotions, it is clear that no image of the gods that would
incite a passionate response can be acceptable. Eupathic dispositions, because
they are not technically classified as passions, play an important role in the Stoic
prescriptions for coping with emotion.[144] Inwood only slightly overstates this
point when he says that the Stoic theory "might be summed up in the slogan
'apatheia is eupatheia'."[145] As disease is to the body, so are πάθη to the soul.
Moderation is only treating the symptom; eradication removes the root cause.
Once the symptom appears, it is too late for preventive treatment, and it is
pointless to reason with anyone in the throes of passion because the passionate
state is a sure sign that, at that moment, he or she is not open to rational
persuasion (SVF 3.390, 474–475). The physician of the soul must choose not
only the right method but also the right time to administer therapy. When an
attack of emotion subsides, it is then possible to supplant the false judgment
constituting the emotion with a true one. Different individuals are also likely to
be more or less susceptible to certain emotions, owing to the different
convictions about the world they embrace. Knowledge of this case history
enables the Stoic to tailor the regimen to the specific needs of the patient.
Continuing with the medical analogy, immunization is best of all because it
prevents the onset of the disease. According to Chrysippus, it is possible to

---

falling from a sagely state of ἀπάθεια is seen in SVF 3.237–244. In addition to
melancholy and drunkenness, lethargy (λήθαργος), torpor (κάρος), and consulting
sorcerers are also mentioned as possible conditions threatening to disturb the preferred
state of ἀπάθεια.

[143] Walter Burkert notes the internalization of the concept of purity, expressed in its
simplest terms in an inscription at the Asclepius sanctuary at Epidauris: "Purity is to think
pious things" (cf. Greek Religion, 77). This strand of thought represents a merging of
ritual and ethical reflection in which the latter adds a deeper dimension to the outward
forms of the former. Though of no avail, the sacrifices of popular religion may be
observed by the Stoic sage on the principle that the divine pervades all phenomena.
Indeed, by means of allegory, traditional religion provides Stoic interpreters of the myths
such as Cornutus with an additional source for discerning the nature of the cosmos.

[144] Unfortunately, Chrysippus's book on the therapy of the passions is not extant (SVF
3.457, 474).

[145] Inwood, Ethics and Human Action in Early Stoicism, 173.

inoculate a person against the passions by imagining and preparing for unexpected circumstances ahead of time.[146] True knowledge of good and evil ought to suppress outbreaks of emotion by equipping the individual with sound judgments about what is and is not a legitimate source of anxiety.

Galen—or perhaps Posidonius, for it is often difficult to discern where Galen is reporting and where he is expanding—raises a valid question at this point: why does the mind assent to false judgments of value in the first place?[147] Chrysippus's answer is that some souls are "flabby" or have weak tension (ἄτονος). But how is it that the soul ever finds itself in this condition? Lack of a proper education in virtue and vice in the early years is one cause, and associating with bad characters is another (SVF 3.229A). But how is it that the first bad characters became bad? To this perennial question, Chrysippus appears to have no fully satisfactory answer, though as Gould observes, Posidonius moves towards a position resembling the Christian doctrine of original sin when he says that every soul is "infested by a bad and godless demon" (SVF 3.460).[148] When pressed to do so Plutarch, who is quick to seize upon any perceived lacuna or inconsistency in the Stoic system, will nonetheless account for personal sin in a strikingly similar fashion (Is. Os. 369C–D).

Epicureanism

Across town from the Stoa, Epicurus began receiving pupils in his garden not long after Zeno had founded his school. Epicurus and his followers would become popular targets of abuse from other philosophers, for their purported atheism and above all for their embrace of a hedonistic lifestyle.[149] While much

---

[146] SVF 3.417, 482; cf. Gould, The Philosophy of Chrysippus, 187–88. By dwelling upon potential misfortunes ahead of time, the experience of misfortune will not provoke a painful emotional response because it will not involve a "fresh" belief. This is the reasoning behind the advice of Epictetus to dwell constantly on death (Ench. 20–21). Cicero also endorses the practice of praemeditatio, defending it against the Epicurean alternative of revocatio, the diverting of one's attention from potential future distress to past pleasures (Tusc. 3.13.28–19.46).

[147] SVF 3.460, 473.

[148] Gould, The Philosophy of Chrysippus, 194–95. For a reconstruction of the debate between Chrysippus and Posidonius, see Richard Sorabji, "Chrysippus—Posidonius—Seneca: A High-Level Debate on Emotion," in Sihvola and Engberg-Pedersen, The Emotions in Hellenistic Philosophy, 149–69; and idem, Emotion and Peace of Mind, 93–98. Posidonius recognizes the role of judgments but argues that they are not a necessary cause of emotion. He accordingly prescribes treatments that focus on both rational judgments and non-rational habituation of the sentiments, for example, by means of musical therapy.

[149] For Epicurus's reputation as an atheist, see Cicero, Nat. d. 1.30.85; 1.44.123–124; Plutarch, Adv. Col. 1119E; and Sextus Empiricus, Math. 9.58, all of whom suggest that

anti-Epicurean sentiment rests on misunderstandings, the hostility between the various schools does in fact stem from real and profound disagreements on matters of substance. At the risk of oversimplifying the contrast, it may be said that Plato, Aristotle, and the Stoics assert that reality possesses an objective quality, however imperfectly humans may be able to perceive it, and that human behavior ought to be brought into conformity with it. This is clearest with the Stoics, who have a detailed view of the nature of the cosmos and claim that the secret to happiness is living according to nature. Of course, this often requires a drastic alteration of one's ideas about happiness. The Stoic definition of happiness is a normative one; without a correct understanding of the cosmos and the picture of happiness that goes with it, a person cannot be truly happy. Epicurus on the other hand approaches philosophy from a different perspective. His primary focus is upon the happiness of the individual, as it should be, he says, for any true philosopher.[150] As he puts it in his letter to Menoeceus, pleasure (ἡδονή) is the beginning and the end (τέλος) of a blessed life (*Ep. Men.* 128). Because his epistemological bias is in the direction of trusting the direct experience of the sense-perceptions of the uncorrupted individual over abstract reasoning, Epicurus sees little need to modify one's natural conception of happiness. What can be more "natural" (and therefore appropriate) than to seek pleasure and avoid pain? And who needs a complicated theory of the emotions in order to know what is pleasant and what is not? Not Epicurus. It is perhaps unfair to explain away Epicurean physics and cosmology as a projection of or an extrapolation from their psychology and ethics, but it is important to keep the focus where they keep it—on the feelings and their implications for a happy life.

No straightforward definition of "emotion" comparable to the ones offered by the Stoics appear in the Epicurean sources. Their use of πάθος reflects the broad semantic range this term covers, including affective reactions to external stimuli as well as the passively endured phenomena (παθήματα) to which fear, joy, and anger are subjective responses. As Annas notes, the Epicurean theory of the emotions is in reality a theory of "feelings," in which emotions, for the sake of comparison with other schools, are best understood as complex states of feeling.[151] The Epicurean taxonomy is a simple one. Pleasure (ἡδονή) and pain

---

he nominally acknowledges the gods' existence only for fear of offending the general public. Giving rise to the charges of profligacy is his acceptance of women into his school.

[150] Porphyry quotes Epicurus to this effect (*Marc.* 31): "Empty are the arguments of that philosopher who offers no therapy for human suffering."

[151] Annas, *Hellenistic Philosophy of Mind*, 189–90; J. Gosling and C. C. W. Taylor, *The Greeks on Pleasure* (Oxford: Clarendon, 1982), 345–64. Philosophical and psychological theories of the relationship between emotion and feeling are examined by Lyons, *Emotion*, 130–43.

(ἀλγηών) are the two basic πάθη (Diogenes Laertius 10.34). Whereas for the Stoics the good ultimately determines whether one ought to regard something as pleasant or unpleasant, for the Epicureans it is just the opposite: that which is pleasant is *ipso facto* good. Every sentient being naturally—that is, before it is contaminated by culture—seeks pleasure as the highest good and avoids pain as the greatest evil (Epicurus, *Ep. Men.* 128–129; Cicero, *Fin.* 1.30; 3.3; Diogenes Laertius 10.137). So self-evident is this truth that Epicurus deems redundant any attempts at elaboration.

Given this natural inclination, how is it that anyone experiences pain? Two related causes emerge. Most obvious of all is the undeniable fact that many things are beyond the control of any individual. Desired goods are sometimes elusive, and unwanted evils are often impossible to avoid. The other cause is a cultural one. Very few people remain in the natural state. Rousseau's noble savage is a hypothetical figure, an ideal never really found in nature. Each person is born and raised in particular contexts not of his or her own choosing and so is unable to escape the taint of human culture. Epicurus advises Pythocles to avoid all culture (παιδεία) because it supplies the misguided opinions responsible for disappointment in the pursuit of pleasure (Diogenes Laertius 10.6; cf. *Vatican Sayings* 58). Culture, by introducing opinions and ideals which lead to unnatural and unnecessary desire such as the desires for wealth, fame, and immortality, is continually a source of pain when these desires go unfulfilled (*Kyriai doxai* 26, 29–30; *Vatican Sayings* 21, 67). Epicurus sides with Aristotle against the Sceptics in the belief that opinions about the good will always be present. Indefinite suspension of judgment is impracticable. Emotions, in contrast to raw feelings of pleasure and pain, require some form of belief or opinion, and these beliefs determine whether a given sensation is experienced as fear, anger, excitement or some other specific emotion. But where Aristotle distinguishes between excessive and moderate emotion, Epicurus emphasizes the distinction between "natural" (φυσικός) and "empty" (κενή) ones that are based respectively upon natural and empty beliefs (κενοδοξία).[152] Empty beliefs are typically false, but not all false beliefs are empty. Emptiness necessarily involves significant harm to the well-being of the individual.

---

[152] This distinction is nevertheless very similar to the one affirmed by Plato and Aristotle between true and false emotions, though Aristotle assigns a prominent role to παιδεία in the formation of beliefs and emotions that are conducive to the good life while Epicurus sees education as a prison from which the sage has been freed. The distinction between natural and empty desire appears frequently in the extant writings of Epicurus (*Kyriai doxai* 29–30). Cf. Julia Annas, "Epicurean Emotions," *GRBS* 30 (1989): 147–53; Nussbaum, *The Therapy of Desire*, 111–14; and Sorabji, *Emotion and Peace of Mind*, 26–27.

What practical criteria enable one to make this crucial distinction? Nature provides a convenient guide: that which is good is easy to get, and that which is difficult to get cannot be very good (*Kyriai doxai* 26; *Ep. Men.* 130, 133). An apparent good is not necessary and hence not truly good if the desire for it is difficult or impossible to satisfy. Natural desires have appropriate limits which are conducive to a pleasant life (*Kyriai doxai* 10–11, 15, 18–21; *Vatican Sayings* 25, 59, 68; *Ep. Men.* 130). Insatiable desires do not have true pleasures as their object, regardless of what the individual may think at the time. Those who see the Epicurean way of life as one of unmitigated hedonism miss this last point. Pleasure for Epicurus is best defined in negative terms as the absence of pain or disturbance (*Ep. Men.* 128–131; *Kyriai doxai* 3, 10). Short-term ἡδονή frequently comes at the sacrifice of long-term ἀταραξία, and so one must calculate the advantages and disadvantages before assenting to any experience (*Ep. Men.* 130–132). As a result, the life of the Epicurean sage will not be one of reckless abandon in pursuit of pleasure but rather one of withdrawal and sobriety so as to avoid unnecessary disturbance. Too often one spoils the good that is present by desiring a supposed good that is absent. Contentment with what comes easily is the path of wisdom (*Vatican Sayings* 35).

Most emotions cause disturbance and for that reason receive a negative evaluation from the Epicureans. Fear receives the strongest disapproval from the Epicureans because it is so pervasive and so serious a threat to human flourishing. They single out two specific fears for special consideration, fear of death and fear of the gods. These are more far-reaching in their effects than any other emotions and on that account receive considerable attention, especially from Lucretius in *De rerum natura*.[153] Their analyses of fear bring to light the substantive belief needed to reinforce the practical guidelines for achieving happiness described in the preceding paragraph. Without the correct antecedent beliefs about the nature of things, an individual remains vulnerable to emotional turmoil.[154]

Fear of the gods is the dysfunctional emotion most closely connected to inculturation. Contrary to the charges leveled by their contemporaries, the Epicureans affirm that the gods exist.[155] Cicero has the Epicurean Velleius say

---

[153] See the discussions of Charles Segal, *Lucretius on Death and Anxiety* (Princeton: Princeton University Press, 1990), 3–25; and Nussbaum, *The Therapy of Desire*, 192–238. Writing in Latin, Lucretius uses both *superstitio* and *religio* in connection with the fear described (in Greek) by Epicurus.

[154] This is most explicit in *Kyriai doxai* 11–13, where Epicurus says that the study of natural science (φυσιολογία) is necessary in order to attain peace of mind. Cf. *Ep. Pythocles* 85–87; Lucretius 6.43–95 and also P.Oxy. 215, attributed to Epicurus by A. J. Festugière (*Epicurus and His Gods* [trans. C. W. Chilton; Oxford: Blackwell, 1955], 63–65), where it is said that "the most blessed gift is to have a clear perception of things."

[155] The objection of ancient and modern critics, namely, that the Epicurean picture of God

that nature itself has imprinted the fact of their existence on the minds of all peoples without exception (*Nat. d.* 1.16.43–17.44). Unfortunately, fear of the gods is as widespread as is belief in their existence. Epicurus himself claims that their existence is self-evident, but goes on to qualify this statement by saying that they are not as the masses believe them to be (*Ep. Men.* 123). Sacrifice and participation in public religious festivals are perfectly acceptable so long as one realizes that there is no need to appease wrathful gods.[156] The conception of the gods as blessed and indestructible to which Epicurus subscribes appears in the very first of his *Kyriai doxai*. That which is blessed and indestructible neither suffers disturbance nor causes disturbance to any other being. By imagining that the gods intervene in the ordinary operations of the universe, the masses open the door to all kinds of unhealthy attitudes affecting every area of life.[157] According to Lucretius, the majesty of nature encouraged belief in the gods among all the peoples of the earth, but it also led them to see the active hand of the divine in every event, especially those in the heavens where the gods make their home (5.156–165, 1161–1193; cf. Epicurus, *Ep. Herodotus* 76; *Kyriai doxai* 12–13). Such powerful beings as the popular myths portray are an unending source of fear and anxiety.

The most important educational task of the philosopher is to undo the damage done by these popular beliefs, replacing them with a proper understanding of the nature of the universe. Like everything else in the universe, the gods exist only as conglomerations of atoms powerless, or at least unconcerned, to exert their will on humans.[158] Beings of this kind should not be a source of fear, a point Lucretius repeatedly makes in his poem. Epicurean gods are free from all disturbances, be they pains, dangers, or emotional upheavals such as anger or worry (2.646–651). They do nothing special to help humans in their unchanging administration of the universe, but neither do they cause any harm (2.1090–1104; 5.165–172). A life worthy of the gods is the type of existence to which humans should aspire (3.321–322; cf. *Ep. Men.* 135). Such was the life of Epicurus, whom Lucretius refers to as a god (5.8, 19) and whose

---

is not a worthy one or is not what most ordinary persons mean by the word "God" and so is tantamount to atheism, is best seen as an argument not about theism and atheism but rather about orthodoxy and heresy. See Dirk Obbink, "The Atheism of Epicurus," *GRBS* 30 (1989): 187–223.

[156] P.Oxy. 215 passim. Taking part in the festivals for the sage is to take part in the very happiness of the gods themselves (cf. Festugière, *Epicurus and His Gods*, 61–64). A more pessimistic view of popular religion is found in Lucretius (5.1194–1240).

[157] *Ep. Men.* 124. Obbink shows how Epicurus's rejection of providence and teleology accounts for his reputation in antiquity as an atheist ("The Atheism of Epicurus," 221–23).

[158] Humans, too, have a purely atomistic existence but are nonetheless willing and able to interfere in the lives of other humans, so it is not clear how Epicurean physics, derived largely from Democritus, necessitates this aspect of their theology.

accomplishments are described as greater than those of Hercules because he has purged the mind—that is, his and his pupils'—of the false beliefs that cause lust, fear, and all other destructive emotions (5.1–54; cf. 3.1–30; 6.1–42).[159]

Fear of death and fear of the gods are inextricably related in Epicurean thought. Paradoxical but true, death is the one constant in human life—"when it comes to death all humans live in a city without walls" (*Vatican Sayings* 31)—and most religions provide answers to the questions it poses.[160] Death and the anxiety it creates drive the masses to the gods for comfort.[161] Gods are, almost by definition, ἀθάνατοι, and it is widely believed that they may, if they so choose, grant some degree of power over death to humans as well.[162] According to Lucretius, fear of death was a feature of life in the state of nature he describes (5.925–1104) prior to the advent of religion. Thus it is chronologically prior to and more basic than fear of the gods. The primordial source of the former cannot be found in the latter.[163] Historically speaking, fear of the gods is a result of fear of death, but once religion is introduced the myths

---

[159] Is divinity an image or a projection of the good life described by Epicurus and nothing more? A. A. Long and D. N. Sedley interpret the ambiguous evidence in this fashion and draw the controversial conclusion that the gods of Epicurus are "thought-constructs" whose "primary existence is as a moral concept, not as a specially privileged extraterrestrial life-form" (*The Hellenistic Philosophers* [2 vols.; Cambridge: Cambridge University Press, 1987–88], 1:144–49).

[160] Recent biomedical advances in areas such as genetic engineering suggest that physical immortality may be a more than purely hypothetical possibility in the future. These developments make the philosophical debate about death and its relevance to the meaning of human life more than idle conjecture. Is the prolongation of human life desirable? If human life expectancy is greatly, but not indefinitely, lengthened, will this decrease the anxiety associated with death? Or does it only postpone inevitable fears? If it is the physical suffering accompanying the dying process that is feared rather than death itself, will the elimination of all suffering leading up to death then inadvertently increase the anxieties caused by death, since its approach will be all the more anticipated and the life of which one is deprived will be all the more pleasant? These and other pressing questions are the subject of much speculation in recent thanatological literature. Cf. O. H. Green, "Fear of Death," *Philosophy and Phenomenological Research* 43 (1982): 99–105; A. Brueckner and J. M. Fischer, "Why is Death Bad?" *Philosophical Studies* 50 (1986): 213–21; Fred Feldman, *Confrontations with the Reaper: A Philosophical Study of the Nature and Value of Death* (Oxford: Oxford University Press, 1992), 11–21, 89–105; Nussbaum, *The Therapy of Desire*, 204–17; and Leon R. Kass, "L'Chaim and Its Limits: Why Not Immortality?" *First Things* 113 (May 2001): 17–24.

[161] If Epicurus sounds very "modern" on this point, it should be recalled that Marx's 1841 Berlin dissertation was on Democritus and Epicurus.

[162] Cf. Emily Vermeule, *Aspects of Death in Early Greek Art and Poetry* (Berkeley: University of California Press, 1979), 121–22.

[163] According to the Epicureans, at any rate; cf. Nussbaum, *The Therapy of Desire*, 200. An echo of this debate is heard in Plutarch, frg. 177–178 (Sandbach).

it promulgates provide an additional source of fear about dying. Epicurus wants to free humans from this vicious cycle of belief and anxiety, depicted at great length and in rich detail by Lucretius.

Why is fear of death more to be dreaded than death itself, to borrow the phrase of the first-century aphorist Publilius Syrus (*Sententiae* 511)? Just as it is with fear of the gods (Lucretius 6.58–79), the Epicurean response is a consequentialist one. It is bad to fear death because the practical effects of such fear are undesirable. Dying brings life to an end, to be sure, but fearing death casts a pall over life while one still has it. Even if one does not agree with the Epicurean view of death, on empirical grounds it is difficult to deny this part of their argument. Fear, whether or not it is well-founded, is an unpleasant emotion and for that very reason is an impediment to the enjoyment of life, which is of paramount importance for Epicurus. Hell does not exist, Lucretius insists, but by fearing what may come in the afterlife one makes life on earth into a sort of living hell. Tantalus, Tityos, and Sisyphus are mythical figures in stories told by priests and poets and nothing more. Yet life cruelly imitates art when humans allow their consciences to gnaw at them or sublimate their fear of death in frantic activity aimed at denying the mortality they so resent (3.870–1023). Though arising out of a desire to make sense of death, religion has actually made matters much worse. Traditional Greek theology, eschatology, and soteriology have caused more concrete harm than good in the here and now (1.62–126). Book three of *De rerum natura* opens with a catalogue of the ways in which fear of death indirectly robs humans of their *joie de vivre* and leads to morally repugnant behavior (3.31–93): it causes humans to break the bonds of friendship, to betray parents and country, to break the law in the pursuit of fame and power, and even to rejoice at the death of a sibling, presumably because it removes a rival heir and thereby increases one's own inheritance.[164]

This diagnosis is drawn primarily from Lucretius but is implicit in the extant writings of Epicurus. Lucrétius lays a heavy emphasis on the ills of religion that is largely missing from Epicurus, though this lacuna may be due to the fact that most of Epicurus's vast output, including treatises "On the Gods" and "On Piety," has not survived.[165] Whereas Lucretius is concerned with tracing the bad effects of the religious response to fear of death, Epicurus is more interested in explaining why fearing death is irrational. Because he shares with other schools the conviction that one's beliefs and emotions fit together in a coherent and generally predictable fashion, and that emotional well-being hinges upon having true beliefs about the world, his ideas about what happens at death form a seamless whole with his prescriptions for coping with the emotions.

---

[164] Segal, *Lucretius on Death and Anxiety*, 20–24.

[165] Diogenes Laertius reports that Epicurus was one of the most prolific authors in antiquity, having written approximately 300 scrolls without ever quoting another author (10.26–28).

How is it that Epicurus can say, as he must have been fond of saying if the frequency with which it is repeated is any indication, that "death is nothing to us" (*Ep. Men*. 124; *Kyriai doxai* 2; Lucretius 3.830; Cicero, *Tusc*. 1.8.15)? The realization that death is nothing, he says, makes the mortality of life enjoyable by removing the yearning for immortality. At the time of death, the individual ceases to exist as such because body and soul are nothing more than an impermanent configuration (ἄθροισμα) of atoms that disperses, thereby removing all sensation and consciousness (*Ep. Herodotus* 40–44, 63–65). If this premise is accepted, then the rest of Epicurus's argument falls into place (*Ep. Men*. 125). Death is nothing because "when we exist, death is not yet present, and when death is present, then we do not exist. Therefore, it is relevant neither to the living nor to the dead, since it does not affect the former, and the latter do not exist." No event can be bad (and hence fearsome) if no one exists to experience (and hence to fear) it, and so it makes no sense to fear one's own death.[166] Fear of death, then is an empty emotion, based on false and debilitating beliefs and impossible to satisfy; its cure is to memorize and observe the so-called "fourfold remedy" (τετραφάρμακος): don't fear God, don't worry over death, remember that the good is easy to get, and that evil is easy to endure.[167] In so doing one will lead a genuinely philosophical life, one that consists of continual—yet in no way morbid or depressive—meditation on death (*commentatio mortis*: Cicero, *Tusc*. 1.30.74; cf. Plato, *Phaed*. 67D–E). Their peculiar solution to the problem of morbid fears enable Plutarch to make the observation—unfair because it rests on semantic sleight of hand—that death is most assuredly something, and not nothing, to the Epicureans because they talk about it so much (*Suav. viv*. 1092C–D).

Summary

To sum up, while the various schools of thought informing Plutarch's critique of superstition argue over points of theory and practice, they agree on a basic level on a number of core issues. On the structure of occurrent emotions, Aristotle and especially the Stoics, who carry on a vigorous intramural debate, go to great lengths to understand what constitutes an emotional response. Virtually every Greek writer, Epicurus included, recognizes the physical component of emotions but locates their root cause in cognitive or mental operations and the substantive beliefs, judgments, and opinions into which these processes crystallize, in stark contrast to reductionistic analyses in the fields of neuropsychology, biochemistry, and psychopharmacology. The shape of a

---

[166] See especially S. Rosenbaum's exposition of the Epicurean position in "How to Be Dead and Not Care: A Defense of Epicurus," *American Philosophical Quarterly* 21 (1986): 217–25.

[167] Quoted in Philodemus, *Adv. soph*. 4.9–14 (in Pap.Hercul. 1005).

person's beliefs plays a far greater role in determining emotional disposition than does body temperature or the balance of humors.

Aristotle is the most optimistic about the role of the πάθη in the good life, though he is also wary of their irruption at the wrong time and in the wrong form, and tries accordingly to distinguish, for example, true from counterfeit courage. The Epicureans heartily affirm the pleasant passions, seeking them as the highest good. But because these are usually fleeting and cause pain upon withdrawal, true pleasure consists in knowing one's human limitations and living calmly within them. Coping with emotions, because they develop out of one's beliefs about the world, involves education, or re-education in many cases since traditional beliefs are so often mistaken and hence responsible for unhealthy emotions. These must be stripped and replaced with a right view of the world and of the nature of the good, which in turn vary according to the school. For most of these thinkers, their appraisals of fear fit within this general framework. Plato and Aristotle reserve a place in their systems for appropriate forms of fear. They regard fear of shame in a positive light because it promotes civic responsibility. Aristotle also accommodates feelings of fear within his account of virtue. Brave men experience rational fear, though only on momentous occasions. Only when the end is a truly good one does reason demand fearlessness in the face of extraordinary pain or impending doom. The Stoics concur on this point but are more discriminating when it comes to circumstances in which fear is permissible. Virtue is the highest good, therefore vice alone is to be feared with the caveat that εὐλάβεια, and never simple φόβος, is rational "cautiousness." Their qualifying remarks make plain the fact that, here again, belief as to the good distinguishes disapproved fear from its corresponding approved eupathic disposition.

While each school promulgates a theory of the emotions on the basis of core beliefs about ultimate reality, it is evident that, with the exception of Plato, the emphasis in their accounts is on the practical, ethical aspect. To varying degrees, the emotions are inconvenient because they disrupt the smooth flow of a happy life and are suspicious because they are at odds with a normative conception of virtue. Rational or not, the type of fear these philosophers discuss is an unpleasant feeling that usually signals some deficiency in the cardinal virtue of courage. It may or may not have death or the gods as its object. Little or no specifically religious element attaches to it except in a negative sense. Plutarch takes over this philosophical estimation of fear, makes certain modifications, and applies it to popular religious beliefs and observances in his essay on superstition.

Plutarch on Superstition as Inappropriate Fear

Prior to an examination of the main witness to Plutarch's thought on δεισιδαιμονία, it is first necessary to justify its place in the discussion. Did he or did he not write *De superstitione*?

The Question of Authenticity

The question of Plutarch's consistency on matters of religion has caused some scholars to wonder whether *De superstitione* truly belongs in the Plutarchan corpus.[168] Plutarch was widely read during the Renaissance, and this, along with the specific subject matter of this essay, accounts for the lively debate his writings occasioned during the Enlightenment, when the debunking of superstitions became a popular pastime.[169] The nature of the problem is easy to grasp: a number of statements made by Plutarch in his attack upon superstition seem to contradict statements he makes on similar subjects in other essays. Some of these contradictions, moreover, are not on the periphery but rather touch upon his central thesis, that atheism is to be preferred to superstition because the former is simply an intellectual error, a form of blindness, while the latter is an error compounded by unhealthy πάθος. It is a greater impiety, according to *De superstitione*, to think evil of the gods, as does the superstitious person, than to disbelieve in their existence. "The atheist thinks there are no gods," writes Plutarch, but "the superstitious man wishes there were none" (170F). But elsewhere Plutarch appears to argue the opposite point, namely, that fear of the gods is the lesser of two evils and therefore to be preferred to atheism (*Suav. viv.* 1101C; *Adv. Col.* 1124D–1125A). In other passages he attacks superstition and atheism with equal zeal (*Adul. amic.* 66C; *Is. Os.* 355D, 378A, 379E). Plutarch also ridicules a number of popular religious practices in the essay on superstition that, in other writings, he endorses. Throughout the *Lives* he reports without embarrassment numerous omens and dreams, and describes without condemnation various superstitious actions taken by his heroes.[170] His

---

[168] Only M. Smith ("De Superstitione," 1–7) and J. J. Hartmann (*De Plutarcho Scriptore et Philosopho* [Leiden: Brill, 1916], 110–13), however, go so far as to deny that Plutarch is the author.

[169] Octave Greard, *De la Morale de Plutarque* (Paris: Hachette, 1866), 284–93. More generally on Plutarch's legacy in the early modern period, see Edmund G. Berry, *Emerson's Plutarch* (Cambridge: Harvard University Press, 1961), 1–34. On attitudes towards superstition during the Enlightenment, see Monter, *Ritual, Myth and Magic in Early Modern Europe*, 114–29.

[170] Prophetic dreams: *Them.* 30.1; *Cor.* 24.2–3 (in connection with a dream vision in which Jupiter appears to Titus Latinus, who—unexpectedly, given this context—has just been described as free from superstition); *Sull.* 28.4; *Cic.* 4.4; *Ti. C. Gracch.* 1.6. Omens:

preoccupation with demons and the fate of the soul after death also strikes many readers as inconsistent with his critique of δεισιδαιμονία.[171]

How is one to reconcile these apparent contradictions? It is not always simply a matter of determining which speaker in a dialogue represents Plutarch's own views. F. E. Brenk sees three separate but related approaches that have been taken to account for his inconsistencies.[172] One is the source-critical approach, which tries to explain the data by appealing to Plutarch's incompetence at incorporating the conflicting views of other authors whose works he has used, an approach taken by Abernetty but now generally rejected.[173] A second approach emphasizes the essay's rhetorical character. *De superstitione* in this interpretation is a product of Plutarch's early period and bears the marks of a school exercise such as the use of stock examples and the absence of counter arguments.[174] It does not exhaustively treat the topic or consider possible objections from interlocutors, and some have suggested that Plutarch intended to follow his essay on superstition with others on atheism or piety.[175] The inconsistencies, then, are explained by the exaggerations common in such rhetorical presentations. A third approach seeks to trace Plutarch's development from the early scepticism of the Academy to his later tenure as

---

Thes. 36.2; *Cor.* 38.4; *Dion* 24.5; *Tim.* 8.2; *Pyrrh.* 31.3; *Mar.* 17.4. Oracles: *Lys.* 22.5; *Phoc.* 8.3. His description of Nicias at Syracuse implies that the expedition would not have been such a disaster had his regular diviner Stilbides not already died (*Nic.* 23.1–5).

[171] The topic of Plutarch's demonology has been the object of much scrutiny. Important works include those of Guy Soury (*La Démonologie de Plutarque* [Paris: Les belles lettres, 1942]), R. Flacelière ("Plutarque et la Pythie," *REG* 56 [1943]: 72–111), and Brenk (*In Mist Apparelled*, esp. 49–64). The critical issues involved are legion. For an introduction, see R. M. Jones, *The Platonism of Plutarch* (Menasha, Wisc.: Banta, 1916), 27–40; Dillon, *The Middle Platonists*, 216–24; and Brenk, "An Imperial Heritage: The Religious Spirit of Plutarch of Chaironeia," *ANRW* 36.1:275–94.

[172] Brenk, *In Mist Apparelled*, 9–15. These issues and approaches are not peculiar to the study of Plutarch. Most can also be seen in scholarly treatments of early Christian and Jewish authors as well (cf. Heikki Räisänen, *Paul and the Law* [WUNT 29; 2nd rev. ed.; Tübingen: Mohr-Siebeck, 1987], xi–xxxi, 1–15).

[173] G. Abernetty, "De Plutarchi qui fertur de superstitione libello" (Diss., Königsburg, 1911), 79–100. Cf. Ziegler, "Plutarchus von Chaironeia," 826.

[174] Greard, *De la Morale de Plutarque*, 284–93; Jones, *The Platonism of Plutarch*, 27; Flacelière, "Introduction Générale," cxxxiii–cxxxv; and Oakesmith, *The Religion of Plutarch*, 185–87, though he disagrees that it is a school exercise in which the orator is required to defend a paradox through rhetorical ingenuity. Although the observation is a common one, only Klauck, "Religion without Fear," 113–19, analyzes the essay in light of the standards found in the handbooks of classical rhetoric.

[175] Robert Klaerr, introduction to "De la superstition," in *Plutarque: Oeuvres Morales*, vol. 2 (ed. J. Defradas et al.; Paris: Les belles lettres, 1985), 244; and, briefly, Moellering, *Plutarch on Superstition*, 112. Against this suggestion, it should be noted that no essays on these topics are mentioned in the catalogue of Lamprias.

priest at Delphi and the interest in oracles and prophecies that go with it, an approach especially popular among previous generations of German interpreters.[176] This evolution would thus account for the coexistence in Plutarch's corpus of harsh attacks on superstition and earnest discussions of post-mortem punishment, omens, dream interpretation, and other phenomena usually falling under the rubric of superstition, both for modern readers and for the author of *De superstitione*.

While this last strategy has, in some form, commanded a consensus of scholarly opinion, it is nevertheless not immune to criticism. Morton Smith remains unconvinced by theories of clumsy borrowing or spiritual development on Plutarch's part; the differences on fundamental subjects between the "early" and the "mature" Plutarch are too great to be explained away so easily. Some attempts at harmonizing, indeed, are patently circular.[177] Assigning a late date to essays containing superstitious elements and then using this to support a dating for *De superstitione* early in Plutarch's career is one such example. Relative dates can be determined for many, but not all, of Plutarch's writings, and external evidence allows only for an absolute chronology of some of the later essays.[178] Smith also sees in the atypical self-reference of *Mor.* 170A an awkward attempt by a forger to pass the work off as Plutarch's.[179]

Other scholars take issue with developmental hypotheses not because they fail to account for the evidence but rather, invoking Ockham's razor, because they are not strictly necessary. While not denying certain tensions between *De superstitione* and the later writings, Brenk, Erbse, and others see in the work as many continuities as discontinuities. Brenk observes that mystical tendencies are not confined to the later period but can be seen in the Neopythagorean elements evident in his writings on animals and vegetarianism.[180] It is inconsistent to put

---

[176] For a survey, see Brenk, "From Mysticism to Mysticism: The Religious Development of Plutarch of Chaironeia," *SBL Seminar Papers, 1975* (2 vols.; SBLSP 12; Missoula, Mont.: Scholars Press, 1975), 1:193–98; idem, "An Imperial Heritage," *ANRW* 36.1:256–62. Proponents of this view include R. Hirzel, *Plutarch* (Leipzig: Dieterich, 1912), 8–10; Flacelière, "Plutarque et la Pythie," 104–8; Moellering, *Plutarch on Superstition*, 153; Klaerr, "De la superstition," 244; D. A. Russell, *Plutarch* (London: Duckworth, 1973), 80; Froidefond, "Plutarque et le platonisme," *ANRW* 36.1:210, 228; and Elisabetta Berardi, "Plutarco e la religione, l'εὐσέβεια come giusto mezzo fra δεισιδαιμονία e ἀθεότης," *CClCr* 11 (1990): 141–70.

[177] Smith, "De Superstitione," 4 n. 4; Brenk, *In Mist Apparelled*, 12.

[178] Cf. Jones ("Towards a Chronology of Plutarch's Works") who does not settle on a definite date for *Superst.* but confidently places a number of the essays with which it is in tension late in Trajan's principate and thus near the end of Plutarch's life.

[179] Ziegler, ("Plutarchus von Chaironeia," 190), however, sees this as an indication that it is a product of Plutarch's youth.

[180] Brenk, *In Mist Apparelled*, 68–69, 79–83; "An Imperial Heritage," *ANRW* 36.1:256–57.

these essays in Plutarch's early period and at the same time to see a shift from youthful scepticism (seen in *Superst.*) to a mature mysticism. Plutarch's contempt for the notion of punishments in the afterlife also has parallels in the later writings.[181] Erbse likewise minimizes the differences over the course of Plutarch's development and identifies several ideas in his writings echoing those in *De superstitione*, such as condemnation of human sacrifice (*Sera* 552A; *Marc.* 3), preference for scientific explanations of natural phenomena (*Quaest. nat.* passim), and, in a specific historical reference, bewilderment at the refusal of the Jews to defend themselves on the Sabbath (*Stoic. rep.* 1051E).[182] Opsomer focuses on what he sees as mischaracterizations of the New Academy and argues that the rationalist and religious elements in Plutarch's thought are not mutually exclusive and that neither strand is confined to one period of his career.[183] Another approach, less concerned with chronology, is that of Aurelio Pérez Jiménez.[184] Paying closer attention to the *Lives* than to the *Moralia*, Pérez Jiménez makes sense of the seemingly arbitrary distinction between acceptable and unacceptable forms of δεισιδαιμονία with reference to Plutarch's social and political concerns that arise in the course of writing biography.

A somewhat different tack is taken by A. G. Nikolaidis, who argues that "inconsistency" is the rule for Plutarch and not the exception.[185] He assembles a wide array of contradictory texts on subjects ranging from the most trivial (e.g., the propriety of flute-playing at dinner parties) to the most fundamental (e.g., the value of allegorical interpretation of myths) and concludes that they are to be explained by the differing demands posed by the different problems he treats. Though Plutarch imposes it upon the philosophical schools with which he disagrees, theological consistency is not the ruling principle he follows in forming his opinions. Above all it is the practical considerations of the situations he addresses that determine his positions.[186] Though a Platonist, for example, Plutarch is not hostile to every tenet of Stoicism or Epicureanism across the board; rather, he opposes these schools when he sees their teachings leading to practical consequences he finds morally repugnant or nonsensical. He sometimes sounds like a Stoic when attacking the Epicureans, and like an Epicurean when attacking Stoics. These types of inconsistencies cannot be

---

[181] *Lat. viv.* 1130C–E; *Suav. viv.* 1104A–1107C; *Virt. mor.* 450A; *Adol. poet. aud.* 17C.
[182] Erbse, "Plutarchs Schrift *Peri Deisidaimonias*," *Hermes* 80 (1952): 300–14.
[183] Opsomer, "Divination and Academic 'Scepticism' according to Plutarch," 174–76.
[184] A. Pérez Jiménez, "Δεισιδαιμονία: el miedo a los dioses en Plutarco," *Studia Hellenistica* 32 (1996): 195–225. Like Alan Wardman's (*Plutarch's Lives* [Berkeley: University of California Press, 1974], 86–93), his focus is on the political, though Wardman is not interested in the question of pseudonymity.
[185] A. G. Nikolaidis, "Plutarch's Contradictions," *Classica et Mediaevalia* 42 (1991): 153–86, esp. 164–67.
[186] Ibid., 174–77.

charted along any simple line of development over the course of Plutarch's career.

Nikolaidis's purpose is not to answer the question of authenticity but his conclusions clearly demonstrate that contradictions are not peculiar to *De superstitione*. Inconsistencies—and not just minor ones—may be found in almost any of Plutarch's essays. By identifying contradictions, Smith does not thereby prove that this essay is spurious. His argument can cut in more than one direction, though this fact has not been generally recognized by critics. If the presence of contradictions is by itself evidence of spuriousness, then virtually any of Plutarch's essays might in principle be spurious. Exaggerating the differences between *De superstitione* and his other writings obscures this and also diverts attention from the fact that there are almost no other positive reasons to believe it is a forgery. No one has made a serious case on linguistic grounds that the Greek style deviates from Plutarch's other writings. The manuscript tradition provides no evidence of alternative attribution of authorship, nor is it left out of the Lamprias or Planudean catalogues. Finally, there were no doubts in antiquity as to its authenticity. In sum, the case for pseudonymity is not nearly as decisive as it may at first seem, and the consensus view that *De superstitione* is an authentic work of Plutarch remains the most plausible.

Plutarch's Argument: Summary and Analysis

Though well aware of the difficulties involved, D. Z. Phillips says of religion and superstition that "the important point is simply that we do draw a distinction."[187] Most of his fellow analytic philosophers would likely disagree, but not Plutarch. His treatise on δεισιδαιμονία is his most thorough treatment of the topic. In point of fact, it is the lengthiest discussion that has survived from antiquity. It lacks the humor of Theophrastus's character sketch because superstition is not a purely theoretical issue for Plutarch. He sees it as something more than the silly yet harmless habits and notions of the common people. So dangerous is it that he writes, with surprising vehemence, this piece of epideictic rhetoric wherein he argues that atheism is actually the better way. It is a *tour de force*. Its urgent tone obscures the way in which his remarks are generally in continuity with more measured statements in other essays. A summary of the argument will bring to light those states of mind and heart that are constitutive of δεισιδαιμονία and also provide the opportunity to reflect upon Plutarch's running dialogue with his philosophical predecessors about the emotions, a dialogue in which he broadens the conversation to include their role in religion.[188]

---

[187] Phillips, *Religion without Explanation*, 110.
[188] More concise summaries of *De superstitione* may be found in Braun, "Plutarch's Critique of Superstition," 1–4; and Klauck, "Religion Without Fear," 113–19.

Superstition and the Emotions

Atheism and superstition, according to Plutarch (*Superst.* 164E–F), both derive from a common source: ignorance and blindness concerning the gods (περὶ θεῶν ἀμαθία καὶ ἄγνοια). Whereas atheism begins and usually ends as a false judgment (κρίσις ψευδής) and is on that account cause for grief (μοχθηρός), superstition is worse because it is compounded by emotion (πάθος). Why does this make superstition the worse of the two? Because every emotion is like a festering delusion (ἀπάτη φλεγμαίνουσα) or a perversion of the soul (διαστροφαὶ τῆς ψυχῆς). Epicurean atomism illustrates that false reasoning is a necessary but not sufficient component of δεισιδαιμονία. The Epicurean theory of the origin of the universe is not correct, but neither is it accompanied by wounds, throbbing, or agitation (ἕλκος οὐ ποιεῖ οὐδὲ σφυγμὸν οὐδ' ὀδύνην ταράττουσαν).[189] He says the same of the Stoic position on the corporeality of virtue and vice (165A; cf. *Comm. not.* 1084A). It is mistaken and even a disgrace but no cause for lament. False assumptions that paralyze, distract, disturb the sleep, and drive one into a frenzy (οἴστρων ἐμπίπλησιν), on the other hand, are venomous. Such is the false assumption that wealth is the *summum bonum* (cf. *Sera* 556B). One may be in error as to the real nature of virtue, but Plutarch does not see this as the worst case if it dissuades from vice. Some errors are worse than others, and those that engender disordered emotions are most of all to be avoided. Plutarch refuses to put atheism at the top of this list (*Superst.* 165B). Although it is a careless judgment (κρίσις φαύλη) that consists of disbelief (ἀπιστία) in the divine, it leads only to indifference (ἀπάθεια). By not believing in the gods, the atheist obviously avoids fearing them. Superstition, on the other hand, is an emotional opinion (δόξα ἐμπαθής) concerning the gods, an assumption productive of fear (δέους ποιητικὴ ὑπόληψις). Plutarch concludes this opening section by returning to the theme of ignorance. For the atheist, ignorance produces disbelief in the one who helps. For the superstitious, it produces the added belief in a god who hurts (165C). The ideas of the one are dismissive and deficient, while those of the other are superfluous and defamatory. From this it follows that "atheism is falsified reason (λόγος διεψευσμένος), and superstition is an emotion

---

[189] This clear rejection of Epicurean physics undermines R. Flacelière's contention that Plutarch has used Epicurean literature in support of his case in *De superstitione* ("Plutarque et l'épicurisme," in *Epicurea in memoriam Hectoris Bignone* [Genoa: Istituto di filologia classica, 1959], 198–99). Nevertheless, it remains possible that he eclectically uses some Epicurean arguments when they serve his rhetorical purposes and rejects the rest.

engendered from false reason (πάθος ἐκ λόγου ψευδοῦς ἐγγεγνημένον)."[190]

This definition marks the subtle difference between Plutarch's view of the emotions and that of the Stoics. The standard Stoic analysis collapses all distinctions between the judgments generated by reason and the emotion related to them. For example, the judgment that the gods are easily offended and prone to vent their anger against humans, and the variety of fear called δεισιδαιμονία, are in reality one and the same phenomenon. Seeming evidence that the emotions act contrary to one's reason is to be explained by sudden shifts of the rational faculty pulling now in one direction (because it is judged to be advantageous or desirable), now in another (because of a change in judgment). Judgments about the state of things inform reason, which explains how one can think and act "rationally," that is, in perfect accord with one's presuppositions, yet still entertain bizarre ideas and behave in a reckless manner. That Plutarch understands this much of the Stoic view is evident from *Virt. mor.* 441C–D. Much of this essay on moral virtue is a brief against the Stoic equation of reason and emotion, largely on the grounds that it implies a view of the soul at odds with Plato's.[191] He maintains the technical distinction in *Superst.* 165C, but it makes very little impact on the line of his argument. Undergirding nearly every point he makes is the assumption that a change in the empty beliefs of the superstitious ought to be sufficient to wipe out the superstition itself, with all its injurious consequences. A correct understanding of the gods as benevolent will not engender the emotion of fear at the heart of δεισιδαιμονία. Right reason, while distinct from the emotions, controls the emotions by providing true beliefs (*Tranq. an.* 465C).

---

[190] At *Superst.* 167D, he attributes πάθος to atheists only to contrast this "feeling" with that of the superstitious. The only clue as to the πάθος he has in mind is in the remark that atheists disregard (παρορῶσιν) the gods, which perhaps indicates scorn or contempt. It is unlikely that Plutarch regards all atheists as utterly apathetic after the fashion of a Stoic sage. Complete apathy is not a realistic ideal in his view. The general attribution of apathy to the atheist is a part of the larger comparison in which the superstitious are presented negatively as given to histrionics. Very little has been written on the psychology of atheism in antiquity. Robin Le Poidevin, *Arguing for Atheism* (London: Routledge, 1996), 114–21, 135–46, discusses the emotional aspects of atheism from a modern philosophical perspective.

[191] Babut, *Plutarque et le Stoïcisme*, 266, believes that Plutarch has done his best to comprehend Stoic sources (cf. Diogenes Laertius 7.180; 10.27, on Chrysippus's lack of clarity) and that he is a generally accurate reporter of Stoic doctrine, while Ziegler, "Plutarchus von Chaironeia," 756, regards his approach as overly literal and missing many of the finer distinctions they make, either by honest misunderstanding or by purposefully lampooning beliefs he does not hold. See H. Cherniss, *Plutarch's Moralia*, XIII, Pt. 2 (LCL; Cambridge: Harvard University Press, 1976), 401–6, for a balanced discussion of Plutarch's reliability.

Why does its status as an emotion make δεισιδαιμονία more dangerous than atheism? This is the point Plutarch develops in the following paragraphs. Fear is one genus of emotion, and superstition is in turn a special species of fear.[192] He sounds like a Stoic when he decries all emotions; they forever keep the soul in a state of restlessness and thus strain one's reasoning faculties (165C–D). Throughout the essay Plutarch uses many of the same terms as Aristotle and the Stoics, but it is doubtful that he is using πάθη here in the same technical sense as the Stoics or that he really means it when he says that "all distempers and emotions of the soul (πάντα τὰ τῆς ψυχῆς νοσήματα καὶ πάθη) are disgraceful." This is likely an example of hendiadys where the clearly negative term νοσήματα colors the generic term πάθη, which can be positive, negative, or neutral for Plutarch, depending on the situation. He does not bother with the Stoic distinction between πάθη and eupathic dispositions sometimes mistaken for πάθη. Such qualifications do not serve the purposes of the polemic. Plutarch's criticism of atheism for detracting from the joy of festal gatherings shows furthermore that he welcomes pleasant and edifying emotions.

A study of Plutarch's writings reveals a considerable degree of ambivalence concerning the emotions. On the negative side, he has much to say about the dangers they pose, especially to those in pursuit of virtue. Speaking boldly under the influence of alcohol (so he admits), in first person Plutarch states sweepingly that "all emotions, after having been a long time in the mind, produce evil conditions" (*Quaest. conv.* 682C–D; cf. 681F; *An virt. doc.* 439B; *An. corp.* 501E; *Curios.* 515D, 518C; *Vit. pud.* 528D). They usually result from defective reasoning and, once set in motion, further impair one's ability to make sound decisions (*Adul. amic.* 61F; *Tranq. an.* 475–C; *Vit. pud.* 536C; *Quaest. conv.* 714D). One may become aware of progress in virtue through their abatement (*Virt. prof.* 79C, 84A, 85B). So long as passions fester in the soul, any efforts one makes at escaping vice merely delay the inevitable relapse into anxiousness (*Virt. vit.* 101C; *An. corp.* 500E–501E; cf. the inclusion of δεισιδαιμονία at 100F). Insofar as the goal of human life is to aspire to likeness to God (*Sera* 550D–E), and not Stoic conformity with nature, the passions are a detriment because they constitute the human component of mixed *daimones*, intermediate beings between God and humans (*Is. Os.* 360E; *Def. orac.* 416C–D, 417B–D,

---

[192] Throughout the essay, Plutarch favors the familiar term φόβος, unlike Theophrastus who uses the stronger term "cowardice" (δειλία). Plutarch uses δειλία only once here (169C). His usage elsewhere conforms to standard descriptions of cowardice: it is due to ignorance (*Adol. poet. aud.* 31F); it is a vice antithetical to the vice of rashness (*Virt. mor.* 445A); it accompanies superstition (*Sera* 556B); and it is a terrible liability during battles (*Nic.* 8.2; *Dem.* 20.1; *Brut.* 46.5 et al.). He also explains the ability of chamelions and octopi to change colors as a function of their cowardly nature (*Quaest. nat.* 916B; *Soll. an.* 978E).

420E).[193] Like Aristotle and the Stoics, Plutarch regards training and education
(παιδεία) by which one learns what is properly delightful and distressing as the
surest way to cure or prevent emotional upset (*Conj. praec.* 145E; *Virt. mor.*
452D; *Curios.* 520D). This education provides in advance the resources
necessary to stave off the tumult brought on by superstition and other fears
(*Tranq. an.* 465B–D).

From this dim view of the emotions one might expect Plutarch to embrace
the Stoic ideal of ἀπάθεια, but again the evidence is mixed.[194] His remarks in
De superstitione are neutral; the indifference of the atheist is not admirable but it
is better than the alternative he depicts. It is desirable in that it makes one
immune to any number of vices (*Adul. amic.* 56A; *Virt. prof.* 83B; *Cor.* 1.4; *Cat.
Min.* 1.3) but it is perhaps an unrealistic ideal attainable only by the likes of
Socrates (*Adul. amic.* 72A–B; *Virt. prof.* 83E; *Gen. Socr.* 588D–E; *Quaest.
conv.* 711B). Apathy is not a naturally occurring state of the soul, which
Plutarch sees as tripartite in line with the traditional Platonic view (*An virt. doc.*
439B; *Am. prol.* 495A; frg. 200); where it does occur it may reflect indifference
to a salutary sense of shame at wrongdoing (*Rect. rat. aud.* 46D); and it is
neither possible nor expedient to eradicate the passions as a hard and fast rule
(*Virt. mor.* 443C–D)

Many, though by no means all, of his objections to ἀπάθεια come as part
of his general attack on inconsistencies in the Stoic system, but Plutarch has
more than merely reactive reasons for his ambivalence. What is there to
commend about the emotions that renders ἀπάθεια a problematic ideal? While
Stoics regard extirpation of passions as necessary for virtue, Plutarch believes
they are a natural part of the soul and so incorporates them into his theory of
virtue. His disagreement with the Stoics is in no small part a disagreement over
the definition of what is "natural." Reason does not demand the absence of
passion but rather uses prudence (φρόνησις) to develop the capacity
(δύναμις) for passion into a good disposition (ἕξις), he argues, using
thoroughly Aristotelian language (*Virt. mor.* 443C–D; cf. Aristotle, *Eth. nic.*
2.5.1–6). If one's passions are trained well, they develop into virtues. When

---

[193] On "likeness to God" (ὁμοίωσις θεοῦ or ἐξομοίωσις θεοῦ [cf. Plato, *Theat.*
176B]) as a Middle Platonic concept, see Dillon, *The Middle Platonists*, 192–93; idem,
"*Metriopatheia* and *Apatheia*," in *Essays in Ancient Greek Philosophy* (2 vols.; ed. J. P.
Anton and A. Preus; Albany: SUNY Press, 1983), 2:508; Froidefond, "Plutarque et le
platonisme," *ANRW* 2.36:210–11; and Babut, *Plutarque et le Stoïcisme*, 388–440, who
say that he tends towards moderation and regards extirpation as a counsel of perfection
not really meant for the average person.

[194] Cf. Spanneut, "*Apatheia* ancienne," *ANRW* 2.36:4704–7 (on Plutarch), 4708–11 (on
other Middle Platonists); and Babut, *Plutarque et le Stoïcisme*, 323–33.

tamed and under the control of reason, the passions intensify the virtue by bringing them into a state of moderation (451D–452A).[195]

Positive and Negative Fear

Some emotions may therefore have redeeming side effects. But not so with fear, he says at *Superst.* 165D, because it is wanting in boldness (τόλμα) as well as in reason (λογισμός). It robs the soul of sleep but keeps it from accomplishing anything by its wakefulness because it is impotent (ἄπρακτον), helpless (ἄπορος), and hopeless (ἀμήχανος).[196] Δεισιδαιμονία makes the gods into the cause for such debilitating anxiety (165D–166E).

Here again, Plutarch oversimplifies for the sake of rhetorical effect. On numerous occasions in the *Lives*, of course, fear is a negative character trait. More often than not it is the product of a "flabby" (ἄτονος) character that allows its reason to be overwhelmed by empty beliefs (*Tranq. an.* 476D). Stoics and Epicureans both use such language in their discussions of the emotions. But Plutarch also takes frequent note of the positive value of fear. Reverence (αἰδώς) and fear often play complementary roles in cultivating a healthy sensitivity to the divine (*Suav. viv.* 1101B–F; *Adv. Col.* 1126E). This combination, common in children but usually fading by early adulthood, can also function to reform behavior by encouraging repentance (*Cohib. ira* 459D; cf. [*Lib. ed.*] 12D; *Rect. rat. aud.* 37D; *Virt. vit.* 101A). Fear of shame (τὸ αἰσχρόν) and blame (ψόγος) are admirable traits whereas fear of danger and suffering is base, especially if it ceases to function as a catalyst to action (*Adol. poet. aud.* 29E, 30E; *Virt. mor.* 452D; *Princ. iner.* 781C–F; and *Adv. Col.* 1124E, where he connects fear of shamefulness and trust in the benevolent rule of the gods; cf. also Plato, *Euthyphr.* 12B–C).

Plutarch's approval of certain varieties of fear, namely those that dissuade one from a life of vice, recalls the Stoic approval of the three eupathic dispositions, joy, volition, and caution (εὐλάβεια). These are "good feelings," but not technically πάθη according to the Stoics because they are in tune with right reason. Plutarch ridicules them for what he sees as euphemisms contrived for the purpose of preserving the consistency of their ethical theory without rejecting universally acknowledged virtues (*Virt. mor.* 449A–C; *Stoic. rep.* 1038A). But apart from the polemical context of this and the other anti-Stoic treatises, he rarely disapproves of the "good fear" designated by εὐλάβεια. Though he does not use the term in the passages alluded to above, his commendation of fear felt in the face of shame and proper blame puts him in

---

[195] He quotes Homer (*Il.* 13.284) approvingly and points out that he does not do away with the fear of the courageous man, only excessive fear (ἄγαν φόβον) and rashness.

[196] The examples he cites at *Superst.* 165D–E are taken in part from Aristotle's discussion of courage as a mean in *Eth. nic.* 3.7.7.

agreement with the Stoics, who define αἰδώς, one of the two sub-species of εὐλάβεια, in the same way. In the many passages where Plutarch uses εὐλάβεια, he usually presents it favorably (*Marc.* 9.3; *Nic.* 2.4; *Caes.* 14.6; *Pel.* 20.7; *Pomp.* 57.7; *Comp. Ag. Cleom. cum Ti. Gracch.* 4.3; *Galb.* 3.3).[197] Those who possess it fear shamefulness (*Phoc.* 3.5; *Mulier. virt.* 249C, where it is stronger than fear of death) and are on constant guard against vice (*Adul. amic.* 71B, 85E; *Inim. util.* 90A). Because it is rightly aligned with reason (*Inim. util.* 87E; *Quaest. conv.* 706A; *An seni* 788C) it is conducive to the attainment of the mean position in virtue (*Cam.* 6.4; *Adol. poet. aud.* 29B; *Rect. rat. aud.* 44A; *Cohib. ira* 463C). In religious matters, Plutarch speaks of the exemplary εὐλάβεια of his fellow philosophers in the Academy that consists in their hesitance to assume anything but the best in their speculations about the divine (*Sera* 549E, 551C, 558D). Numa's εὐλάβεια is visible in his religious devotion in stark contrast to the δεισιδαιμονία into which his successor is driven by πάθη (*Num.* 22.7; cf. *Cam.* 21.2; *Cor.* 25.2; *Quaest. rom.* 269E). Conservative adherence to ancestral tradition is also a sign of prudent fear (*Aem.* 3.3; *Is. Os.* 354D, 382E). On this principle Plutarch even prefers the fearfulness of Nicias to the rashness of Crassus because it is motivated by respect for ancient religious custom (*Comp. Nic. Crass.* 5.2).

The habit of consulting charlatans and witches is one such common symptom of superstitious fear, as are the continual ablutions, prostrations, and incantations of the kind described by Theophrastus. These, Plutarch says, impugn "the god-given ancestral dignity of our religion" (165B). False assumptions about the gods sustain this unfortunate condition (166D–E):

> [T]o find a god whom he shall not fear is impossible for
> him who fears the gods of his fathers and his kin, who
> shudders at his saviours, and trembles with terror at those
> gentle gods from whom we ask wealth, welfare, peace,
> concord, and success in our best efforts in speech and
> action.

The temperament of the superstitious borders on the masochistic in that the gods inspire dread yet it is to the temples that they flock. Their conflicted flurry of emotion (πολυπάθεια, 167E) has them fearing the gods one moment and fleeing to them for help the next.[198] In the sanctuaries they come closest to the

---

[197] This is not to say that Plutarch always uses it in the same technical sense as the Stoics. On occasion he refers to ill-timed or excessive εὐλάβεια as a negative trait (*Nic.* 14.2; *Caes.* 39.8; *Cic.* 43.7). By definition, Stoic εὐλάβεια is never excessive since it is always reasonable. It is not possible to have too much of such a good thing. For Plutarch, then, εὐλάβεια sometimes functions as a generic, less pejorative synonym for fear, as in *Superst.* 167A, where the negative element appears in the qualifier περιττῇ.

[198] Such vacillation is at odds with the *constantia* accompanying the eupathic dispositions endorsed by the Stoics (cf. Cicero, *Tusc.* 4.6.14).

gods who are, so it is believed, the source of vivid post-mortem punishments, thus the false notions associated with δεισιδαιμονία make fear last longer than life (166F–167A; cf. Lucretius 3.37).

Fear of Death

Fear of the gods and fear of death are naturally related in Greek religion, but 166F–167A is the only point in the essay where the latter comes explicitly to the fore. Plutarch does not believe in a physical Hades where humans will be punished. This much is evident from his advice on reading poetry (*Adol. aud. poet.* 17A–F). Tales of netherworldly punishments are combinations of fiction and genuine ignorance on the part of the poets. They generate emotions which make one even more susceptible to outlandish stories about what comes after death. It is better to follow the example of Socrates and disavow any claims to sure knowledge of what awaits humans in the hereafter (17E; cf. Plato, *Phaed.* 69D; *Resp.* 3.386B–387C). Plutarch sounds this same note of caution in *De sera numinis vindicta* (549E–550C, 558D). This enigmatic work in the form of a dialogue concludes with a lengthy myth (563B–568A) containing descriptions of gruesome punishments in Hades and ending with a humorous scene in which Nero is reincarnated as a reward for his benefactions to the Greeks. This myth is reported as the near-death experience of a profligate man turned pious, the friend of a friend of his father, and so should not be taken as a presentation of Plutarch's own beliefs about the afterlife.[199] Most of this dialogue "on the delays of divine vengeance" probes a question of theodicy: why don't bad things happen to bad people, at least not in this lifetime? The interlocutors cite various moral factors to account for the apparent slowness of God to punish the wicked. God's slowness to wrath serves as a model to humans who also should learn to keep their passions in check (550D–551C). Like God, humans should also, where possible, approach the wicked not with merely punitive aims but with an eye to their recovery, and this frequently takes a lot of time (551C–552D). These speculations about post-mortem punishment of vice, especially the first one, derive from ethical and theological concerns in equal parts, as do the comments on superstition and fear of death at *Sera* 556A–D. Rather than allow the assumption that the wicked receive retribution after they die to stand unchallenged, which would seem to provide a reasonable basis for fearing death, Plutarch (in his own voice) argues that the vicious life of evildoers constitutes in itself a hellish existence while still on earth (554A–555C; cf. Plato, *Theat.* 177A). Vice is its own reward (cf. *An. corp.* 498D–500A; *Suav. viv.* 1101C–1103BA, both of which mention δεισιδαιμονία). If this is true, then

---

[199] Brenk, "An Imperial Heritage," *ANRW* 36.1:283.

delayed vengeance is not really delayed at all and God's justice remains unimpeached.[200]

Plutarch decries the way in which superstition extends fear to matters beyond the grave for reasons different from those put forth by the Epicureans. For the Epicureans, death is nothing to fear since the individual is merely a temporary formation of atoms that disperses at the point of death. Despite the remark at *Superst.* 166F to the effect that "death is the end of life for all humans"—taken from Demosthenes (*Cor.* 18.97)—Plutarch does not share the Epicurean view of the soul that dispenses with morbid fears. He is stating a truism that supports his point about the paradoxes of superstitious fear rather than adumbrating a formal thanatological principle. In the opening paragraphs of the essay, he has already rejected the atomistic theory on which the Epicureans base their view of death. Plutarch's antipathy toward the Epicureans on these points derives from the practical ethical consequences to which their philosophy leads as well as from his own view of the soul as immortal inherited from Plato.

The practical difficulties Plutarch sees with the Epicurean rejection of morbid fear come to light in *Non posse suaviter vivi secundum Epicurum* (esp. 1103C–1107C). The title of the essay—"That Epicurus Actually Makes a Pleasant Life Impossible" (LCL)—indicates that Plutarch's primary concern here is not the truth or falsity of Epicurean teachings about the fate of the individual after death but rather the internal inconsistency of their positions.[201] He takes this tack with the Stoics as well. Consistency of life and doctrine is the chief standard by which to judge a philosophical system (*Stoic. rep.* 1033A–B). Any philosophy not striving to attain this end is merely sophistry practiced for its own sake. Plutarch tries to show that Epicurean philosophy is to be rejected because, when judged by its own criterion of pleasure, its basic premises do not lead to a life free from fear and anxiety about death.[202] Deliverance from the vicissitudes of life ultimately takes the form of total annihilation of the self (*Suav. viv.* 1103E). This, Plutarch says, is hardly a comforting thought. Longing for existence (ὁ πόθος τοῦ εἶναι), the oldest and strongest of all loves, is far too strong to be disturbed by myth-inspired fears of post-mortem punishment.[203]

---

[200] Plutarch generally prefers to see retribution take place prior to death (cf. Brenk, "An Imperial Heritage," *ANRW* 36.1:327–30).

[201] Cf. Jackson P. Hershbell, "Plutarch and Epicureanism," *ANRW* 2.36:3378. On Plutarch's own inconsistencies, see Nikolaidis, "Plutarch's Contradictions," 153–86.

[202] Retorsion is the name given in logic to the strategy, employed here by Plutarch, of answering an argument by converting it into an argument against one's opponents. On his use of the related Sceptic strategy of ἰσοσθένεια, see Babut, *Plutarque et le Stoïcisme,* 45–46, 124–25.

[203] Plutarch also taunts the Epicureans by saying that, since inactivity is the most pleasant mode of life in their way of thinking, they ought to welcome superstition because fear of punishment in Hades has a paralyzing effect (*Suav. viv.* 1104B).

Anything is preferable to the annihilation and oblivion Epicurus promises on the other side.[204] Thus Epicurus, while he believes he is removing the basis for fearing death, actually confirms the worst fears of all humans and thereby makes a pleasant life practically impossible (1105A). He heightens this most basic existential anxiety as he simultaneously deprives the ordinary person of the most pleasant of hopes—belief in immortality—a hope that consoles the unfortunate in this life by promising a better fate in the next one.

In spite of deceptively similar language in *Superst.* 166F–167A, Plutarch's objection to superstitious fear of death does not issue from any sympathy with Epicureanism. He states that the superstitious look at "the moment of ceasing from trouble" as the beginning of unceasing troubles.[205] The first phrase refers only to the cessation of or respite from activity or troubles (ὅτε παύεται πραγμάτων), not to the obliteration of the individual, a crucial distinction because it allows him to reject superstitious notions about the afterlife without abandoning his belief in the immortality of the soul.[206] And while the details of his view of the soul and the quality of perpetual existence it possesses are not always clear, Plutarch is utterly convinced that the endurance of physical harm will not be a part of its experience, nor will the enjoyment of physical delight. Only that part of the soul that does not co-mingle with the body survives (cf. *Gen. Socr.* 591D–F; *Fac.* 943A–945C). Thus in *Lat. viv.* 1130E–C, fame and being belong to the pious dead, while the impious have their souls—but not their bodies—thrust into a dark pit that engulfs them in obscurity and oblivion. No vultures tear at their livers for there is nothing left of the body to receive such torture.[207] Living according to the Epicurean precept "live unknown" (λάθε βιώσας), that is, a retiring lifestyle free from striving after fame and worldly success, Plutarch says, ultimately ends in oblivion, a death where one is not remembered—a convenient pun suggested by the mythological river Lethe, the river of forgetting.[208] Tensions remain in Plutarch's discussions of what comes

---

[204] Annihilation and oblivion are similar but not identical states. Annihilation refers to a state of non-existence, while oblivion, as distinguished from obliteration, is a state of forgetfulness or of having been forgotten. To be in a state of oblivion it is helpful, but not strictly necessary, to be in a state of annihilation. Plutarch responds to Epicurus by calling annihilation the strongest of fears at *Suav. viv.* 1103E, while he refers to "insensibility, oblivion, and knowing nothing" (ἀναισθησία καὶ λήθη καὶ ἄγνοια) as universal fears at 1104E. On fear of annihilation as a fundamental human fear, see van der Leeuw, *Religion in Essence and Manifestation*, 2:465.

[205] Note the word-play: "connecting with death (θανάτῳ) the thought of undying evils (κακῶν ἐπίνοιαν ἀθανάτων)."

[206] Cf. Dillon, *The Middle Platonists*, 211–14, on Plutarch's picture of the soul.

[207] The concluding description of the fate of the impious dead in *Lat. viv.* 1130E has points of contact with the superstitious fears mentioned in *Superst.* 167A, but the former lacks the motif of active torture present in the latter.

[208] Cf. Brenk, *In Mist Apparelled*, 22–27. Plutarch regards fearlessness in the face of

after death.[209] He is typically cautious in making definitive pronouncements in this area, though preferring to risk error in an optimistic direction (*Tranq. an.* 476A–B):

> But he who understands somehow or other the nature of the soul and reflects that the change it undergoes at death will be for the better, or at least not for the worse, has no small provision to secure tranquility of mind for facing life—fearlessness towards death.

In a physical sense, we are constantly, if figuratively, dying, passing slowly but surely from one stage in the rhythm of organic existence to the next. Death, in the worst possible scenario, is just one further step in this natural evolution and not to be feared.

Atheism and Superstition Compared: Theological and Practical Aspects

The remainder of the treatise is an extended comparison and contrast of superstition and atheism.[210] Plutarch returns to his distrust of the emotions for his first proposition. The atheist's ignorance is distressing (χαλεπός)—distressing for Plutarch, that is, but not for the atheist. It is the lack of distress that, all things considered, makes it worse to have no conception of the gods than to have the conception usually engendered by the distress (ἑλκῶδης), disturbance (ταρακτικόν), and mental enslavement (καταδεδουλωμένον τῇ δόξῃ) of superstition (167B). Right thinking about the gods, like good music, ought to dispel such ill tempers from the soul.[211]

---

death as a necessary virtue for the active life he admires in contrast to Epicurus (cf. *Alex. fort.* 342F, 345B; *Phoc.* 3.5; *Dion* 21.8).

[209] As they do also in Plato's (*Phaed.* 114A–D; *Gorg.* 524B–527E; *Resp.* 1.330D; 10.614B–621D). It is important to remember that Plato and Plutarch are not the only ones able to tolerate discrepancies between formal beliefs articulated in philosophical literature and those implied by the familiar practices of popular religion. The Hellenistic world contains a surprisingly wide range of inconsistent ideas about post-mortem existence standing side by side without any comment; see Keith Hopkins, *Death and Renewal* (Cambridge: Cambridge University Press, 1983), 226–35.

[210] Moellering suggests that a better translation of the essay's title is "Comparison and Contrast of Atheism and a Piety of Dread" (*Plutarch on Superstition*, 31).

[211] The calming effect of music seems to apply only to humans, as the example of tigers driven mad by drumbeats shows (167B). But the verse from Pindar quoted by Plutarch (here and at *Quaest. conv.* 746B; *Suav. viv.* 1095E) appears to suggest that music soothes the nerves only of those beloved of Zeus while it has the opposite effect on others. Plutarch often uses anecdotal evidence from the animal kingdom in support of his arguments and so it is not necessary to see him trying to make a case for the aesthetic sensitivity of tigers here. Elsewhere he argues that music tames the irrational part of the

Nevertheless, the indifference (ἀπάθεια), distrust (ἀπιστία), and insensitivity (ἀναισθησία) of the atheist are preferable to the deformed sense of the superstitious, who regard the benevolent gods as agents of evil (167C–F).

If Plutarch can be said to have a litmus test for orthodoxy, it is evident in his repeated insistence that the gods are benevolent without exception. Many of his accusations against the Stoics presuppose divine beneficence (*Stoic. rep.* 1048C–1050D; *Comm. not.* 1075E). Conflicting evidence suggesting the contrary found in the poets should always be interpreted so as to give the gods the benefit of the doubt (*Adol. poet. aud.* 20C–21A, 23D–E; *Stoic. rep.* 1049E; the poets, Plutarch is certain, do not really imagine that they contrive evil for humans). Whenever the description is appropriate (τό προσῆκον) one may safely assume that the poet is referring to an actual god (*Adol. poet. aud.* 24B). This hermeneutical principle gives a clear indication of Plutarch's bottom line. All good things, and only good things, come from the gods (*Is. Os.* 351C; *Def. orac.* 423D; *Suav. viv.* 1102E–F).[212] Even in their apparent absence or inactivity, he finds reasons for trusting in the gods' beneficence. Plutarch chastises those who complain that the oracles at Delphi are no longer delivered in verse (*Pyth. orac.* 407D–F). The ambiguity, vagueness, and obscurities characteristic of poetry had their function in the past—namely, to confound despots and enemies—but the present time calls for direct, unadorned language. The gods know best and always use the most appropriate instrument for communicating with mortals (405A, 409C–D). He also gives the gods the benefit of the doubt in cases of inequitable treatment of humans. Often it seems that the wicked

---

soul—against the Stoics who see the soul as unitary and rational—thereby enabling it to cooperate with the rational part in learning philosophy (*Virt. mor.* 441E), since reason alone cannot bring all parts of the soul from vice to virtue. This availability of alternate, non-rational ways of inculcating virtue makes it possible for Plutarch, for the sake of the argument, to prefer atheism to superstition in *De superstitione* 167B–C. Reason, though the greatest aid in the acquisition of virtue, is not self-sufficient for this task and, moreover, it may itself become perverted. Something like this has happened with atheists, who display insensitivity by their disbelief. But this insensitivity, unfortunate though it is in Plutarch's eyes, is preferable to the hypersensitivity of the superstitious. Because reason does not carry the entire burden in moral education, but can rely on other, non-rational modes such as music (cf. [*Mus.*] 1145E–1146D) and the imitation of exemplary figures from the past such as are depicted in the *Lives*, all hope is perhaps not lost for the atheist.

[212] Legendary tales suggesting otherwise should be taken as referring to *daimones* (*Is. Os.* 360E–361C; *Def. orac.* 417E; *Fac.* 944D). The same belief was prevalent also in the classical period (J. D. Mikalson, *Athenian Popular Religion* [Chapel Hill: University of North Carolina Press, 1983], 59–60, 66). In the Homeric tradition, Zeus himself is understood as the one who sends both good and evil to humans (*Il.* 15.109; *Od.* 20.199–203; cf. esp. *Il.* 24.525–33, mentioned by Plutarch at *Adol. poet. aud.* 24B; [*Cons. Apoll.*] 105C; *Exil.* 600D).

prosper, never molested by the gods. His response is to urge caution (εὐλάβεια) and to affirm divine providence (*Sera* 549E–550C; cf. 551C, 558D): there is a time for everything though God's timing sometimes seems odd from a human point of view. To "curable" sinners God can grant more time for reform without worrying that they will escape judgment, while the incorrigible will receive poetic justice at the right time and in a fitting manner (551C–D, 553D–F).

The Stoics fail to recognize this aspect of God's goodness and even make the problem of divine punishment worse by their view that the universe is completely in line with the will of Zeus. This, says Plutarch, makes Zeus ultimately responsible for the very evil which he then unfairly punishes (*Stoic. rep.* 1050E–1051A; *Comm. not.* 1076C–1077A; cf. *Adol. poet. aud.* 33E–F). Plutarch prefers to admit that some circumstances are not the will of Zeus. It is impossible, he says, "for anything bad whatsoever to be engendered where God is the Author of all, or anything good where God is the Author of nothing" (*Is. Os.* 369A–B). Since in Plutarch's eyes there is undeniably much that is bad in the world, Zeus must not be responsible for everything that is. As a Platonist, this is in line with his general view of God's transcendence and goodness (cf. Plato, *Resp.* 379A–380C), and the imperfection of the material universe. His subsequent discussion of *daimones* posits a dualistic explanation of the reality of evil in the world that exculpates the gods of all ill will (369C–D).[213]

Plutarch follows this theological critique of δεισιδαιμονία with a litany of examples illustrating the relative superiority of atheism from a practical standpoint. When confronted by misfortune, the atheist will at worst rail against blind fate but will generally search for workable solutions to whatever problems have arisen. The gods—if they exist—help them who help themselves.[214] The superstitious, however, blame the gods for their afflictions rather than fate or themselves, and perform all kinds of bizarre operations in the hope of warding off the punishments that they deserve and that the gods are eager to impose (168A–B). Examination of conscience leads the atheist to the path of self-reformation, but the superstitious wallow in self-pity (not to mention the muck and mire) and reject the counsel of philosophers and physicians they need most,

---

[213] Plutarch's dualistic interpretation of *daimones* in the context of his attack on Stoicism is treated exhaustively by Babut, *Plutarque et le Stoïcisme*, 388–440, who sees any similarities between them as superficial ones. Briefer treatments focussing on this passage from *De Iside et Osiride* are found in Froidefond, "Plutarque et le platonisme," *ANRW* 2.36:215–22; and U. Bianchi, "Plutarch und der Dualismus,"*ANRW* 2.36:354–59. A slightly different way of accounting for the origin of evil is found at *An. procr.* 1015B. On Plutarch's Platonism regarding God and the material world, see Christoph Schoppe, *Plutarchs Interpretation der Ideenlehre Platons* (Münster: Lit, 1994), 139–50, 182–95.

[214] Usually attributed to George Herbert or Benjamin Franklin, almost identical statements of this axiom are found in Aesop (*Hercules and the Waggoner*), Aeschylus (frg. 223), and Hippocrates (*De victu* 4.87.14–16).

sometimes with fatal consequences (168C–169B).[215] Nicias, whose fearful reaction to the eclipse at Sicily in 413 resulted in his death and that of his fleet, is invoked as an object lesson. An eclipse should be no cause for alarm, "but frightful is the darkness of superstition falling upon man, and confounding and blinding his power to reason in circumstances that most loudly demand the power to reason."[216] Plutarch also mentions the Jewish refusal to fight on the Sabbath as a case of turning God into a pretext for cowardice (δειλίας πρόφασις).[217] These are infamous—but not exceptional—examples of fear that leads the religious sense astray not only by degree by also by injecting it into affairs where it has little place. So much for superstition and atheism in times of adversity. How do they compare under happier circumstances? Whereas the only disadvantage for the atheist is that he is deprived by his religious doubt of the joy that comes from festive occasions, the superstitious by their theophobia disprove the Pythagoraean claim that humans are at their best when approaching the gods (169E; cf. *Def. orac.* 413B).[218]

Superstitious beliefs that lead to the horrific practice of human sacrifice provide Plutarch with his strongest evidence that it is the greater impiety (170B–171E). Notorious examples of this crime against humanity appear throughout Plutarch's corpus, where it is sometimes stated that *daimones*, not the true gods, call for such sacrifices (*Pel.* 21; *Def. orac.* 417C–D; *Quaest. rom.* 284C).[219] Plutarch often takes what might be called a consequentialist approach

---

[215] This is a specific application of the principle that πάθη of the soul are worse than those of the body (*An. corp.* 500D–501B). Bodily afflictions are very difficult to ignore, but psychic ones often escape the notice of the sufferer since they infect the rational faculty, which is the very thing that ought to detect the problem. To be rid of the disease, one must first be aware of the condition and, second, realize that the condition is in fact a disease (*Virt. prof.* 81F–82A; cf. *Garr.* 510C).

[216] On this passage, see R. Bodéüs, "Un aspect du platonisme de Plutarque?" *Les Études classiques* 42 (1974): 362–74.

[217] *Superst.* 169C; cf. 1 Macc 2:32–36; Josephus, *C. Ap.* 1.209–210.

[218] Elsewhere Plutarch emphasizes the way in which Epicurus's practical atheism unduly dispenses with joy at festivals in its effort to root out fear. Any anxiety, he says, is driven out by the conviction that the gods are present and is far outweighed by the pleasure to be had on holidays (*Suav. viv.* 1100F–1102D).

[219] The vexed question of Plutarch's precise beliefs about demons influences how one reads these passages but is outside the reach of this chapter. He distinguishes between gods and *daimones*, to be sure, but a close reading of the relevant texts, especially those in the *Lives*, reveals a healthy scepticism on the alleged demands made by evil *daimones*. See Brenk, *In Mist Apparelled*, 53–64, for a critical review of the texts connecting the *daimones* to human sacrifice. While human sacrifice exercises Plutarch more than any other practice, many scholars point out how rare ritual killings are among Greeks in non-mythical settings. Dennis D. Hughes and others argue that human sacrifice in Greek sources is almost always a mythical or imaginative exaggeration; see *Human Sacrifice in*

in his thinking about religion and especially about superstition. A consequentialist approach is one in which preference for one theological position over another is, if not determined, at the very least heavily conditioned by the fact that it leads to a more preferable ethical outcome than the alternative. There can be perceived in Plutarch's thought a dialectical relationship between the practical and the theoretical aspects of religion. Actions have theoretical implications; they make manifest or countenance some idea about the nature of reality. And ideas have practical implications; they lead ineluctably to certain kinds of behavior. But at this point Plutarch leaves the argument from practical results and returns to his fundamental theological objection that superstition slanders the gods. The superstitious man, even while holding the view that the gods delight in cruelty and then acting accordingly, no doubt sees his actions as fulfilling the requirements of piety. After relating a story from Homer (*Il.* 24.602–17) about Leto, Plutarch tries to turn this argument back upon the δεισιδαίμων (170C):

> For if it were really true that the goddess cherishes anger,
> and hates wickedness, and is hurt at being ill spoken of, and
> does not laugh at man's ignorance and blindness, but feels
> indignation thereat, she ought to require the death of those
> who falsely impute to her such savagery and bitterness, and
> tell and write such stories.

Plutarch's basic argument is in the form *a minore ad maius*: if it is slanderous to ascribe such traits to a human, how much more so is it to ascribe them to the gods? To defame the gods is impious, and the repercussions are far more serious than in ordinary cases involving defamation of human character.[220] Abject fear of the gods as rash, faithless, fickle, vengeful, and easily offended gives rise to hatred of the gods, which convicts the superstitious of bad faith and hypocrisy, sins of which the atheist is not guilty (170F): "The atheist thinks there are no gods; the superstitious man wishes there were none, but believes in them against his will; . . . by preference [he] would be an atheist, but is too weak to hold the opinion about the gods which he wishes to hold."

To this Plutarch adds the charge that superstition is in fact a contributing cause of atheism (171A–E). He invokes the main tenet of natural theology, that God is knowable through the beauty and providential order of the created world, and claims that, were it not for the barbarous practices of the superstitious and the aspersions they cast upon the divine, atheism would be without its strongest support. Better no god at all, he says, than such gods as these (cf. [*Apoph. lac.*]

Ancient Greece (London: Routledge, 1991), 185–93. On archaeological evidence suggesting the possibility that life on occasion imitated myth, cf. 13–24, 60–65.

[220] For this argument to work, however, Plutarch must rely on fear of the very kinds of divine punishments that he ridicules throughout the rest of the essay.

228E; *Amat.* 763C–D; *Adol. poet. aud.* 21A; and also *Is. Os.* 379C; *Stoic. rep.*1049E, where the emphasis is on the normative definition of deity: "If the gods do something shameful, they're not gods.").

The preference here for atheism is jarring given Plutarch's remarks expressing the opposite preference at *Suav. viv.* 1101B–D on the grounds that Epicurus does away with joy as well as fear in his presentation of the gods. But the difference between the two here is softened by the organic relationship he sees between them. The superstitious secretly desires to be an atheist, Plutarch says, and this should come as no surprise if δεισιδαιμονία objectively fosters atheism in the way he describes. If the evil of superstition consists in large part in the fact that it gives rise to atheism, it can hardly be said that Plutarch enthusiastically endorses atheism or that he is only concerned with the practical consequences of superstition. Rather, as Moellering observes, "he concedes only so much praise as is required to denounce the *deisidaimon*."[221] His theological objections to superstition are thus every bit as strong as his objections from the standpoint of practicality. After describing approvingly interpretations of Egyptian myths in which unworthy traits are transferred from the deities to mortals, Plutarch hesitates because he worries that such demythologization opens the door to the atheism of Euhemerus (*Is. Os.* 359E–360B).[222] He likewise warns against the equation of the traditional gods with various forces of nature because this, too, engenders "fearful atheistic opinions" (366F–377E; cf. *Amat.* 757B–D).[223] Both of these critiques appear without any special stress laid upon the practical or ethical problems created by atheism. In this light, his objections to superstition on the grounds that it leads to atheism appear to be driven by narrowly theological concerns rather than by the practical concerns of law and order that dominate, for example, Plato's rejection of atheism in the *Laws*.[224]

---

[221] Moellering, *Plutarch on Superstition*, 111; cf. Babut, *Plutarque et le Stoïcisme*, 460.
[222] Cf. Jean Hani, *La Religion Égyptienne dans la Pensée de Plutarque* (Paris: Les belles lettres, 1976), 131–41. Plutarch takes Euhemerus as representative of traditional religion's "cultured despisers," to use Friederich Schleiermacher's phrase, but he also concedes that there may be backward tribes somewhere in the world who share this blindness to the gods' existence (*Comm. not.* 1075A–E).
[223] Plutarch's ambivalence about the evil of atheism is perhaps due to the different possible senses of the term ἄθεος. It can mean either the denial of the traditional gods or the philosophical position denying any and all ideas of the gods' existence; cf. A. B. Drachmann, *Atheism in Pagan Antiquity* (Chicago: Ares, 1977), 1–4.
[224] Plato, *Leg.* 10.885B–888D, 907A–909D; 12.948C–D, 966C–D. It should be noted, however, Plutarch elsewhere warns of the corrosive social effects of atheism. Colotes, by advocating pleasure as the highest good and simultaneously denying divine providence, would return humans to a Hobbesian state of nature where life is poor, nasty, brutish, and short (*Adv. Col.* 1124D–1125E). Belief in the gods is universal and essential to the survival of civilization. His diagnosis anticipates that of Dostoevsky, who has Ivan Karamazov say that, without belief in God and immortality, "everything is permitted."

Piety as a Mean

He concludes with a plea for moderation (171E–F). Δεισιδαιμονία is an
error-ridden, high-strung pathology (πολυπλανὲς καὶ πολυπαθὲς νόσημα)
at one extreme end of the religious spectrum. Harsh, stubborn atheism
(ἀθεότης τραχύς καὶ ἀντίτυπος) lies at the other end, with genuine piety
(εὐσέβεια) in between. Smith's hypothesis, that this Peripatetic notion of the
mean has little to do with the main course of the argument and is likely an
editorial addition, has no support in the manuscript tradition and raises more
questions than it answers.[225] Has a second writer tampered with the Plutarchan
corpus by altering a forgery? Why is there a need to add the doctrine of the
mean? Atheism is described as "stubborn" at the beginning and the end, and
though not nearly as negative as the portrayal of δεισιδαιμονία, does this not
fit with the negative comments on atheism scattered throughout the essay? Does
the essay not begin and end abruptly if one emends the text as Smith
recommends?

It should hardly come as a surprise to hear from Plutarch an endorsement of
the general principle of μετριοπαθεία typically associated with Aristotle.
"Know thyself" (γνῶθι σεαυτόν) was not the only dictum inscribed at Delphi
where Plutarch served as priest for over twenty years. Alongside it was the
advice to "Avoid extremes" (μηδὲν ἄγαν).[226] When one considers this essay
with an eye on both Plutarch's expressly theological statements as well as the
views on the emotions that are integral to his moral philosophy, the conclusion
is not an incongruous one. Indeed, the disapproval of δεισιδαιμονία earlier in
the essay on the Stoic premise that it involves πάθος, expressed initially in
quite absolute terms, is just as surprising as this conclusion when viewed in the
larger context of Plutarch's corpus because of his tendency to embrace
moderation of the emotions. Progress in virtue, he says (*Virt. prof.* 83E–84A),
has as one of its first results the transformation of the sharpest emotions into
more moderate ones (πάθη μεθισταμένη). His language is more explicitly
Aristotelian in the essay on moral virtue, *De virtute morali*, an extended attack
on the Stoic views of the rational soul and its role in emotion, some of which he
seems to have misunderstood.[227] Moral virtue differs from theoretical virtue in

---

[225] Smith, "De Superstitione," 6 n. 5.

[226] *Sept. sap. conv.* 164B; *E Delph.* 385D; *Pyth. orac.* 408E; *Garr.* 511A–B; cf. Plato,
Prot. 343B; *Charm.* 165A; Aristotle, *Rhet.* 2.12.14. The possibly spurious Plutarcharn
text *Consolatio ad Apollonium* (116C–D) also mentions these two sayings as mutually
explanatory and as the bases for all wise living.

[227] If Hartmann (*De Plutarcho Scriptore et Philosopho*, 203–4), who also doubts
Plutarchan authorship of *Superst.*, is correct in regarding *Virt. mor.* as pseudonymous, the
evidence adduced here is not very helpful in understanding the integrity of his thought.
No one else in the past century has shared his position. On the Aristotelian language of

that it is concerned with the emotions (440D), and these are not to be extinguished but rather present in measured proportion (συμμετρία παθῶν καὶ μεσότης) (443C–D). The passions that are an essential ingredient in moral virtue require practical reason to be moderate; otherwise they will erupt at the wrong time, too violently, too slowly, or in some other undesirable fashion either by deficiency or excess (444B–C; cf. *Mulier. virt.* 250F–251A, 262D; *Cohib. ira* 458C).[228] Emotions like fear, when under the moderating control of reason, intensify the virtues in a positive way.[229]

Plutarch's endorsement of μετριοπαθεία in ethical matters dovetails with his mediating position on more narrowly theological matters. He invokes the example of those who adopt atheism as a way of avoiding δεισιδαιμονία in support of the more general point that vice and virtue are not two extremes on the same moral continuum in the way that flattery and harshness represent two extreme vices occupying contrary positions with respect to appropriate speech (*Adul. amic.* 66C). He makes a more explicitly theological point when, after reporting the odd occurrences with Juno's statue after the Roman sack of Veii, he warns against eager credulity and excessive incredulity, one leading to superstition and the other to contempt for all things supernatural (*Cam.* 6.3–4).[230] Plutarch repeats this warning against the extremes of superstition and atheism (*Is. Os.* 355D; 378A; 379E), frequently with the same imagery he uses at the end of *De superstitione*.[231] The differences between this and Plutarch's other essays

---

this essay, see Babut, "Plutarque, Aristote et l'Aristotélisme," *Studia Hellenistica* 32 (1996): 1–22.

[228] Cf. Dillon, *The Middle Platonists*, 195–96; and idem, "*Metriopatheia* and *Apatheia*," 511–12, on the way in which Plutarch develops the Aristotelian doctrine of the mean and at points contradicts it in *Virt. mor.* 444C–445A. The quotation of Sophocles (*Oed. tyr.* 4–5) illustrating the unstable condition of the soul not in a mean state also appears at *Superst.* 169D.

[229] *Virt. mor.* 451D–452A. This language of "intensity," the ensuing characterization of so-called "moderate" emotions, and the identification of τὸ μέτριον as an essential quality of deity (*Def. orac.* 413F) show that Plutarch does not regard the exercise of virtue as the necessarily tepid mode of living suggested by the Latin *mediocritas* or a form of "bourgeois morality."

[230] Caution (εὐλάβεια) and avoidance of extremes, he says, is the wisest course. In times of calamity, however, he later says that εὐλάβεια and δεισιδαιμονία overflow all proper limits (*Cam.* 19.8). Plutarch is not using εὐλάβεια in the technical Stoic sense because here it can become inappropriate whereas it is a rational and virtuous form of fear by definition for the Stoics.

[231] *Superst.* 171F: atheism takes one into territory with many pitfalls and precipices (βάραθα καὶ κρημνούς) when one overleaps piety; *Is. Os.* 378A: fleeing superstition for atheism is like falling over a precipice (κρημνός). In the course of disputing Stoic construals of the connection between judgments, emotion, and virtue, he also describes those who figuratively hurl themselves down from cliffs (κατὰ τῶν πετρῶν) in order to

thus are balanced by these similarities and are best seen as differences in emphasis.

Conclusion

Though thoroughly acquainted with Latin culture and largely sharing the contempt for superstition of his many Roman acquaintances, Plutarch pays very little attention to the political dimension of *superstitio* in his construal of δεισιδαιμονία.[232] Plutarch's focus is upon the individual, and his critique emphasizes the way in which superstition impedes human flourishing. Accordingly, the analysis he offers draws on strands of thinking which have as their central concern the well-being of the individual. Superstition belongs in the general category of the emotions (πάθη). More specifically, it is a type of fear, typically a negative quality but especially undesirable when it has the gods as its object.

His critique of superstition therefore sits at the intersection of two separate but intimately related types of discourse. One is theological in the literal sense of "thinking about the divine." The other is broadly ethical, that is to say, concerned with what is right, proper, or customary and, by implication, conducive to a truly happy life. Those kinds of fear Plutarch allows—generally, the desire to avoid vice and shamefulness (αἰδώς: cf. *Adol. poet. aud.* 32D; *Rect. rat. aud.* 37D, 39C; *Conj. praec.* 139C, 141E; *Princ. iner.* 781B–C; *Adv. Col.* 1120C)—are in keeping with his practical, ethical concerns. With other Hellenistic thinkers he regularly describes inappropriate emotions, of which δεισιδαιμονία is a prime example, in terms of disease. They are pathological states or dispositions. The best cure, the surest path to spiritual wellness is by way of acquiring the right beliefs and opinions about the nature of the world and, above all, of the gods presiding over it. While the various schools of thought differ over the degree to which rational persuasion is sufficient for ridding a person of adverse emotional conditions, all agree that long-lasting health must involve some kind of education, whether it is in childhood and thus preventive or later in life as a corrective remedy for the harm done by the wrong judgments of fact and value. Plutarch returns again and again to the basic truth that the gods are benevolent, reiterating the fact that there is never any cause for fear in one's relations with them. Fear of this kind is a crippling emotion accompanied by all manner of vicious behavior. Both Plutarch and the Hellenistic philosophical traditions informing his analysis would assent to the statement that "fear of the gods is a bad thing." The difference is one of

---

escape vice, quoting Theognis as emended by Chrysippus (*Stoic. rep.* 1039E–F; *Comm. not.* 1069D; *Virt. mor.* 450A; and possibly *Superst.* 165A–B).
[232] Adverse political consequences often accompany superstition but are not constitutive of it (Pérez Jiménez, "Δεισιδαιμονία: el miedo a los dioses en Plutarco," 225).

emphasis, with the Stoics and Epicureans laying stress on the evil of fear and Plutarch objecting that the gods are least of all to be feared.

For both, however, the degree to which their world view and ethos fit together to "form a gestalt with a peculiar kind of inevitability" is quite impressive. The terminology is that of Clifford Geertz, who defines "ethos" with reference to the moral, aesthetic, and evaluative elements of a given culture, and "world view" with reference to the cognitive, metaphysical elements, the picture of the way the world in its sheer actuality is.[233] Religion establishes powerful moods and motivation as a bond between the two. In religious belief and practice, "the ethos is made intellectually reasonable by being shown to represent a way of life implied by the actual state of affairs which the world view describes, and the world view is made emotionally acceptable by being presented as an image of an actual state of affairs of which such a way of life is an authentic expression."[234] Because of its circularity, Geertz's theory is inadequate if one is seeking after the ultimate origin of religion, yet it gives a compelling picture of how, once in motion, religious systems work and make sense to those participating in them. It works equally well in describing systems not typically considered religious like those of the Stoics and Epicureans.

Plutarch's religion, as seen through his critique of δεισιδαιμονία, coheres so tightly that it is difficult to determine whether world view or ethos is primary. His insistence on the unwavering goodness of the gods, his conviction that "belief in their true nature" is the most pleasing service humans can render to the gods (*Is. Os.* 355C–D), his allowance of rational fear (εὐλάβεια) as an appropriate attitude in apprehending the divine (*Sera* 549E, 551C, 558D), and his objection to superstition in part on the grounds that it leads to disbelief—all point to theology as the trump card in matters of religion. Within the framework of the analysis of emotions, his theological concerns are certainly stronger than those of his philosophical interlocutors.

But as soon as one decides that he is more theologian than ethicist or moral philosopher, epistemological questions give cause for second thoughts: how is one to know the will of the gods? It is a given that the gods would not perform or demand anything wicked or immoral, as the superstitious often suggest by their words and deeds, or else they would not be gods. But this appears to subordinate the gods to human standards of morality, unless, that is, one holds to a theory of special revelation wherein the gods reveal moral norms to humans who in turn judge the gods according to their own laws. This conundrum finds

---

[233] C. Geertz, "Ethos, World View, and the Analysis of Sacred Symbols," in *The Interpretation of Cultures* (New York: Basic, 1973), 130.

[234] Ibid., 127. Cf. also 126: "The powerfully coercive 'ought' is felt to grow out of a comprehensive factual 'is.'" The relationship he describes is similar to Peter Berger's analysis of religion and "world-construction" (*The Sacred Canopy* [New York: Doubleday, 1967], 3–28 et passim).

its classic expression in Plato's *Euthyphro*, where Socrates argues that the good is not good because the gods approve of it, but rather the gods approve of it because it is good. Modern philosophers refer to the opposing view—that the content of morality derives exclusively from the directives and prohibitions of God—as divine command morality.[235] Plutarch does not squarely confront all the theoretical problems posed by the superstitious when they claim to act as they do because they are obeying the divine will. He instead presupposes the Socratic position and judges various manifestations of religiosity according to a basically Aristotelian theory of virtue only faintly informed by theistic reasoning. Still, he maintains a belief in divine providence that allows for human freedom and absolves the gods of all responsibility for evil in the world. To account for the undeniable existence of evil, Plutarch adverts in some passages to explanations involving malevolent *daimones* but not the gods themselves. This creates a tension in Plutarch's thought since the existence of devious spirits bent on interfering in the lives of humans would seem to give rise to quite rational fears, however much he may protest in *De superstitione* that behavior to counteract such spirits is foolish and unhealthy.[236] Plutarch seems not to have noticed the problem he created in trying to solve the problem of evil. Perhaps the virtue to which he exhorts his audiences will protect them from the interference of meddling *daimones*. Perhaps his talk of *daimones* is symbolic for the emotional upheaval that poses a threat to the acquisition of virtue. And perhaps the mean he endorses at *Superst.* 171F is a way of negotiating the difficulties attending the position of the enlightened theist: in the absence of a clear and incontrovertible sign from above, how does one understand the relationship of the divine to the created order, and what manner of life—thinking, acting, feeling—does this relationship demand?

---

[235] Janine M. Idziak, *Divine Command Morality* (New York: Edwin Mellen, 1979), 1–38, provides an overview of the philosophical debate but does not pay attention to the ancient discussions, presumably because most adherents of divine command ethics from the medieval period forward operate from within the Judeo-Christian tradition and so assume that the Bible is the source of this view.

[236] Cf. Soury, *La Démonologie de Plutarque*, 50–51; and Moellering, *Plutarch on Superstition*, 120–37, 156. C. S. Lewis, in the preface to his fictional correspondence between two demons, is perhaps the closest to the golden mean proposed by Plutarch. "There are two equal and opposite errors into which our race can fall about the devils," he writes. "One is to disbelieve in their existence. The other is to believe, and to feel an excessive and unhealthy interest in them" (*The Screwtape Letters* [rev. ed.; New York: Macmillan, 1982], 3).

Chapter Three

Freedom from Fear as a
Christian Ideal in Hebrews

Introduction

Does the author of Hebrews really mean it when he says that "it is a fearful thing to fall into the hands of the living God" (10:31), or is he simply, for maximum rhetorical effect, playing upon the superstitious ideas entertained by his audience? Is the notion that God is to be feared the kernel—to use the metaphor of Harnack and Bultmann—or is it part of the mythological husk that may be discarded as peripheral, superfluous, or even incompatible with his main point, what he really meant to say? Answers vary. Evaluations of fear language in Hebrews present in microcosm many of the larger contemporary debates over "God-talk" and its implications for the life of the church. Theologians have in different ways addressed the criticisms put forward by Bertrand Russell and many others to the effect that religion generally, and Christianity preeminently, is a deplorable superstition founded on fear and given to cruelty.[1] Pastors and editors of lectionaries sometimes simply omit from the liturgy so-called imprecatory psalms (Pss 83, 109, 137, 139, and others in which the psalmist calls on God to punish the wicked, frequently in quite graphic terms) on the

---

[1] B. Russell, *Why I Am Not a Christian* (New York: Simon & Schuster, 1957), 20–22, 24, 54 et passim. Oskar Pfister, for example, who wishes "to determine the effect of Christianity upon fear and of fear upon Christianity" by means of depth psychology from a Freudian psychoanalytic perspective, laments at great length the ways in which Christianity ceased to be a religion of love and became a religion of fear, contrary to the spirit of its founder, and as a consequence "has the appearance of a gigantic misunderstanding or of a pathology" (*Christianity and Fear* [trans. W. H. Johnston; New York: Macmillan, 1948], 22–24, 33). Most of Christian history, he contends, consists of a cyclic development in which the actions tending to alleviate fear and transform it into happiness are regularly followed by a much longer period during which fear is generated (36–37; the same is also said of Judaism, but according to Pfister it is in Catholicism where fear is by far the most pervasive; cf. 157, 271).

grounds that they conflict with the NT emphasis on God's love and Jesus' command to love one's enemies (Matt 5:44; John 3:16; 1 John 4:16 et al.). But some see this practice as a dangerous flirtation with the Marcionite rejection of the OT and the God of the Jews. The value of these texts for Christian theology, argues Erich Zenger, lies precisely in their "foreignness," experienced most palpably in the picture of a God who knocks out the teeth of the reprobate and sanctions the slaughter of the enemy's infants (Ps 58:6; 137:9).[2] Still others regard the frightful image of God as a "consuming fire" (Heb 12:29) merely as a vestige of Jewish apocalypticism or as a rhetorical scare tactic still employed by preachers to this day.[3] Whereas these modern responses reflect uneasiness with the ethical and aesthetic qualities of a god who inspires fear, ancient writers more often had trouble explaining divine anger due to the Greek philosophical conception of an impassible deity which conditioned their reading of the OT.[4]

This and the following chapter will consider the motif of fear in its various manifestations in Hebrews, an epistolary homily composed in Greek in which the author reflects on several OT texts and their implications about God's dealings with humanity. How does the problem of fear propel the argument forward, what does the author want to say about the propriety of fear in light of the Christ event, and how might his approach influence an outsider's decision to label Christianity a superstition? The testimony of Hebrews is seemingly mixed, seeking at times to inculcate an ethic devoid of all traces of fear (3:6; 4:16; 10:19, 35) while at other times to instill an image of God that would evoke a fearful reaction from anyone paying close attention to the author and taking his message seriously. But in the absence of a systematic treatment of the kind found in *De superstitione*, the author's treatment of fear retains elements of ambiguity and ambivalence. At certain points in Hebrews, the author's meaning is fairly clear but the feelings expressed or evoked are anything but simple, straightforward, or easily reducible to pure categories like "positive" or "negative."[5] Nevertheless, this and the following chapter divide the evidence of

---

[2] E. Zenger, *A God of Vengeance? Understanding the Psalms of Divine Wrath* (trans. L. M. Maloney; Louisville: Westminster John Knox, 1996).

[3] Cf. Braun, "Plutarch's Critique of Superstition," 4–5; and Jean Delumeau, *Sin and Fear: The Emergence of a Western Guilt Culture* (trans. E. Nicholson; New York: St. Martins, 1990), 493–504.

[4] Cf. Ermin F. Micka, *The Problem of Divine Anger in Arnobius and Lactantius* (Washington, D.C.: Catholic University of America Press, 1943). Recent decades have witnessed thinkers from across the theological spectrum (e.g., Cone, Moltmann, Pannenberg, Wolterstorff) espousing the view that God undergoes changes of emotional state.

[5] It is thus not surprising to find occasional references to Rudolf Otto and the *mysterium fascinans ac tremendum* in studies of thought and imagery (e.g., Braun, *Hebräer*, 447; Weiss, *Hebräer*, 695; John Dunnill, *Covenant and Sacrifice in the Letter to the Hebrews* [SNTSMS 75; Cambridge: Cambridge University Press, 1992], 72). For Otto's own

Hebrews into two broad streams. This chapter considers those passages which point to freedom from fear as a Christian ideal and thus would seem well suited for deflecting accusations of δεισιδαιμονία directed at the church. The next chapter considers the ways in which the author seems to preserve the element of fear as a part of one's proper stance in the presence of a god who sends his son to die as a sacrifice. In each case, the author's mode of expression, assessment, and proposals for coping with fear will be carefully examined, as will the degree to which his approach to fear is integrated with the overarching argument of the letter. When one pays special attention to this register of language and explores parallel patterns of religiosity in Hebrews and its Hellenistic context, that is, by considering the culturally proximate range of alternatives, the particular logic of each pattern begins to make more sense.[6]

Fear of Death (Heb 2:15)

Death is the object of the fear first mentioned in Hebrews: "Since, therefore, the children share flesh and blood, he himself likewise partook of the same things, so that through death he might destroy him who has the power of death, that is, the devil, and free those who all their lives were held in bondage by the fear of death" (2:14–15). Religions take on their peculiar character in no small part as a result of the ways in which they make sense of death and the anxiety it

---

references to Hebrews (10:31; 12:28–29), see his chapter on the "numinous" in the NT in *The Idea of the Holy* (trans. J. W. Harvey; 2nd ed.; New York: Oxford University Press, 1950), 84; and for a critique of facile appropriations of Otto's conception of God in the Bible as "the wholly Other" (*das ganz Andere*), see Hans Urs von Balthasar, *The Christian and Anxiety* (trans. D. D. Martin and M. J. Miller; San Francisco: Ignatius, 2000), 55–56. More generally on the ambivalence of fear in a religious context, see van der Leeuw, *Religion in Essence and Manifestation*, 2:463–66; and Kierkegaard's definition of angst (Danish: *Angest*) as "a sympathetic antipathy and an antipathetic sympathy," generated and sustained by the uncertainty arising out of the possibility of freedom (*The Concept of Dread* [trans. W. Lowrie; Princeton: Princeton University Press, 1944], 38). The most sophisticated modern treatment of this ambivalence from a philosophical vantage point is that of Martin Heidegger, who says that anxiety discloses the true precariousness of one's being and that authentic existence is possible only when one lives in constant anticipation of death (*Being and Time* [trans. J. Macquarrie and E. Robinson; New York: Haper & Row, 1962], esp. 293–95). Psychological perspectives may be found in Carroll E. Izard, *Human Emotions* (New York: Plenum, 1977), 366–69.

[6] This way of framing the investigation draws on the methodological insights of Jacob Neusner, "Alike and Not Alike: A Grid for Comparison and Differentiation," in *Take Judaism, for Example: Studies toward the Comparison of Religions* (South Florida Studies in the History of Judaism 51; ed. J. Neusner; Atlanta: Scholars Press, 1992), esp. 233–34.

creates.[7] It is thus not surprising to see numerous attempts to find a correlation between religious orientation and fear of death.[8] Needless to say, no such survey can be conducted among the recipients of the Letter to the Hebrews. The following pages seek to understand the nature of the fear mentioned in Heb 2:15 in its cultural and literary context. Once this is ascertained, it will be possible to see whether the author gives fear a positive or negative evaluation and what he proposes as an antidote to it.

Sources of Fear of Death

Fear of death was a common topic among ancient writers, many of whom describe at length its object, its causes, its subjective quality, and the beliefs about the world it betrays.[9] Because fear, like any emotion, is more than a purely physical sensation, different kinds of fear take on their special qualities with respect to the objects at which they are directed. At the risk of belaboring the obvious, it must be kept in mind that to understand the nature of fear as it appears in Heb 2:15 one must understand the assumptions regarding death that make it such an undesirable prospect. Hebrews subscribes to the general rule that "it is ordained that humans die once" (9:27), notwithstanding notable

---

[7] Cf. Berger, The Sacred Canopy, 23, 43–44, 55.

[8] Whereas some studies find a positive correlation between Christian faith and anxiety about death (H. Feifel, "Attitudes Toward Death in Some Normal and Mentally Ill Populations," in The Meaning of Death [ed. H. Feifel; New York: McGraw-Hill, 1959], 114–29), many others find no significant relationship between intrinsic, as opposed to extrinsic, religious commitment and death fears (L. Cerny, "Christian Faith and Thanataphobia," Journal of Psychology and Theology 3 [1975]: 202–9; R. D. Kahoe and R. F. Dunn, "Fear of Death and Religious Attitudes and Behavior," JSSR 14 [1975]: 379–82; M. Bolt, "Religious Orientation and Death Fears," RRelRes 19 [1977]: 73–76). Other surveys suggest that the intrinsic-extrinsic model is arbitrary and ill-suited for comparison between different religious-cultural contexts (J. W. Patrick, "Personal Faith and the Fear of Death Among Divergent Religious Populations," JSSR 18 [1979]: 298–305) or that the only conclusion supported by the data is that, under different conditions, religious commitment may either induce or attenuate death anxiety (L. D. Nelson and C. H. Cantrell, "Religiosity and Death Anxiety: A Multi-Dimensional Analysis," RRelRes 21 [1980]: 148–57; J. W. Hoelter and R. J. Epley, "Religious Correlates of Fear of Death," JSSR 18 [1979]: 404–11). For an overview and extensive bibliography, see P. Pressman et al., "Religion, Anxiety, and Fear of Death," in Religion and Mental Health (ed. J. Schumaker; New York: Oxford University Press, 1992), 98–109; and J. A. Thorson, "Religion and Anxiety: Which Anxiety? Which Religion?" in Handbook of Religion and Mental Health (ed. H. G. Koenig; San Diego: Academic, 1998), 147–60.

[9] For lists of relevant texts by Greco-Roman and Gnostic writers, see Spicq, Hébreux, 2:44–45; and Braun, Hebräer, 66–67. This subject is present though less pervasive in Jewish texts; cf. Wis 1:12–2:24; Sir 40:1–7; 41:1–4; Philo, Prob. 22.

exceptions who do not die, like Melchizedek (7:3) and Enoch (11:5). Jesus' vicarious death for everyone (ὑπὲρ παντὸς) presupposes this near-universal truth (cf. 2:9). It is something to be suffered (5:7–8; 11:37a) and not eagerly anticipated as a peaceful slumber or as a way of escaping the troublesome realities of bodily existence as in some intellectual traditions.[10] Faith may make it possible to overcome death or to nullify some of its effects (11:4, 5, 12, 13, 19, 21, 29, 31, 35) but not to prevent its occurrence in the first place.[11]

Death is a fearful prospect presumably for two reasons. One reason is that it is followed by judgment (9:27). The notion that one is judged and punished after death is rejected by Epicureans on physical grounds and by Plutarch on theological grounds, but the author does not elaborate on the nature of this final reckoning.[12] That there is a final judgment—"the Lord will judge his people" (10:30)—and hence a pressing need for the cleansing from sin effected by Jesus (9:28), is more important than the details of any such forensic proceeding.[13] Instruction about "eternal judgment" is listed among the elementary teachings the author expects his readers to have mastered (6:2). "The God of all" and the judge are one and the same (12:23); "the immoral and the adulterous" are among those who will be judged (13:4). That day is drawing near (10:25) on which those not covered by Christ's sacrifice face "a fearful prospect of judgment and a furious fire" (v. 27; cf. 6:7–8).

The demonic power active in death is the second factor contributing to its fearsomeness. Holding the power of death is the devil (2:14); God did not introduce death and in no way delights in it (cf. Gen 3:1–19; Wis 1:13–14; 2:23–24; 1 Cor 5:5). There is a loose connection here between judgment and the devil's power, as the LXX and NT use διάβολος to translate the Hebrew שׂטן,

---

[10] Diodorus Siculus 15.25.2; Plato, *Phaed.* 67D–E; Plutarch, *Tranq. an.* 476B; Dio Chrysostom, *Or.* 6.47; Epictetus, *Diatr.* 4.7.12–21. Grässer refers to the latter view as "ein zentrales Theologumenon" of Hebrews taken over from Gnostic sources but cites few primary texts where fear of death is mentioned ("Die Heilsbedeutung des Todes Jesu in Hebräer 2,14–18," in *Theologia Crucis-Signum Crucis: Festschrift für Erich Dinkler zum 70. Geburtstag* [ed. C. Andresen and G. Klein; Tübingen: Mohr-Siebeck, 1979], 183); cf. Käsemann, *The Wandering People of God*, 157–62, for a similar analysis of Heb 2 against the Gnostic background.

[11] To suggest that death is avoidable would not really help the author's argument. After all, the new "testament" (διαθήκη) cannot take effect until there is a death (9:15–17).

[12] The Epicureans, of course, also object on theological grounds that the gods are not vengeful and hence not eager to punish mortals, but they emphasize the fact of annihilation and consequent removal of consciousness at the moment of death. This, Plutarch says, makes matters worse since it is annihilation that humans fear most (*Lat. viv.* 1103E, 1104E).

[13] The idea of a final judgment is firmly entrenched in Jewish and early Christian tradition (Wis 4:20–5:23; *T. Levi* 3.2–3; *4 Ezra* 7.33–44, 62–69; *2 Bar.* 51.1–6; John 5:25–29; Rom 2:5–10; 2 Cor 5:10; 1 Pet 4:5–6).

who acts as the "accuser" of humans in the heavenly court [14] By granting the power of death to the devil, Hebrews partially avoids the problem of theodicy that would arise from making God the source of evil (in the form of death).[15] Martin Luther also connects the two motifs when he notes that death is the hour of greatest trial, when Satan attempts to plunge the individual into despair by bringing to mind one's sins, God's wrath, and the fires of hell.[16]

Subjective Quality of Fear of Death

In terms of subjective experience, fear of death is characterized as a form of slavery (δουλεία), a common motif in popular and philosophical discussions.[17] In dying a human death Jesus liberated "the seed of Abraham," though syntactically it is uncertain from what or whom they have been set free (ἀπαλλάξῃ).[18] "Slavery" is the natural choice, though "the devil," "death," and "fear" are also possibilities. Grammatically, "fear of death" (φόβῳ θανάτου) is subordinate to the clause "subject to bondage" (ἔνοχοι ἦσαν δουλείας), leading most interpreters to render the phrase in this way: " . . . free those who through fear of death were subject to lifelong bondage" (RSV). The difference between this and the alternative construction is negligible. Moffatt translates 2:15 so as to identify more explicitly "fear of death" as the form and substance of the slavery abolished by Jesus: " . . . and release from thraldom those who lay under a life-long fear of death."[19] Even if the first construction is favored, one will look in vain for an experiential form other than fear of death that this bondage would take. The use of the imperfect (ἦσαν) and the modifying phrase "lifelong" (διὰ παντὸς τοῦ ζῆν; Vulg.: *per totam vitam*) distinguish this fear as an enduring characteristic of humans as such from periodic outbreaks of fear such as occur in dangerous situations.[20] This interpretation fits with the emphasis

---

[14] Job 1:6–2:6; Ps 109:6; and Zech 3:1–10, where the high priest Joshua (LXX: Ἰησοῦς) is opposed by the devil. In the NT, compare 1 Tim 3:6–7; and Rev 12:9–10 with Heb 2:14, suggesting a play on words in which the accuser (ὁ κατήγωρ) is destroyed (καταργήσῃ). The involvement of the devil in "testing" (πειρασμός: cf. Heb 2:18) is seen in Matt 4:1, 3; 1 Cor 7:5; 1 Thess 3:5; Rev 2:10.

[15] For death personified as a quasi-demonic being, see 1 Cor 15:26; Rev 6:8; 20:13.

[16] Discussed by Fred Berthold, Jr., *The Fear of God: The Role of Anxiety in Contemporary Thought* (New York: Harper, 1959), 45–46.

[17] Euripides, *Orest.* 1520–24; Plato, *Resp.* 3.387B–C; Philo, *Prob.* 22; Seneca, *Ep.* 24.4; Plutarch, *Adol. poet. aud.* 34B; [*Cons. Apoll.*] 106D; Epictetus, *Diatr.* 4.7.17–18.

[18] The object of the preposition (ἀπό: Luke 12:58; Josephus, *Ant.* 11.270) which normally accompanies the verb would usually make this clear.

[19] Moffatt, *Hebrews*, 28.

[20] This notion deviates from Aristotle's basic definition of fear as "a painful or troubled feeling caused by the impression of an imminent evil" that appears to be not far off but near at hand and threatening (*Rhet.* 2.5.1). As an example he then mentions fear of death.

throughout the pericope on the physical, emotional, and spiritual experience shared by Jesus and God's other children.[21]

Scope: Whom Does Fear of Death Affect?

Hebrews 2:16 reinforces the element of fear characteristic of the mortal human nature Jesus assumes in order to redeem it. Nearly all commentators read "Jesus" as the subject in 2:16, but the flexibility of the verb ἐπιλαμβάνεσθαι—it can mean to grasp (physically or mentally), to seize in a hostile manner, to take hold, to surprise, to attack, or to obtain—leaves some room for doubt. The RSV and NRSV render it respectively "concerned with" and "help," reflecting the interpretive decision to see "Jesus" as the subject as there is otherwise weak lexical support for these options if one translates literally.[22] Though alone in seeing "fear of death" as the subject of ἐπιλαμβάνεται, Gudorf's recent arguments based on comparisons with the use of γὰρ δήπου (2:16a) in classical Greek are quite strong.[23] Since this phrase usually follows the clause with which it is interacting, "fear of death" emerges as the most likely subject of the sentence.[24] He thus translates v. 16: "For it [fear

All know that they must eventually pass away but are usually untroubled by this fact since death is not near at hand (cf. Philodemus, *Mort.* 37.20). The acknowledgement of death's inevitability, though unpleasant, is not a chronic psychological problem for most people. One might expect that, like the "fresh beliefs" (πρόσφατος δόξα) mentioned by Posidonius (*SVF* 3.481), it would fade in intensity over time, flaring up and reaching a fever pitch only when danger approaches. By contrast, the author of *4 Ezra*, likely a contemporary of Hebrews, develops the notion that judgment underlies the anxiety about death that characterizes the human condition as such. Unlike the animals, humans experience mental torment "because we perish and we know it" (7.64). Animals enjoy a happier life "for they do not look for a judgment, and they do not know of any torment or salvation promised to them after death" (7.66, 69). The thought of post-mortem judgment is necessarily a fearful prospect for humans since "all who have been born are entangled in iniquities" (7.68).

[21] Jesus' conformity with human nature so that he might become a "merciful (ἐλεήμων) and faithful high priest" (2:17) also fits with Aristotle's simplified definition of τὰ φοβερά as those things which appear pitiable (ἐλεεινή) and evoke compassion in others (*Rhet.* 2.5.12).

[22] Cf. Spicq, *Hébreux*, 2:45.

[23] Gudorf, "Through a Classical Lens," 105–8. Moffatt, *Hebrews*, 36–37; and Ellingworth, *Hebrews*, 178, acknowledge the possibility that "fear of death" is the implied subject only to reject it out of hand.

[24] One might make a similar case for "death" or "slavery" if, as Gudorf says, the author is employing a form of brachylogy in which a preceding noun in an oblique case is carried over as the subject of the following clause without use of a referential pronoun (cf. BDF §483). The Peshitta Syriac version reads "death" as the subject of ἐπιλαμβάνεται in 2:16 (A. Bonus, "Heb. II.16 in the Peshitta Syriac Version," *ExpTim* 33 [1921–22]:

of death] clearly does not seize angels, but it does indeed take hold of the seed of Abraham." It is customary to be "seized" prior to being taken captive, and so such a rendering is more faithful to the basic meaning of ἐπιλαμβάνεσθαι and also complements the enslavement image of the preceding verse.[25] In this reading, v. 16 functions as an interjection acknowledging the elementary fact that angels are not affected by fear of death as are human beings, those who have become "for a little while lower than the angels" (2:6b).[26] It furthermore specifies what the author means in v. 17 when he says that Jesus had "to become like his brothers," that is, the seed of Abraham, "in every respect" (κατὰ πάντα). But having become "for a little while lower than the angels" (2:9), Jesus himself thereby became subject to this anxiety along with all the other παθήματα bound up with flesh and blood existence (2:10; the same term also appears as a variant in v. 14 in D* b [t] vg^ms). As a consequence of having experienced this human weakness, Jesus is "able to help those who are being tested" as a merciful high priest (2:18).

Against Gudorf's position one may cite the evidence of Heb 8:9, the only other occurrence of ἐπιλαμβάνεσθαι in the letter. The context is the author's quotation of Jer 31:31–34 (LXX 38:31–34), where the prophet has God promise a new covenant unlike the one "made with their fathers on the day when I took (ἐπιλαβομένου) them by the hand to lead them out of the land of Egypt." While the author may understand this action as a firm yank on the hands of those with whom God finds fault (8:8)—the obdurate Israelites who subsequently forsake the covenant and are in turn ignored by God (v. 9)—it is hard to deny that the verb connotes a benign act (as in Wis 2:18; Sir 4:11). But since it is quoted verbatim from the LXX, it is not necessary to see the occurrence in 8:9 as determinative of the author's only or preferred usage, especially in light of the wide range of possible meanings for the verb.

234–36): death—not Jesus—"takes hold" of the seed of Abraham but not of angels.

[25] Karl-Gustave E. Dolfe presents more philological evidence against the translation equivalent "help" and in support of this understanding of ἐπιλαμβάνεσθαι as a hostile act; see "Hebrews 2,16 Under the Magnifying Glass," ZNW 84 (1992): 289–94. However, he retains "Jesus" as the subject of the sentence and reaches the surprising (and given the thrust of the passage as a whole, incorrect) conclusion that Jesus and "the seed of Abraham" are in fundamental "disharmony" (292).

[26] The author's quotation of Ps 8:4–6 in 2:6b–8a retains the singular "man" (ἄνθρωπος): "What is man that thou art mindful of him, or the son of man, that thou carest for him? Thou didst make him for a little while lower than the angels, thou hast crowned him with glory and honor, putting everything in subjection under his feet" (RSV; cf. KJV, NIV). He may simply be affirming the general sentiment of the psalmist about the condition of all humans, but he may also have Jesus specifically in view, a strong possibility given the special significance of the phrase "son of man" in the NT. The NRSV completely obscures this option by translating the singular pronouns as plural and "son of man" as "mortals."

Stronger support for reading "Jesus" as the subject of 2:16 is found in the allusion, detected by several commentators, to Isa 41:8–10.[27] This LXX text merits quotation in full on account of a number of similarities between the two passages:

> But you, Israel, my servant, Jacob, whom I have chosen, the seed of Abraham (σπέρμα Ἀβραάμ), whom I have loved; you whom I took (ἀντελαβόμην) from the ends of the earth and called from its farthest corners, saying to you, "You are my servant; I have chosen you and not cast you off. Fear not (μὴ φοβοῦ), for I am with you; be not be led astray, for I am your God. I have strengthened you, I have helped you (ἐβοήθησα; cf. Heb 2:18: βοηθῆσαι), I have established you with my just right hand.

"Seed of Abraham" is the most concrete link, but the motifs noted above of "taking hold," freedom from fear, and "help" find intriguing parallels in Heb 2:14–18. Where Hebrews uses ἐπιλαμβάνεσθαι, however, LXX Isa 41:9 uses ἀντιλαμβάνεσθαι, a cognate with a much narrower range of meaning. The latter verb may mean to take part in an activity or to notice something, but its primary meaning is "to help" (Luke 1:54; Acts 20:35; 1 Tim 6:2; Herm. *Vis.* 3.9.2). The sense of security enjoyed by the faithful remnant—here understood as Abraham's spiritual offspring—comes about as a result of being held in God's hands. Deutero-Isaiah repeatedly makes the point that God's presence drives out all cause for fear (40:9; 41:10, 13, 14; 43:1, 5; 44:2, 8; 51:7; 54:4). If Hebrews wants to evoke this specific imagery in 2:16, why does he use a different verb, one that typically carries a harsher connotation? According to Lane, it reflects the language of LXX Jer 38:32, quoted at Heb 8:9, where God takes Israel by the hand (ἐπιλαβομένου μου τῆς χειρὸς αὐτῶν) to lead them out of Egypt.[28] Jesus as ἀρχηγός (2:10) takes the place of God in leading the children out of slavery.

A good case can thus be made for either option as the subject of 2:16. Grammatically, "fear of death" probably has the strongest support, while "Jesus" is to be preferred if more weight is given to the possible scriptural influences operative in the author's mind. Contextually, the scales tip slightly toward "fear of death" since this makes v. 16 consonant with the thrust of the passage as a whole as a characterization of the human condition entered into by Jesus rather than as an identification of those whom he saves. It is already clear that Jesus came to save humans, not angels, who are themselves "sent to serve for the sake of those who are to obtain salvation" (1:14).

---

[27] E.g., Buchanan, *Hebrews*, 35–36; Braun, *Hebräer*, 68–69; Ellingworth, *Hebrews*, 176.

[28] Lane, *Hebrews*, 1:64; cf. P. C. B. Andriessen, "La teneur judéo-chrétienne de Hébr. I,6 et II,14b–III,2," *NovT* 18 (1976): 308–9, who argues for the influence of the Exodus tradition on the author's linkage of these OT texts.

Assessment: Is Fear of Death Morally Culpable?

Having identified fear of death as a basic element of human existence, Hebrews does not outright condemn it or claim that it never has a legitimate basis. It would be difficult to deem fear of death to be morally culpable at all times and places if it is indeed as natural or universal to be afraid of death as the author implies. Insofar as one's sin incurs an eschatological liability on the day of judgment, fear of death is well founded and perhaps even has value as a proleptic indicator of moral peril. Hence the author tells the audience to stir up one another for love and good works when they assemble together, "all the more so as [they] see the Day drawing near" (10:24–25). Purification for sins has been made "in these last days" (1:2–3). Consciousness of sin, whether it is a lingering pang of conscience over past sins or a fresh feeling of guilt over sins committed in the time after their baptism, seems to have created a sense of alienation from God among the audience.[29] Hebrews tends to speak of sin (ἁμαρτία) not in the singular as an abstract state of alienation but in the plural or using verbal forms, as specific moral failings that accumulate and block access to the throne of grace.[30] Sin in this way leads to fear, not fear to sin, at least not necessarily and not initially, though fear as a result of unatoned sins may lead to further sins.[31]

Jesus experiences fear of death as an essential part of becoming like humans in all respects—all, the author later adds in 4:15, except for sin (χωρὶς ἁμαρτίας), a parenthetical remark probably made to prevent the audience from making a false inference from his comments in 2:14–18.[32] He does not

---

[29] Cf. the comparison of the Levitical rites which "cannot perfect the conscience of the worshiper" and do not do away with "consciousness of sin," with the self-offering of Jesus, which is able to "purify your conscience from dead works" (9:9, 14; 10:2, 22). Lindars, *The Theology of the Letter to the Hebrews*, 59–60, 85–89, sees this lingering conviction of sin, together with the absence of a tangible post-baptismal ceremony in Christian worship for dealing with it, as the reason why the Jewish readers are tempted to seek solace by reverting to Jewish purification rites.

[30] The noun occurs twenty-five times. Of these, ἁμαρτία occurs in the singular only seven times (4:15; 9:28; 10:6, 8; 12:1, 4; 13:11); three of these seven occurrences involve technical terms for OT sin offerings (10:6, 8; 13:11).

[31] Andriessen makes the similar point that sinners are afraid of death because they are in bondage to the devil; they are not in bondage to the devil on account of their fear of death ("La teneur judéo-chrétienne," 305).

[32] So Spicq, *Hébreux*, 2:93–94; Grässer, *Hebräer*, 1:256–58, says that the clause should not be regarded as a casually appended afterthought. Going against a strong theological current in the history of doctrine, however, some scholars argue that the NT nowhere asserts unequivocally that Jesus "never did anything wrong throughout his human life" (Lindars, *The Theology of the Letter to the Hebrews*, 63 n. 53; cf. Buchanan, *Hebrews*, 81–82; Ronald Williamson, "Hebrews 4:15 and the Sinlessness of Jesus," *ExpTim* 86 [1974–75]: 5). Some take a softer stance by interpreting the phrase χωρὶς ἁμαρτίας to

underestimate the severity of mortal fear for to do so would be unrealistic and would also detract from his encomiastic presentation of Christ. To minimize the depth of his empathy with humans in τὸ πάθημα τοῦ θανάτου (2:9) would be to take away from his glory and honor. Jesus sympathizes (συμπαθῆσαι) with human weakness (4:15). His tears and loud cries in the face of death illustrate the genuineness of his emotional experience (5:7). If Jesus experiences fear of death, as appears to be the case also in Gethsemane when he prays for "the cup" to be removed from his lips if it is God's will (Luke 22:42), then by itself the mere feeling cannot be sinful in the author's thought.[33]

But if the expectation of judgment after death is what makes it a terrible prospect, what basis is there for the sinless Jesus to be afraid? This question the author does not answer directly. Because Hebrews is not a set of systematic reflections on the nature of death, it may be too much to expect an exhaustive

---

mean that Jesus never "broke faith" with God even in the face of suffering and death, thus equating sin with a vaguely conceived failure to trust God's promises (V. C. Pfitzner, *Hebrews* [ANTC; Nashville: Abingdon, 1997], 87; cf. Weiss, *Hebräer*, 297). Williamson tries to reconcile the statements about Jesus' sinlessness with those emphasizing his authentic humanity and concludes that Jesus achieved impeccability on the cross, only after struggling with temptation and "learning obedience" (Heb 5:7), which implies that there was a point at which Jesus was not obedient. The gospels contain early traditions in which Jesus himself seems to eschew claims to sinlessness (Matt 19:17; Mark 10:18; Luke 18:19); cf. Theodor Lorenzmeier, "Wider das Dogma von der Sündlosigkeit Jesu," *EvT* 31 (1971): 454–63; and the response of Helmut Gollwitzer, "Zur Frage der 'Sündlosigkeit Jesu'," *EvT* 31 (1971): 496–507. Other passages are more or less explicit in their conviction that Jesus led a morally blameless life (John 8:46; 2 Cor 5:21; 1 Pet 2:22; 3:18; 1 John 3:5). Buchanan, in trying to makes sense of the sacrificial logic of Heb 7:26–28, claims that Jesus as high priest offers a sacrifice for his own sins as well as those of the people (129–31; cf. 155). This runs counter to the direct claim of 7:27 that sacrifice for his own sins was not needed as it was for the Aaronic high priest, and is also hard to square with the statement in 9:14 that Jesus gave himself as a spotless (ἄμωμος) offering since, in Buchanan's view, it is presumably Jesus' own sacrifice that renders him spotless and therefore a worthy sacrifice for the people's sins; see esp. the critique of David Peterson, *Hebrews and Perfection* (SNTSMS 47; Cambridge: Cambridge University Press, 1982), 188–90. Many patristic commentators, partially corrected by the formula of Chalcedon, err in the opposite direction, arguing that Jesus was of necessity without sin on account of Christ's divine nature. It is difficult to understand how Jesus was truly tempted as humans are if his capitulation to sin was a priori impossible. But the objection made by Williamson—that to see Jesus as innately incapable of sin "contradicts . . . the anthropological radicality of sin" and compromises the fullness of his humanity—is equally theological in nature, too acutely sensitive to docetic encroachments on orthodox Christology and uneasy with any suggestion that any human could even potentially lead a morally blameless life.

[33] Jesus' prayer in 5:7, to which God responds positively, will be examined below in chapter four.

account of why a person might be afraid of it. In chapter two the author may simply envision the nonspecific yet near-universal feeling of revulsion at the thought of death such as afflicts even a hero like Achilles, who would rather be a slave on earth than king over all Hades (Homer, *Od.* 11.487–91). It is also quite possible that, like Paul and others, he believes that Jesus, in "tasting death for everyone" (2:9), took to himself the sins of the world and was prepared to bear the eschatological brunt of sin.[34] In this understanding, Hebrews can consistently maintain that Jesus experiences quite reasonable fear (of God's wrath directed at the sin he vicariously bears) without conceding that any sin of his own constitutes the rational basis for that fear. To do so, of course, the author may presuppose in the historical Jesus a conscious awareness of the salvific effects of his own death, as do the gospel writers (e.g., Matt 26:28; Mark 10:45; John 10:11, 15).[35] Paradoxically, then, Jesus is in a unique position to experience a special kind of fear. His atoning death dramatically alters the situation for the faithful, however, by removing the objective basis for heretofore well-founded fear, namely, sin for which there is no availing sacrifice.

Freedom from fear of death entails that one grasp the significance of Jesus' accomplishment and has confidence in it, with the corollary that one also trusts in the goodness of the God who works in such mysterious ways (cf. 11:6). Hebrews does not denigrate fear experienced prior to the cross since, at that time, the real source of fear remained intact. The OT heroes and heroines in chapter eleven are exceptional in that they are ahead of their time. They are praised on account of their prophetic faith by which they saw "from afar" the hoped-for fulfillment of God's promises (11:1, 3).[36] In the present age, however,

---

[34] This thought takes various forms in Paul (Rom 5:6–9; 8:3–4; 1 Cor 15:3; 2 Cor 5:19–21; Gal 1:4; 3:13–14; 1 Thess 5:9–10) and elsewhere (1 Pet 3:18; 1 John 2:2; 4:10). *Diognetus* 9.2–5 contains a catena of similar statements celebrating Christ's voluntary acceptance of "the reward of punishment and death" reserved for sinful humanity.

[35] See Heb 10:5–10, where the author puts words on Jesus' lips from Ps 40 implying conscious awareness that his death serves as a sacrificial offering for sins. A different but not necessarily conflicting explanation of Jesus' fear is suggested by David R. Worley ("God's Faithfulness to Promise: The Hortatory Use of Commissive Language in Hebrews" [Ph.D. diss., Yale University, 1981], 176). The prospect of death is at odds with the characteristic feature of the priesthood "according the order of Melchizedek" promised to God by Jesus: its perpetuity (5:6; 7:3, 17, 20, 25, 28). It is conceivable that Jesus would see death as an impediment to his exercising the very ministry for which he had come into the world. His fear would then be an expression of concern for others since, without some kind of extraordinary intervention, death would hinder his ability "to do [God's] will" (10:7, 9).

[36] Pamela M. Eisenbaum, *The Jewish Heroes of Christian History: Hebrews 11 in Literary Context* (SBLDS 156; Atlanta: Scholars Press, 1997), 179–80, identifies the ability to see into the future as a key characteristic linking the various figures appearing in chapter eleven. This is most conspicuous in the examples of Noah (v. 7), Abraham (vv.

fear of death reflects either inadequate beliefs—recall the Hellenistic equation of emotions with (usually false) judgments—about the cosmic status quo in light of the Christ event, or weak convictions as to the certainty of one's beliefs. While it may not always be possible to suppress the initial, instinctive recoiling at the idea of death, only when one gives assent to the proposition implicit in a cringing reaction does it become blameworthy.[37] Most of those mentioned in Heb 11 die or have near-death experiences yet are unafraid because they perceive far ahead of time that God will keep his promises, albeit in an unexpected manner, namely, through the death and resurrection of Jesus.[38] They looked forward to this unusual fulfillment, and the readers are likewise urged to "look to Jesus" (ἀφορῶντες εἰς . . . Ἰησοῦν) and to "consider (ἀναλογίσασθε) him who endured from sinners such hostility against himself" (12:2, 3).[39] If they are not always rescued from death, like the rest of Jesus' siblings they are at least rescued from the fear of death.

10, 18), Isaac (v. 20), Joseph (v. 22), and Moses (v. 26). In the other cases this capacity is not so clear.

[37] Cf. the Stoic concept of "preliminary passions" (προπάθεια) and the ability of the sage to withhold assent (συγκατάθεσις) to impressions issuing from beliefs that are not true to reality (*SVF* 2.974; 3.63, 177, 189, 459, 548; Cicero, *Tusc.* 3.34.83; Epictetus, frg. 9).

[38] Death or "near-death experience" is another component of the hero profile compiled by Eisenbaum (*The Jewish Heroes of Christian History*, 178–79; cf. James Swetnam, *Jesus and Isaac: A Study of the Epistle to the Hebrews in the Light of the Aqedah* [Rome: Biblical Institute Press, 1981], 88–89; A. D. Bulley, "Death and Rhetoric in the Hebrews 'Hymn to Faith'," *SR* 25 [1996]: 414–18). Although "as good as dead" (νενεκρωμένου), Abraham and Sarah are blessed with a son, a preliminary fulfillment of God's pledge to make their descendants as numerous as the stars (11:12; cf. Rom 4:16–19). Isaac's near-death experience in 11:17–19 is used to illustrate his father's faith. The author also points out that Jacob and Joseph demonstrate their faith at the end of their lives (11:21–22; he omits the detail in the case of Isaac in v. 20). The specter of death hangs over Moses and the Israelites in the allusions in 11:23–29 (the king's edict to slaughter Hebrew infants; Moses' flight to Midian; the first Passover; and the passage via the Red Sea). Rahab escapes certain death by harboring Israelite spies (11:31). The final peroration (11:32–38) contains several examples in which nameless heroes either defy death against all odds or perish under the most terrible of conditions, all without losing faith in God.

[39] Jesus in Heb 12:2 is described as "the pioneer and perfecter of faith," thus linking the audience and the faithful figures on the list in the preceding chapter. The common but inaccurate rendering "*our* faith" (e.g., KJV, RSV, NRSV, NIV, NJB) obscures this crucial connection by deflecting attention away from the OT figures who embody this virtue. The placement of chapter eleven leads Bulley to classify it as a funeral oration that functions epideictically to celebrate urgent behavioral ideals of relevance to the situation of the audience ("Death and Rhetoric," 418–20); see also the more detailed argument of T. H. Olbricht, who on the basis of classical *topoi* introduced by the author believes that the whole letter is modeled after the classical Greek funeral eulogy ("Hebrews as

In the transition from the encomium of faith to the exhortation to perseverance, the reference to the cross in 12:2 and the accompanying motif of Jesus' installment in heaven again calls to mind the purification for sin carried out by Jesus as the prerequisite for taking his seat at God's right hand (1:3; 8:1; 10:12). This is important to keep in view since it is the problem of sin—described as "entangling" or "clinging closely" (εὐπερίστατον)[40] in 12:1—which makes death and the ensuing judgment so frightening. God's provision for the problem of sin is included among the promises that the faithful are said to have anticipated but died with receiving (11:13, 39–40). The theme of promise in Hebrews is wide-ranging and the author's references to it are sometimes vague, such that the content of the promises is not always clear from the context.[41] It is usually interrelated with the themes of inheritance and covenant (4:1; 6:12–15, 17; 8:4, 6; 11:8–9, 12–13; cf. Rom 4:13–14, 16; Gal 3:18–19, 29). Since Jesus' atoning death inaugurates the new (and "better," to use the author's favorite word) covenant, its effects must be "what was promised."[42] The author brings together the themes of promise, inheritance, and covenant in 9:15: "Therefore he is the mediator of a new covenant, so that those who are called may receive the promised eternal inheritance, since a death has occurred which redeems[43] them from the transgressions under the first

---

Amplification," in *Rhetoric and the New Testament* [ed. W. E. Porter and T. H. Olbricht; JSNTSup 90; Sheffield: JSOT, 1993], 375–87).

[40] This verbal adjective, possibly coined by the author, is elsewhere unattested. In spite of the prefix (εὐ-) it is clearly a negative term. Its root is related to the verb περίστημι,"to place around," leading many commentators to see in it the idea of "ensnarement" or "captivation" (Westcott, *Hebrews*, 393–94; MM 264; BDF §117; Weiss, *Hebräer*, 633 n. 11; Croy, *Endurance in Suffering*, 172). This characterization of sin is consonant with that in 2:15, where fear of death is experienced psychologically as a form of enslavement as a result of the liability incurred by sin.

[41] Cf. Koester, *Hebrews*, 110–112, for a short summary of the data; more fully, see Worley, "God's Faithfulness to Promise," 69–108 (on the function of promise language in the references to Abraham and his heirs), 163–216 (on the role of Jesus in God's promises).

[42] In the original Genesis narratives, God's promises include "the promised land," but this element is missing from Hebrews. The land or "city" desired in Hebrews is a heavenly one (11:16; 13:14) where Jesus exercises his priesthood (*contra* Buchanan, *Hebrews*, 188–94, who identifies it as the earthly Palestine or Jerusalem).

[43] "Redemption" (ἀπολύτρωσις) and "to redeem" (ἀπολύω) are terms which in secular contexts refer to release from slavery (cf. the papyrological evidence in Spicq, "λύτρον, *lytron*, etc.," *TLNT* 2:426–27) or imprisonment (2 Macc 12:25; 4 Macc 8:2; Luke 23:16). Here and in 9:12 (λύτρωσις) the author may intend to contrast the eternal liberation from sin and death effected by Jesus with the earthly and provisional liberation of Israel from Egypt (Ellingworth, *Hebrews*, 460). This common way of speaking of the happy consequences of Christ's death again underscores the motif of slavery in 2:15 and the implied notion that death is fearful because of the judgment that follows it.

covenant." This verse nicely encapsulates the argument of 7:1–10:18 leading up to the example list in chapter eleven, and the author does not abandon the main topic of these preceding chapters—how Jesus' death and the new covenant it inaugurates solve the problem of sin—when he fleshes out the meaning of faith. Jesus' death obviates past and present fear of death "for all time" (10:12) by securing forgiveness of sins and cleansing the conscience.[44]

Prescription: How to Be Free From Fear of Death

The author can set up freedom from fear as an ideal because he is addressing a Christian audience composed of those who have already been "enlightened" with the knowledge of Christ's saving achievement.[45] His pastoral strategy for helping his readers attain it is to supply and reinforce the proper judgments about Christ in which their emotional dispositions are grounded. Is the ideal a realistic one? How does he go about helping them to attain it?

"Help in Time of Need": Jesus the Great High Priest

The christological formulation of Heb 2:10–18 contains elements particularly well-suited to the task at hand. Like Aristotle, Hebrews neither rejects manifestations of emotion nor regards fearlessness as a totally elusive or illusory state. Near the end of a detailed enumeration of the circumstances giving rise to φόβος and its contrary, confidence (θάρσος), Aristotle makes the general observation that there are only two conditions under which a person is unaffected by fear (*Rhet.* 2.5.18): either one has not been tested or has some means of assistance (ἢ τῷ μὴ πεπειρᾶσθαι ἢ τῷ βοηθείας ἔχειν).[46] The former implies that fearlessness is not infrequently a function of inexperience or ignorance as to those things which inspire fear in most reasonable persons (cf. *Eth. eud.* 3.1.16, 32; *Eth. nic.* 3.8.16). Aristotle spends little or no time elaborating on this condition. Neither does Hebrews hold out this option as a way of dispelling the fear afflicting his readers; to counsel avoidance of

---

[44] See Worley, "God's Faithfulness to Promise," 192–96.

[45] The metaphor of enlightenment (φωτισμός) frequently connotes a movement from ignorance to knowledge of truth (Heb 6:4; 10:32; cf. Sir 45:17; 2 Cor 4:4–6; Eph 1:18; 3:9; Josephus, *Ant.* 8.143).

[46] While Hebrews may not be directly acquainted with Aristotle's *Rhetoric*, the letter's evident rhetorical sophistication suggests a level of education that would likely have exposed him to Aristotelian ideas. Aristotle's treatise is the most important work for understanding Hellenistic rhetoric, as can be seen in its regular use in later handbooks such as the *Rhetorica ad Herennium*. Works examining Hebrews through the lens of classical rhetoric are surveyed by Duane Watson, "Rhetorical Criticism of Hebrews and the Catholic Epistles Since 1978," *CurBS* 5 (1997): 181–86.

adversity is ignoble, impractical, and cold comfort to those unable to avoid falling into dire straits. Advice of this sort, moreover, comes too late to be of use to his readers since hard times have already hit the community (10:32–39; 12:3–4; 13:3). At any rate, such confidence would be inadequate since it is usually a "false" emotion born of false judgments (Plato, *Phileb.* 36C–39C).

In conjunction with his overarching theological and pastoral aims, Hebrews emphasizes the latter of Aristotle's two conditions for fearlessness, namely, the availability of help. The dominant christological image—unique to Hebrews in the NT—by means of which the author illustrates the superiority of the new over the old covenant is that of the high priest, first introduced in 2:17.[47] Jesus becomes "a merciful and faithful high priest in God's service, to make expiation for the sins of the people." And because he has himself suffered and undergone testing, "he is able to help (βοηθῆσαι) those who are tested" (v. 18), in no small part because he has taken away the sting of death. When the priestly image recurs in 4:14–16, again the accent is upon the timely aid (εὔκαιρος βοήθεια) given by the sympathetic high priest (v. 16). This reference to "timeliness" may simply be a tautology; to be of real help, aid must of course arrive when it is needed. But the author may have in mind a specific point in time, that is, God's judgment after death. On that occasion the ministrations of the heavenly high priest will be most urgently needed. That the author reiterates his earlier remarks about this sympathizing figure immediately after the statement that God's word "judges (κριτικός) the thoughts and intentions of the heart" in 4:12 and the thinly veiled allusion in 4:13 to the final judgment meted out by "the one with whom we have to do" marks another point of contact between the help Jesus provides and human anxieties related to death.[48] Finally, the citation of LXX Ps 117:6 in Heb 13:6 brings together in short compass the motifs of fear,

---

[47] Among the numerous works on the high priest Christology of Hebrews one may consult, in addition to the standard commentaries and works on the letter's Christology, Alexander Nairne, *The Epistle of Priesthood* (Edinburgh: Clark, 1913); Heinrich Zimmermann, *Die Hohepriester-Christologie des Hebräerbriefes* (Paderborn: Bonifacius, 1964); D. G. Dunbar, "The Relation of Christ's Sonship and Priesthood in the Epistle to the Hebrews" (Diss., Westminster Theological Seminary, 1974); Nissilä, *Das Hohenpriestermotiv im Hebräerbrief*; William R. G. Loader, *Sohn und Hoherpriester: Eine traditionsgeschichtliche Untersuchung zur Christologie des Hebräerbriefes* (WMANT 53; Neukirchen-Vluyn: Neukirchener Verlag, 1981), 223–38.

[48] Koester's translation of the final clause of 4:13—"him to whom we must render an account"—brings out the eschatological connotation of the terse Greek phrase πρὸς ὃν ἡμῖν ὁ λόγος (*Hebrews*, 281; cf. also Grässer, *Hebräer*, 1:239: "dem wir Rechenschaft zu geben haben"). Calvin connects 4:13 with 12:23, saying that "the one with whom we have to do" is a judge (*Commentaries on the Epistle of Paul the Apostle to the Hebrews* [trans. J. Owen; Grand Rapids: Eerdmans, 1948], 334). For further analysis of the depiction of God as judge here, see G. W. Trompf, "The Conception of God in Hebr. 4:12–13," *ST* 25 (1971): 125–31.

confidence, and help. God has promised (13:5) never to forsake his people, and so the author can confidently (θαρροῦντας) say, "The Lord is my helper (βοηθός); I will not be afraid (οὐ φοβηθήσομαι)."

Priesthood as Fraternity: Brotherly Love and "The Order of Melchizedek"

In Heb 2:17 the image of Jesus as high priest coincides with the image of Jesus as brother of the faithful. More precisely, fraternal empathy is said to be a prerequisite for the office of high priest: "He therefore had to (ὤφειλεν) become like his brothers in every respect so that (ἵνα) he might be a merciful and faithful high priest in God's service." To grasp the full significance of Christ's priesthood and the way in which it addresses the fear of death, it is therefore obligatory to understand the sibling relationship the author envisions, all the more so since the concept of priesthood "according to the order of Melchizedek" is such a peculiar one, about which so little is known in spite of his mention in the OT (Gen 14:18–20; Ps 110:4) and elsewhere (11QMelch; Philo, *Alleg. Interp.* 3.79–82; Josephus, *Ant.* 1.180; *b. Sukkah* 52b; NHC IX,*1 Melchizedek*). It is not as though its qualifications are familiar or self-evident, even to the original audience, since no one else is known to have held the office.[49] Hebrews offers Jesus' priesthood as a superior alternative to Israel's Levitical priesthood because it provides the help needed to obviate the readers' fear. Any clues the author gives to the nature of this priesthood exercised by Jesus alone demand close attention.

The most important clue comes in emphasis upon Jesus in his role as brother. The sibling relationship between Jesus and the readers, most explicit in 2:10–18 but implied in 12:5–11 and elsewhere in the letter, is not unique within early Christianity (cf. Rom 8:29). It follows rather naturally from the twin propositions that Jesus is the Son of God and that Christians are "children of God" (John 1:12; Rom 8:14–17; Gal 3:26; 4:6–7). Their respective statuses differ by virtue of the fact that Jesus is the "firstborn" (πρωτότοκος: Rom 8:29; Col 1:15, 18; Heb 1:6; Rev 1:5; *Acts Thom.* 48). He is therefore their older brother in Hebrews.[50] Many of the qualities central to this christological

---

[49] A few scholars, however, have suggested that the image of Jesus as a high priest is not the original contribution of Hebrews but rather was part of the liturgy of the primitive church; cf. G. Schille, "Erwägungen zur Hohenpriesterlehre des Hebräerbriefes," *ZNW* 46 (1955): 81–109; and Egon Brandenburger, "Text und Vorlagen von Hebr. V 7–10: Ein Beitrag zur Christologie des Hebräerbriefs," *NovT* 11 (1969): 190–224.

[50] Jesus' temporal priority as elder brother is perhaps suggested by his designation as ἀρχηγός (2:10; 12:2; cf. also πρόδρομος in 6:20). The quotation of Isa 8:18 in Heb 2:13 ("Here I am, and the children God has given me"), placed on the lips of Jesus by the author, should not be understood to mean that Christians have become Jesus' children, *contra* Käsemann, *The Wandering People of God*, 147–48. Such a reading runs counter to

presentation, in which the roles of priest and brother merge in the person of Jesus, may be found in ideal depictions of sibling relationships in Hellenistic literature. The most systematic of these depictions—serendipitously for the present investigation—is that of Plutarch in his essay "On Brotherly Love" (*De fraterno amore* 478A–492D).[51] A surprisingly small number of studies have focused on sibling relationships in Greco-Roman antiquity. Those that examine the metaphor of brotherhood in the NT tend to highlight the horizontal aspects of the kinship language employed in early Christian discourse.[52] They attempt to describe the organization and group dynamics of the "brotherhood" joined by

---

the thrust of the entire passage and the unambiguous statements of 2:11, 12, 17. Moreover, δίδωμι in this verse (τὰ παιδία ἅ μοι ἔδωκεν ὁ θεός) can mean simply "to entrust to one's care," as in John 6:37, 39; 17:6, 9, 12, 24. The Roman legal institution of *tutela impuberum* provided for the guardianship of children who were still minors at the time of the father's death; cf. Richard P. Saller, *Patriarchy, Property and Death in the Roman Family* (Cambridge: Cambridge University Press, 1994), 181–203; Cynthia J. Bannon, *The Brothers of Romulus: Fraternal* Pietas *in Roman Law, Literature, and Society* (Princeton: Princeton University Press, 1997), 44–48. A *tutor*, often an older brother, became responsible for the care of minor children and their inheritance until they reached the age of majority, thus heightening the older brother's natural duty to take care of his younger siblings. Jesus, then, is pictured as the guardian of the audience, those whom God has given him and whom he "is not ashamed to call brothers" (2:11). On the priority of the responsibility of *tutela* above other such social bonds as *hospitium* and *amicitia*, see Aulus Gellus, *Noct. att.* 5.13; Quintilian, *Inst.* 11.1.59; Cicero, *Off.* 3.70; *Nat. d.* 3.30.74.

[51] See the introductory comments on this essay and on the *topos* more generally in Hans Dieter Betz, "De fraterno amore (Moralia 478A–492D)," in Betz, *Plutarch's Ethical Writings and Early Christian Literature*, 231–32; Klaus Schäfer, *Gemeinde als "Bruderschaft": Ein Beitrag zum Kirchenverständnis des Paulus* (Europäische Hochschulschriften XXIII/333; Frankfurt am Main: Peter Lang, 1989), 135–45; Hans-Josef Klauck, "Brotherly Love in Plutarch and in 4 Maccabees," in Balch et al., *Greeks Romans, and Christians*, 144–50; and Reidar Aasgaard, "Brotherhood in Plutarch and Paul: Its Role and Character," in *Constructing Early Christian Families: Family as Social Reality and Metaphor* (ed. H. Moxnes; London/New York: Routledge, 1997), 166–74. See also Malherbe, *Moral Exhortation: A Greco-Roman Sourcebook* (LEC 4; Philadelphia: Westminster, 1986), 93–95, on the shorter writing on the same subject by Hierocles. Plutarch, Hebrews, Hierocles, and the author of 4 Maccabees are all writing on this topic within a few decades of one another.

[52] This is true of Schäfer, *Gemeinde als "Bruderschaft,"* as well as a number of the studies in Moxnes, *Constructing Early Christian Families* (P. F. Esler, "Family Imagery and Christian Identity in Gal 5:13 to 6:10," 121–49; Karl Olav Sandnes, "Equality Within Patriarchal Structures: Some New Testament Perspectives on the Christian Fellowship as a Brother- or Sisterhood and a Family," 150–65; Aasgaard, "Brotherhood in Plutarch and Paul," 166–82; and Lone Fatum, "Brotherhood in Christ: A Gender Hermeneutical Reading of 1 Thessalonians," 183–97).

early Christians by appealing to the socio-historical realities on which the sibling metaphor is based. A few acknowledge the christological grounding of the sibling metaphor[53] but fail to look at the relationship of individual Christians to Jesus in light of the Hellenistic *topos* περὶ φιλαδελφίας.[54] That is to say, most studies take seriously the ethical ideals as well as the social realities of brotherhood when considering the relationship of Christian to Christian within the community but rarely do they apply this same general conception of brotherhood to Jesus' position vis-à-vis individual believers. The aim here is not to uncover the sociological impetus or the ultimate origin of the sibling language in Hebrews—that is, to determine whether individuals of liminal status, attracted by the ethos projected by Christian family language, converted as a form of social compensation[55] or whether conversion created family conflicts that were only subsequently addressed by family metaphors promulgated by the likes of Paul and the author of Hebrews.[56] Rather, the aim is to discern the function of

---

[53] E.g., Schäfer, *Gemeinde als "Bruderschaft,"* 39–128.

[54] Given the relative rarity of this nominal form in extant Greek literature. the author's familiarity with this topic of general interest is initially suggested by his admonition in 13:1 to "let φιλαδελφία continue." Fewer than a dozen or so authors use the nominal form in texts predating the NT, where it occurs six times (Rom 12:10; 1 Thess 4:9; Heb 13:1; 1 Pet 1:22; 2 Pet 1:7 [bis]).

[55] See, e.g., Wayne Meeks, *The First Urban Christians* (New Haven: Yale University Press, 1983), 72–77. Schäfer, *Gemeinde als "Bruderschaft,"* 441–45, does not explain Christian conversion as a result the individual's alienation from traditional family structures but still conceives of Pauline churches as instances of an egalitarian *Kontrastgesellschaft* over against the patriarchal household model.

[56] As suggested by Karl Olav Sandnes, *A New Family: Conversion and Ecclesiology in the Early Church, with Cross-Cultural Comparisons* (Studies in the Intercultural History of Christianity 91; Frankfurt am Main: Peter Lang, 1994), 21–31; idem, "The Role of the Congregation as a Family Within the Context of Recruitment and Conflict in the Early Church," in *Recruitment, Conquest, and Conflict: Strategies in Judaism, Early Christianity, and the Greco-Roman World* (ed. P. Borgen, V. K. Robbins, and D. B. Gowler; Atlanta: Scholars Press, 1998), 334–37. The present study leans toward this second approach, informed by the insights of Peter L. Berger and Thomas Luckmann, *The Social Construction of Reality: A Treatise in the Sociology of Knowledge* (Garden City, N.Y.: Doubleday, 1966), 145–46. They argue that the "success" of religious conversion depends on the individual's ability "to keep on taking it seriously" long after the initial experience. To do so requires a community in which the plausibility of the new world view is nurtured, and the optimal conditions for this process obtain when the setting closely resembles that of one's primary socialization, that is, the family; cf. 119–27, 150–52; esp. 121 on the importance of emotional attachments in primary settings, as opposed to the purely cognitive learning of social roles. The socio-historical variability in the definition of stages of childhood (cf. 125–26) justifies close attention to the particular assumptions about sibling relations in the world in which Hebrews was written.

the brother analogy in Hebrews with reference to its social-cultural context. A closer look at the cultural expectations associated with brotherhood will throw into relief the nature of Jesus' priesthood in Hebrews and the way in which it fulfills the emotional and soteriological needs of the audience generated by their experience of fear.

Hebrews mines the image of Christ as brother more deeply than any other NT writer (with the possible exception of Paul in Rom 8:12–17). While he does not always make explicit the fraternal aspect of the qualities predicated of Jesus, the sheer accumulation in Hebrews of motifs found also in Plutarch's essay on brotherly love is a sign that this is no ad hoc characterization on the part of the author, nor is it merely a projection onto the divine realm of language originally applied only to lateral relations in the community. He takes quite seriously the notion that God's Son is the brother of all the faithful and explores the implications of this image for those fortunate to have the same father. This becomes increasingly apparent as one reads through Plutarch's essay.

Even so simple a matter as identifying the relationship between Jesus and the audience as that of siblings plays on standard elements in discussions of brotherhood. Brothers spring from a common source.[57] This should go without saying, but Hebrews nevertheless calls attention to this fact in 2:11a: "The one [Jesus] who sanctifies and those who are sanctified all have one father."[58] He completes the thought in the second half of the verse by saying that Jesus "is therefore not ashamed to call them brothers." As a Jew, Jesus is naturally part of "the seed of Abraham" (2:16) as are the readers, whether this ancestry is conceptualized as physical (as in Luke 1:73; 3:8; John 8:53; Acts 7:2) or spiritual (as in Rom 4:16; Gal 3:7, 29).[59] Hebrews cements this family bond in 2:12 when he places Ps 22:22 on the lips of Jesus: "I will proclaim your name to my brothers; in the midst of the congregation I will praise you." Given that the author is using sibling images to illustrate the way in which Jesus frees the believer from fear of death, it is not likely that his choice of texts is accidental. Psalm 22, the opening line of which becomes Jesus' cry of dereliction from the cross (Matt 27:46=Mark 15:34: "My God, my God, why have you forsaken me?"), is a poignant plea for help (cf. vv. 1, 11, 19) from God, who saves the psalmist from certain death.

---

[57] *Frat. amor.* 479E; 484F–485A; cf. Aristotle, *Eth. nic.* 8.12.3–4; 4 Macc 13:19–22.

[58] The NRSV supplies "Father," while the NIV says that all are "of the same family." The KJV translates ἐξ ἑνὸς πάντες literally ("are all of one"). The identity of "God" as the "one" fits the context much better than the other possibilities that have been suggested such as Abraham or Adam; cf. Attridge, *Hebrews*, 88–89; Koester, *Hebrews*, 229–30.

[59] Whether the readers, too, were "naturally" to be counted among the seed of Abraham depends upon their ethnic background. For the author's purposes, the persuasive force of the pericope is contingent upon their inclusion.

The common parental bond in tightly knit families promotes feelings of affection and solidarity among brothers, and in turn harmonious sibling relationships bring joy to parents like nothing else (*Frat. amor.* 480A, F). Brotherly love, in fact, is proof of love for father and mother.[60] United "in their emotions and actions" (ἐπὶ τοῖς πάθεσι καὶ τοῖς πράγμασιν), brothers delight their parents most of all when their love for one another is manifest (480B–C).[61] As evidence Plutarch introduces Apollonis of Cyzicus, mother of King Eumenes and his three brothers. Eumenes, he says, is able to pass his days without fear (ἀδεῶς) because he is surrounded by devoted brothers.[62] Because they lack such benefits, those without brothers are said to be most unfortunate (480E).

This last remark obviously presupposes a harmonious sibling relationship as a norm. Enmity between brothers is an ever-present possibility, as familiarity can breed contempt and this contempt frequently takes the form of slander (479B, 481A–B, 482D–E, 483C, 490C–F). In these passages Plutarch repeatedly uses the same word for "slander"—διάβολος or cognates—to be sure, without the same netherworldly connotations with which it appears in Heb 2:14, but striking nonetheless for the way it poses a threat that a model brother is able to neutralize. The devil in Heb 2 is not presented explicitly as the antithesis of the ideal brother represented by Jesus. But when one inquires after the setting in which Jesus is envisioned as "destroy[ing] the one who has the power of death," the idea of a post-mortem judgment for sins in this life returns, where "the slanderer" indicts the sinner in God's presence.[63] Unlike the brother who nurses a grudge by remembering wrongdoings (*Frat. amor.* 481D), Jesus, who has put up with all manner of abuse (Heb 12:3: ἀντιλογία; cf. 6:16; 7:7; in a judicial setting, "rebuttal" would also be an appropriate equivalent), makes sure that his brothers' sins will be remembered no more (8:12; 10:3, 17).[64] He accomplishes

---

[60] The contrary is also true: hatred of one's brother leads to hatred of parents (*Frat. amor.* 450A, D; cf. Betz, "De fraterno amore," 242). Thus in Hebrews one finds apostasy—i.e., rejecting God, "the father of spirits" (12:9)—delineated as a "spurning" of or contempt for the Son (6:6; 10:29) that may result in failure to attend community assemblies (10:25)—i.e., neglect of the relationship with one's heavenly and earthly siblings.

[61] Cf. the commendation at Heb 6:10 and the exhortation to continue in love at 10:24.

[62] See also the advice given by Cyrus to his son (Xenophon, *Cyr.* 8.7.15) that there is no need for a man with a great and powerful brother to fear any harm. On the emotional aspects of the sibling bond, see Aasgaard, "Brotherhood in Plutarch and Paul," 171.

[63] Again, refer to the scene in LXX Zech 3:1–10 where the διάβολος and "Jesus" the high priest contend with one another. The slanderer stands "at his right hand" and thus acts as a rival to the high priest (cf. David L Petersen, *Haggai and Zechariah 1–8* [OTL; Philadelphia: Westminster, 1984], 188–96). See also the similar scenario in Ps 109:6. In Hebrews the devil is presumably among those enemies put under Jesus' feet (1:13; 10:12–13) when he sits at God's right hand. The allusion is to Ps 110:1.

[64] Plutarch uses the term μνησικακία. In Herm. *Mand.* 8.10 one sees a similar

this by his self-sacrifice, an especially fitting form of mediation since the emotional disturbance caused by fraternal enmity is most acute at family gatherings such as the shared sacrifices, when the voice of one's brother, which ought to be the sweetest of all sounds, becomes the most dreadful (φοβερωτάτη) to hear (*Frat. amor.* 481D).[65]

Any number of natural inequalities may disrupt the sibling bond. The inferior brother (ὁ λειπόμενος), for example, through resentment or envy of his brother's δόξα often sinks into disgrace rather than allow himself to be raised up and "augmented" by their shared advantages (485E–F, 486E–F). It is in the course of delineating the many negative possibilities that Plutarch's ideal comes more clearly into focus, and the ways in which brothers overcome these hurdles point to numerous qualities of Jesus in Hebrews that mark him out to be an impeccable example of brotherly love. When one casts Jesus in the role of the superior brother (ὁ ὑπερέχων), his embodiment of the Plutarchan ideal is easy to see. The superior brother—usually but not always the older one—"conform[s] his character" (συγκαθιέντα τῷ ἤθει) to that of the inferior so as "to make his superiority secure from envy and to equalize, so far as this is attainable, the disparity of his fortune by his moderation of spirit (τῇ μετριότητι φρονήματος)" (484D).[66] Jesus likewise humbles himself and becomes like his

---

collocation of respect for ἡ ἀδελφότης and the avoidance of μνησικακία. Just prior to an allusion to Heb 3:12, where the author warns the brothers against falling away from the living God, the shepherd tells Hermas to "no longer bear a grudge (μηκέτι μνησικακήσῃς) against your children, nor neglect your sister, that they may be cleansed from their former sins. For they will be corrected with righteous correction (παιδείᾳ δικαίᾳ), if you bear no grudge (μὴ μνησικακήσῃς) against them. The bearing of grudges (μνησικακία) works death" (*Vis.* 2.3.1). Here and throughout the author is concerned with the theological and pastoral problems of post-baptismal sin, repentance, and apostasy (cf. also Heb 6:4–6; 10:26–31).

[65] One may also take φωνῆς αὐτοῦ in Heb 3:7 (also 3:15; 4:7) as a reference to Jesus' voice rather than to God's (cf. Westcott, *Hebrews*, 80). If the reference is to God's voice, there is an unpunctuated shift in perspective somewhere between v. 7b (where a second person pronoun is used and the antecedent of αὐτοῦ is unclear) and vv. 9–11 (where the pronouns are first person and God is in view). The author is probably exploiting this ambiguity, present in both the MT and the LXX, for the purpose of inserting Jesus into the OT narratives of the wilderness generation, though with more subtlety than Paul does in 1 Cor 10:1–5. God elsewhere speaks by or in (ἐν) his son (1:2), and in 2:3–4 the message of salvation is declared "by the Lord" (διὰ τοῦ κυρίου), an unequivocal reference to Jesus, and so the distinction in 3:7 should not be pressed too hard. Whether the voice is a fearful or a reassuring sound depends on the disposition of the one hearing it.

[66] Plutarch also adduces the example of Polydeuces (Pollux), who refuses to become a god by himself and instead becomes a demigod so that he can participate in his brother's mortality (τῆς θνητῆς μερίδος μετασχεῖν) and share with Castor a portion of his own immortality (ἀθανασία). The verb μετασχεῖν is the aorist infinitive of the same

brothers in all respects (Heb 2:17; cf. 2:7, 9, 14) except for sin (4:15) and is thereby able to "deal gently" (μετριοπαθεῖν) with them (5:2).[67]

One way of avoiding discord is to allow the inferior brother a chance to act as a partner in weighty affairs (*Frat. amor.* 485B–C). The author of Hebrews refers to his audience in 3:1, 14, as "partners" (μέτοχοι) of Christ, and Jesus allows them a crucial role in God's plan in 11:39–12:2. The heroes of faith from chapter eleven constitute the "cloud of witnesses" in 12:1 said to be watching the audience as they endure present difficulties. They have already run their race (note the common ἀγών motif here and in *Frat. amor.* 485B) and now can only look on as the readers run theirs. But they are not disinterested spectators, since so much depends upon the outcome of the "race" mentioned in 12:1. In 11:13 the author says that the heroes of faith saw "from afar" the promises they died without receiving. That these promises remain unfulfilled is again mentioned in 11:39, with the cryptic comment in v. 40 that "apart from us they should not be made perfect." This cloud of witnesses, who appear one by one in the preceding chapter, reemerges in 12:1 as a crowd cheering the readers on as they "run the race." Their perfection, the fulfillment of "what was promised," is now beyond their control and is in the hands of the audience. The author ties the fate of the patriarchs and matriarchs to that of his audience. If the audience does not get to

---

verb, μετέχω, used in Heb 2:14 in reference to Christ's participation in the flesh and blood existence of his brothers (μετέσχεν τῶν αὐτῶν) as the means of destroying the power of death. He is "without end of life" (7:3) and has become high priest "by the power of an indestructible life" (7:16). It is also interesting to note that the Dioscuri, as Castor and Pollux are collectively known, are renowned for their willingness to help those who show religious faith and devotion (Cicero, *Nat. d.* 2.2.6) both in times of distress and during athletic competitions (Pindar, *Nem.* 10.54; cf. Heb 12:1, 12–13) and are referred to as "saviors" (Plutarch, *Superst.* 169B; cf. Burkert, *Greek Religion*, 212–13). Hebrews never refers to Christ as σωτήρ but effectively does so by his use of σωτηρία to describe the benefits that accrue to the believer through Christ's death (1:14; 2:3, 10; 5:9; 6:9; 9:28; cf. 7:25).

[67] For the role of μετριοπαθεία in forgiveness of a brother's sins, see Plutarch, *Frat. amor.* 489C; Hierocles, *On Duties* (in Malherbe, *Moral Exhortation*, 94). As E. J. Yarnold argues, against Westcott, Spicq, Michel, and others, μετριοπαθεῖν and συμπαθῆσαι in 4:15 are not synonyms ("ΜΕΤΡΙΟΠΑΘΕΙΝ apud Heb 5,2," *VD* 38 [1960]: 155). Koester, *Hebrews*, 286, captures the meaning of the former term when he translates it "to curb his emotions" (cf. Yarnold: "iram cohibere;" Plutarch, *Cohib. ira* 458C). Advocated by the Peripatetics against the Stoic ideal of apathy, it denotes a moderation of the passions. This general idea is in view in Heb 5:2 even if the author is not consciously engaged in the inter-school debate over the various ways of dealing with the emotions, with which Philo appears to be acquainted (cf. *Abr.* 257; *Alleg. Interp.* 3.129–134; *Virt.* 195; discussed by Williamson, *Philo and the Epistle to the Hebrews*, 26–30). Though there are grounds for anger and impatience with the wayward on whose behalf he ministers, this does not prevent Jesus from offering the help they need to overcome sin.

the finish line, according to the logic of 11:40, then no one gets there. The consequences of the readers' actions in 12:1–13 thus extend far beyond themselves to all those mentioned in chapter eleven. With this remarkable move the author raises the stakes considerably and seeks to impress upon his audience the gravity of the situation and the crucial role they play in salvation history. In this presentation, then, Christ elevates his brothers by granting them a dignified role in God's plan without in any way diminishing his own unique status (cf. *Frat. amor.* 485C).

Age is the most common of the natural inequalities against which brothers must always be on their guard (486F–487E). Differences in age are absolutely ineradicable and therefore their potential to generate strife is all the more durable. Elder brothers, through their domineering nature, too often create resentment in the younger brother, who in turn ignores the elder's admonitions. Plutarch perhaps urges slightly more leniency with the wayward than does Hebrews; he says that the elder's solicitude for the younger should be that "of one who would persuade rather than command, and would rejoice in a brother's success and applaud them rather than criticize him if he errs and restrain him—a spirit showing not only a greater desire to help, but also more kindness of heart" (487B). Yet the younger is still advised to emulate and most of all to obey (πειθαρχεῖν) the older, and obedience is to be accompanied by reverence (αἰδώς). Obedience is the most highly esteemed "among the many honours which it is fitting that the young render to their elders" (487B–C; cf. Xenophon, *Cyr.* 8.7.16; Cicero, *Quint. fratr.* 1.3.3).

Against this background, the christological perspective of Heb 5:9 takes on new significance. Having himself "learned obedience" (v. 8), Jesus "became the source of eternal salvation to all who obey him." Most commentators ignore this final clause, overly generalize its content, or assign to ὑπακούουσιν a meaning not really permitted by its literal sense.[68] The oversight is likely a result of the heavy emphasis on Jesus in this passage and the theological question about the sense in which he "learned obedience."[69] Braun's gloss—"Man gehorcht ihm, indem man wie er gehorcht"[70]—rightly recognizes the function of Jesus' personal example vis-à-vis Christians but avoids grappling with the plain sense

---

[68] E.g., Calvin, *Hebrews*, 125, says that it is a call to imitate Jesus, while Koester, *Hebrews*, 290, simply says that Jesus' obedience is "the basis for Christian obedience." According to Attridge, *Hebrews*, 154, the phrase τοῖς ὑπακούουσιν αὐτῷ is "a traditional expression." Käsemann, *The Wandering People of God*, 106, is correct that Jesus' obedience "serves the divine saving plan to realize obedience also in the world," but this way of paraphrasing 5:9 is no less vague than these other comments.

[69] This is clearly the case in the otherwise excellent studies of Brandenburger, "Text und Vorlagen von Hebr. V 7–10," 190–224; and Jukka Thurén, "Gebet und Gehorsam des Erniedrigten (Hebr. v 7–10 noch einmal)," *NovT* 13 (1971): 136–46.

[70] Braun, *Hebräer*, 147.

of the verse: those who are to attain salvation must *obey Jesus*. This formula fills a gap created by insistence on the inadequacy of the Mosaic law—at least with respect to its cultic component—and the covenant of which it was a part (7:12, 16, 19, 28; 9:15–22; 10:1, 8). Obedience is always defined with reference to some such notion of authority as law. To answer the question "How are we obedient?" one must eventually consider the question "To what or to whom do we owe obedience?" Grammatically, "obedience" and "to obey" do not stand alone without an assumed understanding of what is to be obeyed.[71] One obeys a rule, a law, or a person. In Heb 5:9 the author makes one of the only unambiguous identifications of whom the readers are to obey, namely, Jesus.[72] This is echoed in 10:28–29, where violation of the law of Moses runs parallel with "spurning" the son of God and "profaning" the blood of the covenant he has instituted. By analogy, obedience to the law of Moses is parallel to obedience to the son of God. While violations of Mosaic law are easy to spot, it is still uncertain what constitutes disobedience to Jesus.[73] For the moment, it is less important to discern the details of Christian obedience vis-à-vis Jesus—neither does Plutarch provide any concrete guidance as to the requirements of fraternal obedience—than simply to notice that this key component structuring the relationship between older and younger siblings applies equally to Jesus and the audience of Hebrews. The brotherliness of Jesus helps to define the nature of his priesthood that in turn enables Christians to enjoy freedom from fear (cf. 4:16).[74]

On the basis of his resemblance to Plutarch's portrait, Jesus is the consummate older brother. Plutarch readily admits that the portrait is an ideal one for which very few in his day are qualified to sit as a model (*Frat. amor.* 478C). Bad brothers are much easier to find. What is one who has a bad brother

---

[71] They require some kind of complementary indirect object. The nominal form ὑπακοή is usually followed by the dative or by an objective or subjective genitive, while ὑπακούειν may be followed by the genitive or the dative, as well as by an infinitive expressing the action in which obedience results (BDF §§163, 173, 187).

[72] They are also to obey (ὑπείκετε) and submit (πείθεσθε) to their leaders in 13:17.

[73] In the gospels, the wind, sea, and demons obey Jesus (Matt 8:27; Mark 1:27; 4:41). Obedience to Christ is mentioned elsewhere (2 Cor 10:5; 1 Pet 1:2; *1 Clem.* 20.1; *Diogn.* 7.2) but without specific directives. *1 Clement* (13.3; 59.1) speaks of obedience to Jesus' words and has in view specific injunctions recorded in the canonical gospels.

[74] Note the way in which the author repeatedly brings together the image of Jesus as son with that of the high priest (4:14–15; 5:8–10; 7:3, 28). That this is a deliberate move on the author's part is suggested by his original juxtaposition of Ps 2:7 ("Thou art my son, today I have begotten thee") alongside Ps 110:4 ("Thou art a priest forever, after the order of Melchizedek") in Heb 5:5–6, making explicit a connection already implied in the prologue; for detailed analysis of this connection, see David M. Hay, *Glory at the Right Hand: Psalm 110 in Early Christianity* (SBLMS 18; Nashville: Abingdon, 1973), 114–45.

to do (481F–482A)? In a word, bear with him (ὑπομένειν). When he errs, it is fitting to be patient with him and say, "I cannot leave you in your wretchedness" (482A, adapted from Homer, *Od.* 13.331), though this does not mean that a brother will give utterly free rein to sin (483A–B). Fraternal reprimands, however, should come only after defending the wayward brother before the father and, if necessary, bearing the father's wrath directed at one's brother (482E–483C). In the end the elder brother succeeds not only in lessening the father's anger against the younger brother but also in increasing the father's good will toward himself (483A). The similarities between this picture and Jesus' sympathetic, longsuffering priesthood, as well as the author's conception of the atonement as a vicarious act (cf. Heb 2:9; 6:20; 9:24), should be readily apparent.[75]

Problems associated with inheritance constitute a perennial sore spot between siblings. There are glimpses of this in the NT (Luke 12:13; 15:11–32), and Plutarch says that it is the standard point of departure in discussions of fraternal friction (*Frat. amor.* 482D).[76] He touches on the subject at 482E, where he describes the obsequiousness of the one who ingratiates himself to the parents and in so doing robs his brother of "the greatest and fairest of inheritances," the parents' good will (εὔνοια). Later (483E) Plutarch adds that the best and most valuable part of the inheritance is the brother's friendship and trust (φιλία καὶ πίστις).[77] All too often, however, the day when the father's property is divided

---

[75] Compare the way in which the father's anger abates through the mediation (τῷ διαλλάσσοντι) of the brother (483A) with Jesus' role as μεσίτης (Heb 8:6; 9:15; 12:24), which diverts God's furious judgment of sin (10:27) from his brothers to himself. Note also the forensic language in *Frat. amor.* 483B. An overly critical brother becomes "the most vehement of accusers" who was once "the most zealous advocate before his parents," recalling the idea of the devil as the accuser of humans in the context of eschatological judgment. The obvious difference between this example and Hebrews is that Plutarch allows for circumstances in which the father's wrath is undeserved because of a son's innocence. He also recognizes that parents are sometimes to blame for the shortcomings they punish (482B). Apart from Jesus, Hebrews envisions all humans as deserving of punishment on account of sins (4:15). On the potential conflict between the demands of fraternal and filial devotion, see Bannon, *The Brothers of Romulus*, 35–38.

[76] Such conflict is a common cross-cultural phenomenon. The effect of property transmission on sibling relations is discussed by Hans Medick and David W. Sabean, "Interest and Emotion in Family and Kinship Studies: A Critique of Social History and Anthropology," in *Interest and Emotion* (ed. H. Medick and D. Sabean; Cambridge: Cambridge University Press, 1988), 9–27; and Cheryl A. Cox, *Household Interests: Property, Marriage Strategies, and Family Dynamics in Ancient Athens* (Princeton: Princeton University Press, 1998), 105–29.

[77] In the same spirit is the comment in Xenophon (*Mem.* 2.3.1–4) that a brother is more valuable than material wealth.

is the beginning of strife (483D–484B).[78] Many fathers attempted to preserve harmony between brothers in the disposition of their wills but to little avail.[79]

Jesus, in contrast both to the conniving brothers mentioned by Plutarch and to the negative examples of brotherly love in Hebrews, plays an indispensable role in securing an inheritance for his siblings. Two examples in Hebrews bear mentioning in this connection. Cain appears first, in the commendation of Abel and his sacrifice in 11:4. Cain's anger and God's preference for Abel's sacrifice cause Cain to murder his younger brother (Gen 4:1–10), the incident alluded to also in Heb 12:24. The reasons for God's rejection of Cain's sacrifice in Gen 4:5a are not spelled out and hence occasioned much speculation in Jewish tradition. One possibility is that God disapproved of Cain because of the inferior quality of his sacrifice and the covetousness it reflected (Philo, *Sacr.* 88; *Conf.* 124; Jospehus, *Ant.* 1.54, 61). Rather than taking the initiative in reconciliation, Cain removes his rival for God's favor. For the author of Hebrews, it is unthinkable that Jesus would answer Cain's infamous question—"Am I my brother's keeper?" (Gen 4:9)—in the negative.

The motif of sibling rivalry is more explicitly linked with inheritance in Heb 12:16–17 with the introduction of Esau, the older twin (Gen 25:25–26; 27:32). Esau's rage at his brother, though understandable in light of Jacob's trickery, issues in hatred and a desire to kill (Gen 27:41–45). The author of Hebrews describes him as "immoral and godless," yet the only information he gives is that he sold his birthright (πρωτοτόκια) for a single meal. The reference is to the brief account in Gen 25:29–34. Famished from a day in the field, he agrees to sell his birthright to Jacob for a bowl of stew. The LXX uses the same term, πρωτοτόκια, as in Heb 12:16. His reasoning is logical enough: "I am about to die; of what use is a birthright to me?" Unlike the many figures in chapter eleven who demonstrate their superior faith in the face of death, Esau makes the wrong decision and earns the disapproval of the narrator in Gen 25:34. The right of primogeniture, firmly established later in Deut 21:15–17, is too easily surrendered by Esau, who "despises" (LXX: ἐφαύλισεν) his birthright. To value physical comfort and security over the birthright reserved for a firstborn son reflects misplaced priorities and a wavering faith from which the author of Hebrews seeks to dissuade his audience. When Esau later seeks to inherit his father's blessing, he is rejected (Heb 12:17). Esau's voluntary forfeiture of the birthright that rightfully belongs to him, however, does not take

---

[78] Cf. Cox, *Household Interests*, 108–16, for the detailed arrangements according to Athenian inheritance law, including cases involving sisters. Her use of evidence from orators suggests that the examples she cites were not arcane bureaucratic matters but would rather have been occurrences familiar to the audience. Roman literary and legal texts illustrating the fraternal disputes and financial considerations associated with inheritance are carefully analyzed by Bannon, *The Brothers of Romulus*, 12–61.

[79] Bannon, *The Brothers of Romulus*, 31–32.

place in the interests of forestalling a feud with his brother Jacob over their
father's property, a policy endorsed by Plutarch (*Frat. amor*. 484A–C). Instead
of striving for peace and harmony, he grows into a divisive "root of bitterness"
(Heb 12:14–15; cf. LXX Deut 29:18).

One finds no competitiveness in Jesus' relationship with his brothers—he
has made them his "partners" (3:1, 14)—who owe their promised inheritance to
his offices in both senses of the word, that is, his assistance as well as his
"official" capacities as brother and high priest. Jesus is "the heir of all things"
(1:2) and "has inherited a name" more excellent than that of the angels (1:4),
thus he sits at the right hand of the one who sends angels "for the sake of those
who are to inherit salvation" (1:14: τοὺς μέλλοντας κληρονομεῖν
σωτηρίαν). Apart from the mediation of their devoted sibling, Hebrews
describes no other way by which the readers will receive the promises. The
convergence in the author's mind, in 9;15 and elsewhere, of the ideas of promise
and inheritance has already been observed.[80] Here again, Jesus' status as brother
helps to clarify some of the otherwise confusing inheritance language in
Hebrews.

First, what is the source of the confusion? It has long been noted that in
9:15–17, the author plays fast and loose with the term διαθήκη.[81] Throughout
the LXX, διαθήκη renders the Hebrew ברית, the standard term for God's
covenantal relationship with Israel. Confusion arises from the fact that διαθήκη
can mean both "covenant," in the OT sense of pact or agreement, and "will" or
"testament," in the legal sense, but not normally both at the same time. (Gal
3:15–17 exhibits the same polyvalence.) Contrary to the statement in 9:17, a
"covenant," as the author uses the term in 8:6–9:14, does not require a death in
order to go into effect. The statement is accurate only with respect to wills
outlining the disposition of the testator's estate, as v. 15 suggests. Numerous
commentators have tried to find one inclusive meaning to accommodate the two
differing senses in which the author uses διαθήκη here, none completely
convincing.[82] It is also unfair to assume that the author simply does not
understand the nuances of the Greek language well enough to realize the
apparent mistake he has made. The author's rhetorical sophistication and his

---

[80] Cf. pp. 122–23 above. For the word group ἐπαγγελία/ἐπαγγέλλομαι, see 4:1; 6:12,
13, 15, 17; 7:6; 8:6; 9:15; 10:23, 36; 11:9, 11, 13, 17, 33, 39; 12:26. For the word group
κληρονομέω/κληρόω/ κληρονομία/συγκληρονόμος, see 1:2, 4, 14; 6:12, 17; 9:15;
11:7, 8, 9; 12:17.

[81] Bruce, *Hebrews*, 209–14.

[82] James Swetnam, "A Suggested Interpretation of Hebrews 9,15–18," *CBQ* 27 (1965):
373–90, for example, opts for a consistent reading of διαθήκη as "testament," while J. J.
Hughes, "Hebrews ix 15ff. and Galatians iii 15ff.: A Study in Covenant Practice and
Procedure," *NovT* 21 (1979): 27–96, argues at length that it should always be understood
as "covenant." For a concise review of the debate, see Attridge, *Hebrews*, 254–56.

proclivity for indulgence in word play (seen also in 7:1–10) make this highly dubious. More plausible is the view that in 9:15–17 the author intentionally exploits the polyvalence of διαθήκη for his own purposes. His use here reflects technical legal terminology common in the Hellenistic period.[83]

By virtue of his death, Jesus is the "mediator" (μεσίτης) of this new διαθήκη. Oepke notes the use of the term in a Roman legal context.[84] In a neutral sense, μεσίτης can refer simply to something that establishes a relationship where one would not otherwise exist. A second-century Roman legal commentary suggests a strong possibility for understanding the otherwise uncoordinated images in Hebrews of Christ as brother and mediator. It was a common practice in wills for a father to name two or more grades of heirs, with the lower inheriting should the higher die before the father or for some reason refuse the inheritance, as sometimes happened if acceptance of the inheritance meant that liabilities would outweigh benefits.[85] One form of this was *substitutio pupillaris*, whereby a father named a younger son as the heir of the older son, who stood to inherit should the father die (Gaius, *Inst.* 2.179–80).[86] By so doing, should the older son die before making his own will, the father could ensure that property would go to the younger son instead of inadvertently passing to someone else. *Substitutio pupillaris* in effect allowed the father to make two wills—one on behalf of the older son—with different heirs, to be enacted in two different possible scenarios.[87] In this way, an older brother could be a mediator of another's will in that he stood between the father and the younger son and guaranteed the orderly execution of its terms, even in the event of his own death.

If this early second-century legal precedent cited by Gaius is placed alongside Hebrews, it is possible to make contextual sense of διαθήκη in 9:15–17. It also suggests a way in which Jesus' death puts into effect a new διαθήκη, in both senses of that term. Relative to the Christian audience of Hebrews, Jesus is the older brother, "the firstborn" (1:6) who is not ashamed to call God's other children "brothers" (2:11; cf. 2:10, 12, 17). He is the son "whom God appointed heir of all things" (1:2). The angels are sent to serve

---

[83] J. Behm and G. Quell, "διατίθημι, διαθήκη," *TDNT* 2:105, 124–25; MM 155.

[84] A. Oepke, "μεσίτης, μεσιτεύω," *TDNT* 4:600 n. 2; cf. Ernst Bammel, "Gottes ΔΙΑΘΗΚΗ (Gal. iii. 15–17) und das jüdische Rechtsdenken," *NTS* 6 (1959–60): 313–19.

[85] E. Champlin, "*Creditur vulgo testamenta hominum speculum esse morum*: Why the Romans Made Wills," *CP* 84 (1989): 198–215. Attributed to Benjamin Franklin is the remark that "nothing is certain but death and taxes," in this case both at the same time.

[86] Brothers were given legal priority after the nuclear family in instances of intestate succession in the *Twelve Tables* (5.4–5). Apart from legal provisions, Valerius Maximus says that it was a gross breach of custom not to name one's brother as heir (7.8.4).

[87] For other substitution schemes permissible under Roman law, see Bannon, *Brothers of Romulus*, 13 n. 3, 31 n. 60.

Jesus' younger siblings, "those who are to inherit salvation" (1:14), of which Jesus is the source (5:9). The OT heroes of faith in chapter eleven are in a position analogous to that of the readers with respect to Jesus: he is their older brother, too.[88] Abraham, Isaac, and Jacob are all "joint heirs" of the same promise in 11:9, which makes sense in the OT understanding of διαθήκη but which, apart from the above interpretation, is hard to reconcile with the sense of διαθήκη in 9:15–17 as a will that goes into effect at death.

Inheritance, affection, trustworthiness, sympathy, moral uprightness, accountability, guardianship—Hebrews weaves together these and other concepts related to the role of brother in the Hellenistic world as a means of fleshing out the image of Jesus as high priest. This goes unnoticed if one looks for parallels to the priestly image only among Jewish or Greco-Roman religious texts and institutions. The author of Hebrews, it may be said, offends against rhetorical conventions by mixing his metaphors, but the fault is pardonable when one allows for the novelty of the religious experience giving rise to their common confession of faith, the urgent situation facing his readers, and the relative dearth of literary and pastoral precedents for describing the Christian vision and responding to the challenges it posed. The author understands and explains the unusual in terms of the familiar. Christ's priesthood "according to the order of Melchizedek" is the unfamiliar, almost certainly an appropriation of scriptural traditions originating with the author. His identity as brother of the faithful is the familiar and serves as the key to understanding the nature of his distinctive priesthood. Jesus "had to become like his brothers . . . so that he might become a merciful and faithful high priest in the service of God, to make expiation for the sins of the people" (2:17). Jesus qualifies as a priest uniquely able to deal with the sin underlying their fear of death (2:15). This vision of Christian hope derives from and issues in recognizable cultural formations intersecting at several points—some unexpected and others familiar from Plutarch's critique of superstition—with the concerns and assumptions of the milieu in which it was written. In Heb 2:10–18, Christian hope is articulated in terms of the fears from which Jesus frees the believer. Afterwards the author expresses it in terms of positive emotional dispositions (παρρησία) and the concomitant cultic advantages for which the faithful have been freed.

"Confidence" Before God: ΠΑΡΡΗΣΙΑ in Hebrews

Fear and confidence stand at opposite poles on the spectrum of emotional responses. This is true by definition and in terms of human experience, and the

---

[88] Jesus "perfects" the faith (12:2) of those living under the old covenant as well as the faith of Christian believers, therefore all are in a similar position relative to Christ. That Jesus can somehow be the *older* brother of those mentioned in chapter eleven fits with the intimation in 1:2 of his preexistence.

two are frequently treated as such in ancient rhetorical handbooks as well as in religious and philosophical discussions (cf. 1 John 4:17–18; 4 Ezra 7.98).[89] Plutarch, for example, says that when a man falls prey to superstitious fears, he loses his παρρησία as well (Superst. 165A).[90] The ideas of confidence and fear function together in Hebrews as well. More often than not, the sources and consequences of fear are present, if submerged, in those passages to be discussed below, where the author speaks of the Christian's παρρησία (3:6; 4:16; 10:19, 35).[91]

Confidence as Members of God's Household (Heb 3:6)

A midrashic comparison of Moses and Jesus in 3:1–6, taking Num 12:7 as a point of departure, follows the description of Jesus' relationship with his siblings in 2:10–18. Both Jesus and Moses were πιστός to God "who had appointed" them (3:2). Since the adjective precedes the participial phrase in the dative (τῷ ποιήσαντι αὐτὸν) it is possible that this occurrence of πιστός refers to Jesus' trust in or fidelity to God, perhaps evinced by his successful endurance of the testing mentioned in 2:18.[92] Here and in v. 6a, where Christ is described as "πιστός over God's house as a son," it is also possible to construe it as a comment not on his trusting nature but rather on his inherent trustworthiness or reliability.[93] This latter interpretation is preferred in light of the syntax of v. 6a and what it implies about Jesus' role in God's house. Whereas Moses in v. 5 is said to be faithful in (ἐν) God's house, Jesus is over (ἐπί) the house, thus

---

[89] Sometimes the antithesis involves the term θάρσος and cognates in place of παρρησία (as in Aristotle, *Rhet.* 2.5.16–22), but the two are often used interchangeably or in tandem as in Heb 13:6; cf. Philo, *Her.* 19–29; Josephus, *Ant.* 2.131–133; Epictetus, *Diatr.* 3.22.96; 3.26.24; Lucian, *Demon.* 50.

[90] It is not clear whether Babbitt's translation "freedom of speech" in the Loeb edition is demanded here. From the context, "boldness," "courage," or "confidence" would fit equally as well.

[91] On the term in Hebrews and more generally, see Paul Joüon, "Divers sens de παρρησία dans le Nouveau Testament," *RSR* 30 (1940): 239–41; van Unnik, "The Christian's Freedom of Speech in the New Testament," 466–88; Heinrich Schlier, "παρρησία, παρρησιάζομαι," *TDNT* 5:871–86; Stanley B. Marrow, "*Parrêsia* and the New Testament," *CBQ* 44 (1982): 431–46; C. Spicq, "παρρησία," *TLNT* 3:56–62; and Alan C. Mitchell, "Holding on to Confidence: ΠΑΡΡΗΣΙΑ in Hebrews," in *Friendship, Flattery, and Frankness of Speech* (ed. J. T. Fitzgerald; NovTSup 82; Leiden: Brill, 1996), 203–26.

[92] Cf. Grässer, *Hebräer*, 1:164–65; Koester, *Hebrews*, 243.

[93] Ellingworth, *Hebrews*, 202. The adjective does not appear in the Greek text of v. 6 but is to be supplied from v. 5 in accordance with the μέν . . . δέ construction connecting the two verses.

connoting his role as caretaker of the οἶκος.[94] The greater glory due to Christ is a result of his conscientious performance of the filial household duties imposed on him by God the father on behalf of his brothers. And since the οἶκος is not simply a physical structure but instead consists of those who live in the house, this means that Jesus' "faithfulness" exhibits itself in his "reliability" as a steward or guardian over his siblings, who are addressed as such in 3:1 at the beginning of the pericope. The audience is again reminded of their membership as the section closes: "And we are his house if we hold on to our παρρησία and pride in our hope" (3:6b).

According to this formulation, what could be more important than maintaining a posture of παρρησία? Their very identity as members of God's house hinges upon it.[95] Without a faithful overseer, the house is in jeopardy. The audience is to contemplate (3:1: κατανοήσατε) the fact of Jesus' faithfulness in this role, which provides the basis for their confidence and represents the content of their hope (3:6). So long as they hold on to their confidence, they remain members of the house.[96]

It is tempting to see in the identification of Moses as a servant the notion that he somehow remains a slave to fear of death since this imagery is still fresh in the mind of the audience from 2:15. But the author uses instead of δοῦλος the word θεράπων, which denotes a free person who has voluntarily entered into the service of a superior and enjoys some degree of honor (Exod 4:10; Josh 1:2; Wis 10:16). The label is not intended to denigrate Moses, yet it undeniably places him below Jesus in the hierarchy of agents who act on God's behalf, and so to be content with or to rely on Moses' help is really to forfeit the privileges that come with full membership in the household. As members of the house, Christians are children in full standing alongside Jesus. To renounce this privileged status, then, is in effect to slide back into bondage.

In order to illustrate this point, the author introduces the precedent of the wilderness generation in 3:7–4:13. The citation of Ps 95:7–11 alludes to the rebellion at Meribah recounted in Num 20:1–13, where the Israelites complain that Moses and Aaron have brought them out of Egyptian bondage only to perish in the desert. Over their forty years of wandering, this complaint is heard

---

[94] Cf. S. C. Layton, "Christ over His House (Hebrews 3:6) and Hebrew אשר על־הבית," NTS 37 (1991): 473–77.

[95] Because the possessive in 3:6 is αὐτοῦ, the reference could be either to God's or to Christ's οἶκος. If, as seems most likely, the OT source is Num 12:7, then "God's" is an appropriate rendering, though the distinction is perhaps not so sharp since Jesus is pictured as God's steward.

[96] It makes little difference in meaning whether one reads the conditional ἐάν or the variant ἐάνπερ in v. 6b. The textual history of this verse has been influenced by v. 14, which also led some scribes to interpolate the phrase μέχρι τέλους βεβαίαν in the next line.

several times.[97] They represent the alternative to holding firmly to the παρρησία associated with Jesus, as the author's commentary in 3:12–19 makes clear. (Aside from using ὑπόστασις in place of παρρησία, 3:14 basically recapitulates the message of 3:6b.) Their failure to enter God's rest (3:11, 18; 4:1, 3, 5–6) stems from their "hardness of heart." Hebrews redirects the exhortation of LXX Ps 94:8 (μὴ σκληρύνητε τὰς καρδίας ὑμῶν) at his audience in 3:8 and repeats the warning three more times (3:13, 15; 4:7). Hardness of heart manifests itself in disbelief and disobedience.[98] As a form of intellectual insensitivity or obtuseness, a hard heart is a deleterious condition because it clouds the perceptions and therefore hinders a person from forming the proper judgments about the world which ought to determine how one acts and feels (Prov 28:14; Philo, *Spec.* 1.305; Mark 6:52; 10:5; 16:14; 2 Cor 3:14; Herm. *Vis.* 3.7.6).

The nexus of beliefs, feelings, and actions, familiar from Hellenistic analyses of the emotions, helps to explain the meaning and function of the παρρησία to which Hebrews exhorts his audience in 3:6.[99] In urging them to "hold fast" (κατάσχωμεν; cf. 3:14) to confidence, the author is not merely saying that they should keep an optimistic outlook on life (as if to say, "Don't worry!"). Genuine emotions are not so easy to manufacture on command. They require a reasonable warrant in the form of particular convictions. It makes little sense to expect his readers to maintain an emotional disposition if they do not have the resources for doing so. An emotion like confidence cannot be sustained

---

[97] E.g., Exod 17:1–7; Num 14:1–12, where God, frustrated by their disbelief in spite of the many signs performed for them, responds by threatening to disinherit the people and to make a greater nation out of Moses' descendants (cf. Heb 2:3–4).

[98] There is no sharp dichotomy between faith and obedience in Hebrews. That the author essentially equates faith with obedience, or views them as two aspects of a unitary virtue, is evident from his alternation between the two terms throughout this passage. In 3:12, the author warns the readers not to have an "evil, unbelieving heart" (καρδία πονηρὰ ἀπιστίας) like many in the wilderness generation. God swore "to the disobedient" (τοῖς ἀπειθήσασιν) that they would not enter his rest (3:18). In the following verse, the inability of this same group to enter is attributed to "unbelief" (δι᾽ ἀπιστίαν). Though the equation of disobedience with unbelief in 3:18–19 is potentially open to question, 4:6 leaves little doubt. The syntax of the final clauses of 3:19 (οὐκ ἠδυνήθησαν εἰσελθεῖν δι᾽ ἀπιστίαν) and 4:6 (οὐκ εἰσῆλθον δι᾽ ἀπείθειαν) is identical except that in 3:19, the auxiliary δύναμαι, "to be able," is inserted. Of course, the other crucial difference is the object of the preposition at the end of each clause. In 3:19, denied access into God's rest is "because of unbelief" (δι᾽ ἀπιστίαν). In 4:6, it is "because of disobedience" (δι᾽ ἀπείθειαν). The author in 4:11 again links access to God's rest to the wilderness generation's "example of disobedience" (ὑποδείγματι . . . ἀπειθείας). They had the advantage of ἀκοή (cf. 3:16; 4:2, 6) but did not follow Jesus' example of ὑπακοή; cf. Käsemann, *The Wandering People of God*, 37–38.

[99] Cf. chapter two above, pp. 55–83.

for long without the belief that there exists a real justification for it. Thus the author alternates between exposition and exhortation through the letter, first providing the knowledge needed to inspire his readers to choose the right course of action and then appealing to their bolstered emotions to keep them on their chosen course through good times and bad. To borrow Aristotle's definition of true courage, he wants them to endure or to fear the right things for the right reasons, in the right manner, at the right time, and to act and to feel as the circumstances merit and as principles dictate (*Eth. nic.* 3.6.5). Hebrews cares less about the readers' feelings than about the convictions or beliefs that are part and parcel of those feelings. A hard heart renders the latter, as well as the former by extension, impervious to correction. And since σκληροκαρδία sets in slowly and imperceptibly, they are to exhort one another on a daily basis (3:13).

All emotions are composites of an affective state and the beliefs underlying it, and Hebrews draws these two dimensions together in his characterization of παρρησία.[100] The former consists in the believer's sense of hopefulness and consequent freedom from fear, and is best expressed by the English "confidence" or "boldness," hence its occurrence together with "hope" in 3:6. It should go without saying that such a state is inherently desirable and hardly in need of commendation. Käsemann thus rightly calls inadequate those interpretations (e.g., B. Weiss; Michel; cf. also Braun: *Freudigkeit*) of παρρησία as joyfulness.[101] Chief among the author's tasks is to redefine for his readers the external ground—that is, the necessary and sufficient beliefs—for their internal disposition. In Hebrews one may possess faith, not simply feel it: "One holds it fast . . . by clinging to the presupposition of faith in the promise."[102] Subsumed under the rubric of παρρησία, then, are both their "confidence" and the reality—past, present, and future—of which they are confident. "Conviction" best captures this dual nature.[103]

The hardness of heart presented by the author as antithetical to Christian παρρησία elicits God's wrath (3:10–11; 4:3). That this wrath may be directed at them is an obvious cause for trepidation for the audience. This is the obverse of the author's exhortation to confidence in 3:6: When there are objective grounds for παρρησία, one ought to cling to it and be free from anxiety. If one's convictions waver, fear is entirely appropriate. This is why he says in 4:1, "So while the promise of entering his rest remains, let us fear (φοβηθῶμεν) lest any of you be judged to have failed to reach it." Neither his placement of the

---

[100] Cf. Weiss, *Hebräer*, 250–53; Mitchell, "Holding on to Confidence," 207–17.

[101] Käsemann, *The Wandering People of God*, 41–43.

[102] Ibid., 43.

[103] It also fits the corresponding term ὑπόστασις in 3:14. See also Grässer's equation of παρρησία with πίστις, defined in 11:1 as the ὑπόστασις of things hoped for and the ἔλεγχος of things not seen (*Der Glaube im Hebräerbrief* (MTS 2; Marburg: Elwert, 1965), 16–17, 96–98).

verb in the primary position nor choice of words is accidental here since this is the only occurrence in the NT of the hortatory subjunctive with the verb φοβεῖσθαι. Inclusion in God's house provides the identity at the core of their confidence. It should have the effect of casting out fear. Subsequent occurrences of παρρησία in Hebrews bring out more fully the cultic coloring of the term hinted at by the mention of priesthood in 3:1.

Confidence before the Throne of Grace (Heb 4:16)

With the mention of the "great high priest who has passed through the heavens" in 4:14, the cultic connotations of παρρησία, occurring a few verses later, become more explicit.[104] Because they have such a sympathetic mediator, the author urges his audience to "approach the throne of grace μετὰ παρρησίας, [to] receive mercy and find grace to help in time of need" (4:16). The reassuring tone of these verses represents a shift from that of vv. 12–13, where the word of God is said to "discern the thoughts and intentions of the heart" and "lay bare" all creatures to the piercing gaze of "the one with whom we have to do."[105] So that the heart's thoughts (ἐνθύμησις) and intentions (ἔννοια) will not betray the one standing in God's presence, the Christian should hold fast (κρατῶμεν) to the confession (ὁμολογία). This indicates that the author's use of παρρησία here retains in part its objective character, expressing what the believer possesses.[106] Its content has to do with Christ's priesthood, mentioned only twice previously (2:17; 3:1) and now reintroduced at the beginning of a section that, with a few digressions, will occupy the next six

---

[104] See esp. the analysis of Scholer, *Proleptic Priests*, 103–13.

[105] The image suggested by τετραχηλισμένα in v. 13 is even more ominous than that of the usual rendering "laid bare" (RSV; NRSV; NIV). The root verb often refers to the act of bending back the neck (τράχηλος) of a sacrificial victim so as to slit its throat (Theophrastus, *Char.* 27.5; Diogenes Laertius 6.61) or to a wrestler's overpowering grip on his opponent (Plutarch, *Ant.* 83). The former image is particularly apt in light of the comparison of God's word to a sword.

[106] In this connection, see Schlier's remarks on the possible shades of meaning of παρρησία in the Greek political sphere (*TDNT* 5:872–73). Stress is frequently placed on the idea that "in παρρησία the actuality of things is stated," and in such contexts it "takes on the sense of openness to truth" (cf. Demosthenes, *Or.* 60.26; Lucian, *Vit. auct.* 8). "This openness," he continues, "is controlled by the object and by one's relation to the object to which one turns, and it resists the tendency of things to conceal themselves, and man's tendency to conceal them from himself." Hebrews acknowledges the human inclination to be deceived by sin (3:12–13) and the futility of attempts to conceal one's sin from God (4:12–13), and he also explains why there is no need to do so (4:14–16). Schlier's interpretation makes possible an interpretation of παρρησία in 4:16 that combines honesty before God with the admission that mercy and grace are needed from God.

chapters: they have a priest who has already passed through the heavens, where his sanctifying work on their behalf has already been completed (1:3); the reminder that it is God's son again brings together Christ's inseparable roles as priest and son (and, by implication, sibling).

The content of their confession that undergirds the readers' παρρησία simultaneously conditions their affective experience when contemplating their approach to the throne of grace. While the term συνείδησις does not appear, it is clear that 4:12–13 envisions the examination of the conscience by God's λόγος and hints at its requisite condition for the realization of παρρησία. A clean conscience enables the supplicant to approach the throne without fear. Jesus' priestly work accomplishes this cleansing (cf. 9:9, 14; 10:2, 22; 13:18). As a result, the situation is like that described by Philo of the person who may pray to God with παρρησία "when he is pure from sin and the judgments of his conscience are loyal to his master" (ὅταν ἁμαρτημάτων καθαρεύῃ καὶ τὸ φιλοδέσποτον ἐκ τοῦ συνειδότος κρίνῃ).[107] Freedom of speech, a standard element in the secular use of the term, here factors into the Christian's posture at prayer.[108] Candor and even boldness may characterize the prayer of one aware of the "rights" won through the work of Christ. This coincides with the call to "approach" (προσερχώμεθα) the throne using language redolent of OT calls to prayer (LXX Ps 33:6; Jer 7:16; 49:1–6). In the present tense, προσέρχεσθαι points to the continuance of practices already in place in the community.[109]

Although the author remains silent as to the precise content of their prayers, the expectation of mercy and grace with which they approach the throne demonstrates their firm conviction that God is the source of good things. That such a basic outlook could not be universally presupposed is apparent from the thrust of Hellenistic critiques of superstition.[110] Doubts concerning the deity's beneficence and their consequences for the individual usually registered in the conscience and issued in the apotropaic compulsions ridiculed by Theophrastus and Plutarch. The affirmation of God's goodness in 4:16 thus makes perfect sense alongside the invitation boldly to approach the heavenly throne. Belief in God's goodness also accompanies the approach of the faithful (οἱ προσερχόμενοι) in the author's commentary on Enoch in 11:6. Whereas

---

[107] Philo, *Her.* 6–7, cited by Schlier, "παρρησία," *TDNT* 5:878; cf. also *T. Reu.* 4.2; Josephus, *Ant.* 2.52, 131.

[108] This classical usage is covered by E. Peterson, "Zur Bedeutungsgeschichte von Παρρησία," in *Reinhold Seeberg Festschrift* (ed. W. Koepp; 2 vols.; Leipzig: Scholl, 1929), 1:283–97.

[109] The occurrences in 7:25; 10:22; 11:6, are in the present while 12:18, 22, are in the aorist. The allusion to prayer is most evident in 7:25, where Jesus intercedes (ἐντυγχάνειν) for those who "draw near to God through him."

[110] See also Jas 1:16–17 for the Christian concern to show that God is the source of good; cf. Plutarch, *Suav. viv.* 1102D–F.

Plutarch posits atheism as the lesser evil in his essay on superstition, Hebrews says that "those who would approach God must believe that he exists and that he rewards those who seek him."[111] Nothing else is said of Enoch or of his faith that God found so pleasing that he was taken to heaven ahead of time. So far as Hebrews is concerned, this brief summary encapsulates the entirety of Enoch's faith—that God exists and bestows favor. He is party neither to the old nor to the new covenant, yet he had access to the minimal knowledge needed to please God.[112] The bare propositional component of faith summed up in 11:6 is necessary (δεῖ) but also sufficient for a bold approach to the divine throne. Given their access to the fuller revelation of God's nature through the son, Christians have all the more reason for their παρρησία.[113]

Confidence in the Heavenly Sanctuary (Heb 10:19–31)

The Clean Conscience (Heb 10:19–25)

Nearly all commentators recognize that with 10:19 the author makes a transition from the expository mode that has predominated since 7:1 and begins a new stage of the argument in which he applies the principles derived from his discussions of priesthood, covenant, and sacrifice to the particular needs of his audience. Their παρρησία is foremost in his mind as he addresses the audience as ἀδελφοί and launches into a thematically dense block of paraenesis (10:19–25):

> Therefore, brothers, since we have παρρησία for entering the sanctuary by the blood of Jesus, by the new and living way which he opened for us through the veil, that is, through his flesh, and since we have a great priest over the house of God, let us approach with a true heart in full assurance of faith, with hearts sprinkled clean from an evil conscience and bodies washed with pure water. Let us hold on to the confession of [our] hope without wavering, for the one who has promised is faithful; and let us consider how to stir up one another to love and good works, not

---

[111] LXX Pss 13 and 52 use the same language in bringing together belief in God's existence and seeking after him; cf. also *4 Ezra* 7.22–24, 37; 8.58; 9.10–12; Epictetus, *Diatr.* 2.14.11; *Ench.* 31.1; and the excellent summary in Braun, *Hebräer*, 348–49. See chapter two above for Plutarch's qualifications of his own position on this point.

[112] Enoch, though unnamed, is the subject of Wis 4:10–15, where his "snatching away" by God is depicted as an act of mercy. He is taken up by God "lest evil change his understanding (σύνεσις) or deceit beguile his soul" (v. 11). A deformed understanding of God would have inevitably placed him among the sinners.

[113] See deSilva, *Perseverance in Gratitude*, 183–84, for a similar analysis of this passage that plays close attention to the elements it has in common with deliberative rhetoric.

> neglecting the assembling of yourselves together, as is the habit of some, but encouraging one another, and all the more so as you see the day drawing near.

Most commentators also note the linguistic, conceptual, and structural echoes between this passage and the previous occurrence of παρρησία, 4:14–16.[114] Whereas the cultic component remains largely latent in the earlier texts, here the mention of blood, sanctuary, curtain, priest, sprinkling, and washings makes it conspicuous.[115]

Using thoroughly cultic language, the author is again trying to show the ideal effect of the Christ event upon the emotional disposition of his readers. His mode of argumentation, moreover, reflects the widely held view of emotions as judgments or, at the least, as affective complexes so closely allied with their generative beliefs that the two dimensions become, for all practical purposes, inseparable. Not surprisingly, one finds competing interpretations of παρρησία in 10:19, some emphasizing its characteristic attitudes or behaviors, and others emphasizing the beliefs giving rise to these attitudes and behaviors. In the author's thought the two are complementary.[116] The readers' awareness of their purity provides the grounding for their confidence. Purification takes effect through the agency of Christ's shed blood (v. 19) and is symbolized by a body cleansed in pure water (v. 22). Without this heavenly reality, any feelings of confidence are illusory, but just as essential to any normal sense of the term "confidence" is an awareness of that reality on the part of the one emboldened by it. God, who takes the initiative in sending Jesus to bring about their purification, also takes the initiative in communicating this fact to the people. A consequence of the new covenant inaugurated by Jesus' death is that God "will no longer remember their sins and misdeeds" (10:17, quoting Jer 31:34). Since those who have been, or think they have been, wronged are rightly to be feared (Aristotle, *Rhet.* 2.5.8), this reminder of God's selective amnesia is most reassuring.[117] It creates the requisite condition for the clean conscience

---

[114] For detailed analysis of the parallelism, refer to W. Nauck, "Zum Aufbau des Hebräerbriefes," in *Judentum, Urchristentum, Kirche* (ed. W. Eltester; BZNW 26; Giessen: Töpelmann, 1960), 203–4; Lane, *Hebrews*, 2:285–86; deSilva, *Perseverance in Gratitude*, 334.

[115] The reference to the priest "over (ἐπί) the house of God" in v. 21 once more draws together the christological images of priest and son by picking up the earlier description of Jesus as a faithful son over God's house in 3:6.

[116] Nils A. Dahl is correct in saying that it here includes both the God-given permission to enter and the personal confidence arising from this authority ("A New and Living Way: The Approach to God according to Heb. 10:19–25," *Int* 5 [1951]: 403).

[117] The tenor of the citation from Jer 31, quoted in full at Heb 8:8–12 and excerpted again in 10:16–17, makes it clear that Israel's lack of fidelity to the covenant constitutes a personal affront to God. This is why God "finds fault with them" (8:8), that is, with the

mentioned in v. 22.[118] Hebrews starts from the assumption that a guilty conscience poses an obstacle to true worship of God.[119] Therefore, to "draw near" to God, be it in private prayer or in communal worship, is impossible apart from παρρησία, since the defective conscience now—after Easter—evinces disbelief in one's confession of God as merciful and faithful to the promises (v. 23). For those who approach God with confidence, there is no place for fear as "the day" approaches.[120]

Hebrews recognizes that his audience is only human and that emotions tend to fade over time. Though their initial commitment had been made "with a true heart," the intense affections accompanying it have diminished with the result that some members are neglecting their common assemblies. This "cooling off" process has a circular effect. As members absent themselves from the gatherings, the setting in which their παρρησία originated and is exercised becomes increasingly alien; and without the encouragement provided in that setting, the subjective sense of παρρησία weakens and the plausibility of those counter-definitions of reality in which their confidence is rooted comes into question.[121] The same might also occur in a different way with those who have

---

people and not simply with the old covenant to which they were obligated.

[118] "Conscience" here refers not to the more modern notion of an autonomous faculty within the individual that distinguishes ahead of time good from bad but rather to the consciousness of, and resultant guilt over, one's own sinfulness (cf. 10:2). Weiss recognizes the shoring up of the readers' consciences as integral to the author's paraenetic aims (*Hebräer*, 52–53; cf. 528–30).

[119] C. A. Pierce, *Conscience in the New Testament* (SBT 15; Chicago: Alec R. Allenson, 1955), 100.

[120] In early Christian idiom, "the day," as it almost certainly does here, refers to the eschatological "day of the Lord" (1 Cor 1:8; 5:5; 1 Thess 5:2; 2 Thess 2:2; 2 Pet 3:10; cf. also 1 Cor 3:13; 1 Thess 5:4; and *Barn.* 7.9; 21.3, for the simple phrase, "the day") when God is to mete out justice in accordance with OT prophecy (Isa 2:12–22; Joel 1:15; 3:14; Amos 8:9–14; Zeph 1:14–18 et al.). Depending on the individual, of course, this could result either in retribution (Heb 10:30) or in salvation (9:28). On "nearness" of potential harm as an essential component of fear, see Aristotle, *Rhet.* 2.5.1.

[121] Cf. Berger and Luckmann, *The Social Construction of Reality*, 152; also Koester, *Hebrews*, 450: "Social bonds reinforce belief just as expressions of belief strengthen social bonds." Spending time together seems especially important for the cohesiveness of a group understanding itself to constitute a "household" (3:1–6; 8:8, 10; 10:21). Furthermore, it is impossible to carry out mutual exhortation as recommended by the author (10:24–25; cf. 3:13)—whether or not it included confession of faults, correction, rebuke, and instruction, and played so central a role in their theory and practice as it did in Epicurean psychagogy—unless individuals are present in the same location (cf. also Plutarch, *Virt. prof.* 82A–F; *Adul. amic.* 89B–C, on the personal moral benefits of confessing faults). The medium of the letter is an attempt, though an inadequate one, to make the author present to his audience.

elected to remain in the dwindling group.[122] If, as is often surmised, fear of stigma or persecution is the cause, then any loss of παρρησία due to slack attendance is all the more unfortunate because it compounds the original problem.[123]

Rather than celebrate the weakening of their "fresh beliefs" as a sign of their progress on the road to ἀπάθεια, as would a Stoic, the author seeks to rekindle their prior enthusiasm by providing new reasons for reaffirming the confession made upon their entry into the church. His reminder of the occasion of their baptism in v. 22 serves this purpose. But as Lindars argues, the purpose is not to prove that Jesus' death suffices as an offering for his readers' sin—this was already accepted by the audience in common with much of early Christian preaching.[124] Instead, the author is at pains to show how the salvific effects of the sacrifice are perpetually in force. If Jesus' sacrifice has permanent efficacy, then it is possible to enjoy permanent παρρησία since the one whose promises this sacrifice fulfills is reliable (10:23). Only by such an understanding of the eternal quality of the atonement can the author expect this to be good news to his readers, whose sins had not even been committed at the time when Christ's death took place for their forgiveness.[125] The cross was a "once for all" event (7:27; 9:12, 28; 10:10; 1 Pet 3:18) and extends into the future to cover future sins as well. In this sense "Jesus Christ is the same yesterday and today and forever" (13:8). Because this part of the confession is impervious to change, by clinging to it "without wavering" (ἀκλινῆ) they demonstrate their παρρησία.

Apostasy and the Forfeiture of Confidence (Heb 10:26–31)

The most egregious form of "wavering" is that of apostasy. A majority of commentators agree that the potential "falling away" of the audience is in view

---

[122] See deSilva's paraphrase of John Donne as applicable to their situation: "each member's defection diminishes me" (*Perseverance in Gratitude*, 342). The term used for "forsaking" the assembly (ἐγκαταλείποντες) connotes something far more negligent than the contemporary "skipping church" (cf. LXX Deut 31:6, 8; Josh 1:5; Matt 27:46; Acts 2:31; 2 Cor 4:9; 2 Tim 4:10, 16; Heb 13:5; *Barn.* 11.2). Even the slightly softer variant καταλείποντες (P[46] D*) retains a pejorative sense (cf. Luke 10:40; *Mart. Pol.* 17.2).

[123] Moffatt, *Hebrews*, 147–48, reviews the possible explanations for the abandonment of fellowship alluded to in 10:25. The same concern is evident in the post-apostolic period (*Did.* 4.2; *Barn.* 4.10; Ign. *Eph.* 13.1; *Pol.* 4.2).

[124] Lindars, "The Rhetorical Structure of Hebrews," 395.

[125] The controversy occasioned by Heb 6:4–6 over the possibility of repentance after baptism, beginning at least as early as the *Shepherd of Hermas*, shows that it is quite plausible, as Lindars contends, that the readers may have had worries about the continuing efficacy of Jesus' death.

in 10:26–31, the most severe passage in the entire letter.[126] In these verses the author outlines the circumstances under which Christian παρρησία finds its contrary—well-founded fear of divine judgment, the "day" to which v. 25 refers:

> For if we sin deliberately after receiving knowledge of the truth, there no longer remains any sacrifice for sins, but a certain and terrifying (φοβερά) expectation of judgment and a furious fire which will destroy the adversaries. One who has violated the law of Moses dies without receiving mercy on the testimony of two or three witnesses. How much worse punishment do you think the man will deserve who has trampled on the Son of God, and deemed profane the blood of the covenant by which he was sanctified, and insulted the spirit of grace? For we know the one who said, "Vengeance is mine; I will repay," and also, "The Lord will judge his people." To fall into the hands of the living God is a fearful thing (φοβερόν).

The motif of fear brackets the paragraph near the beginning (v. 27) and at the very end (v. 31). It functions in this passage to specify the nature of the sin—apostasy—which is pronounced unforgivable in 6:4–6. Conversion is a dynamic rather than a static process in that the conditions for peaceful coexistence with God do not remain the same once one has "received knowledge of the truth" and affirmed it by becoming a part of God's people. There is no turning back after crossing the threshold of faith, and it is no longer possible to plead ignorance. The emphasis on God's fearsomeness in 10:26–31, in conjunction with the emphasis on confidence in vv. 19–25 and 32–39,

---

[126] The secondary literature on this question, which also involves the interpretation of 6:4–6, is immense. Controversy over the teaching of Hebrews on repentance for post-baptismal sin has been a constant in the letter's interpretation since the second century and is most heated in the aftermath of the third-century Decian persecutions when debate centers on Christians who had apostatized under coercion and the terms by which they might be readmitted to church fellowship. For a sample of opinions on the matter as they touch on the interpretation of 10:26–31, see, in addition to the standard commentaries, D. H. Tongue, "The Concept of Apostasy in the Epistle to the Hebrews," *TynBul* 5–6 (1960): 19–26; J. C. Adams, "The Epistle to the Hebrews with Special Reference to the Problem of Apostasy in the Church to Which It Was Addressed" (Ph.D. diss., Leeds University, 1964); Grässer, *Der Glaube im Hebräerbrief*, 192–98; J. K. Solari, "The Problem of *Metanoia* in the Epistle to the Hebrews (Ph.D. diss., Catholic University of America, 1970); Ingrid Goldhahn-Müller, *Die Grenze der Gemeinde: Studien zum Problem der Zweiten Busse im Neuen Testament unter Berücksichtigung der Entwicklung im 2. Jh. bis Tertullian* (GTA 39; Göttingen: Vandenhoeck & Ruprecht, 1989), 93–102; and Hermut Löhr, *Umkehr und Sünde im Hebräerbrief* (BZNW 73; Berlin: de Gruyter, 1994), 49–52, 223–25.

underscores the fact that freedom from fear is the ideal, and indifference—whether theological suspension of judgment or Stoic ἀπάθεια—is not an option.

Where knowledge is thought to be equivalent to virtue, v. 26 would sound like nonsense. That is to say, from the perspective of those who believe that knowledge of the truth leads inexorably to a moral way of life structured perfectly in accordance with that truth, it is hard to conceive of such a thing as deliberate sin. Yet this is precisely what Hebrews posits as the alternative to "holding fast to the confession"—not mere weakness of will or slackening enthusiasm, but intentional sin (with ἑκουσίως in the emphatic position). Hebrews inherits from Judaism the distinction between willful (ἑκουσίως) and inadvertent (ἀκουσίως) sins, the latter frequently falling in the category of cultic impurity.[127] It is with the former that the author is more concerned. Under the old covenant, the high priest offered sacrifices for the unintentional sins of the people, which included sins committed in ignorance (Heb 9:7: ἀγνόημα; cf. 5:2; Herm. *Sim.* 5.7.3).[128] That the author means to rule out the excuse of ignorance on the part of his audience is apparent from his statement that they have already received knowledge of the truth.[129] Deliberate sin constitutes an abuse of the παρρησία described in 10:19–25. (At best, it is a miscalculation comparable to that of Paul's interlocutor in Rom 6:1 who asks, "Are we to continue in sin so that grace may abound?") Although the offense in view does not derive from anomalies in the cultic realm, the author frames it in cultic terms ("there no longer remains any sacrifice for sins") parallel to the expression of vv. 19–22. The posture of the sinner in v. 26 may faintly resemble that of boldness, but is in truth more akin to audacity or insolence.[130]

---

[127] The distinction appears, e.g., in Lev 4:1–5:13; Num 15:22–31; Tob 3:3; Philo, *Cher.* 75; for later discussions, cf. Str-B 1:636–38. On this distinction generally, see Robin C. Cover, "Sin, Sinners (OT)," *ABD* 6:34–36; Goldhahn-Müller, *Die Grenze der Gemeinde*, 96–97; and in Hebrews, Löhr, *Umkehr und Sünde*, 22–68. Philo (*Post.* 48) relativizes the distinction somewhat when he contends that the sacrifices on the Day of Atonement cover intentional as well as unintentional sins.

[128] Cf. Löhr, *Umkehr und Sünde*, 41–44.

[129] His chiding of the audience in 5:11–14 likewise signals his assumption that they have already learned "to distinguish good from evil" and so can be expected to act accordingly.

[130] As this passage falls between vv. 19–25 and 32–39, the author likely envisions boldness as embodied in "holding fast to the confession" in the face of persecution. DeSilva, *Perseverance in Gratitude*, 345–46, compares the stance of Hebrews with that of 4 Maccabees. In 4 Macc 8:12–9:9, the brothers refuse to give in to the king's demands even though their capitulation would be due to their understandable fear of torture, an emotion they overcome out of deference to Torah (8:28; cf. 8:14, 25, for the view that neither God nor the law would condemn them for their weakness); see also the Hasideans in 1 Macc 2:42 who offer themselves in the struggle against Antiochus "voluntarily for

Because deliberate sinners act contrary to what they know to be right and just, their future can be described as fearful. They know the truth and therefore will come to realize that their persistence in sin (ἁμαρτανόντων) leads to destruction, thus the emotional response of fear even then is based on an accurate perception. The polyvalence of φοβερά in v. 27 mirrors that of the English "fearful," which can refer both to the capacity of a thing to induce fear and to the subjective response itself. For the one not covered by Jesus' sacrifice, it is almost redundant to describe the "expectation of judgment" (ἐκδοχὴ κρίσεως) as fearful, since fear is itself an expectation of future harm and the divine judgment of the intentional sinner will be a negative one.[131] A "furious fire" (πυρὸς ζῆλος) will accompany judgment, an image most likely borrowed from Isa 26:11. While most commentators (e.g., Spicq; Attridge; Löhr) recognize the allusion, they fail to note that the LXX speaks of how "jealousy will grip an undisciplined people (λαὸν ἀπαίδευτον) and fire will consume the adversaries." The notion that only those without God's παιδεία are exempt from hardships will reappear in 12:5–11.

With the mention of judgment, the author revisits the topic of death since death is fearful primarily because of the judgment that follows. The a fortiori argument in vv. 28–29 serves the same purpose. A sentence of death was the worst possible punishment for sinners under the old covenant (Deut 17:6; 19:15), but the fate of apostates under the new covenant is even more dire. How much worse is it? Details are lacking as the author leaves the question unanswered, but the readers' imaginations would presumably fill in the blank.

Three participial clauses delineate the frame of mind counted worthy of punishment. "Trampling" (καταπατήσας) the Son of God expresses disdain for the one who will, in a cosmic reversal of fortune, use his enemies as a footstool (1:13; 10:13). Literal trampling (as the verb denotes in LXX Isa 26:6; Mic 7:10; Matt 5:13) is obviously not in view, any more than literal "re-crucifying" is envisioned in 6:6. The metaphor presents in physical terms the attitude of the apostate.[132] "Deeming" or "judging to be" (ἡγησάμενος)

---

the sake of the law" (ἑκουσιαζόμενος τῷ νόμῳ). This hard line contrasts with *T. Zeb.* 1.5–6, where Zebulon's fear of being killed by his brothers excuses his failure to speak up when they sell Joseph into slavery.

[131] Contrast the "expectation" (ἐξεδέχετο) of Abraham in 11:10. The enclitic τις in 10:27 intensifies rather than weakens the phrase (BDF §301[1]).

[132] Moffatt, *Hebrews*, 151, notes that καταπατεῖν ὅρκια is the Homeric formula for breaking an oath (*Il.* 4.157). Persecution of Japanese Christians in the seventeenth century made use of *fumie*, a copper plate engraved with an image of Christ on which suspected Christians were compelled to tread under threat of torture. See Shusaku Endo's historical novel *Silence* (trans. W. Johnston; New York: Taplinger, 1969), which vividly portrays the spiritual struggle of a Portugese priest and the effects of his apostasy on the natives he had converted.

profane the blood of the covenant likewise emphasizes the role of substantive beliefs in shaping behavior which incurs God's wrath. Finally, "insulting" (ἐνυβρίσας) the spirit of grace exacerbates the situation of the apostate since, as Aristotle notes (*Rhet.* 2.5.5), "outraged virtue" (ἀρετή ὑβριζομένη) is a source of fear to the one who has committed the outrage, especially when the offended party has been a benefactor and has the wherewithal to satisfy the claims of justice.[133]

The formula in 10:30 introducing the citations from Deut 32 reinforces the premise of v. 26 that the hypothetical apostate sins in full knowledge of the consequences. This particular circumlocution for God seeks to pre-empt a plea of ignorance as "we know (οἴδαμεν) the one who has spoken" thus in Scripture.[134] recontextualization of statements about divine vengeance and judgment draw attention to the profound repercussions he perceives as contingent upon inclusion in God's people. Just as the sacrifice inaugurating the new covenant is once-for-all, so is the decision to become a party to it unrepeatable and non-reversible. In its original setting, Deut 32:35 ("Vengeance is mine; I will repay") foretells the future yet certain destruction of Israel's enemies. Taken out of this context, however, Hebrews is able to turn it into a warning directed to those on the inside who may be considering defection under duress. Put another way, he casts apostates described in v. 29 in the role of the enemy upon whom the Lord will exact vengeance.[135]

Why he bothers to separate this quotation from the quotation of Deut 32:36 in v. 30b by the conjunctive phrase καὶ πάλιν is not perfectly clear, unless it is to give the impression of a multiplicity of scriptural testimonies in support of his argument.[136] Again, the author has redirected the warning and aimed it at insiders. The language of the MT is unambiguous in stating that God will "vindicate" (יָדִין) Israel in the face of its enemies. In using κρινεῖ the LXX permits the negative meaning intended when Hebrews quotes it. (The negative sense of "passing judgment" is the predominant sense of the Greek term.) The excerpt also leaves off the second clause of Deut 32:36 ("and shall console his

---

[133] Noted also by deSilva, *Perseverance in Gratitude*, 353, who supplements his analysis of 10:26–31 in terms of the conventions of the patron-client relationship with observations on the author's rhetorical appeals to emotion (343–55).

[134] Koester, *Hebrews*, 453.

[135] Jonathan Edwards appropriates this verse from Deut 32 in a similar way when he takes it as the text for his famous sermon "Sinners in the Hands of an Angry God." In the very first line he states that it was directed at "wicked unbelieving Israelites" rather than against nations hostile to Israel. Paul quotes Deut 32:35a in Rom 12:19 in exhorting his readers to refrain from avenging themselves against their enemies so that they may "leave room for the wrath of God."

[136] It is unlikely that he uses the device to direct the reader away from Deut 32:36 to a second text, Ps 135:14, where the identical statement appears.

servants") which, in synonymous parallelism with the first clause, reinforces the positive nuance in the original. By choosing and editing a text about God's κρίσις in this way, the author is able to provide proof from Scripture backing up his warning about the "fearful prospect of judgment" in v. 27.

A weighty declaration in v. 31, with φοβερόν placed first for emphasis, concludes the section on a solemn and disquieting note. Swetnam stands almost alone in alleging that the statement ("To fall into the hands of the living God is a fearful thing") is a positive expression of hope.[137] He notes the positive sense of the quotations from Deut 32 in their original context, the polyvalence of φοβερός, and the frequently positive tenor of the phrase "falling into the hands of," and on this basis claims that the warning passage beginning in v. 26 extends only to v. 30a. With the quotation of Deut 32:36 in v. 30b, the author begins a new section aimed at encouragement. Swetnam's cogent arguments notwithstanding, the sentence must be understood as a warning. To argue for a positive interpretation of v. 30b on the basis of the positive sense of the source text is to ignore the plain fact that in v. 30a the author goes against the sense of his source. Second, the meaning of φοβερόν in v. 31 must be determined by the context. The unequivocally negative connotation of φοβερὰ in v. 27 tilts in favor of reading the adjective in v. 31 as "terrifying." Third, while falling into God's hands is sometimes a cause for hope (2 Sam 24:14; 1 Chron 21:13; Sir 2:18), it is just as often a prelude to punishment (2 Macc 6:26; 7:31; cf. Exod 7:4; Wis 16:15), and "falling" (ἐπεσεῖν) usually carries negative connotations.[138]

The author certainly hopes and appears confident that God's righteous anger is not a pressing threat to his audience and thus not a live source of fear. Emotions such as fear are not abstract constructions but are always embodied or experienced by particular persons in particular settings. Because the audience is not in a position vis-à-vis God such that terror is an appropriate response, by rhetorical means the author can only approximate the conditions necessary for the emotion of fear so that they can experience it vicariously through the hypothetical apostate. Such a strategy serves obvious paraenetic purposes, but vicarious experience of an emotion is not the real thing and calling God "fearful" is not sufficient to evoke the response of fear. Perhaps Hebrews is simply trying, to use a modern idiom, to scare his readers into staying in the church, but it seems just as likely that his use of φοβερόν is an attempt to capture a fundamental and objective quality of God which nevertheless takes on a different aspect depending on the position of the observer. Like the gestaltist's familiar drawing that from one angle resembles a duck and from another resembles a rabbit, the description of the living God as φοβερόν may strike the

---

[137] James Swetnam, "Hebrews 10,30–31: A Suggestion," *Bib* 75 (1994): 388–94.
[138] Ellingworth, *Hebrews*, 543–44.

observer either as fearsome or as awesome.[139] Yes, according to Heb 10:26–31, God is fearful in that he poses a real threat to the sinner, whose proper response is one of fear. The faithful envisioned by the author cannot undergo quite the same experience, but upon considering the scenario of vv. 29–31 they cannot help but feel something akin, in English, to awe. Swetnam's reading is partly right, then, though for the wrong reasons. The Greek allows for a positive nuance in v. 31, but the matter is not a merely linguistic one either here or in 12:28–29, where the positive aspect of this awe surfaces in the affirmation that "our God is a consuming fire."

The Reward of Confidence (Heb 10:35)

The setting envisioned for the exercise of παρρησία in 10:35 is a secular one of persecution, in contrast to the three previous occurrences of the term.[140] That is to say, their παρρησία is to manifest itself vis-à-vis human opposition rather than in a sacred setting in the presence of God. After the audience was "enlightened," suggesting that their conversion to Christianity has been taken as a pretext, they were publicly harassed and suffered the confiscation of their property. They submitted to such abuse with joy because they knew they had "a better and abiding possession" (10:34).[141] "Therefore," the author admonishes them, "do not throw away your παρρησία; it has a great reward. For you need endurance, so that when you have done God's will, you may receive what was promised" (vv. 35–36). By way of transition from the previous section, the author might have quoted Jesus' exhortation of his followers in Matt 10:26–31. Persecutions will come, but they are not to be afraid of their human tormentors.

---

[139] As art historian E. H. Gombrich remarks, "We are compelled to look for what's 'really there,' to see the shape apart from the interpretation, and this, as we soon discover, is not really possible" (*Art and Illusion: A Study in the Psychology of Pictorial Representation* [New York: Pantheon, 1960], 6); cf. also L. Wittgenstein, *Philosophical Investigations* (3rd ed.; trans. G. E. M. Anscombe; New York: Macmillan, 1958), 194–96.

[140] The discussion in 10:26–31, however, anticipates the usage of παρρησία in 10:35 by depicting the non-cultic act of apostasy in cultic terms parallel to its usage in 10:19.

[141] Their disposition, expressed by the verbal form προσεδέξασθε, may also be rendered "accepted" or "welcomed." Althhough they are not cognates, προσδέχομαι and προσδοκάω/προσδοκία cover the same semantic range, including the neutral sense of expectation or anticipation (cf. Luke 21:26; Acts 24:15; 2 Pet 3:12–14). Fear and confidence are regularly described in terms of expectation (προσδοκία) of evil or of good (*SVF* 2.98; 3.386, 388, 391, 463; Aristotle, *Rhet.* 2.5.13; *Eth. nic.* 3.6.2; Philo, *Mut.* 163). Whereas it would be perfectly natural to experience fear when anticipating the despoliation of one's property, the audience is commended because they anticipate it "with joy." Their posture in the face of conditions normally inspiring fear defines their confidence.

"Do not fear those who kill the body but cannot kill the soul; rather, fear the one who can destroy both soul and body in Gehenna" (10:28).

It is interesting to note how the Christian's παρρησία, ordinarily exercised in a setting of worship and prayer, translates into non-cultic behaviors. These behavioral correlates will be considered in detail in the following section. For the moment it is worthwhile simply to point out again the way in which the author appeals to the constancy of his readers' convictions as a support for the affective dimension of their παρρησία. Their confidence in the face of brutal treatment should not be a fleeting feeling. Rather, it should take on the constancy and permanency of the "more lasting" hope underlying it (v. 34). Because confidence "has a great reward" (ἔχει μεγάλην μισθαποδοσίαν), it reveals a trust in the goodness of the one bestowing that reward. To "throw away" (ἀποβάλλω) one's παρρησία reveals precisely the opposite, whether the verb refers to active, deliberate disavowal or to a subtler, more passive erosion of faith and confidence.[142] For Hebrews it makes little difference. The author is trying to help his readers understand the consequences of their actions, or rather inaction, if sluggishness and withdrawal from open association with their colleagues are the problem. By letting go of their "boldness," whether they realize it or not, they show their failure to understand the true magnitude of the Christ event and their unwillingness to appropriate it as a means of counteracting quite reasonable fears of persecution.[143] Why should God continue to give to those who have shown their ingratitude by throwing away the unmerited and unmatchable gift of παρρησία?[144]

It is not possible to do justice to the author's mention of παρρησία in 10:35, however brief, without appreciating the conditions calling for it. The following section therefore deals with 10:32–39 and the importance of standing up to persecution.

Fearlessness in the Face of Earthly Dangers

Fear felt in encountering "worldly" adversity is of a different order from the trepidation experienced in contemplating divine wrath. Insofar as the circumstances giving rise to it are fairly constant, the virtue required to overcome the former is readily recognizable. Agreement on such matters is usually easy to come by even among those who disagree as to how, or whether

---

[142] Ellingworth, *Hebrews*, 550–51. It represents the negative alternative to "holding on" (cf. 3:6: κατάσχωμεν; 4:14: κρατῶμεν; 10:23: κατέχωμεν).

[143] The parallel phrase in Dio Chrysostom (*Or.* 34.39) refers to the citizen's abuse of his rights of free speech through exercising it frivolously (cf. Plato, *Resp.* 8.557B; and Isocrates, *Or.* 7.20; 8.14, where he cites the example dramatists who confuse liberty with license; also 11.40, where he bemoans the παρρησία of poets who vilify the gods).

[144] Cf. Spicq, *Hébreux*, 2:330.

there is even any need, to deflect the latter. "Mundane" fear and supernatural fear are obviously directed at different objects, and one may experience one without being troubled by the other. Barbarians, even with their debased notions of the deity, could nonetheless exhibit extraordinary courage in dire straits. Yet Plutarch and other writers suggest that superstitious fear of the gods and lack of courage more commonly go hand in hand.[145] These concerns are manifest in Hebrews under three separate but related headings: (1) the author's desire to provide encouragement in the face of persecution; (2) his use of Moses as an example of fearless defiance of authority; and (3) his call for the readers to regard their sufferings as a necessary part of their education as God's children.

Withstanding Persecution

In connection with the author's attempt to encourage his readers who may be in danger of "shrinking back" in the face of persecution, three passages are worthy of mention: 10:32–39; 11:32–38; 13:6.

Heb 10:32–39

Although the author's rehearsal of the hardships experienced by the community in 10:32–34 is not as detailed as historians would like, it provides just enough information to discern the general outlines of their response. They need not have done anything at all to provoke the abuse they received. Simply identifying themselves as Christians would likely have sufficed.[146] There is little for the author to commend in this scenario since there is nothing inherently virtuous about being a victim, especially of abuse one does not actively court. In vv. 33b–34a, however, there is an indication of proactive behavior worthy of the author's compliments. Once their fellows have been singled out for harassment, the rest, perhaps a separate cell in the larger local congregation, must decide whether they will stand with them or let them suffer alone for their faith. Silence is easy to rationalize; what is the use, one can hear them asking themselves, of more Christians being publicly beaten and ridiculed? Isn't it wiser to lie low until this latest flare-up of anti-Christian (perhaps also anti-Jewish) bigotry dies

---

[145] Plutarch, *Superst.* 169C, cites the case of the superstitious Jews who would not fight to save Jerusalem because the invasion came on the Sabbath as an example of "cowardly excuse" (δειλίας πρόφασις). See also 165D–E, 168E–169C, for the connection between superstition and lack of courage. ·

[146] Grässer, *Hebräer*, 3:65, correlates the experience of the audience with that of the Christians mentioned by Pliny, Tacitus, and Suetonius who are targeted in this way on account of their *superstitio*; see also deSilva, *Despising Shame*, 148–52. A hostile informant may have denounced the Christians to the local authorities (as occurs in Acts 16:16–24) whose cooperation would have been needed in order to detain them.

down, as they usually do? No, says the author, who commends those who "became partners" (κοινωνοὶ . . . γενηθέντες) with the persecuted. Whatever this phrase means, it almost certainly involves some kind of public acknowledgement of one's own Christian allegiance, as would also showing "compassion" for those in prison (τοῖς δεσμίοις συνεπαθήσατε).[147] It need not refer to any formal opportunity to recant. It may be something so simple as showing up for their worship assemblies (cf. 10:25) where abuse was waiting for them.[148] When the author warns them not to throw away their παρρησία in v. 35, then, he would seem to have in mind, in addition to the theological component, the freedoms of speech and assembly that term connotes in the Greek political sphere.[149]

Physically, socially, economically, and psychologically, the nature of the readers' fears is not difficult to appreciate.[150] Despite the abuse it earns them, the author nevertheless exhorts his readers to act on their confidence and to endure by maintaining their faithful profession of faith. When witnessed in a philosopher like Socrates, such uncompromising behavior can take on the character of a virtue, the moral freedom and integrity of the wise man who stays true to his principles in defiance of tyranny.[151] But the same pose, when struck by a member of a subculture like the Maccabean martyrs in devotion to Torah, can be regarded as irrational and fanatical in the worst way. This kind of obstinacy bewildered many observers, like Pliny in his famous letter to Trajan, and contributed to Christianity's characterization as a superstition, especially since such seemingly masochistic tendencies were seen as the very will of God (Heb 10:36).

To press home his point about the need for boldness and endurance, the author adduces evidence from scripture in vv. 37–39 that he then applies to his readers. The quotation is a composite one taken from the LXX: "For yet a very little while, and the coming one will come and will not delay; but my righteous one will live by faith, and if he shrinks back, my soul finds no pleasure with him" (ἔτι γὰρ μικρὸν ὅσον ὅσον, ὁ ἐρχόμενος ἥξει καὶ οὐ χρονίσει· ὁ δὲ δίκαιός μου ἐκ πίστεως ζήσεται, καὶ ἐὰν ὑποστείληται, οὐκ εὐδοκεῖ ἡ ψυχή μου ἐν αὐτῷ). The source for v. 37a is Isa 26:20, quoted in

---

[147] Though the encouragement and material provision implied by this phrase could conceivably come from non-Christian family members, here (as elsewhere: Heb 13:3; Ign. *Eph.* 1.2; Lucian, *Peregr.* 12–13) it clearly indicates care for fellow believers.

[148] This could be the case even without a formal prohibition of assembly as was promulgated by Claudius with regard to the Jews in Rome (Dio Cassius 60.6).

[149] Cf. Plato, *Gorg.* 461D–E; Demosthenes, *Or.* 9.3; 58.68; 60.26; Polybius 2.38.6; and Peterson, "Zur Bedeutungsgeschichte von Παρρησία." 1:283–84.

[150] Cf. deSilva, *Despising Shame*, 154–64, for the kinds of pressures their hardships entailed.

[151] Schlier, *TDNT* 5:874.

full at *1 Clem*. 50.4 but only excerpted in Hebrews, where only the phrase μικρὸν ὅσον ὅσον appears. This fleeting allusion may be intended to evoke the wider context of Isa 24–27 in which Judah pleads for God to judge the wicked of the earth and the prophet reassures the people that they—but not the wicked—will be raised from the dead (26:19). First, however, they must hide themselves away "for a little while" until God's wrath has fallen on the wicked (vv. 20–21). As that time approaches, there will be cause both for joy at God's vindication and for fear of judgment.

By alluding to Isa 26:20, the author may be acknowledging the strategy of some Christians to avoid conflict by withdrawing for a time from public view in light of the impending eschatological conflagration (Heb 10:25, 30), only to subvert it by adding the testimony of Habakkuk 2:3–4 in Heb 10:37b–38.[152] He takes over the messianic tone of Hab 2:3 and amplifies it by adding to the participle ἐρχόμενος the definite article (ὁ), resulting in the substantive, "the coming one." This brings the author's language into line with the christological vocabulary of other NT writers (cf. Matt 3:11; 11:3; Luke 19:38; John 1:27) and has the effect of reminding his readers of the imminent parousia (1:2; 9:28; 10:25).

More importantly, in 10:38 Hebrews follows the LXX but with one crucial modification. He inverts the clauses of Hab 2:4 and in so doing shifts its point of

---

[152] T. W. Lewis, "'And if he shrinks back . . .' (Heb. 10.38b)," *NTS* 22 (1975–76): 91–93. Lane, *Hebrews*, 2:305–6, and Koester, *Hebrews*, 468, dispute Lewis' contention that the author has in mind withdrawal from worldly affairs, saying that withdrawal from community fellowship is what earns his disapproval. However, these two options are not mutually exclusive. Because the community has been thrust into public view by virtue of its persecution by outsiders, withdrawal from fellowship activities at the same time would be in effect withdrawal from "the world." Hebrews raises the stakes in rejecting this option. Although it may not seem like so momentous a decision, the author suggests that to leave one's fellows in the lurch is tantamount to apostasy. One problem with Lewis' argument not noted by Lane or Koester is the vague description of the position Hebrews is seen to be countering. What, precisely, constitutes a "life-style of withdrawal and concealment" in the situation envisioned in Hebrews? In societies where Christianity is already established to some degree, it is easy to imagine what this might mean: cessation of social welfare efforts aimed at assisting the non-Christian needy; removal of signs indicating the presence of a church building; non-participation in civic affairs where the church normally has a representative; setting up a self-sufficient compound that renders most or all contact with the outside world unnecessary. These seem like unlikely courses in the situation facing Hebrews. After the audience has already been identified as Christian, moreover, they would not be relevant unless the purpose of the harassment is to get them to desist from such activities. Whether they like it or not, their identification as Christians for the purposes of persecution puts them in a public space. The only way to "withdraw" from it is to deny, when questioned, that one is a Christian, even if the denial is quite understandably motivated by the desire to avoid ill treatment.

reference. The textual tradition of this verse is a complicated one.[153] Who is "the righteous one" who "shall live by faith"? In the MT, it refers to the fidelity of the prophet who is told to wait patiently for a vision from the Lord. In 1QpHab VIII, 2–3, it is those members of the community who observe the law and will be delivered by God from "the House of Judgment because of their suffering and because of their faith in the Teacher of Righteousness." In the LXX, it seems to refer to a figure in the vision—perhaps the Chaldean king—who will live through God's own fidelity. Inversion of the two clauses in Hab 2:4 makes ὁ δίκαιός μου the subject of both, and so the one who shrinks back is not "the coming one" but rather "my righteous one." This slight modification has the effect of making his audience the subject of the oracle: those who remain faithful in spite of the suffering involved are "my righteous one[s]," while those who do not are "those who shrink back" (10:39).[154]

This reference to "shrinking back" is significant because it signals the integration of the motif of fear with the author's desire to prevent his readers from apostatizing. The attitude underlying the action expressed by ὑποστέλλω/ὑποστολή in 10:38–39 is one of timidity.[155] In the oracle from Habakkuk quoted in v. 38, God is displeased (οὐκ εὐδοκεῖ) with those who shrink back. This thought corresponds chiastically with the first half of v. 39, where the author carries over the idea of shrinking back with the substantive ὑποστολή while amplifying the element of divine displeasure.[156] Not only do

[153] Detailed discussion may be found in Joseph A. Fitzmyer, "Habakkuk 2:3–4 and the New Testament," in *To Advance the Gospel: New Testament Studies* (New York: Crossroad, 1981), 236–46; also Attridge, *Hebrews*, 301–304.

[154] Paul makes a similar move when he cites a version of Hab 2:4 in explicating the nature of faith (Rom 1:17; Gal 3:11). In Romans, however, it is also possible that "the righteous one" refers to Jesus or that Paul intends a double entendre in which it would refer both to Jesus and to the believer.

[155] Demosthenes, *Or.* 4.51; Isocrates, *Or.* 8.41; Wis 6:7; Acts 20:27; Philo, *Mos.* 1.83; Josephus, *Vita* 215.

[156] As in 10:5–9, the author here selects an OT text concerned with how one pleases God (εὐδοκέω). In the former passage, Ps 40:7–9 expresses Christ's desire to please God (vv. 6, 8: εὐδόκησας) by doing his will (vv. 7, 9). The author alludes to divine displeasure in 10:38 to exhort the audience to persevere and "do the will of God" (10:36). Using very similar language in 13:21, the author prays that God will equip them "to do his will, doing in [them] that which is pleasing (τὸ εὐάρεστον) in his sight." Their compassion for their fellows in prison, taking the form of material provision, no doubt performs such a function in this context, as it may also in 13:16 where they are told to "share what [they] have, for such sacrifices please God" (εὐαρεστεῖται ὁ θεός). No such good deed is mentioned in 11:5 of Enoch, who pleased God (εὐαρεστηκέναι τῷ θεῷ) prior to his translation into heaven. The following verse states that those who would approach God (as opposed to shrinking back?) "must believe that he is, and that he is a rewarder of those who seek him," suggesting that faith has a propositional component without which

those who recoil fail to please God—they are also headed for destruction. Although the reference to destruction need not imply that God is the one who actively destroys since it is not in the form of a divine passive but rather occurs in an elliptical prepositional phrase—"shrinking back" or "timidity" is "for destruction" (εἰς ἀπώλειαν)—the author almost certainly means to keep in the minds of his readers the prospect of eschatological judgment, still fresh from his warnings in 10:26–31.[157] It is counter-intuitive that someone would knowingly or intentionally draw back "for" or "towards" ἀπώλεια. After all, it is presumably in order to avoid physical as well as fiscal devastation (10:32–34) that some are tempted to shrink back from conflict generated in part by their profession of faith. The author must be pointing out the cruel paradox exemplified by those who draw back. By shrinking back in fear from religious persecution and the shame associated with it, they have unwittingly leapt out of the proverbial frying pan into the fire.[158] Thinking they have escaped destruction, they will in fact have run headlong into it.

Members of the wilderness generation in 3:7–4:11 provide the prototype of apostasy by wanting to fall back when it is time to press on to the promised land. Rather than persevere with Moses in the desert to claim God's promise for them, they are all too ready to settle for the false security of Egyptian bondage (Num 20:1–6). They lacked faith and as a consequence were unable to enter God's rest (Heb 3:19; 4:2). Their example finds its obverse in 10:39 in the faithful endurance of the audience who thereby "keep their souls" (εἰς περιποίησιν ψυχῆς). The author chooses his words carefully so as to acknowledge their willingness to be dispossessed in light of God's promise to compensate them with "a better and more abiding possession" (10:34–35).[159] Some versions gloss εἰς περιποίησιν ψυχῆς as "saved" (NIV; NRSV), but this conceals the economic aspect of the term περιποίησις, which frequently means "property" or "possession" (Eph 1:14; 1 Pet 2:9; likewise περιποιεῖσθαι: Thucydides

---

"it is impossible to please him" (ἀδύνατον εὐαρεστῆσαι). Worshipping God "in a pleasing manner" (εὐαρέστως) involves the acknowledgement of such heavenly rewards (12:28).

[157] "Destruction" is elsewhere a conventional way of referring to the final judgment; cf. LXX Job 21:30; Matt 7:13; Phil 1:28; 3:19; 2 Pet 3:7; 2 Clem. 1.7. The image, if not the precise language, recalls the fate of apostates in Heb 6:7–8; 10:26–27.

[158] Coincidentally, this aphorism in its Latin form—de calcaria in carbonarium—is attested in Tertullian (Carn. Chr. 6) in reference to the attempt of Apelles to temper Marcion's radical dualism only to fall under the equally heretical influence of the oracular prophetess Philumena.

[159] Cf. T. S. Eliot, in The Four Quartets ("East Coker," 3.140–141): "In order to possess what you do not possess/You must go by the way of dispossession." Worley, "God's Faithfulness to Promise," 72–73, notes that Abraham willingly chooses to be dispossessed of his homeland in 11:8–10, living in tents in foreign countries rather than relying upon the rights and benefits afforded by citizenship.

1.9.2; Herm. *Sim.* 9.26.2). This link with v. 34 is brought out by Lane's rendering, "culminating in the acquisition of life."[160] To help the audience endure in the face of fearful conditions, Hebrews asks them to alter their ideas about true wealth and, indeed, about the very meaning of life; they need to remember that death now plays a pivotal role in defining life since Jesus "through death destroy[ed] the one who has the power of death" (2:14). Without the hope of something better, their capacity to endure present adversity will vanish.[161] Hebrews thus turns on its head the truism, voiced by Terence (*Haut.* 981) and Cicero (*Att.* 9.10) among others, that "where there's life, there's hope." According to Hebrews, where there is hope (and faith), there is true life.

Heb 11:32–38

In order to relativize even further "worldly" distinctions between life and death and in so doing to encourage his readers to withstand persecution without renouncing their faith, the author introduces a litany of examples from Israelite history in the peroration to chapter eleven. "Time permitting" (ἐπιλείψει ὁ χρόνος), the author would gladly retell—his allusive references presuppose prior knowledge[162]—the stories

> of Gideon, Barak, Samson, Jephthah, David, and of Samuel and the prophets, who through faith conquered kingdoms, administered justice, obtained promises, shut lions' mouths, put out raging fire, escaped the edge of the sword, overcame weakness, became mighty in war, scattered foreign armies. Women received their dead by resurrection. Some were tortured, refusing the offer of release so that they might attain a better resurrection, while others experienced ridicule and scourging, and even chains and imprisonment. They were stoned, sawn in two, killed by the sword; they wandered about in the skins of sheep and goats, destitute, afflicted, tormented—of these the world was not worthy—roaming through deserts and mountains and in caves and holes in the ground (11:32–38).

Earlier in the chapter there have appeared numerous examples in which the heroes of faith endure trying circumstances which pose serious obstacles to the fulfillment of God's promises. In these verses the author fixes on dangers most closely resembling those facing his audience at the end of the preceding chapter,

---

[160] Lane, *Hebrews*, 2:274; cf. Buchanan, *Hebrews*, 93: "acquisition of a soul."
[161] Moffatt, *Hebrews*, 156, quoting Maximus of Tyre, *Diss.* 33.
[162] These biblical allusions receive detailed treatment from Bruce, *Hebrews*, 329–42; Braun, *Hebräer*, 390–400; and Lane, *Hebrews*, 2:382–92.

though they have not yet had their own blood shed (12:4) in the course of resistance. Their own story is but the latest chapter in the long story of faith.

Memory in this instance pre-empts the emotion of fear. It doesn't take a coward to be afraid of being thrown to the lions, placed in a furnace, tortured, scourged, imprisoned, or sliced in half with a saw. Threats of such treatment, however, should not take the faithful by surprise. Familiarity with these and other similar narratives from history fosters the necessary resolve to stifle, or at least to survive, one's visceral response to the prospect of abuse. Having already advised them to recall their own persecution in the past to help them remain steadfast in the present and to "anticipate with joy" economic privation (10:32–34), the author now takes a longer view, citing well-known cases from the ancient past to illustrate the persistent incommensurability between righteousness and the prevailing spirit of the age.[163] Since unexpectedness magnifies the emotional disturbance caused by dreadful occurrences, dwelling ahead of time upon such precedents as appear in 11:32–38 blunts the impact when disaster strikes.[164] Likewise, if it appears as if they may pass away without first receiving "what was promised," this should not cause the audience to faint since that fate befell the heroes and heroines of faith (11:39). And since courage does not require that one endure great evils unless the object is exceedingly good (καλός: Aristotle, *Eth. eud.* 3.1.14, 32), the author reminds the audience that a "better" reward awaits them when they finish their race. Hebrews thus points both backward and forward in time to prepare the believer for the experience of fear.

The surest way to forestall the onset of fear and its harmful effects is to have in place the right set of beliefs as a guide for one's emotions. Trust in God to provide "something better" (11:40) is in this respect the most valuable resource, especially to those whose hardships include the suffering of death. This is most apparent in the case of the Maccabean martyrs to which v. 35b refers.[165] They refuse to accept release precisely in order that (ἵνα) they might rise again to a better life. In their refusal to compromise with Antiochus IV

---

[163] Hence their characterization as "strangers and foreigners on the earth" in 11:13–16. Plato holds a similar idea in his description of the righteous man who "does not wish to seem but to be good" (*Resp.* 2.361B). In order to determine whether he acts justly for the sake of δικαιοσύνη or for the sake of the benefits that a reputation for justness brings, one must "deprive him of the seeming." Though in reality above reproach, he must become of ill repute so that he may be tested by experiencing its consequences. The inevitable result is that he "will have to endure the whip, the rack, chains, the branding iron in his eyes, and at last, after every extreme form of suffering, he will be crucified" (2.361E).

[164] This is a Stoic strategy endorsed by Chrysippus (*SVF* 3.417, 482), Cicero (*Tusc.* 3.14.29–16.35), and Epictetus (*Ench.* 20–22).

[165] DeSilva, *Despising Shame*, 195–202, convincingly makes the case for knowledge of this tradition as it is preserved in 2 Macc 6:18–7:42 and 4 Macc 5–18.

Epiphanes and their willingness to undergo gruesome tortures on the way to their deaths, Eleazar, the seven brothers, and their mother all show the depth of their conviction that death is not to be feared since it only marks a transition to a new and better mode of existence for the faithful. As the second brother says to his tormenters, "You dismiss us from this present life, but the king of the universe will raise us up to an eternal renewal of life, since we have died for the sake of his laws" (2 Macc 7:9; cf. 7:14, 23, 29, 36).[166] Like Epicurus, they are able to say, "Death is nothing to us," though not because they believe that all consciousness dissolves along with the body when life ceases. Believing that God is able to suspend or reverse the power of death, they regard their present sufferings "as nothing" (2 Macc 7:12). Hebrews hopes that his readers' "rational piety," in the idiom of 4 Maccabees, will master their emotions and keep them from denying their faith.

Heb 13:6

Shifts in style, tone, and form mark the transition from the first twelve chapters of Hebrews and the last, and lead many scholars to doubt that chapter thirteen is a part of the original document.[167] Against this view that it is a secondary epistolary addition to the homily or treatise that concludes with the end of chapter twelve, the consensus today is that chapter thirteen, on the basis of thematic echoes with the other sections, was written by the same person to the same audience and on the same occasion as the rest of the epistle.[168]

Subdividing it into smaller units, most commentators place v. 6 at the end of the short section opening the chapter. With the exception of v. 4, each of the admonitions recalls some aspect of the persecution undergone by the community and seeks to shape their response to this experience, which may occur again, by means of quite traditional paraenesis.[169] The call to continue in brotherly love

---

[166] In Heb 11:35a, the experience of the women who have "received their dead by resurrection" prefigures the better resurrection mentioned in the second half of the verse. The biblical allusion is to the widow of Zarephath of Sidon, whose son is revived by Elijah (1 Kgs 17:17–24), and to the Shunnamite woman, whose son is raised in a similar fashion by Elisha (2 Kgs 4:17–37). Like Lazarus in John 11, the two sons presumably again die a natural death at a later time and so these miracles are properly understood as instances of resuscitation rather than the full-fledged resurrection hoped for by Hebrews.

[167] This thesis, still followed by Buchanan, *Hebrews*, 267–68, is argued most forcefully by Wilhelm Wrede, *Das literarische Rätsel des Hebräerbriefes* (FRLANT 8; Göttingen: Vandenhoeck & Ruprecht, 1906), esp. 39–73.

[168] Representing this view are C. Spicq, "L'authenticité du chapitre XIII de l'Épître aux Hébreux," ConBNT 11 (1947): 226–36; and Floyd V. Filson, *"Yesterday": A Study of Hebrews in the Light of Chapter 13* (SBT 4; London: SCM, 1967).

[169] The presence of the exhortation to marital fidelity in v. 4 is often attributed to its customary pairing with the topic of greed in Hellenistic moral discourse (Epictetus, *Diatr.*

(v. 1) reiterates the importance of solidarity at a time when external pressures threaten to overwhelm the group. Christianity's rapid geographical expansion, aided by the empire's well-kept system of highways, depended on the hospitality extended to itinerant missionaries by local house churches (as reflected in Rom 12:13; 16:1–2; 1 Cor 16:5–11; Philem 22; 1 Pet 4:9; 3 John 5–8; *Did.* 11:1–6). Worries about infiltration or simply drawing attention to themselves by welcoming strangers may have caused the readers to abandon this practice (v. 2). The reminder of those in prison and those who have been ill-treated (v. 3) repeats in condensed form the concerns of 10:32–34 and reinforces the element of empathy; they are to remember the prisoners "as though imprisoned with them" (ὡς συνδεδεμένοι), and those harassed "as though [suffering] in the body" (ὡς καὶ αὐτοὶ ὄντες ἐν σώματι), just as Jesus voluntarily endured hardships in his priestly service to humans. To be "free from love of money" (ἀφιλάργυρος) in v. 5 makes it easier to "be contented with what [they] have" and to "anticipate with joy" the plundering of their possessions (cf. 10:34). The scriptural support—"I will never fail you nor will I forsake you"—taken from Gen 28:15 or Deut 31:6, 8, or from some other text in a version not extant, forces the readers to decide whether they will trust in their own ability to store up wealth[170] or in the God who has provided "something better" (11:40; cf. 10:34–36).

Whatever its literary source, the assurance of God's continual presence in v. 5 provides the basis for the Christian's confident (θαρροῦντας) declaration in v. 6, " The Lord is my helper; I will not be afraid—what will a man do to me?"

3.7.21; *T. Jud.* 18.2; *T. Levi* 14.6; Philo, *Post.* 116; *Abr.* 133–134; Eph 5:3; Lucian, *Nigr.* 16). Koester, *Hebrews*, 565, suggests other reasons for the unexpected appearance of these remarks about sexual morality in Hebrews more closely connected with the situation facing the audience. Hospitality, which they are to continue in spite of the financial burden in may pose (13:2), involves bringing strangers into the home. This could either give rise to temptation or provide fodder for slanderers ready to defame the Christians should they not otherwise observe the strictest standards of propriety. Imprisonment of a spouse (13:3) would leave the other spouse bereft of conjugal companionship, again leaving room for temptation or, if the free partner is the wife, making it easier for an unscrupulous male to take advantage of a woman left alone. Economic privation may also have induced some women to trade sexual favors for monetary aid. Should such exchanges take place between community members, the scandal would confirm the worst suspicions of outsiders about this exclusive sect. The directive to "let marriage be highly esteemed among all, and let the marriage bed be undefiled," then, is intended for both sexes.

[170] Perhaps as part of a strategy for buying off their attackers, who are extorting money from church members who want to be left alone. Although the practice was prohibited by the *Lex Iulia de repetundis*, Felix leaves Paul in prison for two years in Acts 24:26 because he hopes he will try to buy his freedom (cf. Jospehus, *B.J.* 2.273–276; *Ant.* 20.215).

This statement reproduces verbatim LXX Ps 117:6, which in turn voices the same sentiment as LXX Ps 55:4, 11, and the language of many other passages from the Greek Psalter. Early Christian writers quote or allude to this psalm on several occasions but only Hebrews borrows the motif of God-given courage in the face of mortal enemies.[171] In the Greek version the psalmist repeats four times the acclamation that "the Lord is good" in the verses preceding v. 6. The rest of the psalm praises God for delivering the speaker from death (vv. 17–18) at the hand of his enemies, as does also Ps 22, quoted in Hebrews at 2:12. While the audience does not face the same military crisis as the psalmist, they nevertheless need to recognize the same hierarchy (God is superior to humans), draw from it the logical conclusion (following the reasoning of Paul in Rom 8:31: "If God is for us, who can be against us?"), and allow this conviction to shape their response on the level of the emotions.[172]

The author's invocation of "the Lord" as his "help" (βοηθός) picks up his earlier depiction of Christ's priesthood as one that helps (2:18; 4:16) the individual to overcome fear of death and subsequent judgment, where Jesus provides the solution to the problem of sin. A different kind of help is needed in 13:5–6. Hebrews applies κύριος to both God and Jesus. If he understands the psalm in its original setting, God is the "Lord" who will personally be with the people. If "Lord" here refers to Jesus (as in 2:3; 7:14; 13:20), then the conjoining of the psalm in 13:6 with the quotation in the preceding verse portrays God sending Jesus as a helper of the persecuted faithful.[173] The audience could with reason reply that God's help is of slight value since it has not always protected them in the past nor did it save their leaders, if 13:7 in fact refers to their martyrdom.[174] In chapter twelve, the author takes up this misunderstanding and again urges them to remain steadfast in times of trouble.

---

[171] Appendix IV (*Loci Citati vel Allegati*) of NA[27] lists several NT references to LXX Ps 117: v. 22=Matt 21:42; Mark 12:10; Luke 20:17; Acts 4:11; 1 Pet 2:7; v. 23=Matt 21:42; Mark 12:11; v. 25–26=Matt 21:9; 23:39; Mark 11:9; Luke 13:35; 19:38; John 12:13.

[172] As Attridge, *Hebrews*, 389 n. 82, notes, "the motif of fearlessness inspired by the protection of the Lord, and its grounding in the appropriate fear of the Lord are commonplaces in the Psalms." He cites 3:6; 23:4; 27:1–3; 46:2; 49:5.

[173] *1 Clem.* 36.1 speaks of Jesus as helper, while 59.3 refers to God in this way.

[174] So Moffatt, *Hebrews*, 230–31; Spicq, *Hébreux*, 2:421; and Westcott, *Hebrews*, 434. That they need to "remember" the leaders suggests that they are no longer present and thus probably no longer alive. "Outcome" (ἔκβασις) can be a euphemism for death, as in Wis 2:17 where the ungodly plan to ambush the righteous man and mock his trust in God behind his back: "Let us see if his words are true, and let us test what will happen at the end of his life. For if the righteous man is God's son, he will help him and deliver him from the hand of his enemies. Let us test him with insult and torture, so that we may know his meekness and make trial of his patience. Let us condemn him to a shameful death, for, according to his own claims, he will be protected" (vv. 17–20).

Defiance of Human Authorities: Moses' Fearlessness (Heb 11:23–28)

Closely related to those texts in which the Christian ideal of fearlessness manifests itself in the willingness and ability to withstand persecution is the example of Moses in Heb 11:23–28. In this passage the author accentuates the active defiance of earthly authority in Moses' faithful response to God. Whereas many of the hardships mentioned in Hebrews, especially that of the readers themselves, come uninvited by any particular action on the part of the ones suffering, Moses faces a series of decisions in which he could either take the path of least resistance or stand up to Egyptian rulers and risk incurring their wrath. The author's compositional technique in these verses reinforces the paraenesis of 10:32–39 and calls attention to the way in which acquiescence to the emotion of fear can all too easily take one into the realm of apostasy.

Mary Rose D'Angelo looks only at vv. 23–27 in forming her picture of "Saint Moses the Martyr" in Hebrews.[175] If Moses is the focus, however, it is not clear why v. 28 should be excluded since he is the subject, though unnamed, of this verse referring to the first Passover as well. The description of the exodus in v. 29 along with vv. 30–31 might also be treated as part of the same pericope since they deal with the generations of Israelites who left Egypt under Moses and reached Jericho under Joshua.[176] For the moment, vv. 23–28 will serve as the focus since this block of text explicitly concerns Moses and the quality of the faith by which he defied authority.[177]

Small children make few appearances in chapter eleven because they do not generally exhibit the type of faith the author wants to commend. Baby Moses in v. 23 is the apparent exception that proves the rule. His name appears after the anaphoric πίστει, and Μωϋσῆς is the grammatical subject of the first independent clause. Moses appears frequently in Jewish example lists but his parents do not.[178] Hebrews plays to Jewish expectations by using an episode

---

[175] Mary Rose D'Angelo, *Moses in the Letter to the Hebrews* (SBLDS 42; Missoula, Mont.: Scholars Press, 1979), 17–64. On the basis of external evidence and the author's selection of OT texts, she says that v. 28 and what follows belong to another formal unit (27). With respect to external evidence, she cites only John Chrysostom as an ancient commentator who divides the text between v. 27 and v. 28.

[176] Many commentators (e.g., Buchanan, Hegermann, Weiss, Attridge, Koester) take vv. 23–31 as a single unit. Since the males who had come out of Egypt all died in the wilderness "not having listened to the voice of the Lord" (Josh 5:6–7) and were not among those involved in the conquest of Jericho, one might also make the division after v. 29.

[177] In favor of so dividing the text, one might also point to the *inclusio* formed by the two slaughters in vv. 23 and 28. The threat is to Hebrew children in v. 23, while in v. 28, all first-born children of the Egyptians are killed just prior to the exodus. The poetic justice of this reversal delights the author of the Wisdom of Solomon (18:5–8)

[178] Cf. Eisenbaum, *The Jewish Heroes of Christian History*, 167.

from Moses' life in a hortatory context, but by his use of the passive voice (ἐκρύβη) the author is able to introduce untraditional material in support of the moral-theological point he wants to make. The opening vignette in this section is not about the faith of Moses but about that of his parents.

Moses is hid for three months after his birth "by his parents, because they saw that the child was excellent (ἀστεῖον), and they were not afraid of the decree of the king," who wanted to curtail the growth of the male Israelite population (Exod 1:8–22). The crucial detail that they had no fear is not present in the MT or the LXX of Exod 2:2. Josephus represents a haggadic amplification in a slightly different direction. Moses' father Amram, "fearful" (ὡς δεδιώς) for his nation's survival (*Ant.* 2.210), has a dream in which God foretells the birth of a deliverer. After he tells his pregnant wife Jochebed of the prediction, their fear (δέος) grows even stronger (217).[179] They conceal the infant for three months and then Amram, fearing (δείσας) the king's wrath should they be found out (219), sets Moses afloat on the Nile under Miriam's watch. It is possible to view the father's actions in a cynical light as motivated by an instinct for self-preservation and the thought that abandoning the child would constitute the lesser of two evils since their detection by Pharaoh would mean certain death for both parent and child.[180] Josephus, however, sees their decision as an act of faith that God would find a way of protecting Moses and hence of fulfilling the prediction that the Israelites would be redeemed from slavery (219–23).

Perhaps as a function of the narrative brevity required in the composition of an example list, Hebrews, unlike Josephus and Pseudo-Philo (*L.A.B.* 9), does not elaborate here on the parents' trust in God's fidelity in the face of daunting obstacles. Instead, the author's bare report stresses only their fearless refusal to obey the king. The unexpected appearance of this motif is due solely to the author, who has likely translated the midwives' fear of God in LXX Exod 1:17, 21, into the ethical correlative of courage on the part of Moses' parents. Because of the exceptional risk involved, they must have based their course of action on some perception of great value or else moral philosophers, as well as ordinary citizens, would have considered them foolhardy. Amram and Jochebed "saw that the child was ἀστεῖον." To render the adjective "beautiful" (RSV; NRSV; cf. Spicq: *joli*; Buchanan: "attractive;" Lane: "uncommonly striking;" Weiss:

---

[179] Their fear is mixed with joy at the greatness held in store for Moses, and their "anxiousness" (εὐλαβεῖς) is a sign of prudent precaution taken lest God's plan for the child and for Israel be thwarted.

[180] This is essentially the view of Philo (*Mos.* 1.10). Although they resist the king's order for as long as possible (1.9), they abandon him in the fear (φοβηθέντες) that their efforts to save the baby would in the end cause themselves to perish as well. Philo's portrayal of the parents emphasizes their guilt over exposing Moses and so consigning him to the same fate as the rest of the Hebrew infants, thus it lacks completely the element of trust in God's providence.

wohlgestaltet) attributes to Moses' parents superficial and misguided priorities which are incompatible with the exercise of true virtue (Aristotle, *Eth. nic.* 3.8.16). Testimonies to Moses' beauty as a baby notwithstanding (Jospehus, *Ant.* 2.225, 230–32; Philo, *Mos.* 1.9), it is highly unlikely that Hebrews means to hold up for emulation their pride as new parents. Parents love their ugly children, too, so much so that they often seem unaware of their ugliness and are equally as willing to risk their lives for their sake as are the parents of attractive children. Given the emphasis on "the unseen" in definition of faith (11:1), physical beauty would seem an odd motivation for exemplary behavior. D'Angelo, who takes little notice of the parents' fearlessness since her focus is on Moses, is correct to understand ἀστεῖον in Hebrews, as also in Acts 7:20 in reference to Moses (ἀστεῖος τῷ θεῷ), as "signed by God's predilection."[181] His parents' faith consists in a fearlessness rooted in discernment of the divine will and is witnessed in their defiance of the king.

When Moses comes of age in vv. 24–26, he opposes human authority out of deference to God, not in the clandestine manner of his parents but by renouncing his status as the son of Pharaoh's daughter and, by implication, as Pharaoh's heir.[182] The OT does not record any formal act of disassociation nor do the other accounts of Moses' early adulthood. Other authors relate stories of plots concocted by envious Egyptians to discredit him before Pharaoh and thereby portray Moses as reacting only when his hand is forced (Philo, *Mos.* 1.46; Josephus, *Ant.* 2.254–257). Although in vv. 24–26 (and most likely v. 27 as well) Hebrews presupposes but does not rehearse the general story line of Exod 2:11–15 leading up to Moses' flight to Midian, the author presents the entire drama as the result of his freely formed judgments and conscious choices.[183]

---

[181] D'Angelo, *Moses in the Letter to the Hebrews*, 39. Like Bruce, she uses the slightly archaic "goodly" in order to retain the multivalence of both ἀστεῖον and טוב in the LXX and MT of Exod 2:2 that gave rise to much speculation, especially in rabbinic sources, about what Amram and Jochebed saw in their child. The loose rendering, "no ordinary child" (NIV), is in this case an apt equivalent.

[182] The biblical text does not identify the daughter by name. Josephus calls her Thermuthis (*Ant.* 2.224; *Jub.* 47.5 uses the variant form Tharmuth). Artapanus gives her the name Merris (cf. Eusebius, *Praep. ev.* 9.27.3). Hebrews refers to her only by her relation to the king. In the detail that she is Pharaoh's only child who is herself without a child to whom she might pass "the magnificent inheritance of her father's kingdom" (*Mos.* 1.13), Philo supplies information about the magnitude of the wealth that is within Moses' grasp. He also expands upon the daughter's great joy in receiving a son, albeit in an unusual way, and the great lengths to which she goes in protecting Moses and passing him off as her biological child (1.14–17), thus heightening the element of insult to the king's daughter that would have been perceived upon the repudiation of his princely status.

[183] It is uncertain, however, that Hebrews envisions a legal course of action taken by Moses to relinquish his rights as son, *contra* J. Feather, "The Princess Who Rescued

First, he refuses (ἠρνήσατο) to be called the son of Pharaoh's daughter.[184] Second, he "choos[es] (ἑλόμενος)[185] to suffer abuse together with (συγκακουχεῖσθαι) the people of God rather than enjoy the short-lived (πρόσκαιρον) pleasures of sin." Moses' devaluation of fleeting sensations would earn the approval of Epicurus, but his preference for ill-treatment would bewilder most Greeks and Romans, even if it is out of compassion for his brothers (cf. LXX Exod 2:11). But in exchange for eternal salvation—should such a state exist—this choice makes very good sense (cf. Heb 5:9; 9:12, 15; 13:20).[186] Finally, he reasons that "reproach endured for Christ (τὸν ὀνειδισμὸν τοῦ Χριστοῦ) is greater wealth than Egypt's treasures, for he was watching for the reward." As Pharaoh's presumptive heir accustomed to a life of ease, Moses' voluntary forfeiture of his inheritance could easily have led to acute anxiety over the material privation consequent upon his decision. Hebrews reports no such fears as would belie his recognition of true wealth as coming from God.

Only one verb in the indicative (ἠρνήσατο) appears from v. 24 up to the final clause of v. 26, implying that the intervening participial clauses modify and elucidate Moses' renunciation of his Egyptian inheritance. Adoption by the daughter would have been necessary to make him the king's heir, as the extant Jewish sources clearly assume. Hebrews, like Philo and Josephus, is probably ignorant of thirteenth-century Egyptian adoption practices. Insofar as the author contemplates the ramifications of Moses' decision, contemporary customs most likely provide the basic categories by which he understands its significance. One of these is the Roman custom wherein adoption abrogates the adoptee's prior

---

Moses: Who Was She? With a Note on Heb. XI.24–26," *ExpTim* 43 (1931–32): 423–25. When would a specifically legal renunciation have taken place? If it is prior to his murder of the Egyptian, it is doubtful that he could have remained in the oversight capacity implied by the narrative. Had he renounced his status after fleeing Egypt to escape punishment, such a proclamation would surely have been unnecessary.

[184] The verb ἀρνέομαι appears frequently in the NT to denote denial (of Christ: Matt 10:32–33; 26:70, 72; Luke 12:8–9; John 13:38; Acts 3:13–14; 2 Tim 2:12; Jude 4). Second-century writers employ it almost as a technical term to describe the improper response to persecution designed to elicit such denials (esp. Herm. *Vis.* 2.2.7–8; *Sim.* 9.26.3–8; *Diogn.* 7.7; 2 *Clem.* 3.1). The author may thus be contrasting Moses' action with the potential apostasy of his readers who must decide whether to acknowledge or to disavow their allegiance to Christ.

[185] As D'Angelo notes, the use of this aorist participial form of αἱρέω situates the verse within the realm of Hellenistic Jewish moral discourse (*Moses in the Letter to the Hebrews*, 28). Her observation accords with the argument of H. Riesenfeld against Feather that ἠρνήσατο in the previous verse denotes a moral rather than a legal decision (cf. "The Meaning of the Verb ἀρνεῖσθαι," ConBNT 11 (1947): 218.

[186] Likewise, on the "lasting" (μένουσαν) nature of the benefits had by the faithful, see 10:34; 12:27; 13:14; and Thompson, "'That Which Abides,'" passim.

status in his or her biological family.[187] Subsequent *emancipatio* from the adoptive family, for whatever reason, likewise entailed the relinquishing of the privileges had in that family as well.[188] The decision facing Moses therefore determined his true sonship, with all the rights and responsibilities pertaining thereto. The audience, though some are unaware of it, faces the same decision, as the author later explains in 12:1–13. Not "to share ill-treatment together with the people of God," then, is a sin, of omission rather than of commission, and as such is tantamount to apostasy.[189] Continually fluctuating between rival families as fortunes change is not an option for those with faith (cf. Jas 1:2–8).

Hebrews does not spell out the events precipitating his break with Pharaoh's household. A few manuscripts (D* 1827 it[d] vg[ms]) fill out the narrative after v. 23, adding that "by faith, when he had grown up, Moses killed the Egyptian when he saw the humiliation of his brothers." This variant certainly deserves attention by the text-critical rule stating that the harder reading is to be preferred (*difficilior lectio potior*), since it is difficult to square the author's exhortation of his readers to endure suffering willingly in solidarity with their fellow Christians with praise for Moses' "murder by faith," even if it is justifiable homicide (as described in Exod 2:11–12; Acts 7:24; Philo, *Mos.* 1.44).[190] External criteria as well as considerations of context and coherence nevertheless trump the criterion of difficulty in this instance.

Manuscripts containing the scribal insertion after v. 23 seem to regard the entire section beginning with the added material and continuing to the end of v. 27 as referring to the episode in Exod 2:11–15 and expanding on Moses' motivations for acting as he did. Many scholars, however, wonder about the specific allusion contained in v. 27. Is the departure from Egypt a reference to his flight to Midian after his murder of the harsh taskmaster or does it refer to the exodus in Exod 12–14?[191] In LXX Exod 2:14–15, Moses becomes afraid (ἐφοβήθη) when he learns that his crime has been discovered, and he runs away when Pharaoh hears the news and seeks to kill him.[192] This creates an obvious

---

[187] Noted in passing by D'Angelo, *Moses in the Letter to the Hebrews*, 43.

[188] Cf. Adolf Berger et al., "Adoption, Roman," *OCD* 13.

[189] Cf. deSilva, *Despising Shame*, 193.

[190] Brevard S. Childs lists Augustine (*Faust.* 22.70) and a number of other exegetes who find fault with Moses over the murder, (*The Book of Exodus* [OTL; Philadelphia: Westminster, 1974], 41–42).

[191] Moffatt, *Hebrews*, 181–82; and Braun, *Hebräer*, 382, associate it with the flight to Midian, as do all patristic commentators. Westcott, *Hebrews*, 373; and Buchanan, *Hebrews*, 198, associate it with the exodus. For references to ancient, medieval, and early modern commentators on both sides of the question, see Spicq, *Hébreux*, 2:359; and Koester, *Hebrews*, 503.

[192] Philo (*Mos.* 1.47) deftly passes over Moses' decision-making process and simply says that he "retired" (ὑπανεχώρησεν) to Arabia while his enemies were plotting against him. He subsequently describes Moses as an aspiring Stoic spending his time in the

problem if one sees the earlier incident as the background since Hebrews states flatly that Moses left Egypt "unafraid of the king's anger" (μὴ φοβηθεὶς τὸν θυμὸν τοῦ βασιλέως). On the other hand, if v. 27 refers to the exodus of the people after the final plague, there is a chronological jumble when v. 28 returns to the eve of the Passover which takes place prior to their passage through the Red Sea (Ex 12:1–28). The comment on Moses' fearlessness, moreover, would appear to be superfluous if the exodus is in view; there was very little need for fear on that occasion since, after the tenth plague which resulted in the death of the Egyptians' firstborn, the pharaoh and his subjects were all too eager to see the Israelites go (Exod 12:31–33).[193]

A number of commentators see in v. 27 a general reference to the whole sequence of events in Moses' early life up to and including the exodus, especially his encounters with the king and the ensuing departures.[194] But the following mention of Passover and exodus in vv. 28–29 seriously militates against this hypothesis: why, if v. 27 is a summary, would the author immediately go back and take up these two episodes for special treatment?

On the whole, the arguments strongly favor the flight to Midian as the intended allusion. Hebrews undoubtedly knows what Exod 2:14 says and must be aware that his epitome in 11:27 appears to conflict with the biblical account.[195] The author does not readily contradict the Scriptures, so it must be asked how he understands his use of Moses as an example of fearless faith to be a legitimate interpretation of the text. Even if it receives more earnest attention from previous generations of exegetes, the question is not the private concern of

---

wilderness studying philosophy and endeavoring to bring his conduct into conformity with "nature's right reason" (1.48), perhaps in a literary attempt to rehabilitate the biblical Moses after his cowardly behavior when faced with danger. In *Alleg. Interp.* 3.11–14, Philo also eliminates the mention of fear and characterizes Moses' departure as a temporary withdrawal for the purpose of forming the proper judgments whereby he might master his passions and then return to contend with Pharaoh (cf. the similar portrayal of A. S. Peake, *Heroes and Martyrs of Faith* [London: Hodder and Stoughton, n.d.], 123, who believes Moses may have been tempted to lead a slave revolt rather than wait on God and therefore required "the discipline of inaction"). Artapanus (Eusebius, *Praep. ev.* 9.27.18–19) also leaves out Moses' fear, as does Josephus (*Ant.* 2.256–257), who turns his flight into a show of endurance (καρτερία) by the addition of the detail that he set out without any provisions.

[193] Cf. Bruce, *Hebrews*, 322–23.

[194] Spicq, *Hébreux*, 2:359; deSilva, *Perseverance in Gratitude*, 412; Koester, *Hebrews*, 503–4; cf. D'Angelo, *Moses in the Letter to the Hebrews*: This sequence of events constitutes "a manifold event with a single meaning," and "while it is virtually certain that 11.27 refers to Ex. 2.14, that does not exclude a reference to Exodus 3 and 10–14 under the same allusion" (59, 62).

[195] The apparent contradiction is not due simply to reliance on an idiosyncratic LXX translation. The MT also says that Moses was afraid (וַיִּרָא).

those committed to preserving the Bible's internal consistency. It sits at the heart of the author's view of the history of Israel, of which Moses is a part and to which the OT is the primary witness, as a kind of *praeparatio evangelica*. One answer is to deny that the author is trying to be faithful to the text; he simply alters the story so that it supports his paraenetic program. A variation on this approach is that of de Wette, who sees no need to counter charges of intentional contradiction because he thinks the author simply forgot that the crucial detail—that Moses experienced fear—appeared in the biblical account.[196] These solutions are inadequate since they ignore his tendency to bend over backwards in order to maintain the integrity of the OT text when Christian beliefs and practices seem to call it into question.[197] One might also speculate that the author is relying on a corrupt LXX manuscript in which οὐκ is interpolated before ἐφοβήθη in Exod 2:14 (reading δέ as adversative), hence he sees no inconsistency; but this is pure conjecture unsupported by any hard evidence.

Attempts to reconcile Hebrews with Exodus typically have the author of the epistle detecting seams in the biblical account and basing his portrait of the courageous Moses on certain silences and ambiguities in the text. The murder and the flight to Midian were firmly entrenched in the tradition, making it difficult if not impossible for Hebrews to ignore it completely in telling even a radically abbreviated version of Moses' story. It would not have been possible to say that "by faith Moses remained in Egypt and there withstood the king's wrath" because everyone knew this to be untrue. By flying "from before the face of the king," Moses made himself less attractive to any writer wanting to use him as an exemplar of fearless faith. Hebrews nonetheless chooses this very episode for precisely this purpose. Upon reading the Exodus narrative, the most natural inference to make is that Moses in 2:14 is afraid that the king will punish him for killing the Egyptian, thus one would expect to hear that Moses left in fear of the king's anger instead of what one finds in Heb 11:27. But Exodus does not explicitly name the cause of Moses' fear; it only says that he was afraid. Arguing from silence, Hebrews may be giving Moses the benefit of the doubt and acquitting him of charges of tyrannophobia due to the fact that the text nowhere unambiguously states that he was afraid of the king's anger when he departed.[198]

---

[196] W. M. L. de Wette, *Kurzgefasstes exegetisches Handbuch zum Neuen Testament* (2nd ed.; 11 vols.; Leipzig: Weidmann, 1846–64), 9:234.

[197] *Contra* Childs, *Exodus*, 37.

[198] The author employs a similar interpretive strategy in 7:3: he can infer that Melchizedek is "without father, without mother, without genealogy, having neither beginning of days nor end of life, but resembling the son of God, he continues a priest forever," because Scripture nowhere records a genealogy, mentions his birth or death, or temporally circumscribes his priesthood. For use of the principle *quod non in thora, non in mundo*, see F. Schröger, *Der Verfasser des Hebräerbriefes als Schriftausleger*

Such creative exegesis has been criticized as "artificial" or "special pleading," and so it may be—on the author's part of the author of Hebrews, that is.[199] But this criticism seems to confuse or combine shortcomings as an interpreter of Exod 2:14 with the shortcomings of later exegetes trying to understand how Hebrews is interpreting the OT. It is not incumbent on the exegete to demonstrate the validity of an author's theological appropriation of a given narrative if the aim is simply to understand that appropriation according to the sense of that author's text. One is a theological or a hermeneutical task, while the other is more narrowly historical. Whatever the weaknesses of those interpretations seeking to reconcile Heb 11:27 with Exod 2:14, they have the merit of taking seriously the two things that are absolutely certain: that the author of Hebrews regards Moses' flight from Egypt as an act of faith, and that he finds something in the story indicating a posture of fearlessness. It is possible, though not likely, that Hebrews is motivated in his selection and editing of the story primarily by a desire to clean up Moses' image. This seems improbable because the author's aims in chapter eleven are hortatory, and presumably there are plenty of other incidents in Moses' life that would foster these aims perfectly well. The rehabilitation of Moses, whose flight might be seen as a sign of cowardice, is therefore of secondary importance if it is in the author's mind at all.

Hebrews selects this specific episode because he sees something in it to commend to his audience. What does he see, and how does it fit into his paraenetic purposes? In v. 27, the author appears to be continuing in the same vein as in vv. 24–26 by elaborating on Moses' embrace of his true sonship. Wickham sees "Egypt" as a kind of synecdoche for the royal palace from which Moses went out (LXX: ἐξῆλθεν) to join his fellow Israelites.[200] This by itself would have provoked Pharaoh. Not only does it threaten to undermine Egyptian security, but on the part of the crown prince it represents the supreme act of disloyalty. The author does not explicitly mention the murder, thus accentuating the way in which Moses takes the initiative. His roles as sympathizer, resister, fugitive, and finally deliverer in Heb 11 do not come to him accidentally. Delitzsch observes that instead of using a verb like φυγεῖν, the author says he

(Biblische Untersuchungen 4; Regensburg: Pustet, 1968), 258; for rabbinic parallels, see Str-B 3:694–95.

[199] For these remarks, see Moffatt, *Hebrews*, 182; and Hugh Montefiore, *The Epistle to the Hebrews* (HNTC; New York: Harper & Row, 1964), 204.

[200] E. C. Wickham, *The Epistle to the Hebrews* (2nd ed.; London: Methuen, 1922), 103–4. He also points out that Goshen, where the Israelites reside (Exod 8:22; 9:26), is associated with Arabia in LXX Gen 45:10. Hebrews, relying on the LXX and its geography, may thus have considered Moses to be literally "leaving Egypt" already when he "goes out" to look at his brothers.

"forsook" (κατέλιπεν) Egypt without fearing the king.[201] Hebrews might concede that Moses "fled" temporarily in fear due to the shock received from the unexpected disclosure of his crime, but he chooses, understandably, not to focus on this aspect. By using καταλιπεῖν, the author implies that Moses willfully leaves behind Egypt, "forsaking" it and all it represents, devaluing it in favor of something he deems more desirable, namely, "the unseen."[202]

Thus, the king's wrath (θυμός) of which Moses is said to be unafraid, rather than displeasure at his murder of a low-level Egyptian supervisor, in Hebrews is fatherly indignation at a rebellious son's ungrateful rejection of his parents. The murder itself would seem to constitute little cause to fear Pharaoh. Revenge by the victim's family is a more likely worry, and even this could be subject to legal constraints since the murder was not premeditated. Personal offense against the king, on the other hand, could be prosecuted as an act of treason and punished by death or confiscation of property.[203] This, in addition to the harsh sanctions attached to dishonor of parents in antiquity, is a more probable source for Moses' fear. If Hebrews conceives of the relationship between Moses and Pharaoh through the lens of the Roman institution of *patria potestas*, then the declaration of fearlessness is at the same time a declaration of independence, or more accurately, it is a statement that Moses was undeterred by any of the harsh consequences that would surely attend his unilateral abrogation of familial ties with Pharaoh and (re)incorporation into the household of God (cf. Heb 3:1–6). Moses left Egypt "though not afraid of the king's wrath" (taking μὴ φοβηθείς as a concessive participle) at his impudence; he endured "as though he saw the unseen" (τὸν ἀόρατον ὡς ὁρῶν), perhaps an allusion to

---

[201] Franz J. Delitzsch, *Commentary on the Epistle to the Hebrews* (trans. T. L. Kingsbury; 3rd ed.; 2 vols.; Edinburgh: Clark, 1883), 2:266. The LXX says Moses departed (ἀνεχώρησε) in language that supports Delitzsch's argument about the distinctive thrust of the passage in Hebrews.

[202] The reference to τὸν ἀόρατον in 11:27 may refer to God, the invisible King, as in most translations rendering it "*him* who is invisible" (KJV; ASV; RSV; NIV; NRSV), or to "the reward" mentioned in v. 26, as in those that render it generically "the invisible" (Buchanan; Eisenbaum). In favor of the distinction seen by Delitzsch in the nuance of καταλιπεῖν are those occurrences where it connotes disdain for that which is "abandoned" and preference for something else. LXX Deut 29:24 uses it to describe disregard for the covenant, as does Josephus (*Ant.* 8.190) in reference to Solomon's moral downfall. In reference to the rejection of virtue or vice, see *T. Iss.* 6.1; *2 Clem.* 10.1. Hermas uses it to describe those who abandon the truth under the influence of riches and eventually become apostate (*Sim.* 8.9.1; 9.26.4). Finally, Philo says Moses "gave up (κατέλιπεν) the lordship of Egypt" and renounced his inheritance, and was rewarded by God with leadership of Israel (*Mos.* 1.148–49).

[203] Cf. Raymond Westbrook, "Punishments and Crimes," *ABD* 5:550–51. This would also be essentially true if Hebrews is reading later Roman custom back into the Exodus account; cf. Adolf Berger et al., "Law and Procedure, Roman," *OCD* 833.

the theophany in the burning bush at Horeb (Exod 3:1–4:17) which had not yet taken place. Without referring to the power of life and death (*ius vitae necisque*) possessed by the *paterfamilias*, Peake nevertheless captures the dynamic at play when he says that Hebrews sees Moses as separating fearlessly from one king because he has his sights set on an invisible king "who held life and death more firmly in His hand."[204] Moses had much to lose and faced an adversary of legendary fierceness and might. If he is able to endure in obedience to God, then the readers, blessed as they are with an even fuller revelation of God's plan, should be able to withstand their persecution without falling away (cf. 10:32–39).

In 11:28, the author passes over the whole series of face to face meetings with Pharaoh leading up to the eve of Israel's departure.[205] By faith Moses "performed the Passover and the sprinkling of blood so that the destroyer of the firstborn would not touch them." He relays the command to smear lamb's blood on the doorposts of the houses in order to avert the tenth and final plague from the Israelites (Exod 12:7, 13). "The destroyer" (ὁ ὀλοθρεύων) in Heb 11:28 comes from LXX Exod 12:23, where Moses tells the community elders that the Lord will pass by to strike the Egyptians down but will see the blood "and not allow the destroyer to enter" their houses. Unlike in Exod 12:13, 27, the Lord and the avenging angel are closely linked yet still distinct, and Hebrews plays down God's active involvement in the slaughter.[206]

The only other biblical appearance of this figure is in Wis 18:25. Although there is no explicit mention of fear in Heb 11:28, the haggadic midrash on the Passover story contained in Wis 17–18 suggests a background for an implicit contrast between the terror-stricken Egyptians and the confident Israelites.[207]

---

[204] A. S. Peake, *Hebrews* (NCB; Edinburgh: Jack, n.d.), 220–21.

[205] John Chrysostom believes that it was these encounters after his return from forty years in exile that Moses did not fear when he left Egypt the first time (*Hom. Heb.* 26.5). If this is true, the cynic might reply that Hebrews harmonizes his account with Exodus on a technicality since the king at the time of his first departure is dead by the time he returns, and thus is not to be feared (Exod 4:19). Interestingly, this detail in God's command to return—that all those who sought Moses' life were now dead—highlights the element of personal affront in the conflict that led to his departure in the first place. The fact of his crime has not changed, but since it never comes up in his meetings with the new pharaoh, it must not have seemed so great a matter even to the Egyptian authorities. It was his rejection as heir apparent of his adoptive grandfather that was most heinous.

[206] As do versions of the story which feature an "angelic avenger": Ps 78:49–51; *Jub.* 49.2; Ezek. Trag., frg. 13, l. 33; *Exod. Rab.* 17:5. Later rabbinic sources tend to emphasize God's direct activity; cf. Judah Goldin, "'Not by Means of an Angel and not by Means of a Messenger'," in *Religions in Antiquity* (ed. J. Neusner; Leiden: Brill, 1968), 414–18.

[207] Though he nowhere quotes it, familiarity with the Wisdom of Solomon is quite plausible. Its inclusion in the Muratorian Canon attests to its popularity in early Christian

Darkness is the ninth and penultimate plague visited upon Egypt (Exod 10:21–23), and its treatment in Wis 17:1–18:4 sounds a note of dread that continues to resonate in 18:5–25 in the description of the final plague, referred to in Heb 11:28. The Egyptians' fear is mentioned repeatedly (17:3–4, 6, 8–15, 19; 18:17).[208] In the dead of night, God's all-powerful λόγος "leapt from heaven out of the royal throne, like a fierce warrior into the midst of a land of destruction (ὀλεθρία)" (18:14–15). This word is pictured as wielding a "sharp sword" (ξίφος ὀξύ) that somehow induces the Egyptians to have nightmares in which they foresee their deaths and learn that their wickedness is the cause.[209] When the destroyer later threatens the Israelites in the desert, Aaron, "a blameless man," averts disaster through his priestly functions (18:20–25).[210]

Hebrews has Moses performing the ritual that does away with all need for fear on the eve of Passover. After the death of the firstborn and the beginning of the exodus, the Israelites, who have gone out "boldly,"[211] approach the Red Sea when Pharaoh changes his mind and pursues them (Exod 14:8; cf. Num 33:3). In 11:29, Hebrews leaves out the fact that they lapse back into fear when the Egyptians approach (Exod 14:10, 13), mentioning only that faith enables them to cross over "as if on dry land." The Egyptians are drowned when they try to do the same. The author recounts this happy ending in the briefest of terms, and by using the passive (κατεπόθησαν) he minimizes God's active involvement in their destruction and mutes the vengeful tone that pervades Exod 15. Hebrews is not as concerned to address the fate of those who oppose the people of God as he is to underscore the ways in which faith helps the readers to endure such opposition without losing trust in their heavenly Father, a theme he takes up at the beginning of chapter twelve.

---

circles. The indices of NA[27] list over a dozen possible NT citations to chapters 17–18 alone. Clement of Rome, the first writer to quote Hebrews, is also the first to quote Wisdom (cf. *1 Clem.* 27.5, quoting Wis 11:21; 12:12, just after quoting Heb 6:18). Irenaeus, in a book no longer extant, also quotes Hebrews in tandem with Wisdom, according to Eusebius (*Hist. eccl.* 5.26.3). At the very least, Hebrews inherits images and ideas from the same fund of Hellenistic Jewish traditions.

[208] Their haunted sleep (17:14–15; 18:19) is reminiscent of Plutarch's description of the effects of superstition (*Superst.* 166C). The pangs of conscience (17:11), the paralysis (17:17–18), and the definition of fear (17:12) as "an abandonment of the helps that come from reason" (προδοσία τῶν ἀπὸ λογισμοῦ βοηθημάτων) likewise recall the Hellenistic analyses which inform Plutarch.

[209] The image of God's word as a sword, as well as its function in relation to the human conscience, is found also at Heb 4:12–13.

[210] Not all are saved, however (v. 20, 23; cf. 1 Cor 10:10).

[211] Literally, "with a hand held high" (ἐν χειρὶ ὑψηλῇ), connoting a defiant pose.

Reinterpreting Adversity as God's Education (Heb 12:5–11)

There is no explicit mention of fear in Heb 12:5–11.[212] From his allusion in 12:4 to their "resistance," however, it is evident that the author is addressing those circumstances which inspire fear in the readers. His response furthermore reflects a worry that they may begin to confuse natural objects of fear with supernatural ones. In the time since their conversion, the audience has undergone unaccustomed abuse—though not to the point of bloodshed—and they have two basic options for interpreting this experience: they can look at their suffering as ultimately meaningless, without any purposive relationship to the deity, who in turn may be conceived of as noninterventionist or nonexistent; or, still worse, they can look on it as a sign of displeasure and chastisement in which God has an active hand. Those whom Plutarch labels superstitious choose the second option (*Superst.* 165B, 168A–C, 170E et al.). The frequent outcome of this form of piety, as Plutarch observes, is embittered atheism, where a man resents the gods in whom he no longer believes. Hebrews presents a third way. The author urges his readers to regard their hardships as a necessary part of their education as God's legitimate children.

A lingering consciousness of past sin or a fresh distress over sins committed since baptism may make the temptation to view their afflictions as God's punishment an especially strong one. The sense of the text certainly permits such a punitive understanding of their suffering by its repeated use of παιδεία and cognates in 12:5–11:

> And you have completely forgotten the exhortation which reasons with you as sons: "My son, do not disregard the παιδεία of the Lord, nor be discouraged when rebuked by him. For the one he loves the Lord disciplines (παιδεύει), and he chastens every son whom he accepts." Endure for the sake of discipline (εἰς παιδείαν). God is dealing with you as sons, for what son is there that a father does not discipline (παιδεύει)? But if you are without παιδεία, in which all have a share, then you are illegitimate and not legitimate sons. Moreover, we have had our natural fathers as disciplinarians (παιδευτάς) and we respected them. Should we not all the more be subject to the father of spirits and live? For they applied discipline (ἐπαίδευον) for a short while as they thought best, but he does so for our benefit so that we might share in his holiness. Though for the moment, all παιδεία appears to be not joy but grief,

---

[212] One possible exception is ἐκλύομαι, "lose heart," in v. 5 (cf. Deut 20:3; 1 Macc 9:8). This term falls in the same broad semantic field but, as it occurs in a quotation of Prov 3:11, it does not reflect the author's special usage.

later it yields a peaceful fruit of righteousness in those who
have been trained by it.

The key term in Greek may refer either to the physical discipline or correction of an errant child, or more inclusively and positively to the general process of education and upbringing. (The Vulgate leans in the direction of the latter by consistently using *disciplina*.) Interpreters from the patristic period to the present have offered differing assessments of the meaning of παιδεία in Heb 12:5–11. Does Hebrews envision the role of suffering in παιδεία as essentially retributive or punitive in nature, or is it more appropriate to read this passage as supporting a non-punitive understanding of suffering in which the formative, educative aspect is primary?[213] The former plays into the hands of those ready to paint Christianity as δεισιδαιμονία, while the latter, by invoking the shibboleth of cultured Greeks, would conceivably go a long way toward removing the stigma of superstition.

Croy forcefully argues for the primacy of the non-punitive interpretation on the basis of the author's recontextualization of a proverb expressing the punitive view common in Jewish wisdom literature.[214] With a minor alteration, Heb 12:5–6 quotes Prov 3:11–12, which clearly contains the element of punishment seen also in many other proverbs (6:23; 12:1; 13:18, 24; 15:10; 19:18; 23:13–14). Hebrews follows the LXX, which intensifies this punitive aspect by using the verb μαστιγοῖ ("whips" or "flogs") in v. 6 to render כְּאָב instead of reading it as a prepositional phrase ("as a father") as in the pointing of the MT.[215] In light of his reliance on the Greek, the absence of any elaboration on God's corrective discipline is particularly striking. All other Jewish and Christian allusions to Prov 3:11–12 take over the punitive element from the original context.[216] The author's editorial activity, resulting in the downplaying of an image of God that would smack of superstitiousness, therefore has all the marks of a deliberate interpretive strategy.

Although Hebrews is capable of attributing punishment to God, as in the warning passages directed at potential apostates (6:4–8; 10:26–31), he refrains from doing so in chapter twelve. In those passages describing the fate of apostates, the type of fear in view has a supernatural entity as its object. Here and elsewhere, the objects of fear are the physical, earthly ones associated with persecution. God's fearsome qualities do not appear in 12:5–11, yet the author appears to be sensitive to a possible misconstrual. Yes, sufferings will come; and yes, they are in some sense a function of their status as God's children. But God

---

[213] For the history of interpretation on this question, see Croy, *Endurance in Suffering*, 9–34.

[214] Ibid., 88–89, 196–200.

[215] Schröger, *Der Verfasser des Hebräerbriefes als Schriftausleger*, 188–89.

[216] Croy, *Endurance in Suffering*, 210–13. Hebrews stands closer to first-century pagan Greeks, whose usage appears to have been overwhelmingly non-punitive (196).

is not the proximate cause of their sufferings, nor is their sin mentioned as the reason God is allowing them to be afflicted (in which case one might expect a call to repentance, as in those OT texts where Israel's afflictions are said to serve as punishment for the sins of the people; e.g., Jer 2:1–4:4; Hos 5:15–6:6; Amos 4:6–12).[217]

Rather than allow their hard experiences to nurture seeds of doubt about their relationship to God, they are to recognize that the testimony of Scripture trumps their experience in this instance.[218] The author injects his audience into the sacred text when he introduces the citation of Prov 3:11–12 by saying that it addresses (present tense) them as children. Hebrews also personalizes the statement by adding the possessive μου after υἱέ, though it is not clear if this is the influence of the MT, a variant LXX reading, or the author's own modification. In its original setting, God is not understood to be the speaker. In Hebrews, however, God the father becomes the speaker, and the sapiential vocative "my son" takes on a deeper significance in light of the connection between Jesus' sonship and that of the readers. If Scripture identifies them as sons, then they are in fact God's sons and they must remember to filter their experience through this reality. Instead, they have forgotten this exhortation. The perfect ἐκλέλησθε expresses the completeness of their forgetfulness: they have not momentarily forgotten but are in danger of developing amnesia.[219] Instead of suggesting that the audience has forgotten this particular verse from the OT, it is more likely that the author is saying that in their current circumstances they will have the chance to show by their response whether they remember its gist. Despair reflects a lack of trust in the parent's love which always operates—even when appearances are to the contrary—in pursuit of the child's best interests.

Whereas Heb 12:5–6 focuses on the means, v. 7 reflects the polyvalence of the term παιδεία by pointing also to the end of divine discipline. Originally denoting only the process of education, by the first century παιδεία came to include the objective content of education as well.[220] When the author exhorts

---

[217] Cf. Croy, *Endurance in Suffering*, 83–133 for a thorough survey of Jewish perspectives on suffering.

[218] In his *Treatise of the Fear of God*, John Bunyan likewise makes biblical revelation the supreme guide to interpreting personal experience: "Let the Word be true, whatever thy experience is" (in *The Miscellaneous Works of John Bunyan* [ed. R. Sharrock; Oxford: Clarendon, 1981], 9:35).

[219] The syntax suggests that v. 5a is declarative, but it should not be taken too literally as the author sometimes describes hypothetical scenarios in the indicative as a means of impressing upon his audience the urgency of his exhortations; cf. C. E. Carlston, "Eschatology and Repentance in the Epistle to the Hebrews," *JBL* 78 (1959): 296–302.

[220] Diodorus Siculus 12.13.4; Josephus, *Vita* 359; *C. Ap.* 1.73; cf. W. Jaeger, *Paideia: The Ideals of Greek Culture* (3 vols.; trans. G. Highet; New York: Oxford University Press, 1939–44), 1:303.

his readers in v. 7a to endure εἰς παιδείαν, the preposition may be taken as purposive ("for the purpose of an education") or causal ("because of discipline").[221] Whether they can endure because they already (as sons) have discipline (without which they could not endure) or they are acquiring discipline as a part of their becoming sons is not clear, and consequently the reality or potentiality reflected in the phrase ὡς υἱοῖς is likewise unclear. The argument of Hebrews is characterized by a tension between the status already effected by Jesus' once-for-all sacrifice and the future attainment of the promises. One might paraphrase the author in this passage to be saying, "Be patient and endure until you become who you really are." The analogy in v. 7c suggests that discipline is a natural and expected component of the father-son relationship, not that discipline makes one a son who is not otherwise a son. Being a son has as its corollary the privilege of an education, and the inherent value of this παιδεία provides the motivation for which the audience can endure fearful things.

The final clause of v. 7 is a reminder that the need for such endurance should not come as a surprise to them. To expect anything else is to betray an appalling ignorance of the implications of their sonship. To wish for anything different is tantamount to forfeiting one's status as son and heir.

This is the slant of v. 8, which answers the question posed in v. 7: "But if you are without παιδεία, in which all have a share, then you are illegitimate (νόθοι) and not legitimate sons."[222] This is the only NT occurrence of νόθος, but the term is common in Greco-Roman literature in reference to children born out of wedlock or, more generally, to that which is in some sense "counterfeit" (Plato, *Tim.* 52B; *Leg* 741A).[223] Such children were often the offspring of a slave and thus were automatically illegitimate by law.[224] The silver lining in the dark cloud of illegitimacy in ancient Rome had to do with the exemption of bastard children from the power of the *paterfamilias*.[225] By law and by custom, the institution of *patria potestas* invested the oldest male in Roman families with almost absolute power over all his descendants, including the families of male

---

[221] Lane, *Hebrews*, 2:401, surveys the interpretive options.
[222] The logic of the verse requires that "sons" be coordinated with πάντες since the final clause makes clear that not everyone has undergone the discipline of a legitimate son.
[223] Cynthia B. Patterson ("Those Athenian Bastards," *Classical Antiquity* 9 [1990]: 40–73), however, shows how νόθος, while reflecting inferior status, is not always strictly equivalent to "born out of wedlock." Aside from Hebrews, the only biblical use of the word is in Wis 4:3, but the word is otherwise so common and the similarities so general in nature that Ellingworth's claim of an intentional echo between the two passages is quite plausible but inconclusive (cf. *Hebrews*, 652).
[224] Suzanne Dixon, *The Roman Family* (Baltimore: Johns Hopkins University Press, 1992), 124.
[225] As Braun, *Hebräer*, 413–14; and Grässer, *Hebraer*, 3:263–65, note.

offspring but excluding married daughters, who fell under the *patria potestas* of another *paterfamilias*.[226] All legitimate children were under this jurisdiction from birth, and reaching the age of majority did not abrogate the obligations it imposed on a child.[227] Only death, formal *emancipatio*, adoption into another family, or the father's insanity suspended *patria potestas*. A *paterfamilias* possessed power of life and death (*ius vitae necisque*) over his children, who could not technically own their own property or make legally valid wills. A father could deny marriage, compel divorce, and even sell his children. Saller argues that the image of the Roman family as nothing more than a paternal despotism is something of an exaggeration, but the caricature is nevertheless rooted in the ancient sources and thus would have conditioned how the parental language in Hebrews was received.[228]

This image and experience of fathers affects how one understands the father-son analogy in Heb 12:8, especially since the *paterfamilias* was ultimately responsible for the rearing and education of children.[229] The author of Hebrews presupposes on the part of the audience an experience of parental discipline that corresponds to what one finds reflected in contemporaneous Greek and Roman moralists. Seneca (*Ira* 2.21.1–6) believes that fathers should not be too strict with their children but, for the children's sake, neither should they be too lenient. He contends that a father's love and his severity with his children are in direct proportion to one another, just as "the Lord disciplines whom he loves" (Heb 12:6a; cf. *Prov.* 1.5). Maximus of Tyre (*Diss.* 4.7) likewise argues that the desire to give pleasure is an unreliable indicator of true parental affection. Minus the specifically Christian elements, Heb 12:7–11, could have been written by almost anyone in the Roman Empire.[230]

---

[226] On the institution in general, see J. A. Crook, "*Patria Potestas*," *CQ* 17 (1967): 113–22; and E. Eyben, "Fathers and Sons," in *Marriage, Divorce, and Children in Ancient Rome* (ed. B. Rawson; Oxford: Clarendon, 1991), 114–43.

[227] In fact, it went into effect before birth since a woman having an abortion without the husband's consent could be held liable under Roman law on account of its interference in inheritance schemes (cf. Dixon, *The Roman Family*, 195 n. 17).

[228] Saller, *Patriarchy, Property and Death in the Roman Family*, 114–32, 225–32. Infamous examples of the public exercise of *ius vitae necisque* also made a strong impression on the collective Roman consciousness, even if such cases were the exception and not the rule. Valerius Maximus records a number of well-known instances (*Factorum ac dictorum memorabilium* 5.8.1–3). Augustus's law against adultery (*lex Iulia*) even gave *patresfamilias* license to kill daughters and sons-in-law caught in the act. Under the law's terms, he later exiled his own daughter.

[229] The same is true of Jewish fathers; cf. André Lemaire, "Education (Ancient Israel)," *ABD* 2:306.

[230] Saller balances these texts with others where authors condemn the practice of corporal punishment with slaves and children alike because of the need to differentiate between the two; cf. *Patriarchy, Property and Death in the Roman Family*, 134; idem, "Corporal

Discipline as part of education was sometimes delegated to slaves. According to Plutarch, Cato the Elder himself undertook his son's education because he thought it unseemly for his son to be disciplined by a slave, "to have his ears pulled for being tardy at his lessons" (*Cat. Maj.* 20.4–7; cf. the rebuke of negligent fathers in [*Lib. ed.*] 9D). Heb 12:9 has in mind just such a scrupulous parent. The author reminds the audience that they had fathers—not slaves—"as disciplinarians" (παιδευτάς). Many fathers failed to find the right balance between severity and affection. Pseudo-Plutarch (*Lib. ed.* 9B) describes fathers who

> in their eagerness that their children may the sooner rank first in everything, they lay upon them unreasonable tasks, which the children find themselves unable to perform, and so come to grief; besides being depressed by their unfortunate experience, they do not respond to the instruction they receive.

This author's use of athletic terminology in the context of a discussion on parenting and its unintended effects on the child bears a resemblance to the race metaphor in Heb 12:1, 12–13, and to the intervening discussion of παιδεία, with its concern about the child's discouragement in vv. 3 and 5.[231] Finally, the analogy between the human and the divine made in Heb 12:5–11 is matched closely by Seneca (*Prov.* 2.6; cf. 1.6; 4.7, 11–12), who describes God as a loving father who says of humanity, "Let them be harassed by toil, by suffering, by losses, in order that they may gather true strength," a sentiment echoed in the exhortation of 10:32–39 as well.[232] Along with the obedience it entails, *pietas* towards a gentle father is admirable, but towards a harsh father is even more laudable, particularly when it is out of love and not with an eye to increasing

---

Punishment, Authority, and Obedience in the Roman Household," in *Marriage, Divorce, and Children in Ancient Rome* (ed. B. Rawson; Oxford: Clarendon, 1991), 144–65. While he is right to view with scepticism those approaches which fail to distinguish between case law and sociological description, Saller too quickly accepts these parental ideals of the nobility as reality. The need to state the ideal indicates that it was not always followed and that corporal punishment did in fact take place, though to what extent is impossible to gauge. Seneca allows that it is sometimes in order with very young children due to the ineffectiveness of rational correction (*Constant.* 12.3; cf. *Clem.* 1.14.1; Cicero, *Tusc.* 3.27.64; Seneca the Elder, *Controv.* 9.5.7). Eyben documents the survival of the traditional view supporting the appropriateness of corporal punishment of one's own children ("Fathers and Sons," 125–32).

[231] Note also the final remark about unresponsiveness to instruction and the pedagogical concern of Heb 2:1; 5:11–14; 6:11–12.

[232] On Seneca and the similarities between the vantage point of *De providentia* and Hebrews, see Croy, *Endurance in Suffering*, 148–50, 205.

one's share of the inheritance (Valerius Maximus, *Factorum ac dictorum memorabilium* 5.4.3).

Though spared many of the unpleasant aspects of *patria potestas*, bastards occupied a precarious position in Roman society because of the deleterious consequences of illegitimacy in terms of inheritance rights. They were usually left out of a father's will and had few rights should the father die intestate.[233] Unless explicitly and intentionally left out of a will (*exheredatio* or *abdicatio*), by contrast, all legitimate children were *sui heredes* and had a share in the father's estate. Of course, the connection between legitimacy and inheritance is also present in the OT tradition.[234] The implications of legitimate sonship hinted at in the rhetorical question in Heb 12:8 point again to the inheritance motif, thus supplying the motivation to endure the hardships they face.

Hebrews appropriates but redefines conceptions of inheritance found in the Greco-Roman and Jewish contexts. On the Gentile side, Hebrews uses terminology that evokes the topics of discipline and inheritance as prevalent concerns of sons. But in its conception of what constitutes true παιδεία and a valuable inheritance, Hebrews is obviously far from typical in the Greco-Roman world. Jewish notions are much closer to Hebrews, which is concerned with clarifying the true character of παιδεία and its connection with true wealth and inheritance. Over against the caricature shared by many contemporary Jews and Christians of pagans as greedy and profligate with misplaced priorities, Hebrews sees worthwhile possessions as something other than material wealth.[235] This

---

[233] Cf. Spicq, *Hébreux*, 2:393–94; Dixon, *The Roman Family*, 62. The plight of bastards was typically worse in classical Greece than in Rome; see the law cited by Demosthenes (*Macart.* 51): "No illegitimate child (νόθος) . . . shall have the right of succession either to religious rites or civic privileges."

[234] In Deut 23:2, illegitimate children are denied admittance into the assembly of the Lord "even to the tenth generation." The sentence of death for breaking the seventh commandment (against adultery) is likely a function of the importance accorded to the sexual integrity and economic security of the family (Deut. 22:22). Children owe honor and obedience to their parents (Lev 20:9; Deut 5:16; 27:16). Rebellious sons, while legally entitled to an inheritance if the firstborn (Deut 21:15–17), may nonetheless be stoned to death (Deut 21:18–21), in which case inheritance rights become the least of their concerns. The family played a pivotal role in Israel's covenant with Yahweh. Thus in Jewish tradition, the social, economic, and theological aspects of parent-child relationships are interconnected in ways that have parallels in Roman society and in Hebrews, where the two traditions converge in the first century. The theological element is naturally much less prominent in Greco-Roman tradition. In Rome, where the gods were closely identified with the state, family relations instead assumed a political or patriotic function (cf. D. L. Balch, *Let Wives Be Submissive: The Domestic Code in 1 Peter* [SBLMS 26; Atlanta: Scholars Press, 1981], 21–62).

[235] Indeed, this is the major theme of Prov 3, from which Hebrews quotes in 12:5–6. Note the promise to "make straight your paths" (Prov 3:6; cf. Heb 12:13), the prospect of

broad likeness notwithstanding, Hebrews diverges from the Jewish idea of "promise" and inheritance in a few ways. The land of Canaan, "the promised land," is the most common referent of "inheritance" in the OT. Some writings describe the Law as Israel's inheritance (Sir 24:23). In Hebrews, Noah—living before the establishment of the Abrahamic covenant—is an heir, though an heir "to righteousness which comes by faith" (11:7). Hebrews 11:10 suggests that the promised inheritance is a "city with foundations, whose architect and builder is God" instead of Canaan. Sometimes the content of the "inheritance" is quite simply "the promise" (6:12, 17). Most significantly, the inheritance in Hebrews comes through Jesus, who is "the mediator of a new covenant, so that those who are called may receive the promised eternal inheritance" (9:15).

By transforming such received notions of inheritance, the author of Hebrews is able to counter the doubts raised by whatever persecution his audience is facing and to allay the natural fears arising out of it. The redefinition of "inheritance" as something more spiritual accomplishes two things. First, it makes empirical disconfirmation of God's promises more difficult than if "inheritance" is equivalent to possessing the land. Second, it makes the fulfillment of inherited promises independent of external circumstances and, at least in part, within the control of the community since it is realized in the formation of an ἐκκλησία characterized by the behaviors suggested, for example, in 13:1–19. "The peaceful fruit of righteousness" and the prospect of "sharing in his holiness" (12:10–11) produced by God's discipline should enable the audience to face their present persecution with the "confidence" that they will receive "the promise" (10:35–36), as should the knowledge that their discipline will last only "a short while" (πρός ὀλίγας ἡμέρας).[236] Their willingness to be dispossessed is an indication to the author that his readers are not afraid of the wrong things and that they perceive their sufferings as firm but loving παιδεία administered by God the father, who truly knows best.[237] And

---

healing and refreshment (Prov 3:8; cf. Heb 12:12–13), and the description of wisdom as a way of pleasantness and peace (Prov 3:17; cf. Heb 12:11).

[236] Cf. the saying attributed to Aristotle by Diogenes Laertius (5.18) that the roots of παιδεία are bitter but the fruit is sweet. Likewise, the assurance in 12:11 that God's discipline, in the form of suffering, is only grievous "momentarily" (πρὸς τὸ παρόν) aims to inspire the audience to be brave until conditions improve since it suggests that relief is in sight (cf. Aristotle, *Rhet.* 2.5.16–17). Without this assurance, they remain mired in grief (λύπη), which along with disturbance (ταραχή) forms the vocabulary by which Aristotle characterizes the emotion of fear (2.5.1). That it only "seems" (δοκεῖ) to be so painful underscores the notion that emotion is founded on a false judgment. Hebrews describes the preferred alternative state in 12:11 as "peaceful" (εἰρηνικόν).

[237] Earthly fathers discipline their children "as they think best" (κατὰ τὸ δοκοῦν αὐτοῖς) but are far from perfect (12:10). Moffatt detects in the phrase an allusion to the arbitrariness of *patria potestas*, as is suggested by the RSV's "at their pleasure" (*Hebrews*, 203–4). The discipline of the heavenly father is objectively "for our benefit"

like the philosopher Stilpo, whose property had been plundered when Ptolemy Soter captured his hometown of Megara, they can say that they need not be compensated for their losses since no one has taken their παιδεία.[238]

Conclusion

The motif of fear pervades the argument in Hebrews at almost every turn, even when the explicit language is missing. Its place among the author's chief concerns is further suggested by his coordinated discussions of Christian "confidence" and his editorial decisions in such passages as the retelling of the Moses story in 11:23–28. Sources of fear fall into two broad categories: "natural" fear, which includes the ordinary human desire to avoid physical pain, economic deprivation, humiliation, and the like; and "supernatural" fear, the primary manifestation of which is fear of divine judgment after death. Between these two heuristic categories there is, not surprisingly, some degree of overlap. Fear of death, though primarily concerned with what comes after death in Hebrews, naturally participates in both types. In one form or another, thanatophobia and its effects drive the arguments the author tailors to his audience, who have "not yet" had to withstand persecution to the point of bloodshed (12:4). Fear in Hebrews is itself an undesirable state and usually serves as an indicator either of potential peril or of disordered priorities.

The author's approach to fear is not like that of the school philosophers who assert that it is a ready indicator of superstitiousness and that the emotion has no rational or legitimate basis.[239] He is closer to the more balanced approach one finds in Aristotle in his analysis of the conditions giving rise to fear and his proposed solutions to the problem it presents. The contours of the letter's Christology fit especially well within a theological and paraenetic program designed to achieve an ideal of fearlessness. Because of the specific claims about the nature of the Christ event, the theological aspect has profound "practical" implications. No longer does "natural" fear excuse one from moral responsibility for capitulation to human forces seeking to dishonor God. This

---

(ἐπὶ τὸ συμφέρον); on the Stoic resonance of this phrase and its similarities with Hebrews, see W. Jentsch, *Urchristliches Erziehungsdenken: Die Paideia Kyriu im Rahmen der hellenistisch-Jüdischen Umwelt* (BFCT 45/3; Gütersloh: Bertelsmann, 1951), 161–68; and Croy, *Endurance in Suffering*, 204–5. See also the concluding remark of Plutarch's *De virtute morali* (452D) that the goal of the free-born child's παιδεία is to make him take joy in honorable things and to be vexed only at dishonorable things.

[238] Diogenes Laertius 2.115. The story is also mentioned by Seneca, *Ep.* 9.18–19; and Ps.-Plutarch, *Lib. ed.* 5F–6A.

[239] However, one does not find the kind of explicit engagement with Hellenistic analyses of emotional response as one finds, for example, in Clement of Alexandria (*Strom.* 2.7–8).

kind of fear bears an inverse relationship to faith, "without which it is impossible to please God" (11:6).

So in one respect, that is, in its insistence that fear is no longer an appropriate component of human engagement with the divine, Hebrews is in agreement with Plutarch. But the qualifier "no longer" would likely be the stumbling block for a contemporary Greek because it points to what has become known as "the scandal of particularity." Fearlessness is an achievable goal only because of what has transpired with Christ and not because it was a mistake ever to believe that fear once had any objective grounding. In an imaginary debate, then, one can see Plutarch complaining that Hebrews hasn't gone far enough in expunging fear and has in fact compounded the problem by granting legitimacy to those beliefs underlying the gravest fears in the first place. And to this Hebrews might respond that fear cannot be so easily explained away, and that Plutarch wants the brand of Protestantism whose credo, in the critical summary of H. Richard Niebuhr, can be reduced to this: "A God without wrath brought men without sin into a kingdom without judgment through the ministrations of a Christ without a cross."[240] In spite of attempts to dispel his readers' fears, then, it is hard to imagine his sermon earning the approval of the author of *De superstitione*.

---

[240] H. Richard Niebuhr, *The Kingdom of God in America* (New York: Harper, 1937), 193.

Chapter Four

Reverence and Awe:
Fear as an Appropriate Response to God in Hebrews

Introduction

Inasmuch as "fear" denotes an inherently unpleasant state, one does not find it listed among those dispositions to be cultivated as intrinsically beneficial by Hellenistic moral philosophers or counted as "fruits of the spirit" by early Christian writers. Plutarch's recognition of this basic fact of human nature accounts for the caustic tone of his attack on superstition on the grounds that it generates needless fear and anxiety. Objects of rational fear certainly exist, but there is no reason to inject it into the religious realm. On this Plutarch stands closer to Aristotle than to the Stoics or Epicureans, who generally hold that all emotions are unreliable indicators of the true nature of things. Hebrews does not denigrate or dismiss the response of fear as such, that is, not on the grounds that it is a πάθος and therefore not to be trusted in any way as a guide for thinking and acting. When it appears in Hebrews, the motif of fear occasions talk of some manifestly disagreeable or disadvantageous condition—for example, eschatological doom, misguided judgments of value, lack of faith, subjection to demonic forces, the threat of physical harm, or the human condition prior to the advent of Christ. Fearlessness, then, is the author's holistic ideal in that it includes an internal sense of confidence and also results from (necessarily so, in the author's mind) an awareness of Christ's accomplishments as high priest.

Nevertheless, there are a few passages in Hebrews where apparent manifestations of fear are suggestive of something the author regards in a positive light. The task of this chapter is to examine these texts in order to complete the picture begun in the previous chapter. Even when fear seems to play a salutary role in his vision of Christian faith, however, the author tends to shy away from the word φόβος and not once does he use the standard phrase, "fear of the Lord" (φόβος κυρίου/θεοῦ), which occurs so frequently in the OT as to be a virtual synonym for "true religion."[1] Nor does he refer to the faithful as "those who fear the Lord," a designation very common in the Psalms but not to be confused with the technical term for Gentile proselytes in the Hellenistic period, "God-fearers" (οἱ φοβούμενοι/σεβόμενοι τὸν θεόν). This seeming avoidance is somewhat surprising since fear of God or Christ as an explicit expression for Christian piety appears in so many strata of early Christian literature.[2] Could it be due to the negative valence of φόβος and its association with δεισιδαιμονία among educated Greeks? Perhaps. This chapter thus will also explore the ways in which Hebrews, even when assigning a constructive role to fear, may be equipped to neutralize the charge of δεισιδαιμονία. One area of focus has to do with the example of Jesus (5:7). A second area of focus has to do with human responses to God and Jesus (12:28–29).

Jesus' "Godly Fear" (Heb 5:7)

Because he has been declared sinless in Heb 4:15, the apparent predication of fear on the part of Jesus a few verses later seems to be at worst a morally neutral description. While on earth, Jesus "offered prayers and supplications, with a loud cry and tears, to the one able to save him from death and was heard ἀπὸ τῆς εὐλαβείας" (5:7). The solution to the exegetical crux represented by the final phrase determines whether one rightly treats it as a part of the emotional texture of the letter and whether Jesus' disposition in fact gains divine approval.

Lexical, grammatical, syntactical, text-critical, and contextual considerations all come to bear upon the decision of the translator in 5:7, and the flexibility of the key term—a rare one in the NT[3]—seems to allow for the

---

[1] References to the hundreds of primary texts, as well as overviews of the broad semantic territory covered by the phrase in the OT, the pseudepigrapha, and at Qumran, may be found in B. J. Bamberger, "Fear and Love of God in the OT," *HUCA* 6 (1929): 39–53; G. Wanke and H. Balz, "φοβέω κτλ.," *TDNT* 9:201–207; S. Terrien, "Fear," *IDB* 2:257–59. Biblical Hebrew has a far richer vocabulary for speaking of fear than does the Greek. G. A. Lee, "Fear," *ISBE* 2:289–91, lists over a dozen different words from the MT for the experience of fear for which the LXX can muster only a handful translation equivalents.

[2] Luke 1:50; 18:2, 4; Acts 9:31; 10:35; Rom 3:18; 2 Cor 5:10; 7:1; Eph 5:21; Col 3:22; 1 Pet 2:17; Rev 11:18; 14:6; 15:4; *1 Clem*. 3.4; 21.6–8; 22.1; 23.1; 28.1; 57.5; Pol. *Phil.* 4.2; *Did.* 4.9–10; *Barn.* 1.7; 4.11; 10.10–11; 11.5; 19.2–7; 20.1–2; Herm. *Man.* 7.1; 8.9; 10.6.

[3] Outside of Hebrews (5:7; 11:7; 12:28), cognates appear only at Luke 2:25; Acts 2:5; 8:2; 22:12. For the classical and Hellenistic usage, see R. Bultmann, "εὐλαβής κτλ.," *TDNT* 2:751–53; BAGD, s.v.; and C. Kerényi, *The Religion of the Greeks and Romans* (trans. C. Holme; London: Thames and Hudson, 1962), 97–103, who comments on the relationship of εὐλάβεια and δεισιδαιμονία.

differences seen in various versions.[4] The element of fear is visible in many versions such as in the KJV (" . . . and was heard in that he feared").[5] Most versions render εὐλάβεια so as to accentuate the notion of "religiousness," for example, as "piety" (NASB), "reverence" (Douay-Rheims), *reverentia* (Vulg.), or "reverent submission" (NIV; NRSV). Still others attempt to combine the two elements in the idiom "godly fear" (RSV; Moffatt).[6] The overarching question to be considered here has to do with the author's evaluation of the disposition denoted by this term. Answering this basic question necessarily involves coming to terms with the text-critical and grammatical challenges presented by the immediate context. Once it is understood whether Hebrews positively assesses the fear one sees in 5:7, it will be possible to ascertain which aspects of Jesus' εὐλάβεια are central to the author's exposition and which may be appropriate for the audience's emulation.

What Does Jesus Pray For and How Is He "Heard"?

What does the author mean when he says that Jesus "was heard for his godly fear" (εἰσακουσθεὶς ἀπὸ τῆς εὐλαβείας), as the RSV puts it? Is this in fact what the author meant to say? Before determining what the "hearing" of Jesus' prayers implies, it is necessary to decide whether God is actually presented as hearing them. Harnack first suggested that the text had been corrupted and should be emended by the insertion of the negative οὐκ before the

---

[4] For an overview of the exegetical problems to be solved in vv. 7–8 and the theological ramifications of translators' decisions, see Adolf Harnack, "Zwei alte dogmatische Korrekturen im Hebräerbrief," in *Studien zur Geschichte des Neuen Testaments und der alten Kirche* (Arbeiten zur Kirchengeschichte 19; Berlin and Leipzig: de Gruyter, 1931), 245–52; Spicq, *Hébreux*, 2:114–18; J. Jeremias, "Hbr 5,7–10," *ZNW* 44 (1952–53): 107–111; Brandenburger, "Text und Vorlagen von Hebr. V 7–10," 191–99; P. Andriessen and A. Lenglet, "Quelques passages difficiles de l'Épître aux Hébreux (5,7–11; 10,20; 12,2)," *Bib* 51 (1970): 208–212; Christian Maurer, "'Erhört wegen der Gottesfurcht', Hebr 5,7," in *Neues Testament und Geschichte* (ed. H. Baltensweiler and B. Reicke; Tübingen: Mohr-Siebeck, 1972), 275–84; N. Lightfoot, "The Saving of the Savior: Hebrews 5:7ff.," *ResQ* 16 (1973): 166–73; Braun, *Hebräer*, 140–46; Ward Allen, "The Translation of ἀπὸ τῆς εὐλαβείας at Hebrews 5.7," *Bulletin of the Institute for Reformation Biblical Studies* 1 (1989): 9–10; Grässer, *Hebräer*, 1:302–5; Lane, *Hebrews*, 1:119–21; Ellingworth, *Hebrews*, 286–93; James Swetnam, "The Crux at Hebrews 5,7–8," *Bib* 81 (2000): 347–50; and Koester, *Hebrews*, 288–90.

[5] Notes taken at the 1610 meetings of the King James translation committee show that this rendering is somewhat ambiguous by design. In fact, it was a stated principle of the committee to render ambiguous Greek into ambiguous English and to avoid being too specific when the original does not provide a sufficient basis (Allen, "The Translation of ἀπὸ τῆς εὐλαβείας," 9).

[6] Cf. also Spicq (*crainte de Dieu*); Braun (*Gottesfurcht*).

passive participle εἰσακουσθείς in 5:7.[7] Such an emendation would obviously change the meaning of the verse entirely. The logic of this position is fairly straightforward: Jesus prays to God, "the one who is able to save him from death." Jesus dies. Therefore, he cannot have been heard by the one able to save him from death. In this view, the verse ought to conclude, " . . . and was *not* heard because of his εὐλάβεια." While allowing that transcriptional probabilities could conceivably account for the received text, Harnack does not believe it is accidental that οὐκ has dropped out, thereby removing a theologically embarrassing statement suggesting the inadequacy of Jesus' prayers.[8] This view presupposes that the content of Jesus' prayer was for avoidance of death (hence Harnack's inclination to see an allusion to Gethsemane[9]) and that "hearing" the prayer takes the form of a specific "answer," namely, the prevention of Jesus' death on the cross. It also assumes an essentially negative meaning for εὐλάβεια, as Jesus' "Furcht und Sorge" were not worthy of a divine "hearing."[10]

The most serious drawback to Harnack's proposal is its conjectural status. No extant manuscripts preserve his proposed reading, and no patristic citations indicate the existence of a textual tradition supporting it. His case rests upon two contested points of grammar and syntax. First, to make sense of the clause in question, he changes the conventional punctuation of the passage so that καίπερ ὢν υἱός goes with v. 7 ("he was [not] heard though he was a son") rather than with what follows in v. 8 ("he learned obedience from what he suffered"), claiming that καίπερ always introduces clauses that modify a preceding main verb (in this instance, [οὐκ] εἰσακουσθείς instead of ἔμαθεν). The LXX and non-biblical authors, however, frequently break this rule and so the force of this

---

[7] Harnack, "Zwei alte dogmatische Korrekturen," 249–50. Harnack's proposal is accepted by Hans Windisch, *Der Hebräerbrief* (2nd ed.; HNT 14; Tübingen: Mohr-Siebeck, 1931), 43–44; Bultmann, *TDNT* 2:753; and Felix Scheidweiler, "ΚΑΙΠΕΡ: nebst einem Exkurs zum Hebräerbrief," *Hermes* 83 (1955): 225–26.

[8] Harnack, "Zwei alte dogmatische Korrekturen," 249. In the same article, he also appeals to early christological considerations in arguing for the emendation of 2:9 (236–45). Scheidweiler, "ΚΑΙΠΕΡ," 226, similarly notes the potential embarrassment caused by the picture of Jesus' seeming lack of trust in the face of death.

[9] Harnack, "Zwei alte dogmatische Korrekturen," 245. Also identifying an allusion to Christ's agony in Gethsemane are Bruce, *Hebrews*, 98–100; T. Lescow, "Jesus in Gethsemane bei Lukas und im Hebräerbrief," *ZNW* 58 (1967): 223–39; and A. Feuillet, "L'évocation de l'agonie de Gethsémane dans l'Épître aux Hébreux (5,7–8)," *Esprit et vie* 86 (1976): 49–53. On the inconclusive character of this identification, see Attridge, *Hebrews*, 148–51.

[10] Harnack, "Zwei alte dogmatische Korrekturen," 247. The logic of the passage resulting from Harnack's emendation precludes an interpretation of εὐλάβεια as "piety" (or *Gottesfurcht*) since it would create an even larger problem to say that Jesus was not heard because of his piety.

argument is weakened considerably.[11] The second point at which Harnack's interpretation is vulnerable is related to the meanings he assigns to εἰσακούω and to ἀπό. He takes the verb as a pregnant construction indicating that Jesus "was heard (and consequently delivered) from" his fear.[12] Except for the negative particle οὐκ, then, Harnack construes the phrase in the same way as do scholars who see God's deliverance of Jesus from the clutches of fear (if not from death itself) as the way in which his prayer is heard. Since εἰσακούω does not connote the act of "delivery," this aspect cannot be assumed. It is inferred by interpreters who read ἀπό as "out of" or "away from." But for ἀπό to have this sense, it requires some verb expressing the idea of separation.[13] Since εἰσακούω does not by itself express this notion, such a reading of ἀπό seems forced.[14] These considerations of grammar, therefore, do not favor the emendation suggested by Harnack.

Solutions to many of the exegetical conundrums in this passage hinge on the meaning one assigns to εὐλάβεια even after the text-critical question is settled in favor of the traditional reading. For this very reason, however, it is best not to begin by prescribing a specific definition that will prematurely determine how one construes the other elements of the passage. Momentarily, then, judgment on the meaning of the phrase ἀπὸ τῆς εὐλαβείας will be withheld. It is wiser to look first to the other elements which may shed light on Jesus' εὐλάβεια. Two such elements concern the content of Jesus' "prayers and supplications" and the manner in which they are "heard." The second of these is less problematic and only partly contingent upon how one handles the first. Because of the particular circumlocution for God in 5:7—"the one able to save him from death" (πρὸς τὸν δυνάμενον σῴζειν αὐτὸν ἐκ θανάτου)—it is most natural to assume that the hearing of Jesus' prayer consists in some fashion in God's saving him ἐκ θανάτου. The preposition ἐκ can support either of two meanings. Here it may denote intervention to prevent Jesus from dying (cf. Sir 51:12; John 12:27; 2 Cor 1:10; Jas 5:20). Prevention of death in the absolute

---

[11] So Maurer, "'Erhört wegen der Gottesfurcht'," 276–78; see the texts adduced by Jeremias, "Hbr 5,7–10," 108; Brandenburger, "Text und Vorlagen von Hebr. V 7–10," 220; Lane, *Hebrews*, 1:110; and Ellingworth, *Hebrews*, 289. M. Rissi ("Die Menschlichkeit Jesu nach Hebr 5,7–8," *TZ* 11 [1955]: 42) and deSilva (*Perseverance in Gratitude*, 192–93) agree with Scheidweiler that καίπερ qualifies the preceding clause but do not adopt the emended text.

[12] Cf. Attridge, *Hebrews*, 151. Harnack renders the emended phrase "und von der Angst weg *nicht* erhört wurde," in accordance with the Old Latin (*exauditus a metu*) and Calvin (*ex suo metu*); so also Thurén, "Gebet und Gehorsam," 141; and Buchanan, *Hebrews*, 97–98.

[13] BAGD, s.v. "ἀπό," I.1. Without such a verb, this translation would result in an awkward ellipsis; cf. Harold W. Attridge, "'Heard Because of His Reverence' (Heb 5:7)," *JBL* 98 (1979): 90.

[14] Swetnam, *Jesus and Isaac*, 178–79; BDF §211.

sense would be odd, though in the OT·both Enoch and Elijah are taken from the earth without dying. The intended reference could also be to a particular kind or instance of death. But the fact that Jesus dies—a fact Hebrews celebrates—precludes this interpretation of ἐκ θανάτου as the mode by which God answers his prayers.[15] The other construal of ἐκ (in spatial terms) is to be preferred, that is, that God answers Jesus' prayers by raising him "out of" death.[16] In early Christian idiom, this would be an overt allusion to the resurrection. Hebrews makes more use of the category of exaltation than that of resurrection in speaking of Jesus' career after the cross, but the author is not a part of a hypothetical "Jesus movement" for which the resurrection was not a fundamental way of understanding the Easter faith.[17] Resurrection is mentioned in a few passages (6:2; 11:19, 35), though these are references to the ἀνάστασις of other people, not of Jesus. Only in the closing benediction in 13:20–21 does Hebrews unambiguously refer to Jesus as having risen from the dead[18]:

> May the God of peace, who brought back from the dead (ὁ ἀναγαγὼν ἐκ νεκρῶν) our Lord Jesus, the great shepherd of the sheep, by the blood of the eternal covenant, equip you with everything good so that you may do his will, working among us that which is pleasing in his sight, through Jesus Christ, to whom be the glory forever and ever.[19]

---

[15] Westcott, *Hebrews*, 126, observes that it is customary to use σώζειν ἀπό in reference to peril "from which" a person is rescued (Matt 1:21; Acts 2:40; Rom 5:9) while in σώζειν ἐκ "the dominant thought is of the peril *in* which the sufferer is immersed." This view is qualified somewhat by Bruce, *Hebrews*, 100 n. 51.

[16] Ellingworth, *Hebrews*, 288. Not surprisingly, this meaning for ἐκ θανάτου is much less common outside the NT.

[17] Cf. Luke T. Johnson, *The Real Jesus* (San Francisco: Harper, 1996), 137–38.

[18] It is possible that 7:11, 15, also contain veiled allusions to Jesus' rising.

[19] It is tempting to see these verses as an afterthought with little or no connection to the author's argument or as traditional, possibly hymnic, material that the author has taken over with little regard for how it relates to the rest of the letter. On these grounds one might object that it therefore cannot be used as a source for the author's thought. Three answers can be given to this objection. First, that the benediction is traditional material does not in principle disqualify it as a clue to the mind of the author. He may have chosen it precisely because of what the tradition contained. Second, "traditional" material in the early church did not spontaneously generate itself. Someone had to put it into writing, and it is quite possible that the author of Hebrews, whose literary skill is manifest throughout the letter, was one of those responsible for the extant form of the church's "tradition." (Buchanan, *Hebrews*, 98, argues that Heb 5:7 is an original hymn of thanksgiving based on an earlier creed.) Third, to disregard what the benediction contains as mere formalities is to beg the question. As Attridge notes, the references to peace,

God here takes the initiative in raising Jesus from the grave, thus providing support for viewing the resurrection as the answer to Jesus' prayers.[20]

Working backwards, if the resurrection constitutes the divine response to Jesus' prayer, it may seem most reasonable to assume that the thrust of his prayer was to be raised from the dead—Jesus got exactly what he asked for, in other words.[21] This view is certainly superior to some of the other theories about the content of his prayer that have little discernible basis in the text.[22] It is important here to make a careful distinction. For a modern scholar to say that Hebrews attributes to Jesus belief in his own resurrection and trust in God to

---

God's will, and covenant bring together three of the letter's central themes (*Hebrews*, 405).

[20] What "resurrection" meant for the author and his readers, however, is not self-evident. C. F. Evans discusses the various forms the resurrection belief takes in the NT, and it is instructive to compare these with the perspective of Hebrews (*Resurrection and the New Testament* [SBT, 2nd ser. 12; London: SCM, 1970], 132–69). A "rudimentary" form is one he calls the "re-active." This understanding focuses upon the divine reversal of the evil done by humans in crucifying Jesus. Interpreting the resurrection in this way is compatible with what one finds in Heb 13:20 in that it sees resurrection as primarily an act of God. But insofar as it sees the crucifixion as something only to be reversed, it is inadequate for expressing the author's thought. Jesus' death and suffering in Hebrews have positive salvific consequences.

Another aspect of resurrection mentioned by Evans is more helpful in understanding its function in Hebrews. Resurrection suggests, among other things, the raising of a particular person. It looks backward as well as forward and draws attention to the death in a way that exaltation does not because death is implicit in the idea of resurrection. Death need not play any part whatsoever in exaltation. Since resurrection is the reversal of a particular death, it emphasizes the particular life which has been cut short. The sheer fact of death has a different meaning when considered apart from the identity of the one experiencing it. Viewed from this perspective, the author's often underappreciated interest in the earthly career of Jesus ("the days of his flesh") comes into clearer focus (cf. E. Grässer, "Der historische Jesus im Hebräerbrief," *ZNW* 56 [1965]: 82–88; B. L. Melbourne, "An Examination of the Historical-Jesus Motif in the Epistle to the Hebrews," *AUSS* 26 [1988]: 281–97). It was important not only that Jesus *died*, but that *Jesus* died as well. Jesus was a descendent of Abraham (2:16–17). He endured testing and suffering (2:18). He was from the tribe of Judah and not, as his priestly status might suggest, a Levite (7:14). He was crucified (12:2). His crucifixion took place specifically "outside the city gate" (13:12). It is the peculiar quality of this life that contributes to the efficacy of his death.

[21] See also Jeremias, , "Hbr 5,7–10," 109–110; Attridge, *Hebrews*, 150. Speculation as to the content of Jesus' prayer began at least as early as John Chrysostom (*Hom. Heb.* 8.3) and so is not peculiar to modern commentators; cf. Westcott, *Hebrews*, 126.

[22] Attridge, *Hebrews*, 150, and Koester, *Hebrews*, 288, cite earlier studies specifying the content of Jesus' prayer as, e.g., a request for strength to withstand suffering, for victory over Satan, or for rescue from premature death in Gethsemane.

bring it to pass is not the same as to say that the historical Jesus himself held such convictions. Confident expectation of his own resurrection as reflected in his prediction of this event recorded in the gospels (Mark 8:31; 9:9, 31; 10:34; 14:28 and parallels) is usually dismissed as *vaticinia ex eventu* formulated by the early church. This presents no problem for the present discussion since it is the aim to uncover what one segment of the early church (that represented by Hebrews) thought about Jesus and not what he may have thought about himself. Nor is it relevant to object on theological grounds that firm hope on Jesus' part of being resurrected detracts from his true humanity by mitigating his subjective sense of anxiety over the prospect of death.[23] Such an objection embodies a sweeping claim in both metaphysical and existential terms. Who is to say what is "truly human" or how Jesus may have been spiritually or psychologically affected by any foresight of the resurrection. Moreover, countless individuals over the centuries—including the fourth of the Maccabean martyrs in 2 Macc 7:14 (cf. also Heb 11:35)—have been utterly convinced, with or without good reason,[24] of their own future resurrections without becoming "less human" by virtue of any resultant relativization of their anxiety. There is thus no a priori reason to believe that the author of Hebrews would have intended to detract from Jesus' humanity by suggesting that he asked, and fully expected, to be raised from the dead.[25] Prophetic foresight in the face of death is a faculty possessed by many of the faithful in chapter eleven, and so it would be curious to deny it in this instance to Jesus.

Since Hebrews envisions Jesus as praying to be resurrected, he further implies that Jesus is acquiescing in his own death. This follows because the concept of resurrection requires that a death has occurred. Swetnam pushes the point even further: in acquiescing to the idea of his own sacrificial death, not only is Jesus not asking God to prevent him from dying; rather, he is actually asking to be allowed to die.[26] This hypothesis takes care of many of the

---

[23] This is implied in Oscar Cullmann's treatment of Heb 5:7, which, along with 2:17, "is perhaps the boldest assertion of the completely human character of Jesus in the New Testament" (*The Christology of the New Testament* [trans. S. C. Guthrie and C. A. M. Hall; London: SCM, 1959], 95). Interpretations seeking to minimize Jesus' fear, he says, lean dangerously in the direction of Docetism (cf. 96–98).

[24] Socrates' interlocutor in *Phaed.* 87A–88B says that no one but a fool can face death with confidence unless he can prove the immortality of the soul. More accurately, perhaps, is to say that no one ought to face death confidently without being able to prove the immortality of the soul; many people in fact feel confidence even when they lack good reason for doing so.

[25] Especially since Jesus appears to have agreed with the Pharisees over against the Sadducees on the resurrection (Mark 12:18–27 and parallels).

[26] Swetnam, *Jesus and Isaac*, 182–84. A variation of this argument is offered by John Chrysostom (*Hom. Heb.* 8.3), who suggests that Jesus prays for death but did not need to pray for resurrection since this was in his own power.

difficulties already mentioned: Jesus is "heard" in that he is permitted to die by "the one who is able to save him from death." It becomes possible to take καίπερ ὢν υἱός from v. 8a as a concessive clause describing the dynamic between God and Jesus, as God hears and grants his unusual request to die "although he was a son."[27] Jesus' willingness to die may also account for the efficacy of his death as compared with that in 11:19 of Abraham's offering of Isaac—whom the patriarch received "back from the dead" (ἐκ νεκρῶν), though only "figuratively speaking" (ἐν παραβολῇ)—since only an actual death could be the source of real salvation (cf. 5:8–9; 9:17–22).[28]

Swetnam's proposal fits better if Jesus' prayer takes place in some setting other than Gethsemane as described in the Synoptic Gospels.[29] As noted above, there is no scholarly consensus concerning the setting Hebrews envisions. Gethsemane poses a problem for Swetnam because Jesus appears to be pleading for his life, not for his death. Even so, if Hebrews does have Gethsemane in mind, it may be that he focuses on the second half of the prayer ("nevertheless not my will, but yours, be done") instead of the first half ("if you are willing, remove this cup from me"). Thus Hebrews could conceivably construe the conditional nature of the petition to mean that Jesus was effectively asking to die. When Judas hands over Jesus immediately after the prayer in Matthew's version and one of the disciples cuts off the ear of his would-be captor, Jesus rebukes him and says that, if he so wished, he could ask God to rescue him (26:53): "Do you think that I am not able to appeal to my father, and he will at once send me more than twelve legions of angels?" He could have pleaded for his life, Jesus implies, but he did not because it was not the divine will.[30] In Heb 10:5–10, the author places LXX Ps 39:7–9 on the lips of Jesus, twice (vv. 7, 9) citing the line, "Behold, I have come to do thy will" (ἰδοὺ ἥκω τοῦ ποιῆσαι τὸ θέλημά σου).[31] He prefaces the section by stating that Christ expressed this

---

[27] His suggested solution is less helpful in clarifying the rest of v. 8. This is not to say that he is necessarily off the mark in interpreting v. 8—only that his novel interpretation of v. 7 adds relatively little to the discussion of the following verse.

[28] Swetnam, *Jesus and Isaac*, 184; idem, "The Crux at Hebrews 5,7–8," 356.

[29] Matt 26:36–46; Mark 14:32–42; Luke 22:29–46. John's account in 18:1–11 does not describe Jesus at prayer but does retain a statement about the necessity of drinking "the cup" God has given him.

[30] In a similar passage in John, though not set in the garden, Jesus contemplates his glorification, by which he means his death (12:27): "And what will I say? 'Father, save me from this hour'? No. It is for this reason that I have come to this hour." Jeremias puts special emphasis on this passage for understanding Heb 5:7, which he tends to associate with Gethsemane ("Hbr 5,7–10," 109). Cf. Bruce, *Hebrews*, 102 n. 63, for the observation that in Matt 4 (esp. vv. 3, 6) Jesus similarly refuses to exploit his special stastus as God's son though tempted to do so by the devil.

[31] The alterations made by Hebrews in citing the LXX, especially the deletion of ἐβουλήθην, have the effect of more closely connecting Jesus' entry into the world to his

sentiment "when he came into the world" (εἰσερχόμενος εἰς τὸν κόσμον), thus Hebrews regards it as a guiding principle in interpreting Jesus' motivations covering his entire life. These remarks in chapter ten occur in the context of characterizing Jesus' priesthood and its superiority over the Levitical cult. Because Jesus' prayer in 5:7 is likewise a function of his unique priesthood (cf. 4:14–5:6; 5:10), it makes good sense to see him seeking God's will here as well.[32]

It is perhaps imprudent to concentrate too narrowly on Gethsemane as the *Sitz im Leben* for Jesus' prayer envisioned by Hebrews in light of the very real possibility that the letter was written prior to the gospels. While it is highly probable that this tradition circulated in oral form and as part of a primitive passion account prior to its incorporation into the Synoptic Gospels[33] and thus may have been familiar to the author of Hebrews in a variety of forms, conclusions based on his hypothetical exegesis of the details of the scene rightly remain tentative. There is little way of knowing with adequate precision what it might have looked like even when one grants his familiarity with some version of the story.

Likewise, it is possible to be overly precise in specifying the content of the prayer since the author sees fit not to dwell on it at any length. That Jesus dies, according to Hebrews, that he serves as both priest and victim and offers himself for the sins of the people, that he prays to God and is "heard," that he seeks to accomplish God's will from the moment he enters the world until the time he leaves it and beyond, that he returns from the dead, and that he serves as an exemplar for the readers— all may be safely assumed since the author states these propositions more or less explicitly in the letter. The challenge is to determine whether there is a way of understanding the ambiguities—namely, the details of Jesus' prayer and the nature of his εὐλάβεια—in a way that is both consonant with those aspects of the author's argument that are clear and indisputable, and also intelligible against the background of assumptions about

---

express purpose to do God's will, which is for Jesus' sacrifice of himself and not for the inadequate burnt offerings and sin offerings made under the old covenant; cf. Schröger, *Der Verfasser des Hebräerbriefes als Schriftausleger*, 173–75; Lane, *Hebrews*, 2:263–64.

[32] Westcott's formulation is a variation of the position taken here: "True prayer—the prayer which must be answered—is the personal recognition and acceptance of the divine will . . . . It follows that the hearing of prayer, which teaches obedience, is not so much the granting of a specific petition, which is assumed by the petitioner to be the way to the end desired, but the assurance that what is granted does most effectively lead to the end" (*Hebrews*, 127).

[33] So R. Bultmann, *History of the Synoptic Tradition* (rev. ed.; trans. J. Marsh; Oxford: Blackwell, 1963), 267–68; and Vincent Taylor, *The Gospel According to St. Mark* (London: Macmillan, 1959), 551.

the emotions and their religious value current in the broader milieu when he is writing.

The author's extensive and creative use of the OT, especially the Psalter, in presenting and interpreting the Christ event suggests a possible alternative to the hypothesis that Gethsemane provides the only or most appropriate lens through which to view the interaction between God and Jesus in Heb 5:7. Just as the Synoptic passion narratives combine description of events with citation of and allusion to specific biblical texts, the two need not be automatically regarded as mutually exclusive in Hebrews.[34] A brief look at the psalms that likely influence the language of this tightly constructed scene will help to determine whether it is necessary to go all the way with Swetnam's strong reading of Jesus' prayer (as a plea for, not from, death) in order to make sense of the author's message.

Commentators have identified several psalms of which echoes can be heard in 5:7.[35] Two psalms merit special attention, Pss 22 and 116 (LXX 21 and 114–115). Strobel, followed by Brandenburger and Buchanan, see LXX Ps 114 as the source of the language in Hebrews.[36] The psalmist sings praises "because the Lord will hear (εἰσακούσεται) the sound of my supplication (τῆς δεήσεώς μου)" (114:1). He had been surrounded by the snares of death and Hades, and the Lord saved (ἔσωσέν) him (vv. 3, 6). The Lord delivered his soul from death (ἐκ θανάτου) and his eyes from tears (ἀπὸ δακρύων) (v. 8).[37]

Equally striking are the verbal affinities with Ps 22 (LXX 21), which begins with the familiar cry of anguish, "My God, my God, why have you forsaken me?" and continues in v. 3, "I will cry (κεκράξομαι) to you by day but you will not hear (οὐκ εἰσακούσῃ)."[38] Their ancestors, he says in v. 6, cried (ἐκέκραξαν) to God and were saved (ἐσώθησαν). But for the psalmist, things get worse before they get better: he is without any help (v. 12), and though surrounded by ravenous enemies, it is God who brings him down "to the dust of death" (v. 16). In v. 23 (quoted earlier in Heb 2:12) the tone turns hopeful, and

---

[34] See esp. A. Strobel, "Die Psalmengrundlage der Gethsemane-Parallele Hebr. 5,7ff.," ZNW 45 (1954): 252–66.

[35] Bruce, Hebrews, 101 n. 54, and Schröger, Der Verfasser des Hebräerbriefes als Schriftausleger, 120–21, mention Pss 31; 39; 69. Koester, Hebrews, adds Ps 42.

[36] Strobel, "Die Psalmengrundlage der Gethsemane-Parallele," 254–65; Brandenburger, "Text und Vorlagen von Hebr. V 7–10," 211; Buchanan, Hebrews, 97–98.

[37] In its original setting, this verse probably referred to deliverance after a close brush with death (so Strobel, "Die Psalmengrundlage der Gethsemane-Parallele," 260–61, against Attridge, Hebrews, 150 n. 167). The snares of Hades (κίνδυνοι ᾅδου) in v. 3 refers to the risk of death, not necessarily to the actual experience of death. One might expect even greater rejoicing if something more like resurrection were in view; cf. the possible allusion to v. 3 in Acts 2:24, followed by the citation of LXX Ps 15:8–11.

[38] Justin Martyr, Dial. 99, associates this verse with Gethsemane; cf. Bruce, Hebrews, 101 n. 55.

in v. 25 he declares, "The Lord has not turned his face from me, and when I cried (κεκραγέναι) to him, he heard (εἰσήκουσή) me."

Nothing from either psalm appears in direct, unmistakable quotation in Hebrews. If the question is framed in terms of demonstrable familiarity or likely influence, the scales tip towards Ps 22. Not only does Hebrews quote this psalm (in 2:12); it is moreover the primary text read by the early church as a description of Jesus' passion.[39] Swetnam, in his most recent article, argues that v. 25 is the intended allusion in Heb 5:7 and that the *Sitz im Leben* is the cross.[40] So precise an identification, however, seems to weaken somewhat his earlier claim (which, while radical, had a considerable degree of logical consistency) since the psalm gives little or no indication that the speaker wants to die. The emphasis falls almost entirely on the fact of his suffering and on the deliverance he seeks from God. The habit of early Christian writers like Hebrews to find significance beneath the surface of, and often in conflict with, their OT sources sometimes detracts from the exegetical yield to be had from the identification of these sources. That is to say, if Swetnam can posit Ps 22 as the background for Heb 5:7 and still assert that Jesus is praying expressly for his own death, it becomes difficult in principle to rule out more arbitrary interpretive decisions. Accordingly, it is more advisable to stop short of Swetnam's position on the content of the prayer and say only that here Jesus assents to his death and looks forward to a "better resurrection."

The Exemplary Function of Jesus' Submission

Jesus' "humble submission" (NEB) and trust in God in the face of suffering and death characterize the εὐλάβεια that gains a positive hearing, hence its common rendering as "reverence" or "piety." What of his "loud cry and tears"? Are not such physical symptoms suggestive of a quivering anxiety, the likes of which Hebrews wants to dispel? Not necessarily. Attridge has demonstrated the way in which the description of Jesus' prayer in 5:7 conforms to a pattern found in Hellenistic writings delineating the ideal prayer of a pious Jew.[41] He adduces evidence from Philo (*Her.* 1–29) which portrays the exemplary prayers of Abraham and Moses as characterized by boldness (παρρησία), loudness, and emotion.[42] In *Her.* 22–29, Philo adds that εὐλάβεια also accompanies the bold

---

[39] Quotations of Ps 22 in the NT (according to Appendix IV in NA[27]): v. 2=Matt 27:46; Mark 15:34; v. 14=1 Pet 5:8; v. 19=Matt 27:35; Mark 15:24; Luke 23:34; John 19:24; v. 22=Heb 2:12. Possible allusions: v. 3=Luke 18:7; v. 6=Rom 5:5; v. 7=Mark 9:12; v. 8=Matt 27:29, 39; Mark 15:29; Luke 23:35; v. 9=Matt 27:43; v. 21=2 Tim 4:17; v. 23=Rev 19:5; v. 28=Rev 11:15.

[40] Swetnam, "The Crux at Hebrews 5,7–8," 356–60.

[41] Attridge, "'Heard Because of His Reverence'," 90.

[42] N.B. esp. *Her.* 14–16, where the faithful should "not only speak with ordinary

prayer of the faithful, tempering it in a way that is fitting when approaching a fearful master. One who makes petition tacitly acknowledges the Lord's sovereignty and terrible power (τὸ φοβερὸν τῆς δυναστείας): "I come before Thee in fear and trembling (δεδιὼς καὶ τρέμων), and yet again I am confident (θαρρῶ)."[43] Fear and confidence are not, as it were, at war within the individual but are "blended in a harmony" such that one's speech is "neither bold without caution, nor cautious without boldness" (μήτε ἄνευ εὐλαβείας παρρησιάζεσθαι μήτε ἀπαρρησιάστως εὐλαβεῖσθαι). Confidence to approach God results from perceiving and confessing one's nothingness (*Her.* 29).

It is doubtful that Hebrews is dependent on this passage, yet the correspondence in implicit attitude and action makes it clear that both authors regard the quality denoted by εὐλάβεια as a virtue and not a vice, one that is moreover perfectly compatible with confidence. Epictetus takes the perceived incompatibility between confidence (θάρσος) and εὐλάβεια as the subject of a discourse (2.1), recognizing that most people consider paradoxical the Stoic assertion of their essential complementarity. Confidence, he says, is the appropriate disposition in matters outside of one's control since things that lie outside the sphere of choice (τὰ ἀπροαίρετα) are ἀδιάφορα (neither good nor evil; cf. *SVF* 3.118 et al.), while εὐλάβεια is appropriate in matters in which an actor may exercise the will (τὰ προαιρετικά) since evil consists only in making bad choices (2.1.4–7). The canonical Stoic distinction between passions and the three εὐπαθείαι ("good feelings") obviously informs his treatment in this essay. Chrysippus (*SVF* 3.175) and others define εὐλάβεια as εὔλογος ἔκκλισις ("rational avoidance") and, as one of the eupathic dispositions unlike φόβος, consider it a praiseworthy quality perfectly conducive to the exercise of virtue.[44]

Needless to say, it is even more doubtful that Hebrews is drawing on Epictetus in his characterization of Jesus in 5:7. There are nonetheless significant points at which the portrayal of Jesus harmonizes with the Stoic

---

gentleness but shout with a louder cry (κραυγῆς μείζονος)." God, the hearer (ὁ ἀκροατής), is said to ask of the one who prays, "Is it in supplication for ills to be averted, or is in thanksgiving for blessings imparted, or in both?" Also 19, where Philo writes that "the virtuous man uses such παρρησία as not only to speak and cry out, but even to advance positive claims with true confidence and genuine feeling (ἀπὸ γνησίου τοῦ πάθους)" (trans. Yonge). See also 2 Macc 11:6; 1 Esd 5:62; Philo, *Det.* 92; *Alleg. Interp.* 3.213; *Cher.* 47. Earlier than Attridge, Dey, *The Intermediary World*, 224, noted similar language describing pious prayer in Philo (*QG* 4.233) and in 3 Macc (1:16; 5:7, 25).

[43] Walter Grundmann comments on this passage, "If εὐλάβεια expresses the sense of distance, the *tremendum*, θαρρεῖν expresses the *fascinosum*" ("θαρρέω," *TDNT* 3:26).

[44] On Stoic descriptions of εὐλάβεια, see above in chapter two, pp. 71–74.

notion of εὐλάβεια. Hebrews places Jesus in the arena of choice in his
encounter with death, which, according to Epictetus, is appropriate to the
exercise of εὐλάβεια by the virtuous. Only if Jesus' obedience is a function of
his free will—meaning that his compliance with the divine will was not
foreordained and wholly inescapable but rather truly voluntary—is it genuine
obedience and therefore worthy of praise.[45] He voluntarily submits his will to
God's when he offers himself as propitiation for sin (9:26; 10:5–10).[46] Jesus
performs his role as "pioneer and perfecter of faith" in 12:2 "for the sake of the
joy set before him," implying that he had the option, if he so chose, to avoid the
shame of the cross.[47] When faced with the prospect of death, he exhibits
εὐλάβεια in making the right choice (to assent to suffering and death in
accordance with God's will) and is consequently "perfected" (τελειωθείς).
Apart from the obvious differences, such as their respective notions of the divine
and of what it might mean to live "in accordance with nature," Hebrews departs
from the description of Epictetus in making the experience of death non-
compulsory for Jesus *qua* human, even if it is absolutely necessary in order to be
designated "high priest according to the order of Melchizedek." Because of this
key difference, however, the predication of εὐλάβεια on the part of Jesus is at
least partly intelligible alongside the Stoic concept of appropriate emotion
(εὐπάθεια).

    Does this mean that Jesus is afraid of death in 5:7? Koester points out that
εὐλάβεια and cognates can be used to express a fear whose unstated object is
death, but he misreads Epictetus when he cites *Diatr.* 2.1.14 as an example of
this usage.[48] Epictetus states in this passage, "Our confidence (θάρσος) ought,
therefore, to be turned toward death, and our caution (εὐλάβεια) toward the
fear of death." He is not equating fear of death with εὐλάβεια as a cursory
reading might suggest. After all, εὐλάβεια is a good thing for Stoics and
φόβος, like all emotions, is a very bad thing. Rather, in the first clause he is
arguing in good Stoic fashion that death, as it is an inescapable and "natural"
fact for all humans, is not an evil to be dreaded but should be welcomed without
any dismay. When he continues that εὐλάβεια should be directed at fear of

---

[45] The same is true in the case of the other NT references to his obedience (Rom 5:19;
Phil 2:5–11).

[46] This takes place "by that will" (ἐν ᾧ θελήματι) according to 10:10, which leaves it
ambiguous as to whether it is God's or Jesus' will. At any rate, in the context the two
wills have merged to form a united will and so no distinction is needed. Attridge,
Hebrews, 276 n. 105, notes the development of this theme in John (4:34; 5:30; 6:38–40).

[47] It is possible to take ἀντὶ τῆς προκειμένης αὐτῷ χαρᾶς as either "for [i.e., in
exchange] the joy" (RSV and most modern translations) or "rather than the joy" (Lane);
cf. Croy, *Endurance in Suffering*, 4–25, for the history of interpretation on the question.
In either case, Jesus is presented as making a choice to endure the cross.

[48] Koester, *Hebrews*, 289, correctly citing Sir 41:3; 2 Macc 8:16.

death, he is saying that one should be cautious or wary about being afraid to die; in other words, when it comes to death, one should be afraid of being afraid. This may seem odd but it fits seamlessly within the Stoic view of the emotions and within the context of Epictetus's argument: Desire to avoid death in the absolute sense will leave one continually subject to fear and perturbation since that eventual fate is ultimately beyond any human's control (2.1.13). Therefore, the formation of opinions (δόγμα) concerning death must take place not in a careless manner (2.1.14–15) but "cautiously" (εὐλαβῶς). One's opinions, and hence one's emotions, fall within the power of the individual, thus the ideal of self-sufficiency (αὐτάρκεια) will be attainable by "those who are being truly educated" (τοῖς τῷ ὄντι παιδευομένοις).[49] The exercise of εὐλάβεια, then, involves careful discernment concerning future circumstances that are truly evil and, at least in theory, avoidable.

Jesus represents a special case not envisioned by Epictetus in that he need not be bound by mortality unless he chooses to fulfill the role of high priest. He thus satisfies the requisite conditions for the exercise of εὐλάβεια, which involves much more than a subjective response to perceived harm. Philo's usage shows that the "loud cry and tears" can actually be a function of the petitioner's piety expressive of boldness rather than excessive agitation or anguish, though the use of εὐλάβεια certainly allows for some element of fear.[50] Its use to describe the extreme grief as is purportedly witnessed in the physical state of Jesus in Heb 5:7, however, is quite rare. Cognate forms in the LXX most often carry the neutral sense of wariness or caution (1 Sam 18:25, 29; Sir 22:22; 1 Macc 3:30 et al.). Frequently they express the familiar notion of "fear of the Lord" as a synonym for Israelite religiosity (Prov 2:8; 30:5; Isa 57:11; Nah 1:7; Hab 2:20; Zech 2:13; Mal 3:16; Sir 7:29), which is often indistinguishable from more general expressions conveying the sense of conscientious observance of the law (Lev 15:31; Josh 22:24; Prov 28:14; Mic 7:2; Sir 11:17; 2 Macc 6:11). Only at Wis 17:8 does it clearly refer to the kind of fear and anxiety from which, according to Bultmann's interpretation, one would need to be "liberated."[51]

Likewise among pagan authors, the occurrence of εὐλάβεια to denote a particularly undesirable disposition or affective state is relatively uncommon. Cognate forms occur most often with the generic meaning of "carefulness" or

---

[49] *Diatr.* 2.1.21–22. The "fruit" (καρπός) of this teaching, says Epictetus, is tranquility (ἀταραξία), fearlessness (ἀφοβία), and freedom (ἐλευθερία). Cf. the conclusion to the argument in Heb 12:4–11 aimed at persuading the audience to regard hardship as a necessary component of the freeborn son's education: God's παιδεία will yield "a peaceful fruit of righteousness."

[50] On the hypothesis that Ps 22 provides the background for Heb 5:7, it is also noteworthy that the author of Hebrews has not taken over the extreme manifestations of distress one finds in vv. 12–21 in describing Jesus' prayer.

[51] Bultmann, *TDNT* 2:753.

"vigilance" concerning some matter, in both sacred and secular contexts, without any noticeable sense of disapproval, in fact, with the occasional nuance of conscientiousness.[52] Within this very broad category, Bultmann notes many different nuances in meaning that are frequently difficult to perceive even when one checks his references to primary texts. This is especially the case in those instances where he characterizes a usage as "fear" or "anxiety." In a great number of these texts, nothing so extreme or pejorative is necessarily implied at all. This is the case in the description of Nicias in Diodorus Siculus (13.12.7), where εὐλάβεια occurs together with δεισιδαιμονία. The tone is not judgmental or condescending, and only if one comes to this passage presupposing (or sharing[53]) the low opinion of Nicias found in other versions of his story does the description necessitate a negative interpretation of εὐλάβεια.[54] Counterbalancing this purported equation is Plutarch's portrait of Numa, whose initiative in promoting the national cult in Rome's earliest days is referred to as his εὐλάβεια and is compared favorably to the pitiful δεισιδαιμονία of his successor (Num. 22.7). In fact, when Plutarch uses the term, it is almost always with a positive valence. He regularly uses it in association with careful avoidance of shame and vice and also in religious discourse, where it refers to the conscientious desire to think the right things

---

[52] In this general sense, see Demosthenes, Or. 18.159; 19.206, 262; 23.15; Plato, Phaed. 89C; Ion 537A; Gorg. 519A; Prot. 321A; 333E; Pol. 311A–B; Leg. 3.691B; 11.927C; Aristotle, Pol. 1269A; 1315A; Eth. nic. 4.1.39; 4.7.8; Polybius 1.16.7; 3.111.1; Diodorus Siculus 2.13.4; 16.22.2; Plutarch, Per. 7.1; Brut. 12.2; Epictetus, Diatr. 4.13.4; Diogenes Laertius 7.116; Herodian 2.8.2; 5.2.2; for other references, cf. Bultmann, TDNT 2:751–52.

[53] This is probably the case with Bultmann. The final sentence of his TDNT entry gives cause for questioning his objectivity in presenting and interpreting the evidence. He notes that εὐλάβεια is the common word for piety in present-day Greece, "where religion consists essentially in δεισιδαιμονία." The first half of the statement is true enough. The second half is astonishingly patronizing, especially in a dictionary article. One might give Bultmann the benefit of the doubt if in modern Greek εὐλάβεια and δεισιδαιμονία were more or less synonymous. They are not. Orthodox Christianity in contemporary Greece does not describe itself as δεισιδαιμονία. Just as in the Hellenistic period, today it still has the same meaning as "superstition" has in English, without any positive or even neutral connotation. In this instance (and others), Bultmann confuses description with prescription; that is, in mistakenly citing this as an example where εὐλάβεια has a pejorative sense, he is stating how he thinks Diodorus Siculus ought to have evaluated Nicias but presenting it as though this is how he did in fact evaluate Nicias.

[54] The difficulties in distinguishing the views of Diodorus Siculus from those of his sources are discussed by Robert Drews, "Diodorus and His Sources," AJP 83 (1962): 383–92. Martin, "Hellenistic Superstition," 121–22, has observed how he can even speak of the ways in which δεισιδαιμονία results in confidence instead of fear.

about the gods and to conservative adherence to ancestral tradition.[55] The usage of Philo runs the same gamut of emotions and attitudes as the Jewish and Greco-Roman traditions to which he is heir.[56] All in all, the neutral or positive sense of εὐλάβεια is much more common in biblical and non-biblical Greek than the negative.

Clearly there exists more than ample precedent for viewing the description of Jesus in Heb 5:7 as something other than a picture of cowering fear in the face of death. Similarly, each NT occurrence of the adjectival form εὐλαβής outside of Hebrews is unequivocally positive and appears in reference to devout Jews who recognize, or come to recognize, the spirit of God at work in Jesus or his followers (Luke 2:25; Acts 2:5; 8:2; 22:12).[57] In Heb 11:7, too, the use of the verbal form (εὐλαβηθείς) is an endorsement of Noah's response to God's voice. God sends warning of the imminent flood to Noah, who discerns the signs of the times, "takes heed," and builds the ark for the salvation (σωτηρία) of his household. His actions prefigure those of Christ, whose εὐλάβεια also leads to σωτηρία (5:9) for his οἶκος (3:1–6; 10:21). As this vignette appears as an illustration of praiseworthy faith in God, "fear" would seem to be an inappropriate rendering. At the same time, Noah provides an example for the audience in their present situation—living near the end of an epoch, having received special revelations from God, subjected to the dominant culture's ridicule, and looking forward to salvation for themselves and judgment of the adversaries.[58] One is therefore able to draw a line, running from Jesus to Noah to the audience—who are to worship God "with reverence and awe" (μετὰ εὐλαβείας καὶ δέους)—which marks out the contours of an appropriate Christian response to God when faced with the prospect of death.

Subtle verbal echoes between 5:7–10 and vv. 11–14 further signal that the author wants his audience to learn from and follow Jesus' example of εὐλάβεια, which leads him on a course of voluntarily endured suffering. He refers to his readers in v. 13 as "infantile" (νήπιος), a pejorative term that contrasts with the designation of Jesus as "son" in v. 8. They are not yet ready for solid food as are "the mature" (τελείων), a substantive in v. 14 from the same root as the participle (τελειωθείς) in v. 9 describing Jesus' perfection. There is also the rebuke in v. 12 in which the author expresses his disappointment that the readers still have need of a teacher when they ought to

---

[55] See *Cam.* 21.2; *Aem.* 3.2, in addition to the references contained in the above discussion of Plutarch's use of εὐλάβεια (chapter two, pp. 93–94).

[56] Bultmann, *TDNT* 2:752.

[57] Cf. also *Mart. Pol.* 2.1, referring to the propriety of recognizing God's sovereign will, even in the sufferings of martyrs.

[58] Matt 24:37–39 (=Luke 17:26–27) cites Noah as an example of prudent action in view of the Son of Man's coming to usher in the day of judgment. An analogy between the flood and the salvific effects of the baptismal waters is seen in 1 Pet 3:20–21.

have become teachers themselves. The stark description of Jesus' own "learning" in v. 8 is still ringing in their ears when he berates them for still having much to learn. Instead of having learned their lessons, in v. 11 they have become "dull of hearing" (νωθροὶ . . . ταῖς ἀκοαῖς). The dullness of their ἀκοή stands in contrast to Christ's exemplary ὑπακοή in v. 8. In 6:1 the implicit comparison becomes a more explicit call to imitation with the appeal to press on to perfection (τελειότης). Inasmuch as Christ's perfection derives from the fact of his obedient suffering and death (2:10; 5:8–9; 7:27–28), the author may be hinting that the readers' perfection involves their willingness to run the same risk by remaining true to their confession.[59] Their perfection will not of necessity involve their own deaths, but suffering voluntarily endured does play an important role "as an encouraging proof of sonship."[60] Since the readers exercise some measure of control in determining whether they suffer by virtue of their decision to remain faithful and not apostatize under pressure, they will have ample opportunity to demonstrate their capacity "to distinguish good from evil" (5:14), a phrase which, rather than carrying purely ethical connotations, may indicate a Christ-like commitment to doing God's will (10:36; 13:21) wherever it may lead them and in spite of their instinctive aversion to the attendant pain and suffering.[61]

Bultmann asks why εὐλάβεια is so rare in the religious sense in early Christian literature given that it seems to have been suited for this role by its Hellenistic usage.[62] The main reason, he speculates, is that "the decisive element . . . is the negative aspect of nervous caution, as may be seen from the connection between εὐλάβεια and δεισιδαιμονία," adding that it thus comes as little surprise that Jews are called εὐλαβεῖς. But as was shown above, the equation of εὐλάβεια with δεισιδαιμονία is rarely, if ever, made in the way Bultmann and others[63] suggest, and when it is in reference to Jews, εὐλαβεῖς is

[59] On the association of Jesus' death with his perfection, see Peterson, *Hebrews and Perfection*, 68–69; and deSilva, *Perseverance in Gratitude*, 197–99. Most succinct are the final words of Jesus on the cross in John 19:30, "It is finished" (τετέλεσται). Given the comparison in Hebrews of Jesus' priesthood with the Levitical priesthood, the statement at Philo, *Alleg. Interp.* 3.45, that Aaron is made perfect (τελειωθῇ) when he dies is intriguing but otherwise without any discernible relationship to the discussion of death in Hebrews. More generally on the use of τελειόω and cognates in reference to death, see Attridge, *Hebrews*, 85–86; and Koester, *Hebrews*, 124–25.

[60] Peterson, *Hebrews and Perfection*, 175. Again, this is also the thrust of 12:5–11.

[61] See Allen Wikgren, "Patterns of Perfection in the Epistle to the Hebrews," *NTS* 6 (1959–60): 159–67, on the relationship between the perfection of Christ and that of the believer.

[62] Bultmann, *TDNT* 2:753–54.

[63] E.g., Andriessen and Lenglet, "Quelques passages difficiles," 208–12. While they do not make the explicit equation, their interpretation of ἀπὸ τῆς εὐλαβείας is such that εὐλάβεια takes on all the disagreeable nuances, such as terror and paralysis, that attach

usually used by other Jews and so should be deemed a compliment and not an insult. Moreover, if the negative aspect of fear is indeed the dominant one, it is odd that the word group appears only in Hebrews and Luke-Acts, arguably the two most skilled Greek stylists among the NT authors who would presumably be well aware of the impression made by the words they chose. Of all people, surely they ought to know better than to use so negative a term in such a complimentary way. The fact that they apparently do not use it in this way adds to the likelihood that the prevalence of the negative aspect of εὐλάβεια has been much exaggerated.

Much more likely is the thesis that Hebrews chooses εὐλάβεια to characterize Jesus in 5:7 precisely because, while allowing for some element of reasonable apprehension in view of the fate awaiting him, it emphasizes the measured quality of his fear and his reverent subordination of his will to God's. So measured is his fear that he actually acquiesces in his own death, thus he is able to overcome any instinctive human revulsion he may experience at the thought of dying.[64] However well it may accord with Hebrews' usage, it is not necessary to assert that the author is consciously adapting the technical term used by Stoics of the eupathic dispositions since the positive sense of εὐλάβεια was in such wide circulation.[65] Far from introducing the potentially embarrassing note of terror, the author's choice of terms avoids giving this impression. In a way that φόβος is not able, εὐλάβεια conveys the idea of healthy caution together with that of reverent attentiveness to the divine will. Finally, if the author has LXX Ps 21:25 in mind ("The Lord has not turned his face from me, and when I cried to him, he heard me")—and this is quite likely given the popularity of this psalm in early Christian circles and given the fact that Hebrews quotes v. 23 earlier in the letter—this may explain why Hebrews does not attribute φόβος τοῦ κυρίου to Jesus, as vv. 24 and 26 of the psalm would lead one to expect.

---

to δεισιδαιμονία (cf. also the Weymouth version: " . . . was delivered from the terror from which He shrank").

[64] His moderation is all the more impressive if one sees Hebrews as agreeing with the notion, implicit in the Synoptic accounts, that Jesus regards his own death not as simply an ordinary human death—horrible though even that would be—but as the consequence of God's wrathful judgment on sin (cf. Taylor, *St. Mark*, 554); cf. also Otto, *The Idea of the Holy*, 84–85.

[65] See E. Vernon Arnold, *Roman Stoicism* (Cambridge: Cambridge University Press, 1911), 420 n. 20, for the claim that Hebrews knowingly invokes Stoic terminology in order to present the Christian faith in a form that would win the intellectual assent of the Roman world.

Fear as a Concomitant of Revelation and Worship (Heb 12:18–29)

In 12:18–29, a pericope beginning and ending with fire imagery for the divine, two final occurrences of the motif of fear deserve attention. The fear and trembling of Moses in v. 21 may be categorized as a form of theophanic fear, though this variety of fear is not easy to distinguish from that which is to accompany true worship of God in vv. 28–29.[66]

Moses' "Fear and Trembling" at Sinai (Heb 12:21)

Whereas Hebrews goes out of the way in chapter eleven to expunge all traces of fear from Moses' record, no such attempt is made in 12:21. The author catalogues a number of phenomena familiar from Israel's encounter with God at Sinai and explains that "the spectacle was so terrifying (οὕτω φοβερόν) that Moses said, 'I tremble with fear' (ἔκφοβός εἰμι καὶ ἔντρομος)." No OT text is an exact match for this statement. To appreciate the nature of Moses' fear and its place in the author's argument, it will be helpful to consider which texts may underlie the scenario Hebrews envisions.

Although never identifying the site by name, the author appears to have combined elements from a handful of episodes taking place at Sinai-Horeb in the pentateuchal narratives.[67] The blazing fire, darkness, gloom, and whirlwind in v. 18 derive from accounts in Deuteronomy (4:11–12; 5:22–25) as does the mighty voice in v. 19. The trumpet's blare is taken from Exod 19:16–19, so loud that it causes the people to tremble (ἐπτοήθη). Thunder and lightning, the sound of trumpets, and smoke also accompany Moses' delivery of the Ten Commandments in Exod 20:18–19 and evoke the fear of the people, who ask Moses to speak to them because God's unmediated word is too much for them to bear (cf. Deut 4:33; 5:23–26). Hebrews 12:19–20 traces the thread of the Exodus narrative back again to Exod 19:12–13 to explain why those hearing the voice "begged that no further messages be given to them": God had ordered that "if even a beast touches the mountain, it shall be stoned." Their awe before the divine presence is mixed with fear driven by the instinct of self-preservation.[68]

The language of v. 21 presents a problem in identifying the intended allusion and hence the source of Moses' fear. While the people are said to be terrified at God's descent at Sinai, nothing is said in the aforementioned texts of fear on the part of Moses, who exhorts the Israelites not to be afraid. Only later,

---

[66] See Terrien, *IDB* 2:257–58.

[67] Ellingworth, *Hebrews*, 676; Koester, *Hebrews*, 543–44.

[68] The prohibition in Exod 19:12–13 against crossing the boundary and setting foot on the holy mountain applies to both animals and humans. If unwitting transgression by an animal is punished by death, Hebrews implies, then the consequences of the willful disobedience of the people would be all the more terrible.

after Moses has been on the mountain for forty days to receive the stone tablets of the law and the people have prevailed upon Aaron to fashion the golden calf to receive their offerings, does the OT attribute fear to Moses with words resembling those of Hebrews. The story appears first in Exod 32. When it is retold by Moses in Deut 9, he quotes himself in v. 19 as having said, "I am afraid" (ἔκφοβός εἰμι). Moffatt remarks that the author forgets that Moses utters his cry of horror not at the Sinai theophany but on this separate occasion some time later, when God's wrath against Aaron and the people terrifies Moses and leads him to intercede on their behalf.[69] Also lacking from Deut 9:19 is the "trembling" (ἔντρομος) of Heb 12:21.[70]

These inconsistencies lead most commentators to the broad conclusion that Hebrews simply wants to highlight the terror felt in the theophany at Sinai by expanding it to include Moses as well as the people.[71] While this is true, it overlooks certain aspects of the author's handling of the tradition. There is actually little need to go outside of Deut 4 to account for the way in which the author of Hebrews collapses separate episodes taking place at Sinai into a unified yet complex scene in 12:18–21. His use of fire imagery in Heb 12:29 ("Our God is a consuming fire")—an allusion to Deut 4:24—to form an *inclusio* with 12:18, which draws on language found in Deut 4:11–12, strongly suggests that Hebrews has dwelt at length upon this specific recapitulation of the Sinai narrative. Moses reminds the people of the portents surrounding the giving of the law (4:10–14) and then reinforces the injunction against idolatry (vv. 15–31). God had grown angry with Moses when they fell into idolatry during his time on the mountain, which leads to his exclusion from the promised land (vv. 21–22).[72] The episode with the golden calf is clearly in view here, even if it is not described as fully as in the retelling of Deut 9. The verbal detail of Moses' fear (ἔκφοβος) comes from 9:19, where he is said to intercede for them as well as for Aaron, but God voices no intention of making Moses pay for their sin; to the contrary, God plans to blot out the people's name and make a great nation out of him in their place (9:14; cf. Exod 32:7–10). The earlier passage, then, makes explicit the cause for Moses' fear, which is only implied in Deut 9:19: through no fault of his own, God is angry with Moses because of the people and vows to bar him from leading them into the land of rest (4:21; cf. 1:37; 3:26).

---

[69] Moffatt, *Hebrews*, 216.

[70] Acts 7:32 uses the word to describe Moses' reaction to the burning bush in Exod 3. For ἔντρομος, some manuscripts (א D*) read ἔκτρομος at Heb 12:21.

[71] Lane, *Hebrews*, 2:464; cf. Attridge, *Hebrews*, 374.

[72] Other accounts (Num 20:6–12) cite Moses' disobedience and lack of faith—seen in his decision to strike the rock to provide water in the desert instead of speaking to it as commanded by God—as the reason for his exclusion.

In the Deuteronomistic as well as in the Yahwist-Elohist traditions, Moses could thus be seen as a mediator and intercessor between God and the people.[73] He is quite conscious of this role in the pentateuchal narratives upon which Hebrews relies (e.g., Exod 32:30–34; Deut 5:22–27) and of the personal suffering its performance may necessitate. His awareness of the nature of his role no doubt helps to explain his fear in Heb 12:21. The posture of a mediator, moreover, is heavily conditioned by the position of the two parties between whom he is mediating, and Moses' fear serves as an index of the relationship that obtains between God and Israel. His trembling is entirely appropriate in light of God's holiness disclosed at Sinai to the consternation of all present; anything less would suggest a failure to appreciate the absolute qualitative distinction between the human and the divine.[74] It is in this regard that Luther says that to have no anxiety is the worst anxiety of all.[75] At the same time Moses' fear evinces an awareness of the enormity of the task he has taken on as an intercessor for Israel, whose depravity provokes God's wrath. Nothing in Heb 12 hints that his uneasiness is without good cause.[76] Though decidedly superior to his brother Aaron in this capacity—the Lord is so angry with Aaron the high priest for his role in Israel's idolatry that he is ready to destroy him (Deut 9:20)—Moses is nevertheless an imperfect mediator when compared with Christ (Heb 12:24).

While the superiority of Jesus and the new covenant he mediates is an integral part of the equation in vv. 18–24, the antithesis marked by the adversative ἀλλά in v. 22 is not simply between a fearful Moses and a fearless Jesus. It is rather one between a scene which evokes wonder and terror and another which is even more awe-inspiring.[77] The scene at Mount Zion in vv. 22–24 is a crowded one which overwhelms the reader. In arriving at "the city of God, the heavenly Jerusalem," they have come

> to myriads of angels in festal gathering, and to the
> assembly of the firstborn enrolled in heaven, and to a judge
> who is God of all, and to the spirits of the righteous who

---

[73] See Dewey M. Beegle, "Moses (Old Testament)," *ABD* 4:915.

[74] Thus, while the element of fear in the ἔκφοβος and ἔντρομος of Heb 12:21 is more pronounced than in the related φόβος καὶ τρόμος elsewhere in the NT (1 Cor 2:3; 2 Cor 7:15; Eph 6:5; Phil 2:12), they still retain the element of "respect" or "reverent awe." See Willem S. Vorster, "*Phobos kai Tromos*: A Greek Idiomatic Expression with a Semitic Background," *Theologia Evangelica* 5 (1972): 39–48.

[75] "Nulla tentatio—omnis tentatio." Quoted in Berthold, *The Fear of God*, 41.

[76] The same is true of the fear of the people. In Deut 5:28, God tells Moses that their refusal to hear the divine voice without mediation for fear of perishing is based on an accurate perception.

[77] That Moses—whom the author elsewhere praises for his courage—trembles with fear functions to heighten this sense of awe.

have been made perfect, and to Jesus, the mediator of a
new covenant, and to sprinkled blood that speaks better
than the blood of Abel.

Decidedly more festive in tone than the foreboding clouds and faceless voice at
Sinai, the presence of the divine judge[78] in v. 23 nonetheless serves to temper the
celebratory mood, as may also the mention in v. 22 of "the living God," a phrase
which frequently describes the wrathful aspect of the deity.[79] Zion was identified
as the site of God's future judgment according to Jewish apocalyptic traditions
contemporaneous with Hebrews (4 Ezra 13:35–39).[80] By allowing this
undercurrent to come to the surface at this juncture, the author reminds the
readers how much more fearful it will be for them if they now "refuse him who
is speaking" (12:25). Now that they have come to Zion, the consequences of
falling away for those who have been privileged with God's definitive revelation
will be even more dreadful than the fate of those who turned away at Sinai. The
note of fear sounded in 12:18–21 continues to reverberate, softly in vv. 23–24
but more audibly again in vv. 25–26, as fitting accompaniment for the disclosure
of the divine plan (cf. 2:1–4).

Worship in the Last Days: "Reverence and Awe" (Heb 12:28–29)

A final instance where fear assumes a positive function comes at the very
end of the twelfth chapter. After he quotes Hag 2:6 in 12:26 ("Yet once more I
shall shake not only the earth but also the heaven") the author adds a note in the
following verse identifying the future event to which the prophecy points. Its
fulfillment will come with the sweeping away of the created order which will
take place at the end of time to clear a way for "that which cannot be shaken"
(τὰ μὴ σαλευόμενα). The coda in vv. 28–29 looks forward to the dawning of
this eschatological reality—which has in fact already begun to take
effect[81]—and lays out the fitting Christian response: "Therefore, as we are
receiving an unshakeable kingdom, let us give thanks through which we might
offer worship to God in a pleasing manner, with reverence and awe (μετὰ
εὐλαβείας καὶ δέους); for our God is a consuming fire."

To describe acceptable worship, the author uses the same term as in 5:7,
where Jesus' εὐλάβεια is the reason for God's hearing of his prayer. Whereas
the relative flexibility of the single term in the earlier passage gave rise to

---

[78] There is little warrant for understanding κριτής as "avenger" or "vindicator" rather
than as "judge" in this context (Attridge, *Hebrews*, 376 n. 80).

[79] E.g., Josh 3:10; Jer 10:10; cf. Buchanan, *Hebrews*, 222.

[80] Lane, *Hebrews*, 2:470, but see already Ps 48:11 for the identification.

[81] The present participle παραλαμβάνοντες suggests that they are already in the
process of receiving an unshakeable kingdom and that this will continue into the future;
cf. Lane, *Hebrews*, 2:484; Ellingworth, *Hebrews*, 690.

conflicting understandings of the nature of Jesus' experience, in 12:28 two words come into play. One (εὐλάβεια) allows for more of a religious interpretation[82] while the other (δέος) sits more squarely in the sphere of the emotions. Translations of μετὰ εὐλαβείας καὶ δέους join the two in various ways, with most renderings avoiding the stronger nuance of "terror" which frequently attaches to δέος.[83] Some interpreters see the two terms coming together to form a hendiadys ("with reverent awe").[84]

Already in the textual history of v. 28 one finds variant readings which subtly downplay the element of fear. While some manuscripts simply reverse the order of the terms, several substitute αἰδώς ("respectfulness") for δέος.[85] Attridge explains this variant as a case of dittography (of αι from the preceding καί).[86] The resulting text (μετὰ εὐλαβείας καὶ αἰδοῦς) also conveniently yields a phrase emphasizing reverence over fear. As was noted above in chapter two, both terms represent positive analogues to the emotion of fear for the Stoics. That so many copyists retained αἰδώς in v. 28 suggests that it was perceived to fit the context very well.[87] External attestation for δέος is nevertheless quite strong[88] and is to be preferred as the original reading.

The source of the fear in view should by this point in the letter be readily apparent. Fear accompanies thankful worship "because our God is a consuming fire." Hebrews here returns to Deut 4 for the image of God as a πῦρ καταναλίσκον. The divine flame usually strikes out in judgment and devours the ungodly, but as it does here and at Deut 4:23–24, where it supports the continued injunction against idolatry, the metaphor also expresses the dire consequences awaiting the people of God when they forsake the covenant.[89] Instead of dwelling on God's judgment of the wicked who oppress the faithful, Hebrews addresses those whom God has addressed (12:25). Thus one finds the

---

[82] See C. Spicq, "Religion (Vertu de)," *DBSup* 10:230–32.

[83] Most common is "with reverence and awe" (NASB; NIV; RSV; NRSV); cf. KJV ("with reverence and godly fear"). Luther ("mit Zucht und Furcht") as well as Windisch and Braun ("in Scheu und Furcht") bring out the aspect of fear more forcefully. For δέος—a NT *hapax*—as "fear" or "dread," see Herodotus 4.115; Plato, *Euthyphr.* 12B–C; *Prot.* 358D; 2 Macc 3:17; 12:22; Epictetus, *Diatr.* 2.23.38.

[84] Attridge, *Hebrews*, 383 n. 78; also Ellingworth, *Hebrews*, 691.

[85] א² D¹ P 0243 614 945 1739 1881 *pc* d. A few mss also transpose these terms (K L Ψ). At least one ms has only εὐλαβείας (1845), while one reads φόβου for δέους (241). See Braun, *Hebräer*, 446.

[86] Attridge, *Hebrews*, 379 n. 12.

[87] Note the same pairing in Philo, *Mut.* 201; and *Legat.* 352, where the delegation of Jews from Alexandria approach the emperor μετ' αἰδοῦς καὶ εὐλαβείας.

[88] P⁴⁶ א* A C D* 048 33 81 1175 1241ˢ *pc* saᵐˢˢ bo.

[89] For the "devouring" of outsiders, see Deut 9:3; 2 Sam 23:6–7; Ezek 38:19; Sir 45:19; *Pss. Sol.* 15.4–13; 2 Thess 1:7; 2 Pet 3:7. In Isa 33:11–14, however, the fearful and trembling who will be consumed are "the sinners in Zion;" cf. Deut 32:22; Jer 4:4.

fire metaphor employed in 6:8 (to describe the fate of the hypothetical apostate) as well as in 10:26–30 (where the language of judgment is explicit and is turned towards those on the inside).[90] Vögtle and Lane also see a figurative expression for the effects of divine judgment in 12:27.[91] The exegetical comment in this verse substitutes participles formed from σαλεύειν for the verb σείειν in the Haggai prophecy quoted in the preceding verse, and this brings the author's language into closer conformity with LXX descriptions of God's judgment as a "shaking."[92]

If fearlessness is the ideal state the author wants to cultivate in his readers, why at this critical juncture does he resort to language and imagery connected with judgment which would be a source of excusable trepidation for anyone paying close attention to his homily? His belief that they were living in the last days (1:2) goes a long way toward explaining the note of apprehension that sounds together with that of hope (3:6; 6:11, 18; 7:19). In this regard, the way in which their situation parallels that of Noah in 11:7 is instructive. Noah was warned (χρηματισθείς) by God about an impending cataclysm of global proportions, totally unanticipated by those around him who were to be wiped out by the waters of the flood on account of their wickedness (cf. Gen 6:5–8; Josephus, *Ant.* 1.75–76). Understandably concerned (εὐλαβηθείς),[93] he took prudent precautions and constructed the ark to save his family. "By this" (δι' ἧς), the author says, Noah "condemned (κατέκρινεν)[94] the world and became

---

[90] With characteristic exegetical ingenuity, John Chrysostom finds grounds for optimism in the analogy of fruits and thorns in 6:7–8. Land (=the individual soul) that bears thorns (=sin) "is worthless and on the verge of being cursed; its end is to be burned." If one is only "on the verge of being cursed" (κατάρας ἐγγύς), then there is still hope of averting this end (*Hom. Heb.* 10.3).

[91] A. Vögtle, "Das Neue Testament und die Zukunft des Kosmos: Hebr. 12,26f. und das Endschicksal des Kosmos," *BibLeb* 10 (1969): 252; Lane, *Hebrews*, 2:481–82.

[92] 2 Kgs 17:20; Ps 47:6; Lam 1:8. Contrast the "unshakeableness" of the righteous in the Greek Psalter (Ps 14:5; 15:8; 61:3; 65:9; 111:6; 120:3; and 124:1, where "those who trust in the Lord will be like Mount Zion, and he who dwells in Jerusalem will never be removed").

[93] Westcott: "moved with pious care." Moffatt: "reverently." Spicq: "saisi de crainte religieuse." Bruce: "moved with godly fear." Braun: "voll frommer Scheu." Attridge and Koester: "in reverence." Weiss: "als ein frommer Mann."

[94] It is unlikely that the author means that Noah, a mere human, is solely responsible for the judgment and punishment of sinful humanity. Rather, the statement probably alludes to traditions emphasizing his preaching of repentance to his contemporaries and his own exemplary conduct by which he put them to shame (2 Pet 2:5; *1 Clem.* 7.6; *Sib. Or.* 1.125–70). See Jack P. Lewis, *A Study of the Interpretation of Noah and the Flood in Jewish and Christian Literature* (Leiden: Brill, 1968), 101–103; cf. BAGD, s.v. κατακρίνω: "The conduct of one person, since it sets a standard, can result in the condemnation before God of another person whose conduct is inferior."

an heir (κληρονόμος) of the righteousness that is according to faith."[95] The audience is likewise instructed in Heb 12:25 not to turn away from "the one who warns (τὸν χρηματίζοντα) from heaven." Their response is to be characterized by εὐλάβεια. And as part of their inheritance, they are "receiving a kingdom that cannot be shaken."

While the author does not draw explicit attention to the connection between Noah and the audience, he appears to presuppose a historical scheme which places them in analogous positions in the divine plan. Jewish apocalyptic traditions likely shared by Hebrews and 2 Peter (3:5–13) divide history into three epochs separated by two worldwide catastrophes.[96] Noah lived at the end of one age, which was destroyed by the flood. God establishes a covenant with Noah after the flood and promises never again to destroy the world and its inhabitants by water (Gen 9:8–17). The terms of this covenant still made it possible for God to bring the second epoch to a close by means of a fiery conflagration, after which a third and final age would commence.[97] In Heb 12:26–29, the shaking of heaven and earth and the fire imagery hearkening back to earlier passages referring to divine judgment locate the audience near the very end of this second epoch. Judgment will involve the whole creation, and they must survive this divine shaking to come into their heavenly kingdom (cf. 11:13–16). If "shaking" signifies the effects of judgment and also discloses "that which remains,"[98] then judgment and salvation may be seen as concurrent events, taking place at the same time and by the same means.[99]

---

[95] LXX Gen 6:8 states that Noah "found grace" (εὗρε χάριν) with God and became the one through whom a remnant of humanity would survive. It is tempting to see a parallel in the exhortation to "have grace" (ἔχωμεν χάριν) in Heb 12:28. Westcott (*Hebrews*, 422) and Spicq (*Hébreux*, 2:413) construe the phrase in the sense of "enjoying" or "holding on to" divine favor. The hortatory context and the well-attested idiomatic sense of "being thankful" (1 Tim 1:12; 2 Tim 1:3; Phlm 7) call this interpretation, and thus also the specific allusion to Gen 6:8, into question. See Heb 4:16, however, for the phrase χάριν εὑρίσκειν.

[96] See Lewis, *Noah and the Flood*, 169–73; Richard J. Bauckham, *Jude, 2 Peter* (WBC 50; Waco, Tex.: Word, 1983), 299–301.

[97] This widespread notion may be seen, e.g., in 1QHᵃ 3.19–36; *Sib. Or.* 3.84–92; 4.171–192; Josephus, *Ant.* 1.70; in early Christian sources, see 2 *Clem.* 16.3; *Apoc. Pet.* 5; Theophilus, *Autol.* 2.38; Minucius Felix, *Oct.* 11.1.

[98] For a brief account of "what remains," see Attridge, *Hebrews*, 281–82; cf. Lane, *Hebrews*, 2:483, who says that the faithful community itself is what remains, as the cosmic shaking will result in the decisive removal of all who have ignored God's voice (12:25).

[99] See Philip E. Hughes, *A Commentary on the Epistle to the Hebrews* (Grand Rapids: Eerdmans, 1977), 465, for the same point with regard to Noah in 11:7. By building the ark, he simultaneously saves his family and condemns the world. Similarly, Albert Vanhoye believes the author, employing the Jewish technique of interpreting a term in

Their "reverence and awe," then, demonstrates their awareness of living on a threshold, at a point where the old is vanishing and the new is just coming into view (cf. 8:13).[100] They are on the verge of entering the promised rest, as were the Israelites when they faltered in disobedience and failed to enter (3:7–4:11). For this reason, the citation in v. 29 of Deut 4:24 is particularly apt because it comes from Moses' speech to the people as they are about to enter the land.[101] Moses himself is not able to enter, and so the audience must be careful to avoid presumption by assuming that they deserve the kingdom they are receiving by their own merits.[102] Because what they receive is a gift from God, thanksgiving (12:28: ἔχωμεν χάριν) is the proper mode of worship.[103] But their thanksgiving and also the festive mood of vv. 22–24 are not untouched by an element of apprehension. Thus their "reverent awe" and the hope which moves them to give thanks are not two poles between which the Christian continually wavers, but rather they belong together as correlatives because, in Bultmann's words, "the grace that emancipates him is the 'grace' of a Judge."[104] And precisely because the believer has been set free, Bultmann continues, how he conducts himself

---

one passage according to its meaning in another (*gezera shawa*), links Hag 2:6 with LXX Ps 95:9–10 and thereby presents worship and judgment as concomitant events, both coinciding with the shaking of heaven and earth ("L'οὐκουμένη dans l'épître aux Hébreux," *Bib* 45 [1964]: 248–53). In Ps 95:10 the earth (γῆ) will quake, yet strangely, when the Lord establishes his kingdom, the world (οὐκουμένη) will not be shaken (σαλευθήσεται).

[100] By allowing the imagery of a journey nearing its end to overlap with that of the visible, tangible world dissolving to reveal the invisible, intangible world, Heb 12:18–29 is a primary locus for the perceived tension between an eschatological-apocalyptic outlook and a metaphysical-dualistic orientation on the part of the author; cf. J. Cambier, "Eschatologie ou hellénisme dans l'Épître aux Hébreux: Une étude sur μένειν et l'exhortation finale de l'épître," *Salesianum* 11 (1949): 62–86; Barrett, "The Eschatology of the Epistle to the Hebrews," 363–93; Hering, "Eschatologie biblique et idéalisme platonicien," 444–63; Thompson, *The Beginnings of Christian Philosophy*, 41–52; and Hurst, *The Epistle to the Hebrews: Its Background of Thought*, 21–41.

[101] Cf. Lane, *Hebrews*, 2:487–88, citing J. M. Casey, "Eschatology in Heb 12:14–29: An Exegetical Study" (Diss., Catholic University of Leuven, 1977), 570–71.

[102] This caution is especially pronounced in Deut 9:3–7, when Moses reminds the people that it is God who crosses over before them "as a devouring fire" and three times says that it is not on account of their own righteousness that he is fulfilling the promises made to Abraham, Isaac, and Jacob by allowing them to occupy the land.

[103] For Hebrews' emphasis on χάρις, see 2:4; 4:16 (bis); 10:29; 12:15; 13:9, 25. The emphasis in 12:28 is on the believers' gratitude offered in response to the χάρις of their heavenly benefactor; cf. deSilva, *Perseverance in Gratitude*, 473.

[104] Bultmann, *Theology of the New Testament*, 1:321–22. Fear is an indispensable element in faith "inasmuch as it guarantees the centering of the believer's attention upon God's 'grace'" (1:320). His remarks are in reference to Paul but nevertheless apply to the dynamic at work in Heb 12 as well.

now really matters.[105] Hebrews therefore translates "acceptable worship attended by reverence and awe" into practical ethical directives in the thirteenth and final chapter.[106]

Conclusion

D. H. Lawrence quotes Heb 10:31 (RSV) verbatim in the opening line of his poem, "The Hands of God," only to follow it with a second line suggestive of the sometimes ambivalent reactions to the prospect of becoming a child of God in the Letter to the Hebrews: "It is a fearful thing to fall into the hands of the living God/But it is a much more fearful thing to fall out of them."[107] The poem closes with a cry for salvation from "ungodly knowledge": "Let me never know myself apart from the living God!" The primary aim of the author of Hebrews is to assist his readers in experiencing "boldness" by showing them how their brother and high priest has neutralized the most pervasive causes of fear—namely, judgment by God and abuse at the hands of humans. But in order to help them learn who they really are in God's eyes, he must draw on a register of language in some respects expressive, even evocative, of a form of fear.[108] Analyses of this language in Hebrews, however, frequently exaggerate the degree to which it connotes craven terror. The author generally avoids such vocabulary, preferring to use terms (εὐλάβεια) which accentuate the individual's recognition of and submissiveness to the will of God. Jesus models this disposition for his siblings, learning the full meaning of obedience to God from the fearful things he suffered. Some measure of trepidation is not only permissible, it is entirely appropriate when confronted with the auspicious events connected with the new covenant, so long as it does not lead one to seek consolation anywhere other than in the living God.

---

[105] Ibid., 1:321. Again, he quotes Paul (Phil 2:12–13: "Work out your own salvation with fear and trembling, for God is working in you both to will and to work for his good pleasure") but the sentiment could as easily be that of Hebrews.

[106] Koester, *Hebrews*, 561.

[107] *The Complete Poems of D. H. Lawrence* (ed. V. de Sola Pinto and W. Roberts; 2 vols.; New York: Viking, 1964), 2:699.

[108] Much to the chagrin, e.g., of Friedrich Schleiermacher. While "sacred reverence . . . is the first element of religion," fear is "not only not religion itself, it is not even preparatory or introductory" (*On Religion: Speeches to Its Cultured Despisers* [trans. J. Oman; London: Kegan, Paul, Trench, Trubner, 1893], 65).

Chapter Five

Conclusions

While his letter is by no means a formal or systematic treatise such as one finds in the Greek and Roman philosophical schools, the author of Hebrews is deliberate in addressing the problem of fear and its function in one's relationship with the deity. As Braun, Klauck, and Morton Smith recognize in various ways, the motif of fear represents a fundamental category of religious experience and provides the most natural point of contact between Plutarch's thought and that of the early church.[1]

Fear causes disruption in both secular and sacred spheres of activity in Hebrews. It manifests itself in the ordinary, instinctive human desires to avoid physical pain, financial hardship, humiliation before one's peers, and other circumstances in which religious belief and practice play no defining role; and it may also accompany contemplation of divine displeasure and punishment in the hereafter. The author is deeply interested in both species of fear. His concern is most evident when he characterizes the incarnation of Christ, his fraternal empathy, and his unique priesthood in 2:14–18 as parts of a divine plan to deliver humans from the bondage brought about by fear of death. Equally manifest is his desire to mute any sound of fearfulness in retelling the scriptural story of Moses' encounters with Pharaoh in 11:23–28. The author has an unmistakable interest in showing his readers how they are able to say with confidence, "I will not be afraid" (13:6). Sacred and secular fears naturally overlap to some extent. Plutarch (*Superst.* 165D–E, 168E–169C) notes the ways in which their respective causes and cures regularly impinge on one another. The author of Hebrews, too, impresses upon his readers the point that the boundary separating the natural from the supernatural realm is permeable, allowing events in one to nurture either fear or confidence in the other.

With its delineation of proper and improper types of fear and its paraenetic program aimed—at points quite explicitly—at cultivating the grounds for

---

[1] See especially Smith, "De Superstitione," 11–12, who states that "fear of the Father . . . is not only a major motif in the literature, but a major structural factor in the religion which the literature represents."

παρρησία, Hebrews therefore participates in a discussion about the perennial problem of fear which also concerns Plutarch in his attack on δεισιδαιμονία. The author never uses the word δεισιδαιμονία, but since superstition involves labeling the wrong things as objects of fear and then taking the wrong kinds of steps to conquer that fear, Hebrews and Plutarch are engaged in analogous tasks. In analyzing the conditions set right by Jesus' death, Hebrews identifies what is and is not truly fearful, the conditions under which fear is or is not warranted, and the reasons for judging fear to be an appropriate or inappropriate response. He also explains how it is that fearlessness is a realizable goal, how to maintain a posture of confidence in the face of human and even supernatural threats, and what may lead to a relapse into the dire circumstances that had given rise to well-founded fears in the past.

The author's critical yet constructive engagement with the OT is a part of this program. The narratives and psalms that Hebrews sees as pointing to the Christ event do not simply provide illustrations of abstract principles or philosophical doctrines about such matters as sin, salvation, and emotional tranquility.[2] They are the very stuff of divine revelation. If he is going to address the problem of fear, he has to do so within the terms of this tradition he inherits from Judaism. An increased awareness of the ways in which God had dealt with Israel in the past, while absolutely indispensable for appreciating the Christian message contained in the NT, nevertheless brought with it certain complications. It was the rest of the package, so to speak, bought by converts when they became Christian. In many ways the OT testimonies regarding God's ways of relating to Israel in the past looked like a boon. They added to the depth and richness of the good news believers had perceived in the early Christian proclamation. For example, Scripture provided the backdrop for understanding the nature of Jesus' accomplishment in destroying "the one who has the power of death, that is, the devil, and deliver[ing] all those who through fear of death were subject to lifelong slavery" (Heb 2:14–15). At the same time, the Law and the Prophets contained material not so easily integrated into the emerging

---

[2] As it is presented in the OT, the past is a history that contains prophecies finding fulfillment in the present or in the very recent past, namely, in the person of Jesus. For example, the "today" spoken by the Holy Spirit in Ps 95:7–11 is revealed in Heb 4:6–11 (cf. 3:7, 13, 15) to refer to the very situation facing the audience. In 7:1–28 (cf. 5:5–10) the author treats the fleeting OT references to the enigmatic figure of Melchizedek, mentioned only in Gen 14:17–20 and Ps 110:4, as oracles pointing to Jesus' distinctive qualifications for the high priest's office. The promise of a new covenant in Jer 31:31–34, largely neglected by Jewish interpreters prior to 70 C.E., is invoked in Heb 8:6–13 as proof that God's new way of relating to humanity was foreshadowed in the Mosaic law. And in Heb 10:5–10, the author uses Ps 40:7–9 to show how Jesus' first coming was also foretold in scripture, once again a hitherto unrecognized provision mentioned in the old covenant as an admission of its own inherent limitations.

Christian view of history. How, for example, could Jesus fulfill the priestly function vital for the individual's confident approach to the throne of grace when his descent was through the line of Judah instead of Levi? Hebrews' engagement with the OT thus addresses this and other legitimate questions arising out of the emphasis on God's fearfulness throughout the letter and the rest of early Christian literature.[3]

Fear of God, as both Hebrews and critics of superstition like Plutarch usually perceive, is not anxiety directed at a fickle, sadistic, and totally unpredictable deity. More accurately, the gods elicit fear because they are thought to punish wrongdoing, whether in this world or in the next. In this respect, those whom Plutarch and others label superstitious presuppose a degree of predictability on the part of the gods—they are predictably vengeful toward those who displease them. Their relative predictability explains why the habitual practices of the superstitious are deemed effective in averting their wrath. Critics believe that the superstitious are overly sensitive and include too many of the wrong kinds of misdeeds in the category of those that upset the gods. Many critics go further, asserting that the gods never actively punish mortals, no matter how heinous the crime, and hence are never appropriate objects of fear.

Hebrews fits the superstitious profile in that the author connects the fearfulness of God and of death to the divine judgment individual sinners expect to meet at the end of their lives (4:12–13; 9:27; 10:26–31; 12:23; 13:4). Yet Hebrews claims that Jesus' sacrifice has made a decisive difference, cleaning the conscience like no other offering and thereby establishing once and for all the grounds for true and lasting παρρησία. The author reflects this new state of affairs by redefining for his readers what things are and are not rightly feared, from what motives, at what times, and in what manner.[4] The new covenant inaugurated by Jesus, according to Hebrews, finally provides an effective solution for human sin at the root of the gravest fears. By presenting Jesus' accomplishment under its sacerdotal aspect, the author is able to compare the two covenants at precisely the point where the old covenant falls short—in the cultic realm.

It is here, in the lengthy dissection of the Levitical cult in Heb 7:1–10:18, that Hebrews most closely resembles the Hellenistic critiques of popular

---

[3] The author's analysis of the human condition—in particular, his approach to fear—could quite effectively address the perception of superstitiousness on the part of Gentiles learning the implications of their new-begotten faith. Even if they come from a Jewish background, the author and audience still belong to the class of those for whom such a message has relevance. Hellenized Jews, living in close and sustained contact with their Gentile neighbors, would naturally be more sensitive to the scorn of the dominant culture which, in the religious realm, is labeled δεισιδαιμονία and highlights the crippling emotion of fear.

[4] Cf. Aristotle's description of the virtue of courage (*Eth. nic.* 2.6.10–11; 3.7.5).

religion. The author reserves his strongest remarks for the ritual requirements of the first covenant, not for the Law in its totality or for its more narrowly ethical requirements. Greek and Roman writers frequently lampoon the superstitious for their excessive attention to religious ritual.[5] A key component of this critique is that it applies almost exclusively to scruples regarding performance. It is perfectly normal to take an interest in the "deeper" or "true" meaning of religious ritual. When the action itself becomes the main focus, one enters the realm of δεισιδαιμονία. As Plutarch reminds Clea, it is possible to avoid superstition "if you always perform and observe the established rites of worship, and believe that no sacrifice that you can offer, no deed that you may do will be more likely to find favour with the gods than your belief in their true nature," an approach which requires that the myths and rites in question be understood "reverently and philosophically" (ὁσιώς καὶ φιλοσόφως) rather than literally.[6]

Nowhere in Hebrews does the author exhort his readers to be more fastidious in the performance of any recognizable form of religious ritual as a means of freeing themselves from the grip of fear. His indifference to (or lack of familiarity with?) the details of the Jerusalem cult of the first century is often seen as evidence that he is writing later than 70 C.E., when the temple has been destroyed and Jews begin to "spiritualize" the language and imagery of the Israelite cult.[7] The author is indeed keenly interested in the details of priestly duties, especially in 7:1–10:18, but these derive from written sources describing ancient practices in the pre-Solomonic tabernacle. They concern the author only insofar as they prefigure Christ's priestly service, which perfectly fulfills the Levitical requirements and reveals the incompleteness of the old covenant. The author's apparent disinterest in ritual performance in the present exempts him from a charge of superstition, but it is incorrect to see him as denigrating the rituals described in the OT as totally silly or without purpose. Cultic ritual pointed beyond itself and played a crucial part in God's plan.

---

[5] Extremism is the common denominator in virtually every Hellenistic critique of superstition. Adherence to proper forms of ritual, avoidance of defilement, interest in oracles, belief in divine intervention—all are acceptable so long as they are not "excessive." The slur of superstition takes on its special nuance with reference to the specific tendencies in conflict with prevailing notions of normalcy. Extremism is therefore an evaluative category under which various attitudes and practices may be described. Identifying the point beyond which a given practice or attitude becomes "extreme," however, is a highly subjective process.

[6] Plutarch, *Is. Os*. 355D; cf. also *Cupid. divit*. 527F; *De laude* 545A, on the primacy of correct beliefs.

[7] That Philo, who probably dies over twenty years prior to the destruction of the temple, exhibits the same tendency in interpreting those parts of Torah referring to sacrifice weakens the case for a later dating of Hebrews on the basis of alleged evidence of the cessation of cultic activity in Jerusalem.

Most of the rituals alluded to in Hebrews deal with matters of purity. Obsessive preoccupation with moral or physical pollution requiring purification routinely receives attention in Hellenistic critiques of δεισιδαιμονία since the time of Theophrastus and probably even earlier. Purity and pollution are correlative concepts: that which pollutes is an impediment to purity, and that which purifies does away with pollution. Together they represent a terribly complex and far-reaching area of ancient Mediterranean thought and practice. Robert Parker makes this point by way of understatement when he comments that thinking about purity and pollution is "a vehicle for many different concerns: it has no unified origin or history."[8] What pollutes and thus requires purification? Answering this question would require a study not only of Mediterranean religion in its entirety but of many other aspects of culture and society as well. Disruptions such as birth, death, sexual intercourse, murder, illness, and insanity are commonly associated with impurity and generate considerable anxiety about one's standing in the eyes of the gods.[9] Baths, lustrations, fasting, sacrifice, abstinence from sexual activity—all are customary ways of achieving purity in the world's religions, East and West, ancient and modern.

Hebrews' interest in matters of ritual purity is undeniable, yet to ask whether the anxiety his remarks indicate is so extreme as to constitute a form of δεισιδαιμονία elicits a predetermined answer. Systems of purification at or near the heart of many forms of Hellenistic religion represent distinctive conceptions of, and proposals for dealing with, pollution understood in various ways. Different religions assign impure status to different objects and actions. Where they consider the same things impure, they usually mandate different procedures for purifying a given person, place, or thing. Because they have different beliefs about what in particular is impure and what means are effective in restoring purity, adherents of different religions will necessarily view other notions of purity, with their related practices, as odd or, to use the key phrase, superstitious. Jews, Muslims, Zoroastrians, and devotees of Isis can all agree that it is a good thing to be pure. Disagreement, and subsequent derogation as superstitious, comes as soon as the details of what is and is not pure as well as

---

[8] Robert C. T. Parker, "Pollution, The Greek Concept of," *OCD* 1209; cf. idem, *Miasma: Pollution and Purity in Early Greek Religion* (Oxford: Clarendon, 1983), esp. 1–17. The fundamental separation of pure from impure "may be taken as an axiom of ancient religion" (Everett Ferguson, *Backgrounds of Early Christianity* [2nd ed.; Grand Rapids: Eerdmans, 1993], 174). E. R. Dodds brings together different motifs related to superstition when he links fear of the gods in early Greece with the "universal fear of pollution (*miasma*) and its correlate, the universal craving for ritual purification" (*The Greeks and the Irrational* [Berkeley: University of California Press, 1966], 38).
[9] Cf. Burkert, *Greek Religion*, 75–84. Many of these motifs are found together in an inscription at a temple of Athena in Pergamum (*SIG* 3:982).

the appropriate remedies come under debate. It therefore follows that almost any solicitude over pollution and purity evinced by Hebrews would impress an outsider as superstitious.

Even apart from the lengthy excursus in 7:1–10:18 comparing the Levitical priesthood and Jesus' priestly service in heaven, there are a number of passages indicating the author's concern for purity and holiness. He takes over the peculiar Christian self-designation as "the saints" or "the holy ones" (οἱ ἅγιοι: 3:1; 6:10; 13:24). This is no casually chosen nickname but rather a shorthand reference to the source and the goal of Christian existence, as the author's predilection for cognates of ἅγιος attests. Jesus is the one who sanctifies (ὁ ἁγιάζων) with his own blood (2:11; cf. 9:13; 10:10, 14, 29; 13:12). God wants all humans to share his holiness (ἁγιότης), and the author urges his readers to "strive for peace with everyone and for the holiness (ἁγιασμός) without which no one will see the Lord," for they will be defiled (μιανθῶσιν) if bitterness springs up and causes strife (12:10, 14–15).[10]

Cognates from related semantic fields also appear in other descriptions of Jesus' accomplishments. He takes his seat at God's right hand once he has finished making purification (καθαρισμός) for sins (1:3).[11] Especially dense is the cluster of terms in 9:13–14 (cf. also 10:1–2, 22) where the author makes what many take to be his main point:

> For if the sprinkling of defiled persons (κεκοινωμένους) with the blood of goats and bulls and the ashes of a heifer sanctifies (ἁγιάζει) for the purification (καθαρότητα) of the flesh, how much more shall the blood of Christ, who through the eternal spirit offered himself without blemish (ἄμωμον) to God, purify (καθαριεῖ)your conscience from dead works for serving the living God!

A clean conscience is necessary for a fearless approach to the throne of grace since sin stands between God and humans as a barrier that registers at the level of the emotions when the individual is conscious of it. Although the imagery of cleansing is on occasion an allusion to ritual washings of water (6:2; 10:22), the blood is essential, for according to the law, "almost everything is purified with blood, and without the shedding of blood there is no forgiveness of sins" (9:22). So great is the epistle's interest in ritual purity that even "the heavenly things themselves must be cleansed (καθαρίζεσθαι)," a statement that has shocked

---

[10] They are also warned to "let the marriage bed be undefiled (ἀμίαντος)" (13:4; cf. 7:26, for the same quality predicated of the ideal high priest).

[11] Related references to sacrifice for sins are found in 5:1–3; 7:27; 8:3; 9:9, 23, 26; 10:1, 5, 8, 11, 12, 26.

and confused many interpreters because of what it seems to imply about the nature of heaven—that it is somehow susceptible to defilement.[12]

Yet it is difficult to ignore the fact that Hebrews, for all its interest in OT sacrifice and use of cultic vocabulary, refrains from making sacrifice as it was popularly conceived a duty incumbent on the Christian to perform. As Hans-Josef Klauck puts it, the author "uses a thoroughly cultic language to make a deeply uncultic statement."[13] Hebrews has this in common with almost all early Christian literature. The only concrete instruction on sacrifice comes at 13:15–16: "Through him then let us continually offer up a sacrifice of praise to God, that is, the fruit of lips that acknowledge his name. Do not neglect to do good and to share what you have, for such sacrifices are pleasing to God." Praise and benevolence as modes of sacrifice are not ideas peculiar to Hebrews.[14] Nor is the author alone in his endorsement of "spiritual sacrifice," a concept developed in distinctive ways by pagan, Jewish, and Christian writers.[15] This notion often emerges as a positive alternative in the context of religious and philosophical critiques of the sacrificial mindset. In the OT, prophetic critiques emphasize the inadequacy of animal sacrifices unaccompanied by obedience to Mosaic law.[16] The same sentiments are also found at Qumran and in Jewish literature from the dispersion.[17]

Greek and Roman writers direct similar attacks against their own indigenous cults.[18] Their criticism echoes many of the elements in more general Hellenistic attacks on superstition.[19] Popular sacrificial practices reflect

---

[12] Heb 9:23. See Attridge, *Hebrews* 261–62; and Dunnill, *Covenant and Sacrifice*, 117–18, for a summary of the issues involved.

[13] Hans-Josef Klauck, "Sacrifice and Sacrificial Offerings (NT)," *ABD* 5:890.

[14] Sacrifice and praise used in conjunction: Lev 7:12; 2 Chr 29:31; Ps 50:14, 23; Jonah 2:9; 1QS 10.18, 22; Philo, *Spec.* 1.195. Benevolence as sacrificial: Hos 6:6; Matt 9:13.

[15] See Everett Ferguson, "Spiritual Sacrifice in Early Christianity and Its Environment," *ANRW* 23.2:1151–89.

[16] 1 Sam 15:22; Ps 40:6–8; 50:7–23; Prov 21:3; Isa 1:10–17; Hos 6:6; Amos 5:21–24. Sirach 34:18–35:11 offers the most thorough example of this viewpoint. Note especially the priority of obedience over burnt offerings in Jer 7:21–23, which presents in compressed form the same message as in Jer 31:31–34, quoted in full at Heb 8:8–12.

[17] E.g., 1QS 9.4–5, 26; *Ep. Arist.* 234; Philo, *Cher.* 94–96; *Spec.* 1.201, 277 et al. For a fuller study of this theme in Philo, see V. Nikiprowetzky, "La Spiritualisation des Sacrifices et le Cult Sacrificiel au Temple de Jérusalem chez Philon d'Alexandrie," *Sem* 17 (1967): 97–116.

[18] See Frances M. Young, *The Use of Sacrificial Ideas in Greek Christian Writers from the New Testament to John Chrysostom* (Cambridge: Philadelphia Patristic Foundation, 1979), 15–23; and Thompson, *The Beginnings of Christian Philosophy*, 110–113.

[19] The opening paragraph of Lucian's essay *On Sacrifices*, for example, could easily have been written by Plutarch: "In view of what the dolts do at their sacrifices and their feasts and processions in honour of the gods, what they pray for and vow, and what opinions

unworthy notions of the gods as dependent upon the offerings of mortals for sustenance and responsive to bribes rather than sincere piety.[20] If the gods are ἀπαθής or otherwise immutable as the Stoics and Platonists claim respectively (Plutarch, *E Delph.* 393C; *Def. orac.* 420E), it is pointless to expect them to change their minds on account of an especially fine offering; and if inexorable fate rules the universe, then the gods cannot—even if they were so inclined—alter the preordained course of events so as to benefit the worshiper. Moreover, such ministrations are undignified and, because they are material, are ineffective for acquiring moral purity, which alone is pleasing to the gods (Lucian, *Sacr.* 15; Diogenes Laertius 6.42).

Much in Hebrews' discussion of the ancient Israelite cult conforms to this strand of thinking on matters of purity and sacrifice. Above all, the author's preference for the new covenant's way of solving the problem of fear can be seen in his insistence that the normal sacrifices required as a part of the old covenant could not sufficiently repair the damage done by the sin on account of which they were instituted. Under the provisions of the old covenant, "gifts and sacrifices are offered which cannot perfect the conscience of the worshiper" (9:9; cf. 9:13–14). Because the law has "only a shadow of the good things to come" and not their "true form," its sacrifices cannot perfect those who would draw near to God nor do away with the consciousness of sin that gives rise to fear and places a barrier between the individual and God (10:1–2, 22).[21]

This emphasis on the interior state of the individual fits with the philosophical preference for "rational" worship and so might be presumed to preempt charges that the author is encouraging superstitious notions of the role purity and sacrifice play in bridging the divide between the human and the divine. It is important to keep in mind, however, that while the citation of LXX Ps 39:7–9 in Heb 10:5–10 comes very close, Hebrews stops short of condemning outright the sacrificial system of the OT. After all, God had instituted it and so non-performance was not really an option. The author seeks instead to show that the purity requirements of the Israelite cult have now been fulfilled by Jesus in such consummate fashion that any further blood offerings

---

they hold about the gods, I doubt if anyone is so gloomy and woe-begone that he will not laugh to see the idiocy of their actions. Indeed, long before he laughs, I think, he will ask himself whether he should call them devout or, on the contrary, irreligious and pestilent, inasmuch as they have taken it for granted that the gods are so low and mean as to stand in need of men and to enjoy being flattered and to get angry when they are slighted."

[20] Apollonius of Tyana, *Ep.* 26; Euripides, *Herc. fur.* 1345; Plato, *Phaedr.* 279B–C; *Leg.* 716D–717A; Seneca, *Ben.* 1.6.3; Maximus of Tyre, *Diss.* 11; Plutarch, *Is. Os.* 355D.

[21] On the role of conscience, see Pierce, *Conscience in the New Testament*, 99–102; W. G. Johnsson, "Defilement and Purgation in the Book of Hebrews" (Ph.D. diss., Vanderbilt University, 1973), 282–88; and G. S. Selby, "The Meaning and Function of συνείδησις in Hebrews 9 and 10," *ResQ* 28 (1986): 145–54.

are superfluous. Hebrews is in this respect situated between the message of Jesus in the Sermon on the Mount (in Matt 5:17–48) when he says that he has come not to abolish but to fulfill the law, and the *Epistle to Diognetus* (3.3–5), which basically equates Jewish sacrifice with pagan sacrifice to idols and explicitly refers to it as an instance of δεισιδαιμονία.[22] The OT cult had its proper time and place (cf. 7:12, 18; 8:6–7), but after the resurrection and exaltation of Christ the situation has changed dramatically. Hebrews' analysis of the old covenant and its way of dealing with moral pollution thus hinges on a highly distinctive understanding of history—they have entered "the last days" (1:2); the first covenant "is becoming obsolete, growing old, and is ready to vanish" (8:13; cf. 10:9); the καιρός of reformation has arrived (9:10); Jesus' self-sacrifice comes "at the end of the age" (9:26)—quite alien to most Greeks and Romans. Because there is little or no precedent for the special kinds of claims made by the early Christians, however, it is not clear whether the idea that God would grant a special dispensation for the benefit of humans would qualify as δεισιδαιμονία in the eyes of pagan observers.[23]

The recognition that God has in fact acted, quite recently, and in an extraordinary fashion is an integral component of the disposition the author seeks to cultivate in his audience. On the one hand, Jesus' fulfillment and abrogation of the old cult breaks the spell of sin and the fear of God it inspires. On the other hand, the new disclosure of God's plan and the mysterious ways in which it unfolds causes understandable consternation when one realizes that history is at a turning point.[24] God is revealed at the end of the age to be "a consuming fire" who therefore deserves thanksgiving "with reverence and awe"

---

[22] Perhaps Hebrews should be seen as occupying a position on the Law close to that of Paul (in 2 Cor 3:4–18; Gal 3:19–29). Paul's critique covers the Law in its entirety, however, while Hebrews concentrates on its cultic demands and upholds the necessity of obedience. Johnsson, "Defilement and Purgation," 62–68, probes the issue of Hebrews' position on the (dis)continuity of the OT cult and Christianity, arguing that the author appears to share the cultic presuppositions of the Israelites while drawing different conclusions in light of Jesus' death and resurrection.

[23] Christian belief in such a dispensation might engender an attitude of fearlessness in the face of earthly dangers and human judgments—this is unquestionably the hope of Hebrews—yet still strike outsiders as superstitious. Inasmuch as a firm conviction that one's own group enjoys the gods' special favor could engender obstinacy in the face of earthly authorities and military hubris taking the form of armed revolt (such as in the Jewish revolts of 66–70 and 132–135), it is easy to imagine how the eschatological leanings of Hebrews might raise Roman suspicions of *superstitio* on political grounds; see, e.g., Augustus's burning of over two thousand prophetic verses, including some of the Sibylline books, on account of their subversive character (Suetonius, *Aug.* 31.1).

[24] Compare the constant need of God and of angelic messengers in both testaments to admonish those to whom they appear to be unafraid (Gen 15:1; Judg 6:23; Isa 41:10; Luke 1:12–13, 30, 65; 2:10; Rev 1:17).

(12:25–29). Gratitude is in order because the audience is not any longer among those who will be consumed (6:7–8; 10:27). Quite possibly, they had had little idea how close their brush with death and eternal judgment had been prior to their rescue by Christ, understanding only in retrospect the magnitude of the debt of thanksgiving they owe. Like Noah, who approaches the concurrent rescue of his family and the destruction of the world with trepidation (11:7: εὐλαβηθείς), so also is the audience to meditate on God's compound act whereby the faithful are saved and the faithless are rejected with a mixture of joy and fear.

In retaining the element of awe in the appropriate response of the believer to God, Hebrews seeks to instill an attitude closely resembling that which the OT frequently designates as "the fear of the Lord." The phrase as it is used in the OT subsumes a wide range of dispositions—wonder, devotion, loyalty, steadfast love, even dread. It does not appear in Hebrews, but Jesus' "godly fear" (εὐλάβεια) as it is characterized in 5:7 and elsewhere in the letter exemplifies this proper human attitude vis-à-vis God. The key components of this attitude are discernment of the divine will, awareness of the possible adverse consequences of subordinating (or refusing to subordinate) one's own will to that of God, willingness to endure these consequences, and trust in the divine promises even when their fulfillment takes one through the valley of the shadow of death (cf. Heb 11:13–16, 32–40). Wariness when contemplating what sacrifices God's will requires does not necessarily reflect a lack of reverence; rather, it can be an indication that one perceives the seriousness of the situation and the extraordinary lengths to which God has gone to set things in order.

Notwithstanding his obvious intention to persuade his readers that freedom from fear is an obtainable goal—witnessed, for example, in his assurance that they now have access to the heavenly sanctuary and that God "will remember their sins and trespasses no more" (Heb 10:17)—it must be recognized that the author of Hebrews is not primarily concerned to shield them from suffering and death, much less to shelter them from the emotional turmoil that anticipation of worldly and otherworldly adversity normally occasions. Freedom from worry is not the highest good, and Hebrews does not hesitate to recommend a course of action likely to heighten his readers' natural anxieties. On this point Hebrews stands a bit closer to Plutarch than to the less compromising Stoics and Epicureans, who deny any value to fear and marshal various arguments meant to prove how, like nearly all emotions, it reflects a way of thinking that is fundamentally out of kilter. All parties agree, however, that beliefs or convictions more or less determine one's emotional response to a given situation. Emotions originate in beliefs and judgments of value, not as issuances of generic personality types. The emotions, furthermore, ought to correspond to the world as it really is and not to how one wants it to be. Denying reality, as it were, through wishful thinking only delays an inevitable encounter with the brute—and sometimes brutal—facts of the universe. This cannot be done indefinitely nor should it be. Salutary fear, with its image of a god who is at once dreadful and marvelous beyond words, manifests a complex of convictions and sentiments that, according to Hebrews, is simply truer to reality than any alternative response.

One can imagine an interlocutor saying to Plutarch that the harm done by the fear associated with δεισιδαιμονία is negligible and that the superstitious man is merely playing it safe by believing as he does about the gods. In a variation of Pascal's Wager, the superstitious reason in this way: if the gods exist and punish iniquity with furious anger, then we have everything to gain by believing as we do and acting accordingly; if, on the other hand, the gods exist yet are all-beneficent and remain effectively indifferent toward human vice, then we have little or nothing to gain by believing as Plutarch would have us believe and behaving accordingly. After all, an all-beneficent deity, lacking all the fearsome qualities attributed to it by the superstitious, would wink at even the disgraceful beliefs and practices decried by the author of *De superstitione*. Otherwise, it would not be the unconditionally benign being Plutarch describes. Plutarch's rejoinder would be twofold.[25] First, there is intrinsic value in holding the right beliefs about the gods, even if the positive effects of orthodoxy are not empirically demonstrable. Second, δεισιδαιμονία is a pathology which hampers human flourishing in this life, the only one that really matters.

Hebrews and Plutarch part company on the last point. Whether one sees it within a temporal/eschatological or a spatial/dualistic horizon, they differ as to the locus of human fulfillment (τελείωσις or σωτηρία for Hebrews; perhaps εὐδαιμονία for Plutarch). A life well (or poorly) lived is for Plutarch its own reward. For Hebrews, consummation is yet to come. What happens in the here and now is not definitive, thus the author sometimes asks his readers to think and act in ways that subordinate their physical welfare and emotional equilibrium to a higher, still future good visible only to the eyes of faith (11:1–40). The virtue denoted by the term πίστις comprises not only a mode of perseverance in accordance with the divine will but also specific, substantive beliefs about God's dealings with humanity. Belief that God exists, of course, is necessary but not sufficient. To please God, one must also believe "that he rewards those who seek him" (11:6). Implicit in this statement and explicit elsewhere in Hebrews' argument is that God does not reward those who do not seek him or who willfully reject him. For the "good news" (εὐαγγέλιον; cf. 4:2, 6) to be truly good, it has to be better than the alternative. Hebrews follows these propositions to their natural conclusion in the idea of divine judgment in the afterlife. When "the judge who is God of all" (12:23) sets all things in order in the hereafter, the sentence will sound simultaneously a note of joy and of fear. The difficulty of delineating both perspectives at the same time accounts in part for the author's oscillation between evocations of God's fearfulness and

---

[25] See chapter two above, pp. 95–103.

reminders of the boldness his audience enjoys in their approach to the heavenly throne.

Despite the author's insistence upon the once-for-all character of Christ's sacrifice and the way in which it renders superfluous all apotropaic rites aimed at deflecting God's wrath, in the final analysis Hebrews leaves intact the basic premise that the divine can in any fashion be a legitimate source of fear. In fact, God alone—not persecution, not material deprivation or physical abuse, not even death—is truly fearful. The idea appears in a more straightforward fashion throughout the OT, as when Isaiah writes, "Do not fear what this people fears, nor be in terror. But the Lord of Hosts, him you shall regard as holy; let him be your fear, and let him be your terror" (Isa 8:12–13).[26] According to Hebrews, the believer has to travel through fear, not around it, to come out on the other side. This notion, far from allaying any suspicion on other grounds that Christianity is an example of δεισιδαιμονία, effectively confirms it for pagan observers after Plutarch who come into direct contact with Christian thought: it is a decidedly good thing that there is no longer any need to be afraid, but the Christian solution comes at the expense of creating a problem where there should not have been one in the first place.

While Plutarch recognizes the possibility that the deity may feel "that he must no longer help us in the same way, but in a different way," and rebukes those who "yearn for the riddles, allegories, and metaphors" as preferable to the simpler, more direct oracles of first-century Delphi (*Pyth. orac.* 407F, 409C–D), there is of course no sure way of knowing how he would have reacted to God's novel way of speaking and acting through a son (Heb 1:1–2).[27] It is one thing to acknowledge a theological principle and quite another to agree upon a specific instance of that principle at work. It is of the essential nature of special revelation that its content or significance is inaccessible to or unanticipated by unaided reason. Accordingly, it is not possible to tell how a person might have responded to the novel claim that only Jesus—his life, death, resurrection, and priestly office in heaven—relativizes the fearfulness of any earthly danger and does away with all need to be afraid of God's wrath. Like most thinkers in antiquity, the author of Hebrews finds the old to be trustworthy and is cautious

---

[26] This statement occurs just a few lines before the verse (Isa 8:18) quoted in Heb 2:13. See also the allusion to Isa 8:12–13 in 1 Peter's admonition to "have no fear of them [i.e., persecutors], nor be troubled, but reverence Christ as the Lord" (3:14–15).

[27] Attempts to answer this question too frequently turn into speculative historical reconstructions or tend to lapse into projection, that is, the habit of unconsciously substituting one's own tastes and opinions for, in this case, those of Plutarch. See, for example, Oakesmith, who wrote a century ago that "Plutarch suggested a frame of mind rather than inculcated a body of dogma, and in that he resembled the founder of Christianity a great deal more than the most honoured theologians of the Church have done" (*The Religion of Plutarch*, 226).

about anything new, yet in common with the rest of the NT authors, he cannot bring himself to deny that something new has happened and that it is the work of God. He bends over backwards to show how Jesus, while representing God's new way of dealing with humanity, nonetheless fits perfectly with the divine plan related under the old covenant. But rather than downplaying it for apologetic purposes, the distinctive solution to the problem of fear in Hebrews actually underscores the scandal of particularity that the Christian message has caused since its very beginning.

Bibliography

Aasgaard, Reidar. "Brotherhood in Plutarch and Paul: Its Role and Character." Pages 166–182 in *Constructing Early Christian Families: Family as Social Reality and Metaphor*. Edited by H. Moxnes. London and New York: Routledge, 1997.

Abernetty, G. "De Plutarchi qui fertur de superstitione libello." Diss., Königsburg, 1911.

Adams, J. C. "The Epistle to the Hebrews with Special Reference to the Problem of Apostasy in the Church to Which It Was Addressed." Ph.D. diss., Leeds University, 1964.

Allen, Ward. "The Translation of ἀπὸ τῆς εὐλαβείας at Hebrews 5.7." *Bulletin of the Institute for Reformation Biblical Studies* 1 (1989): 9–10.

Almqvist, Helge. *Plutarch und das Neue Testament: Ein Beitrag zum Corpus Hellenisticum Novi Testamenti*. Acta Seminarii neotestamentici upsaliensis 15. Uppsala: Appelbergs, 1946.

Alston, W. P. "Emotion and Feeling." Pages 479–86 in vol. 1 of *The Encyclopedia of Philosophy*. Edited by P. Edwards. 8 vols. New York: Macmillan, 1967.

Andriessen, P. "La teneur judéo-chrétienne de Hé I 6 et II 14b–III 2." *Novum Testamentum* 18 (1976): 293–313.

Andriessen, P., and A. Lenglet. "Quelques passages difficiles de l'Épître aux Hébreux (5,7–11; 10,20; 12,2)." *Biblica* 51 (1970): 207–220.

Annas, Julia. "Epicurean Emotions." *Greek, Roman, and Byzantine Studies* 30 (1989): 145–64.

———. *Hellenistic Philosophy of Mind*. Berkeley: University of California Press, 1992.

Arnim, H. von. *Stoicorum veterum fragmenta*. 4 vols. Leipzig: Teubner, 1903–1924.

Arnold, E. Vernon. *Roman Stoicism*. Cambridge: Cambridge University Press, 1911.

Ashton, John. *The Religion of Paul the Apostle*. New Haven and London: Yale University Press, 2000.

Askevis-Leherpeux, F. "Les corrélats de la superstition." *Archives de sciences sociales des religions* 45 (1978): 65–76.

Attridge, Harold W. "'Heard Because of His Reverence' (Heb 5:7)." *Journal of Biblical Literature* 98 (1979): 90–93.

———. *The Epistle to the Hebrews*. Hermeneia. Philadelphia: Fortress, 1989.

———. "The Philosophical Critique of Religion under the Early Empire." *ANRW* 16.1:45–78. Part 2, *Principat*, 16.1. Edited by H. Temporini and W. Haase. New York: de Gruyter, 1978.

Aune, David E. "Heracles and Christ: Heracles Imagery in the Christology of Early Christianity." Pages 3–19 in *Greeks, Romans, And Christians: Essays in Honor of Abraham J. Malherbe*. Edited by D. L. Balch, E. Ferguson, and W. A. Meeks. Minneapolis: Fortress, 1990.

230 Godly Fear

----. *Prophecy in Early Christianity and the Ancient Mediterranean World*. Grand
Rapids: Eerdmans, 1983.

Babut, Daniel. "Plutarque, Aristote et l'Aristotélisme." *Studia Hellenistica* 32 (1996):
1–28.

----. *Plutarque et le stoïcisme*. Paris: Presses Universitaires de France, 1969.

Bacon, Francis. *The Essays, Or Counsels Civil and Moral*. Edited by B. Vickers. Oxford:
Oxford University Press, 1999.

Balch, David L. *Let Wives Be Submissive: The Domestic Code in 1 Peter*. Society of
Biblical Literature Monograph Series 26. Atlanta: Scholars Press, 1981.

Balthasar, Hans Urs von. *The Christian and Anxiety*. Translated by D. D. Martin and M.
J. Miller. San Francisco: Ignatius, 2000.

Bamberger, B. J. "Fear and Love of God in the OT." *Hebrew Union College Annual* 6
(1929): 39–53.

Bammel, Ernst. "Gottes ΔΙΑΘΗΚΗ (Gal. iii. 15–17) und das jüdische Rechtsdenken."
New Testament Studies 6 (1959–60): 313–19.

Bang, Seongkyou. "Rediscovery of the Fear of God: A Study of *The Sayings of the
Desert Fathers*." Ph.D. diss., Emory University, 1999.

Bannon, Cynthia J. *The Brothers of Romulus: Fraternal Pietas in Roman Law, Literature,
and Society*. Princeton: Princeton University Press, 1997.

Bardy, Gustave. *La Conversion au Christianisme durant les premiers siècles*. Paris:
Aubier, 1949.

Baroja, Julio Caro. *De la Supersticion al Ateismo*. Madrid: Taurus, 1974.

Barrett, C. K. "The Eschatology of the Epistle to the Hebrews." Pages 363–93 in *The
Background of the New Testament and Its Eschatology*. Edited by W. D. Davies and
D. Daube. Cambridge: Cambridge University Press, 1954.

Barrow, R. H. *Plutarch and His Times*. Bloomington and London: Indiana University
Press, 1967.

Barth, Marcus. "The Old Testament in Hebrews: An Essay in Biblical Hermeneutics."
Pages 53–78, 263–73 in *Current Issues in New Testament Interpretation: Essays in
Honor of O. A. Piper*. Edited by W. Klassen and G. F. Snyder. New York: Harper &
Row, 1962.

Bauckham, Richard J. *Jude, 2 Peter*. Word Biblical Commentary 50. Waco, Tex.: Word,
1983.

Bauer, Walter, W. F. Arndt, F. W. Gingrich, and F. W. Danker. *Greek-English Lexicon of
the New Testament and Other Early Christian Literature*. 2nd rev. ed. Chicago:
University of Chicago Press, 1979.

Beaujue, J. "L'incendie de Rome en 64 et les Chrétiens." *Latomus* 19 (1960): 65–80,
291–311.

Beegle, Dewey M. "Moses (Old Testament)." Pages 909–18 in vol. 4 of *The Anchor
Bible Dictionary*. Edited by D. N. Freedman. 6 vols. New York: Doubleday, 1992.

Belmont, Nicole. "Superstition and Popular Religion in Western Societies." Pages 9–23
in *Between Belief and Transgression: Structuralist Essays in Religion, History, and
Myth*. Edited by M. Izard and P. Smith. Chicago and London: University of Chicago
Press, 1982.

Benko, Stephen. "Pagan Criticism of Christianity during the First Two Centuries A.D."
    ANRW 23.2:1054–1118. Part 2, *Principat*, 23.2. Edited by H. Temporini and W.
    Haase. New York: de Gruyter, 1980.
——. *Pagan Rome and the Early Christians.* Bloomington: Indiana University Press,
    1984.
Berardi, Elisabetta. "Plutarco e la religione, l'εὐσέβεια come giusto mezzo fra
    δεισιδαιμονία e ἀθεότης." *Civiltà classica e cristiana* 11 (1990): 141–70.
Berger, Adolf, et al. "Adoption, Roman." Page 13 in *The Oxford Classical Dictionary*. 3rd
    ed. Edited by S. Hornblower and A. Spawforth. Oxford: Oxford University Press,
    1996.
——. "Law and Procedure, Roman." Pages 827–34 in *The Oxford Classical Dictionary*.
    3rd ed. Edited by S. Hornblower and A. Spawforth. Oxford: Oxford University Press,
    1996.
Berger, Peter L. *A Rumor of Angels.* Garden City, N.Y.: Doubleday, 1969.
——. *The Sacred Canopy: Elements of a Sociological Theory of Religion.* New York:
    Doubleday, 1967.
Berger, Peter L., and Thomas Luckmann. *The Social Construction of Reality: A Treatise
    in the Sociology of Knowledge.* Garden City, N.Y.: Doubleday, 1966.
Berry, Edmund G. *Emerson's Plutarch.* Cambridge: Harvard University Press, 1961.
Berthold, Fred, Jr. *The Fear of God: The Role of Anxiety in Contemporary Thought.* New
    York: Harper, 1959.
Betz, Hans Dieter. "Christianity as Religion: Paul's Attempt at Definition in Romans."
    Journal of Religion 71 (1991): 315–44.
——. "De fraterno amore (Moralia 478A–492D)." Pages 231–63 in *Plutarch's Ethical
    Writings and Early Christian Literature.* Edited by H. D. Betz. Studia ad corpus
    hellenisticum Novi Testamenti 4. Leiden: Brill, 1978.
——, ed. *Plutarch's Ethical Writings and Early Christian Literature.* Studia ad corpus
    hellenisticum Novi Testamenti 4. Leiden: Brill, 1978.
——, ed. *Plutarch's Theological Writings and Early Christian Literature.* Studia ad
    corpus hellenisticum Novi Testamenti 3. Leiden: Brill, 1975.
Bianchi, Ugo. "Plutarch und der Dualismus." *ANRW* 2.36:350–65. Part 2, *Principat*, 36.1.
    Edited by H. Temporini and W. Haase. New York: de Gruyter, 1987.
Black, Clifton C. "The Rhetorical Form of the Hellenistic Jewish and Early Christian
    Sermon: A Response to Lawrence Wills." *Harvard Theological Review* 81 (1988):
    1–18.
Blass, F., A. Debrunner, and R. W. Funk. *A Greek Grammar of the New Testament and
    Other Early Christian Literature.* Chicago: University of Chicago Press, 1961.
Bodéüs, R. "Un aspect du platonisme de Plutarque?" *Les Études classiques* 42 (1974):
    362–74.
Bolkestein, Hendrik. *Theophrastos' Charakter der Deisidaimonia als
    Religionsgeschichtliche Urkunde.* Religionsgeschichtliche Versuche und
    Vorarbeiten 21.2. Giessen: Töpelmann, 1929.
Bolt, Martin. "Religious Orientation and Death Fears." *Review of Religious Research* 19
    (1977): 73–76.
Bonus, A. "Heb. II.16 in the Peshitta Syriac Version." *Expository Times* 33 (1921–22):
    234–36.

Brandenburger, Egon. "Text und Vorlagen von Hebr. V 7–10: Ein Beitrag zur Christologie des Hebräerbriefs." *Novum Testamentum* 11 (1969): 190–224.

Braun, Herbert. *An die Hebräer*. Handbuch zum Neuen Testament 14. Tübingen: Mohr-Siebeck, 1984.

——. *Plutarch's Critique of Superstition in Light of the New Testament*. Translated by H. D. Betz and E. W. Smith, Jr. Institute for Antiquity and Christianity Occasional Papers 5. Claremont, 1972. Translation of *Plutarchs Kritik am Aberglauben im Lichte des Neuen Testamentes*. Der Anfang 9. Berlin: Verlag Haus und Schule, 1948.

Brenk, Frederick E. "An Imperial Heritage: The Religious Spirit of Plutarch of Chaironeia." *ANRW* 36.1:248–349. Part 2, *Principat*, 36.1. Edited by H. Temporini and W. Haase. New York: de Gruyter, 1987.

——. "From Mysticism to Mysticism: The Religious Development of Plutarch of Chaironeia." Pages 93–98 in vol. 1 of *SBL Seminar Papers, 1975*. 2 vols. Society of Biblical Literature Seminar Papers 12. Missoula, Mont.: Scholars Press, 1975.

——. *In Mist Apparelled: Religious Themes in Plutarch's* Moralia *and* Lives. Mnemosyne Supplement 48. Leiden: Brill, 1977.

Brennan, Tad. "The Old Stoic Theory of Emotions." Pages 21–70 in *The Emotions in Hellenistic Philosophy*. Edited by J. Sihvola and T. Engberg-Pederson. New Synthese Historical Library 46. Dordrecht: Kluwer, 1998.

Brinton, Alan. "Pathos and the 'Appeal to Emotion': An Aristotelian Analysis." *History of Philosophy Quarterly* 5 (1988): 207–19.

Brown, Raymond E., and John P. Meier. *Antioch and Rome*. London: Geoffrey Chapman, 1983.

Brox, N. "Zum Vorwurf des Atheismus gegen die alte Kirche." *Trier Theologische Zeitschrift* 75 (1966): 274–82.

Bruce, F. F. *The Epistle to the Hebrews*. New International Commentary on the New Testament. Grand Rapids: Eerdmans, 1964.

——. "'To the Hebrews': A Document of Roman Christianity?" *ANRW* 25.4:3496–521. Part 2, *Principat*, 25.4. Edited by H. Temporini and W. Haase. New York: de Gruyter, 1987.

Brueckner, A., and J. M. Fischer. "Why is Death Bad?" *Philosophical Studies* 50 (1986): 213–21.

Buchanan, George W. *To the Hebrews*. Anchor Bible 36. Garden City: Doubleday, 1972.

Bulley, A. D. "Death and Rhetoric in the Hebrews 'Hymn to Faith.'" *Studies in Religion* 25 (1996): 409–23.

Bultmann, Rudolf. *History of the Synoptic Tradition*. Rev. ed. Translated by J. Marsh. Oxford: Blackwell, 1963.

——. *Theology of the New Testament*. Translated by K. Grobel. 2 vols. New York: Scribner's, 1951–55.

Bunyan, John. *A Treatise of the Fear of God*. London: Nathaniel Ponder, 1679.

Burke, Edmund. *Speech of Edmund Burke, Esq., on Moving His Resolutions for Conciliation with the Colonies, March 22, 1775*. London: Dodsley, 1775. Repr., *Speech on Conciliation with America*. Edited by A. S. Cook. New York: Longmans, Green, and Co., 1896.

Burkert, Walter. *Greek Religion*. Translated by J. Raffan. Cambridge: Harvard University Press, 1985.

Burtness, J. H. "Plato, Philo, and the Author of Hebrews." *Lutheran Quarterly* 10 (1958): 54–64.

Busch, Peter. "Der mitleidende Hohepriester: Zur Rezeption der mittelplatonischen Dämonologie in Hebr 4,14f." Pages 19–30 in *Religionsgeschichte des Neuen Testaments: Festschrift für Klaus Berger zum 60. Geburtstag*. Edited by Axel von Dobbeler et al. Tübingen: Francke, 2000.

Buxton, Richard, ed. *From Myth to Reason?* Oxford: Oxford University Press, 1999.

Cairns, Douglas L. *Aidōs: The Psychology and Ethics of Honour and Shame in Ancient Greek Literature*. Oxford: Clarendon, 1993.

Calderone, S. "Superstitio." *ANRW* 1.2:377–96. Part 1, *Von den Anfängen Roms biz zum Ausgang der Republik*, 1.2. Edited by H. Temporini and W. Haase. New York: de Gruyter, 1972.

Calvin, John. *Commentaries on the Epistle of Paul the Apostle to the Hebrews*. Translated by J. Owen. Grand Rapids: Eerdmans, 1948.

———. *Institutes of the Christian Religion*. 2 vols. Edited by J. T. McNeill. Translated by F. L. Battles. Philadelphia: Westminster, 1960.

Cambier, J. "Eschatologie ou hellénisme dans l'Épître aux Hébreux: Une étude sur μένειν et l'exhortation finale de l'épître." *Salesianum* 11 (1949): 62–86.

Carlston, C. E. "Eschatology and Repentance in the Epistle to the Hebrews." *Journal of Biblical Literature* 78 (1959): 296–302.

Casey, J. M. "Eschatology in Heb 12:14–29: An Exegetical Study." Diss., Catholic University of Leuven, 1977.

Catechism of the Catholic Church. The Vatican: Libreria Editrice Vaticana, 1994.

Cerny, Leonard. "Christian Faith and Thanataphobia." *Journal of Psychology and Theology* 3 (1975): 202–209.

Champlin, E. "*Creditur vulgo testamenta hominum speculum esse morum*: Why the Romans Made Wills." *Classical Philology* 84 (1989): 198–215.

Childs, Brevard S. *The Book of Exodus*. Old Testament Library. Philadelphia: Westminster, 1974.

Conley, Thomas. "*Pathe* and *Pisteis*: Aristotle, *Rhet* II 1–11." *Hermes* 110 (1982): 300–15.

Cooper, John. "An Aristotelian Theory of the Emotions." Pages 238–57 in *Essays on Aristotle's Rhetoric*. Edited by A. O. Rorty. Berkeley: University of California Press, 1996.

———. "Posidonius on Emotions." Pages 71–111 in *The Emotions in Hellenistic Philosophy*. Edited by J. Sihvola and T. Engberg-Pederson. New Synthese Historical Library 46. Dordrecht: Kluwer, 1998.

Cosby, Michael R. *The Rhetorical Composition and Function of Hebrews 11 in the Light of Example Lists in Antiquity*. Macon: Macon University Press, 1988.

Cover, Robin C. "Sin, Sinners (OT)." Pages 31–40 in vol. 6 of *The Anchor Bible Dictionary*. Edited by D. N. Freedman. 6 vols. New York: Doubleday, 1992.

Cox, Cheryl A. *Household Interests: Property, Marriage Strategies, and Family Dynamics in Ancient Athens*. Princeton: Princeton University Press, 1998.

Crook, J. A. "*Patria Potestas*." *Classical Quarterly* 17 (1967): 113–22.

Croy, N. Clayton. *Endurance in Suffering: Hebrews 12:1–13 in Its Rhetorical, Religious, and Philosophical Context*. Society for New Testament Studies Monograph Series 98. Cambridge: Cambridge University Press, 1998.

Cullmann, Oscar. *The Christology of the New Testament*. Translated by S. C. Guthrie and C. A. M. Hall. London: SCM, 1959.

Dahl, Nils A. "'A New and More Perfect Way': The Approach to God According to Hebrews." *Interpretation* 5 (1951): 401–12.

Daly, R. J. "The Soteriological Significance of the Sacrifice of Isaac." *Catholic Biblical Quarterly* 39 (1977): 45–75.

D'Angelo, Mary Rose. *Moses in the Letter to the Hebrews*. Society of Biblical Literature Dissertation Series 42. Missoula, Mont.: Scholars Press, 1979.

Deissmann, Adolf. *Light from the Ancient East*. Translated by L. R. M. Strachan. New York: Doran, 1927.

Delitzsch, Franz J. *Commentary on the Epistle to the Hebrews*. Translated by T. L. Kingsbury. 3rd ed. 2 vols. Edinburgh: Clark, 1883.

Delling, Gerhard. "Zum Corpus Hellenisticum Novi Testamenti." *Zeitschrift für die neutestamentliche Wissenschaft und die Kunde der älteren Kirche* 54 (1963): 1–15.

Del Real, Carlos Alonso. *Superstición y Supersticiones*. Madrid: Espasa-Calpe, 1971.

Delumeau, Jean. *Sin and Fear: The Emergence of a Western Guilt Culture*. Translated by E. Nicholson. New York: St. Martin's, 1990.

DeSilva, David A. *Despising Shame: Honor Discourse and Community Maintenance in the Epistle to the Hebrews*. Society of Biblical Literature Dissertation Series 152. Atlanta: Scholars Press, 1995.

———. *Perseverance in Gratitude: A Socio-Rhetorical Commentary on the Epistle "to the Hebrews."* Grand Rapids: Eerdmans, 2000.

Dey, L. K. K. *The Intermediary World and Patterns of Perfection in the Epistle to the Hebrews*. Society of Biblical Literature Dissertation Series 25. Missoula, Mont.: Scholars Press, 1975.

Dill, S. *Roman Society from Nero to Marcus Aurelius*. 2nd ed. London: Macmillian, 1905.

Dillon, John. "*Metriopatheia* and *Apatheia*: Some Reflections on a Controversy in Later Greek Ethics." Pages 508–17 in vol. 2. of *Essays in Ancient Greek Philosophy*. 2 vols. Edited by J. P. Anton and A. Preus. Albany N.Y.: SUNY Press, 1983.

———. *The Middle Platonists*. Ithaca: Cornell University Press, 1977.

Dixon, Suzanne. *The Roman Family*. Baltimore: Johns Hopkins University Press, 1992.

Dodds, E. R. *The Greeks and the Irrational*. Berkeley: University of California Press, 1966.

Dolfe, Karl-Gustave E. "Hebrews 2,16 under the Magnifying Glass." *Zeitschrift für die neutestamentliche Wissenschaft und die Kunde der älteren Kirche* 84 (1993): 289–94.

Dörrie, Heinrich. "Die Stellung Plutarchs im Platonismus seiner Zeit." Pages 36–56 in *Philomathes: Studies and Essays in the Humanities in Memory of Philip Merlan*. Edited by R. B. Palmer and R. Hamerton-Kelly. The Hague: Martinus Nihjoff, 1971.

Drachmann, A. B. *Atheism in Pagan Antiquity*. Chicago: Ares, 1977.

Drews, Robert. "Diodorus and His Sources." *American Journal of Philology* 83 (1962): 383–92.

Dunbar, D. G. "The Relation of Christ's Sonship and Priesthood in the Epistle to the Hebrews." Diss., Westminster Theological Seminary, 1974.

Dunn, James D. G., ed. *Jews and Christians: The Partings of the Ways, A.D. 70–135.* Wissenschaftliche Untersuchungen zum Neuen Testament 66. Tübingen: Mohr-Siebeck, 1992.

Dunnill, John. *Covenant and Sacrifice in the Letter to the Hebrews.* Society for New Testament Studies Monograph Series 75. Cambridge: Cambridge University Press, 1992.

Eagar, A. R. "Hellenistic Elements in the Epistle to the Hebrews." *Hermathena* 11 (1901): 263–87.

Ehrman, Bart. *The New Testament: A Historical Introduction to the Early Christian Writings.* New York and Oxford: Oxford University Press, 1997.

Eisenbaum, Pamela. *The Jewish Heroes of Christian History: Hebrews 11 in Literary Context.* Society of Biblical Literature Dissertation Series 156. Atlanta: Scholars Press, 1997.

Eliot, T. S. *The Four Quartets.* New York: Harcourt Brace Jovanovich, 1943.

Ellingworth, Paul. "Hebrews and 1 Clement: Literary Dependence or Common Tradition?" *Biblische Zeitschrift* 23 (1979): 62–9.

———. *The Epistle to the Hebrews.* New International Greek Testament Commentary. Grand Rapids: Eerdmans; Carlisle: Paternoster, 1993.

Ellis, E. E. *Paul and the Old Testament.* Grand Rapids: Eerdmans, 1957.

Empson, William. *Seven Types of Ambiguity.* 2nd ed. New York: New Directions, 1947.

Endo, Shusaku. *Silence.* Translated by W. Johnston. New York: Taplinger, 1969.

Erbse, Hartmut. "Plutarchs Schrift *Peri Deisidaimonias.*" *Hermes* 80 (1952): 296–314.

Esler, P. F. "Family Imagery and Christian Identity in Gal 5:13 to 6:10." Pages 121–149 in *Constructing Early Christian Families: Family as Social Reality and Metaphor.* Edited by H. Moxnes. London and New York: Routledge, 1997.

Evans, C. F. *Resurrection and the New Testament.* Studies in Biblical Theology, 2nd series 12. London: SCM, 1970.

Eyben, E. "Fathers and Sons." Pages 114–43 in *Marriage, Divorce, and Children in Ancient Rome.* Edited by B. Rawson. Oxford: Clarendon, 1991.

Fairhurst, A. M. "Hellenistic Influence in the Epistle to the Hebrews." *Tyndale Bulletin* 7–8 (1961): 17–27.

Fatum, Lone. "Brotherhood in Christ: A Gender Hermeneutical Reading of 1 Thessalonians." Pages 183–97 in *Constructing Early Christian Families: Family as Social Reality and Metaphor.* Edited by H. Moxnes. London and New York: Routledge, 1997.

Feather, J. "The Princess Who Rescued Moses: Who Was She? With a Note on Heb. XI.24–26." *Expository Times* 43 (1931–32): 423–25.

Feifel, Herman. "Attitudes Toward Death in Some Normal and Mentally Ill Populations." Pages 114–29 in *The Meaning of Death.* Edited by H. Feifel. New York: McGraw-Hill, 1959.

Feld, H. *Der Hebräerbrief.* Erträge der Erforschung 228. Darmstadt: Wissenschaftliche Buchgesellschaft, 1985.

236 Godly Fear

——. "Der Hebräerbrief: Literarische Form, religionsgeschichtlicher Hintergrund, theologische Fragen." *ANRW* 25.4:3522–601. Part 2, *Principat*, 25.4. Edited by H. Temporini and W. Haase. New York: de Gruyter, 1987.

Feldman, Fred. *Confrontations with the Reaper: A Philosophical Study of the Nature and Value of Death.* Oxford: Oxford University Press, 1992.

Ferguson, Everett. *Backgrounds of Early Christianity.* 2nd ed. Grand Rapids: Eerdmans, 1993.

——. "Spiritual Sacrifice in Early Christianity and Its Environment." *ANRW* 23.2:1151–89. Part 2, *Principat*, 23.2. Edited by H. Temporini and W. Haase. New York: de Gruyter, 1980.

Festugière, A. J. *Epicurus and His Gods.* Translated by C. W. Chilton. Oxford: Blackwell, 1955.

Feuillet, A. "L'évocation de l'agonie de Gethsémane dans l'Épître aux Hébreux (5,7–8)." *Esprit et vie* 86 (1976): 49–53.

Feyerabend, Paul K. *Against Method.* 3rd ed. London: Verso, 1993.

Filson, Floyd V. "The Epistle to the Hebrews." *Journal of Bible and Religion* 22 (1954): 20–26.

——. *"Yesterday": A Study of Hebrews in the Light of Chapter 13.* Studies in Biblical Theology 4. London: SCM, 1967.

Finn, Thomas M. *From Death to Rebirth: Ritual and Conversion in Antiquity.* New York: Paulist, 1997.

Fitzmyer, Joseph A. "Habakkuk 2:3–4 and the New Testament." Pages 236–46 in *To Advance the Gospel: New Testament Studies.* New York: Crossroad, 1981.

Flacelière, Robert. "L'état présent des études zur Plutarque." Pages 483–505 in *Actes du VIIIᵉ Congrès G. Budé.* Paris: Budé, 1969.

——. "Plutarque et la Pythie." *Revue des études grecques* 56 (1943): 73–111.

——. "Plutarque et l'épicurisme." Pages 197–215 in *Epicurea in memoriam Hectoris Bignone.* Genoa: Istituto di filologia classica, 1959.

Flacelière, Robert, and Jean Irigoin. Introduction to *Plutarque: Œuvres Morales (Tome 1, 1ᵉʳ Partie).* Paris: Budé, 1987.

Ford, Josephine M. "The Mother of Jesus and the Authorship of the Epistle to the Hebrews." *The University of Dayton Review* 11 (1975): 49–56.

Fortenbaugh, William W. *Aristotle on Emotion.* London: Duckworth, 1975.

——. "Aristotle's *Rhetoric* on Emotions." *Archiv für Geschichte der Philosophie* 52 (1970): 40–70.

Frede, Dorothea. "The Cognitive Role of *Phantasia* in Aristotle." Pages 279–96 in *Essays on Aristotle's de Anima.* Edited by M. C. Nussbaum and A. O. Rorty. Oxford: Clarendon, 1992.

Frend, W. H. C. *Martyrdom and Persecution in the Early Church.* Oxford: Blackwell, 1965.

Froidefond, Christian. "Plutarque et le platonisme." *ANRW* 36.1:184–233. Part 2, *Principat*, 36.1. Edited by H. Temporini and W. Haase. New York: de Gruyter, 1987.

Fuchs, Harald. "Tacitus über die Christen." *Vigiliae Christianae* 4 (1950): 65–93.

Gamble, J. "Symbol and Reality in the Epistle to the Hebrews." *Journal of Biblical Literature* 45 (1926): 162–170.

Gardner, Alice. "Superstition." Pages 120–22 in vol. 12 of *Encyclopedia of Religion and Ethics*. Edited by J. Hastings. 13 vols. New York : Scribner's, 1917–27.

Geertz, Clifford. "Ethos, World View, and the Analysis of Sacred Symbols." Pages 126–41 in *The Interpretation of Cultures*. New York: Basic, 1973.

Gill, Christopher. "Did Galen Understand Platonic and Stoic Thinking on Emotions?" Pages 113–48 in *The Emotions in Hellenistic Philosophy*. Edited by J. Sihvola and T. Engberg-Pederson. New Synthese Historical Library 46. Dordrecht: Kluwer, 1998.

Gladigow, Burkhard. "Aberglaube." Pages 387–8 in vol. 1 of *Handbuch religionswissenschaftlicher Grundbegriffe*. Edited by H. Cancik et al. 4 vols. Stuttgart: Kohlhammer, 1988.

Goldhahn-Müller, Ingrid. *Die Grenze der Gemeinde: Studien zum Problem der Zweiten Busse im Neuen Testament unter Berücksichtigung der Entwicklung im 2. Jh. bis Tertullian*. Göttinger theologischer Arbeiten 39. Göttingen: Vandenhoeck & Ruprecht, 1989.

Goldin, Judah. "'Not by Means of an Angel and not by Means of a Messenger.'" Pages 412–24 in *Religions in Antiquity*. Edited by J. Neusner. Leiden: Brill, 1968.

Gollwitzer, Helmut. "Zur Frage der 'Sündlosigkeit Jesu'." *Evangelische Theologie* 31 (1971): 496–507.

Gombrich, E. H. *Art and Illusion: A Study in the Psychology of Pictorial Representation*. New York: Pantheon, 1960.

Gordon, Richard. "Religion in the Roman Empire: The Civic Compromise and its Limits." Pages 233–55 in *Pagan Priests*. Edited by M. Beard and J. North. London: Duckworth, 1990.

Gosling, J., and C. C. W. Taylor. *The Greeks on Pleasure*. Oxford: Clarendon, 1982.

Gould, J. B. *The Philosophy of Chrysippus*. Albany: State University of New York Press, 1970.

Grant, Robert M. *Greek Apologists of the Second Century*. Philadelphia: Westminster, 1988.

Grässer, Erich. *An die Hebräer*. 3 vols. Evangelisch-katholischer Kommentar zum Neuen Testament 17.1–3. Braunschweig: Benzinger; Veukirchen-Vluyn: Neukirchener, 1990–97.

———. *Der Glaube im Hebräerbrief*. Marburger Theologische Studien 2. Marburg: Elwert, 1965.

———. "Der Hebräerbrief 1938–1963." *Theologische Rundschau* 30 (1964): 138–236.

———. "Der historische Jesus im Hebräerbrief." *Zeitschrift für die neutestamentliche Wissenschaft und die Kunde der älteren Kirche* 56 (1965): 82–88.

———. "Die Heilsbedeutung des Todes Jesu in Hebräer 2,14–18." Pages 165–84 in *Theologia Crucis-Signum Crucis: Festschrift für Erich Dinkler zum 70. Geburtstag*. Edited by C. Andresen and G. Klein. Tübingen: Mohr-Siebeck, 1979.

Greard, Octave. *De la Morale de Plutarque*. Paris: Hachette, 1866.

Green, O. H. "Fear of Death." *Philosophy and Phenomenological Research* 43 (1982): 99–105.

Grodzynski, Denise. "Superstitio." *Revue des études anciennes* 76 (1974): 36–60.

Gudorf, Michael. "Through a Classical Lens: Hebrews 2:16." *Journal of Biblical Literature* 119 (2000): 105–8.

238 Godly Fear

238 Godly Fear

238   Godly Fear

238   Godly Fear

238   Godly Fear

238   Godly Fear

238   Godly Fear

238   Godly Fear

238   Godly Fear

238   Godly Fear

Hadas, Moses. "The Religion of Plutarch." *Review of Religion* 6 (1941–42): 270–82.

Haering, T. "Gedankengang und Grundgedanken des Hebräerbriefs." *Zeitschrift für die neutestamentliche Wissenschaft und die Kunde der älteren Kirche* 18 (1917–18): 145–164.

Hagner, D. A. *The Use of the Old and New Testaments in Clement of Rome.* Leiden: Brill, 1973.

Hamm, Dennis. "Faith in the Epistle to the Hebrews: The Jesus Factor." *Catholic Biblical Quarterly* 52 (1990): 270–91.

Hani, Jean. *La Religion Égyptienne dans la Pensée de Plutarque.* Paris: Les belles lettres, 1976.

Hardie, P. R. "Plutarch and the Interpretation of Myth." *ANRW* 33.6:4743–87. Part 2, *Principat*, 33.6. Edited by H. Temporini and W. Haase. New York: de Gruyter, 1992.

Harnack, A. von. "Probabilia über die Adresse und den Verfasser des Hebräerbriefes." *Zeitschrift für die neutestamentliche Wissenschaft und die Kunde der ältern Kirche* 1 (1900): 16–41.

——. "Zwei alte dogmatische Korrekturen im Hebräerbrief." Pages 245–52 in *Studien zur Geschichte des Neuen Testaments und der alten Kirche.* Arbeiten zur Kirchengeschichte 19. Berlin and Leipzig: de Gruyter, 1931.

Harrison, G. W. M. "The Critical Trends in Scholarship on the Non-Philosophical Works in Plutarch's 'Moralia'." *ANRW* 33.6:4646–81. Part 2, *Principat*, 33.6. Edited by H. Temporini and W. Haase. New York: de Gruyter, 1992.

Hartmann, J. J. *De Plutarcho Scriptore et Philosopho.* Leiden: Brill, 1916.

Hay, David M. *Glory at the Right Hand: Psalm 110 in Early Christianity.* Society of Biblical Literature Monograph Series 18. Nashville: Abingdon, 1973.

Hegermann, H. *Der Brief an Die Hebräer.* Theologischer Handkommentar zum Neuen Testament 16. Berlin: Evangelische Velagsanstalt, 1988.

Heidegger, Martin. *Being and Time.* Translated by J. Macquarrie and E. Robinson. New York: Harper & Row, 1962.

Helmbold, William C., and Edward N. O'Neil. *Plutarch's Quotations.* Baltimore: American Philological Association, 1959.

Hering, J. "Eschatologie biblique et idéalisme platonicien." Pages 444–63 in *The Background of the New Testament and Its Eschatology.* Edited by W. D. Davies and D. Daube. Cambridge: Cambridge University Press, 1954.

Hermann, L. "Sénèque et la superstition." *Latomus* 29 (1970): 389–96.

Hershbell, Jackson P. "Plutarch and Epicureanism." *ANRW* 36.5:3353–83. Part 2, *Principat*, 36.5. Edited by H. Temporini and W. Haase. New York: de Gruyter, 1992.

——. "Plutarch and Stoicism." *ANRW* 36.5:3336–52. Part 2, *Principat*, 36.5. Edited by H. Temporini and W. Haase. New York: de Gruyter, 1992.

Hill, David. *New Testament Prophecy.* Atlanta: John Knox, 1979.

Hirzel, R. *Plutarch.* Leipzig: Dieterich, 1912.

Hodgson, Roger, Jr. "Superstition." Pages 239–41 in vol. 6 of *The Anchor Bible Dictionary.* Edited by D. N. Freedman. 6 vols. New York: Doubleday, 1992.

———. "Superstition and Submission: A Study in Roman Social History and Early Christian Ethics." Unpublished paper. Department of Religious Studies, Southwest Missouri State University, 1990.

Hoelter, J. W., and R. J. Epley. "Religious Correlates of Fear of Death." *Journal for the Scientific Study of Religion* 18 (1979): 404–11.

Hofius, Otfried. *Katapausis: Die Vorstellung vom endzeitlichen Ruheort im Hebräerbrief.* Wissenschaftliche Untersuchungen zum Neuen Testament 11. Tübingen: J. C. B. Mohr, 1970.

Hooker, Richard. *The Works of that Learned and Judicious Divine Mr. Richard Hooker, containing Eight Books of the Laws of Ecclesiastical Polity.* 3 vols. Oxford: Clarendon, 1807.

Hopkins, Keith. *Death and Renewal.* Cambridge: Cambridge University Press, 1983.

Horbury, William. "The Aaronic Priesthood and the Epistle to the Hebrews." *Journal for the Study of the New Testament* 19 (1983): 43–71.

Horst, P. W. van der. "Corpus Hellenisticum Novi Testamenti." Pages 1157–61 in vol. 1 of *The Anchor Bible Dictionary.* Edited by D. N. Freedman. 6 vols. New York: Doubleday, 1992.

———. "Sarah's Seminal Emission: Hebrews 11:11 in the Light of Ancient Embryology." Pages 287–302 in *Greeks, Romans, And Christians: Essays in Honor of Abraham J. Malherbe.* Edited by D. L. Balch, E. Ferguson, and W. A. Meeks. Minneapolis: Fortress, 1990.

Hughes, Dennis D. *Human Sacrifice in Ancient Greece.* London and New York: Routledge, 1991.

Hughes, Graham. *Hebrews and Hermeneutics.* Society for New Testament Studies Monograph Series 36. Cambridge: Cambridge University Press, 1979.

Hughes, J. J. "Hebrews ix 15ff. and Galatians iii 15ff.: A Study in Covenant Practice and Procedure." *Novum Testamentum* 21 (1979): 27–96.

Hughes, Philip E. *A Commentary on the Epistle to the Hebrews.* Grand Rapids: Eerdmans, 1977.

Hume, David. "Of Superstition and Enthusiasm." Pages 3–9 in *Writings on Religion.* Edited by A. Flew. La Salle, Ill.: Open Court, 1992.

Hurst, L. D. "Eschatology and 'Platonism' in the Epistle to the Hebrews." Pages 41–74 in *SBL Seminar Papers, 1984.* Society of Biblical Literature Seminar Papers 23 Chico, Calif.: Scholars Press, 1984.

———. *The Epistle to the Hebrews: Its Background of Thought.* Society for New Testament Studies Monograph Series 65. Cambridge: Cambridge University Press, 1990.

Idziak, Janine Marie. *Divine Command Morality: Historical and Contemporary Readings.* New York: Edwin Mellen, 1979.

Inwood, Brad. *Ethics and Human Action in Early Stoicism.* Oxford: Clarendon, 1985.

Inwood, Brad, and L. P. Gerson. *The Epicurus Reader.* Indianapolis: Hackett, 1994.

Irwin, T. H. "Stoic Inhumanity." Pages 218–41 in *The Emotions in Hellenistic Philosophy.* Edited by J. Sihvola and T. Engberg-Pederson. New Synthese Historical Library 46. Dordrecht: Kluwer, 1998.

Isaacs, Marie E. *Sacred Space: An Approach to the Theology of the Epistle to the Hebrews*. Journal for the Study of the New Testament: Supplement Series 73. Sheffield: JSOT Press, 1992.

Izard, Carroll E. *Human Emotions*. New York: Plenum, 1977.

Jaeger, Werner. *Paideia: The Ideals of Greek Culture*. 3 vols. Translated by G. Highet. New York: Oxford University Press, 1939–44.

Jahoda, Gustave. *The Psychology of Superstition*. London: Allen Lane; Baltimore: Penguin, 1969.

James, William. *The Principles of Psychology*. 3 vols. Cambridge: Harvard University Press, 1981.

Janssen, L. "Die Bedeutungsentwicklung von *superstitio/superstes*." *Mnemosyne* 28 (1975): 135–89.

———. "'Superstitio' and the Persecution of Christians." *Vigiliae christianae* 33 (1979): 131–59.

Jarvis, Peter. "Towards a Sociological Understanding of Superstition." *Social Compass* 27 (1980): 285–95.

Jentsch, W. *Urchristliches Erziehungsdenken: Die Paideia Kyriu im Rahmen der hellenistisch-Jüdischen Umwelt*. Beiträge zur Förderung christlicher Theologie 45/3. Gütersloh: Bertelsmann, 1951.

Jeremias, J. "Hbr 5,7–10." *Zeitschrift für die neutestamentliche Wissenschaft und die Kunde der älteren Kirche* 44 (1952–53): 107–111.

Johnson, Luke T. *The Real Jesus*. San Francisco: Harper, 1996.

———. *The Writings of the New Testament*. Philadelphia: Fortress, 1986.

Johnsson, W. G. "Defilement and Purgation in the Book of Hebrews." Ph.D. Diss., Vanderbilt University, 1973.

Jones, C. P. *Plutarch and Rome*. Oxford: Clarendon, 1971.

———. "Towards a Chronology of Plutarch's Works." *Journal of Roman Studies* 56 (1966): 51–74.

Jones, Roger M. *The Platonism of Plutarch and Selected Papers*. Edited by L. Tarán. New York and London: Garland, 1980.

Joüon, Paul. "Divers sens de παρρησία dans le Nouveau Testament." *Recherches de Science Religieuse* 30 (1940): 239–41.

Jülicher, Adolf. *An Introduction to the New Testament*. Translated by J. P. Ward. New York: Putnam's, 1904.

Kahoe, Richard D., and Rebecca F. Dunn. "Fear of Death and Religious Attitudes and Behavior." *Journal for the Scientific Study of Religon* 14 (1975): 379–82.

Käsemann, Ernst. *The Wandering People of God: An Investigation of the Letter to the Hebrews*. Translated by R. A. Harrisville and I. L. Sandberg. Minneapolis: Augsburg, 1984. Translation of *Das wandernde Gottesvolk*. Forschungen zur Religion und Literatur des Alten und Neuen Testaments 55. Göttingen: Vandenhoeck & Ruprecht, 1939.

Kass, Leon R. "L'Chaim and Its Limits: Why Not Immortality?" *First Things* 113 (May 2001): 17–24.

Kerényi, C. *The Religion of the Greeks and Romans*. Translated by C. Holme. London: Thames and Hudson, 1962.

Kierkegaard, Soren. *Purity of Heart Is to Will One Thing*. Translated by D. V. Steere. New York: Harper & Row, 1956.

———. *The Concept of Dread*. Translated by W. Lowrie. Princeton: Princeton University Press, 1944.

Kippenberg, Hans. "Comparing Ancient Religions: A Discussion of J. Z. Smith's 'Drudgery Divine'." *Numen* 39 (1992): 220–25.

Kittel, G., and G. Friedrich, eds. *Theological Dictionary of the New Testament*. Translated by G. W. Bromiley. 10 vols. Grand Rapids: Eerdmans, 1964–1976.

Klaerr, Robert. Introduction to "De la superstition." Pages 239–46 in *Plutarque: Oeuvres Morales*, vol 2. Edited by J. Defradas et al. Paris: Les belles lettres, 1985.

Klauck, Hans-Josef. *Alte Welt und neuer Glaube: Beiträge zur Religionsgeschichte, Forschungsgeschichte und Theologie des Neuen Testaments*. Göttingen: Vandenhoeck & Ruprecht, 1994.

———. "Brotherly Love in Plutarch and in 4 Maccabees." Pages 144–56 in *Greeks, Romans, And Christians: Essays in Honor of Abraham J. Malherbe*. Edited by D. L. Balch, E. Ferguson, and W. A. Meeks. Minneapolis: Fortress, 1990.

———. "Religion Without Fear: Plutarch on Superstition and Early Christianity." *Skrif en Kerk* 18 (1997): 111–26.

———. "Sacrifice and Sacrificial Offerings (NT)." Pages 886–91 in vol. 5 of *The Anchor Bible Dictionary*. Edited by D. N. Freedman. 6 vols. New York: Doubleday, 1992.

Knuuttila, Simo, and Juha Sihvola. "How the Philosphical Analysis of Emotions was Introduced." Pages 1–19 in *The Emotions in Hellenistic Philosophy*. Edited by J. Sihvola and T. Engberg-Pederson. New Synthese Historical Library 46. Dordrecht: Kluwer, 1998.

Koester, Craig R. *Hebrews*. Anchor Bible 36. New York: Doubleday, 2001.

Koets, P. J. *Deisidaimonia: A Contribution to the Knowledge of the Religious Terminology in Greek*. Purmerend: Muusses, 1929.

Kolakowski, Leszek. *Modernity on Endless Trial*. Chicago: University of Chicago Press, 1990.

Kosman, L. A. "Being Properly Affected: Virtues and Feelings in Aristotle's Ethics." Pages 103–16 in Essays *Essays on Aristotle's Ethics*. Edited by A. O. Rorty. Berkeley: University of California Press, 1980.

Kümmel, W. G. *Introduction to the New Testament*. Rev. ed. Translated by H. C. Kee. Nashville and New York: Abingdon, 1975.

———. *The New Testament: The History of the Investigation of its Problems*. Translated by S. Maclean Gilmour and H. C. Kee. Nashville and New York: Abingdon, 1972.

Labriolle, P. de. *La réaction paienne: Étude sur la polémique antichrétienne du Ier au VIe siècle*. 2d ed. Paris: L'Artisan du livre, 1948.

Lampe, P. *Die stadtrömischen Christen in den ersten beiden Jahrhunderte: Untersuchung zu Sozialgeschichte*. Tübingen: Mohr-Siebeck, 1987.

Lane, William L. *Hebrews*. 2 vols. Word Biblical Commentary 47A–B. Dallas: Word, 1991.

La Piana, George. "Foreign Groups in Rome During the First Centuries of the Roman Empire." *Harvard Theological Review* 20 (1927): 183–403.

Latzarus, B. *Les idées religieuses de Plutarque*. Paris: Leroux, 1920.

Laub, Franz. *Hebräerbrief.* Stuttgarter kleiner Kommentar, Neues Testament 12. Stuttgart: Verlag Katholisches Bibelwerk, 1988.

Lausberg, Marion. "Senecae operum fragmenta: Überblick und Forschungsbericht." *ANRW* 36.3:1879–1961. Part 2, *Principat*, 36.3. Edited by H. Temporini and W. Haase. New York: de Gruyter, 1989.

————. *Untersuchungen zu Senecas Fragmenten.* Berlin: de Gruyter, 1970.

Lawrence, D. H. *The Complete Poems of D. H. Lawrence.* Edited by V. de Sola Pinto and W. Roberts. 2 vols. New York: Viking, 1964.

Layton, S. C. "Christ over His House (Hebrews 3:6) and Hebrew אֲשֶׁר עַל־הַבַּיִת." *New Testament Studies* 37 (1991): 473–77.

Lee, G. A. "Fear." Pages 289–92 in vol 2 of *The International Standard Bible Encyclopedia.* Rev. ed. Edited by G. W. Bromiley. 4 vols. Grand Rapids: Eerdmans, 1979–88.

Leighton, Stephen R. "Aristotle and the Emotions." Pages 206–37 in *Essays on Aristotle's Rhetoric.* Edited by A. O. Rorty. Berkeley: University of California Press, 1996.

Le Poidevin, Robin. *Arguing for Atheism: An Introduction to the Philosophy of Religion.* London: Routledge, 1996.

Lescow, T. "Jesus in Gethsemane bei Lukas und im Hebräerbrief." *Zeitschrift für die neutestamentliche Wissenschaft und die Kunde der älteren Kirche* 58 (1967): 223–39.

Lewis, C. S. *Studies in Words.* 2d ed. Cambridge: Cambridge University Press, 1967.

————. *The Screwtape Letters.* Rev. ed. New York: Macmillan, 1982.

Lewis, Jack P. *A Study of the Interpretation of Noah and the Flood in Jewish and Christian Literature.* Leiden: Brill, 1968.

Lewis, T. W. "'And if he shrinks back . . .' (Heb. 10.38b)." *New Testament Studies* 22 (1975–76): 88–94.

Lightfoot, N. "The Saving of the Savior: Hebrews 5:7ff." *Restoration Quarterly* 16 (1973): 166–73.

Lindars, Barnabas. "The Rhetorical Structure of Hebrews." *New Testament Studies* 35 (1989): 382–406.

————. *The Theology of the Epistle to the Hebrews.* Cambridge: Cambridge University Press, 1991.

Lloyd, A. C. "Emotion and Decision in Stoic Psychology." Pages 233–46 in *The Stoics.* Edited by J. M. Rist. Berkeley: University of California Press, 1978.

Loader, William R. G. *Sohn und Hoherpriester: Eine traditionsgeschichtliche Untersuchung zur Christologie des Hebräerbriefes.* Wissenschaftliche Monographien zum Alten und Neuen Testament 53. Neukirchen: Neukirchener, 1981.

Löhr, Hermut. *Umkehr und Sünde im Hebräerbrief.* Beihefte zur Zeitschrift für die Neutestamentliche Wissenschaft 73. Berlin: de Gruyter, 1994.

Long, A. A., and D. N. Sedley. *The Hellenistic Philosophers.* 2 vols. Cambridge: Cambridge University Press, 1987–88.

Lorenzmeier, Theodor. "Wider das Dogma von der Sündlosigkeit Jesu." *Evangelische Theologie* 31 (1971): 454–63.

Lubac, Henri de. *Surnaturel: études historiques.* Paris: Aubier, 1946.

Lührmann, Dieter. "Superstitio—die Beurteilung des frühen Christentums durch die Römer." *Theologische Zeitschrift* 42 (1986): 193–213.

Luther, Martin. *Luther's Works*. Edited by J. Pelikan et al. 55 vols. St. Louis: Concordia; Philadelphia: Fortress, 1958–86.

Lyons, William. *Emotion*. Cambridge: Cambridge University Press, 1980.

MacIntyre, Alasdair. *Whose Justice? Which Rationality?* Notre Dame: University of Notre Dame Press, 1988.

Mackay, B. S. "Plutarch and the Miraculous." Pages 93–111 in *Miracles: Cambridge Studies in their Philosophy and History*. Edited by C. F. D. Moule. London: Mowbray, 1965.

Macmullen, Ramsay. "Conversion: A Historian's View." *The Second Century* 5 (1985–86): 67–89.

———. *Enemies of the Roman Order*. Cambridge: Harvard University Press, 1966.

———. *Paganism in the Roman Empire*. New Haven and London: Yale University Press, 1981.

Malherbe, Abraham J. "Greco-Roman Religion and the New Testament." Pages 3–26 in *The New Testament and Its Modern Interpreters*. Edited by E. J. Epp and G. W. MacRae. Atlanta: Scholars Press, 1989.

———. *Moral Exhortation: A Greco-Roman Sourcebook*. Library of Early Christianity 4. Philadelphia: Westminster, 1986.

———. Review of H. D. Betz (ed.), *Plutarch's Ethical Writings and Early Christian Literature*. *Journal of Biblical Literature* 100 (1981): 140–42.

Malul, Meir. *The Comparative Method in Ancient Near Eastern and Biblical Legal Studies*. Alter Orient und Altes Testament 227. Kevelaer: Butzon & Bercker, 1990.

Manson, W. *The Epistle to the Hebrews: An Historical and Theological Reconsideration*. London: Hodder and Stoughton, 1951.

Marrow, Stanley B. "*Parrêsia* and the New Testament." *Catholic Biblical Quarterly* 44 (1982): 431–46.

Martin, Dale B. "Hellenistic Superstition: The Problems of Defining a Vice." Pages 110–27 in *Conventional Values of the Hellenistic Greeks*. Edited by P. Bilde et al. Aarhus: Aarhus University Press, 1997.

Marx, Karl. "Contribution to the Critique of Hegel's *Philosophy of Right*: Introduction." Pages 11–23 in *The Marx-Engels Reader*. Edited by R. C. Tucker. New York: Norton, 1972.

März, Claus-Peter. *Hebräerbrief*. Neue Echter Bibel 16. Würzburg: Echter, 1989.

Maurer, Christian. "'Erhört wegen der Gottesfurcht', Hebr 5,7." Pages 275–84 in *Neues Testament und Geschichte*. Edited by H. Baltensweiler and B. Reicke. Tübingen: Mohr-Siebeck, 1972.

McCullough, J. C. "Hebrews in Recent Scholarship." *Irish Biblical Studies* 16 (1994): 66–86, 108–20.

Medick, Hans, and David W. Sabean. "Interest and Emotion in Family and Kinship Studies: A Critique of Social History and Anthropology." Pages 9–27 in *Interest and Emotion*. Edited by H. Medick and D. Sabean. Cambridge: Cambridge University Press, 1988.

Meeks, Wayne A. *The First Urban Christians*. New Haven and London: Yale University Press, 1983.

——. *The Origins of Christian Morality*. New Haven and London: Yale University Press, 1993.

Meissner, W. W. *The Cultic Origins of Christianity: The Dynamics of Religious Development*. Collegeville, Minn.: Liturgical, 2000.

Melbourne, Bertram L. "An Examination of the Historical-Jesus Motif in the Epistle to the Hebrews." *Andrews University Seminary Studies* 26 (1988): 281–97.

Meslier, Jean. *Superstition in All Ages*. Repr., New York: Arno, 1972.

Micka, Ermin F. *The Problem of Divine Anger in Arnobius and Lactantius*. Washington, D.C.: Catholic University of America Press, 1943.

Mikalson, J. D. *Athenian Popular Religion*. Chapel Hill: University of North Carolina Press, 1983.

Mitchell, A. C. "Holding on to Confidence: ΠΑΡΡΗΣΙΑ in Hebrews." Pages 203–26 in *Friendship, Flattery, and Frankness of Speech*. Edited by J. T. Fitzgerald. Novum Testamentum Supplements 82. Leiden: Brill, 1996.

——. "The Use of πρέπειν and Rhetorical Propriety in Hebrews 2:10." *Catholic Biblical Quarterly* 54 (1992): 681–701.

Moellering, H. Armin. "Deisidaimonia: A Footnote to Acts 17:22." *Concordia Theological Quarterly* 34 (1963): 466–71.

——. *Plutarch on Superstition*. Rev. ed. Boston: Christopher, 1963.

Moffatt, James. *A Critical and Exegetical Commentary on the Epistle to the Hebrews*. International Critical Commentary. Clark, 1924.

Monter, William. *Ritual, Myth and Magic in Early Modern Europe*. Athens, Ohio: Ohio University Press, 1984.

Montefiore, Hugh. *A Commentary on the Epistle to the Hebrews*. Harper's New Testament Commentaries. London: Black, 1964.

More, Henry. *An Antidote Against Atheism*. 3rd ed. London: James Flesher, 1662.

Muth, Robert. "Vom Wesen römischen 'religio'." *ANRW* 16.1:290–354. Part 2, *Principat*, 16.1. Edited by H. Temporini and W. Haase. New York: de Gruyter, 1978.

Nairne, Alexander. *The Epistle of Priesthood*. Edinburgh: Clark, 1913.

Nauck, W. "Zum Aufbau des Hebräerbriefes." Pages 199–206 in *Judentum, Urchristentum, Kirche*. Edited by W. Eltester. Beihefte zur Zeitschrift für die Neutestamentliche Wissenschaft 26; Giessen: Töpelmann, 1960.

Nelson, L. D., and C. H. Cantrell. "Religiosity and Death Anxiety: A Multi-Dimensional Analysis." *Review of Religious Research* 21 (1980): 148–57.

Nestle, W. "Die Haupteinwände des antiken Denkens gegen das Christentum." *Archiv für Religionswissenschaft* 37 (1941–42): 51–100.

Neusner, Jacob. "Alike and Not Alike: A Grid for Comparison and Differentiation." Pages 227–35 in *Take Judaism, for Example: Studies toward the Comparison of Religions*. South Florida Studies in the History of Judaism 51. Edited by J. Neusner. Atlanta: Scholars Press, 1992.

Neusner, Jacob, and E. S. Frerichs, eds. *"To See Ourselves as Others See Us": Christians, Jews, "Others" in Late Antiquity*. Chico, Calif.: Scholars Press, 1985.

Neyrey, J. H. "'Without Beginning of Days or End of Life' (Hebrews 7:3): Topos for a True Deity." *Catholic Biblical Quarterly* 53 (1991): 439–55.

Niebuhr, H. Richard. *The Kingdom of God in America*. New York: Harper, 1937.

Nikiprowetzky, V. "La Spiritualisation des Sacrifices et le Cult Sacrificiel au Temple de Jérusalem chez Philon d'Alexandrie." *Semitica* 17 (1967): 97–116.

Nikolaidis, A. G. "Plutarch's Contradictions." *Classica et Mediaevalia* 42 (1991): 153–86.

Nissilä, Keijo. *Das Hohenpriestermotiv im Hebräerbrief: Eine exegetische Untersuchung.* Helsinki: Oy Liiton Kirjapaino, 1979.

Nock, Arthur Darby. *Conversion: The Old and New in Religion from Alexander the Great to Augustine of Hippo.* Oxford: Clarendon, 1933.

Nussbaum, Martha C. *The Therapy of Desire.* Princeton: Princeton University Press, 1994.

Oakesmith, John. *The Religion of Plutarch: A Pagan Creed of Apostolic Times.* London: Longmans, Green, and Co., 1902.

Obbink, Dirk. "The Atheism of Epicurus." *Greek, Roman, and Byzantine Studies* 30 (1989): 187–223.

———. "The Origin of Greek Sacrifice: Theophrastus on Religion and Cultural History." Pages 272–95 in *Theophrastean Studies*. Edited by W. W. Fortenbaugh and R. W. Sharples. Rutgers University Studies in Classical Humanities 3. New Brunswick, N.J.: Transaction, 1988.

Oesterle, J. A. "Fear (Moral Aspect)." Page 864 in vol. 5 of *New Catholic Encyclopedia*. Edited by W. J. McDonald et al. 14 vols. New York: McGraw-Hill, 1967.

Olbricht, T. H. "Hebrews as Amplification." Pages in *Rhetoric and the New Testament* Edited by W. E. Porter and T. H. Olbricht. Journal for the Study of the New Testament: Supplement Series 90. Sheffield: JSOT, 1993.

O'Neil, Mary R. "Superstition." Pages 163–66 in vol. 14 of *The Encyclopedia of Religion*. Edited by M. Eliade. 16 vols. New York: Macmillan, 1986.

Opsomer, Jan. "Divination and Academic 'Scepticism' according to Plutarch." *Studia Hellenistica* 32 (1996): 165–94.

Otto, Rudolf. *The Idea of the Holy.* Translated by J. W. Harvey. 2nd ed. Oxford: Oxford University Press, 1950.

Otto, W. "Religio und Superstitio." *Archiv für Religionswissenschaft* 12 (1909): 533–54.

Parke, H. W., and D. E. W. Wormell. *The Delphic Oracle.* 2 vols. Oxford: Blackwell, 1956.

Parker, Robert. *Miasma: Pollution and Purification in Early Greek Religion.* Oxford: Clarendon, 1983.

———. "Pollution, The Greek Concept of." Pages 1208–9 in *The Oxford Classical Dictionary*. 3rd ed. Edited by S. Hornblower and A. Spawforth. Oxford: Oxford University Press, 1996.

Patrick, J. W. "Personal Faith and the Fear of Death among Divergent Religious Populations." *Journal for the Scientific Study of Religion* 18 (1979): 298–305.

Patterson, Cynthia B. "Those Athenian Bastards." *Classical Antiquity* 9 (1990): 40–73.

Patterson, Richard. "Plato on Philosophic Character." *Journal of the History of Philosophy* 25 (1987): 325–50.

Peake, A. S. *Hebrews.* New Century Bible. Edinburgh: Jack, n.d.

———. *Heroes and Martyrs of Faith.* London: Hodder and Stoughton, n.d.

Pears, David. "Courage as a Mean." Pages 171–87 in *Essays on Aristotle's Ethics*. Edited by A. O. Rorty. Berkeley: University of California Press, 1980.

246					Godly Fear

Pease, Arthur S., ed. *M. Tulli Ciceronis De divinatione, Libri Duo.* Darmstadt: Wissenschaftliche Buchgesellschaft, 1963.

Pérez Jiménez, Aurelio. "Δεισιδαιμονία: el miedo a los dioses en Plutarco." *Studia Hellenistica* 32 (1996): 195–225.

Petersen, David L. *Haggai and Zechariah 1–8.* Old Testament Library. Philadelphia: Westminster, 1984.

Peterson, David. *Hebrews and Perfection.* Society for New Testament Studies Monograph Series 47. Cambridge: Cambridge University Press, 1982.

Peterson, E. "Zur Bedeutungsgeschichte von Παρρησία." Pages 283–97 in vol. 1 of *Reinhold Seeberg Festschrift.* Edited by W. Koepp. 2 vols. Leipzig: Scholl, 1929.

Pfaff, I. "Superstitio." Columns 937–39 in vol. 14.A.1 of *Paulys Realencyclopädie der classischen Altertumswissenschaft.* Edited by G. Wissowa. Munich: Druckenmüller, 1931.

Pfister, Oskar. *Christianity and Fear.* Translated by W. H. Johnston. New York: Macmillan, 1948. Translation of *Das Christentum und die Angst.* Zurich: Artemis, 1944.

Pfitzner, V. C. *Hebrews.* Abingdon New Testament Commentaries. Nashville: Abingdon, 1997.

Phillips, C. R. "The Sociology of Religious Knowledge in the Roman Empire to A.D. 284." *ANRW* 16.3:2680. Part 2, *Principat*, 16.3. Edited by H. Temporini and W. Haase. New York: de Gruyter, 1986.

Phillips, D. Z. *Religion without Explanation.* London: Blackwell, 1976.

Pierce, C. A. *Conscience in the New Testament.* Studies in Biblical Theology 15. Chicago: Alec R. Allenson, 1955.

Pirot, L., and A. Robert, eds. *Dictionnaire de la Bible: Supplément.* Paris: Letouzey et Ané, 1928–.

Pohlenz, Max. *Die Stoa.* 2nd ed. 2 vols. Göttingen: Vandenhoeck & Ruprecht, 1959.

Pressman, Peter, et al. "Religion, Anxiety, and Fear of Death." Pages 98–109 in *Religion and Mental Health.* Edited by J. Schumaker. New York: Oxford University Press, 1992.

Räisänen, Heikki. *Paul and the Law.* Wissenshaftliche Untersuchungen zum Neuen Testament 29. 2nd rev. ed. Tübingen: Mohr-Siebeck, 1987.

Ray, R. J. "Crossed Fingers and Praying Hands: Remarks on Religious Belief and Superstition." *Religious Studies* 26 (1990): 471–82.

Reasoner, Mark. *The Strong and the Weak: Romans 14:1–15:13 in Context.* Society for New Testament Studies Monograph Series 103. Cambridge: Cambridge University Press, 1999.

Ren, Jiyu. "Religion and Superstition" (transcript of interview). *Ching Feng* 26 (1983): 158–59.

Riddle, Joseph. *The Natural History of Infidelity and Superstition in Contrast with Christian Faith.* London: Parker, 1852.

Riesenfeld, H. "The Meaning of the Verb ἀρνεῖσθαι." Coniectanea Biblica: New Testament Series 11 (1947): 207–19.

Riess, Ernst. "Aberglaube." Columns 29–93 in vol. 1.1 of *Paulys Realencyclopädie der classischen Altertumswissenschaft.* Edited by G. Wissowa. Stuttgart: Druckenmüller, 1893.

Riggenbach, E. "Der Begriff der ΤΕΛΕΙΩΣΙΣ im Hebräerbrief: Ein Beitrag zur Frage nach der Einwirkung der Mysterienreligion auf Sprache und Gedankenwelt des Neuen Testaments." *Neue kirkliche Zeitschrift* 34 (1923): 184–95.

Rissi, Mathias. "Die Menschlichkeit Jesu nach Hebr 5,7–8." *Theologische Zeitschrift* 11 (1955): 28–45.

———. *Die Theologie des Hebräerbriefes*. Wissenshaftliche Untersuchungen zum Neuen Testament 44. Tübingen: Mohr-Siebeck, 1987.

Rist, J. M. *Stoic Philosophy*. Cambridge: Cambridge University Press, 1969.

Roeth, E. M. *Epistolam vulgo "ad Hebraeos" inscriptam non ad Hebraeos, id est Christianos genere Judaeos sed ad Christianos genere gentiles et quidem ad Ephesios datam esse demonstrare conatur*. Frankfurt am Main: Schmerber, 1836.

Rorty, Amélie Oksenberg. "Aristotle on the Metaphysical Status of *Pathê*." *Review of Metaphysics* 38 (1984): 521–46.

———, ed. *Essays on Aristotle's Ethics*. Berkeley: University of California Press, 1980.

———, ed. *Essays on Aristotle's Rhetoric*. Berkeley: University of California Press, 1996.

Rose, Larry L. "Toward a New Supernaturalism." Ph.D. diss., The Claremont Graduate School, 1967.

Rosenbaum, S. "How to Be Dead and Not Care: A Defense of Epicurus." *American Philosophical Quarterly* 21 (1986): 217–25.

Russell, Bertrand. "An Outline of Intellectual Rubbish." Pages 71–111 in *Unpopular Essays*. New York: Simon and Schuster, 1950.

———. *Why I Am Not a Christian*. New York: Simon & Schuster, 1957.

Russell, D. A. *Plutarch*. London: Duckworth, 1973.

Saller, Richard P. "Corporal Punishment, Authority, and Obedience in the Roman Household." Pages 144–65 in *Marriage, Divorce, and Children in Ancient Rome*. Edited by B. Rawson. Oxford: Clarendon, 1991.

———. *Patriarchy, Property and Death in the Roman Family*. Cambridge: Cambridge University Press, 1994.

Salevao, Iutisone. *Legitimation in the Letter to the Hebrews: The Construction and Maintenance of a Symbolic World*. Journal for the Study of the New Testament Supplement Series 219; Sheffield: Sheffield Academic, 2002.

Salzman, Michele R. "'Superstitio' in the *Codex Theodosianus* and the Persecution of Pagans." *Vigiliae christianae* 41 (1987): 172–88.

Sanders, E. P. *Paul and Palestinian Judaism*. Minneapolis: Fortress, 1977.

Sandmel, Samuel. "Parallelomania." *Journal of Biblical Literature* 81 (1962): 1–13.

Sandnes, Karl Olav. *A New Family: Conversion and Ecclesiology in the Early Church, with Cross-Cultural Comparisons*. Studies in the Intercultural History of Christianity 91. Frankfurt am Main: Peter Lang, 1994.

———. "Equality within Patriarchal Structures: Some New Testament Perspectives on the Christian Fellowship as a Brother- or Sisterhood and a Family." Pages 150–65 in *Constructing Early Christian Families: Family as Social Reality and Metaphor*. Edited by H. Moxnes. London and New York: Routledge, 1997.

———. "The Role of the Congregation as a Family within the Context of Recruitment and Conflict in the Early Church." Pages 333–46 in *Recruitment, Conquest, and Conflict: Strategies in Judaism, Early Christianity, and the Greco-Roman World*.

Edited by P. Borgen, V. K. Robbins, and D. B. Gowler. Atlanta: Scholars Press, 1998.

Schadewalt, W. "Humanitas Romana." *ANRW* 1.4:43–62. Part 1, *Von den Anfängen Roms biz zum Ausgang der Republik*, 1.4. Edited by H. Temporini and W. Haase. New York: de Gruyter, 1973.

Schäfer, Klaus. *Gemeinde als "Bruderschaft": Ein Beitrag zum Kirchenverständnis des Paulus*. Europäische Hochschulschriften XXIII/333. Frankfurt am Main: Peter Lang, 1989.

Schäfer, Peter. *Judeophobia: Attitudes Toward the Jews in the Ancient World*. Cambridge: Harvard University Press, 1997.

Scheidweiler, Felix. "ΚΑΙΠΕΡ: nebst einem Exkurs zum Hebräerbrief." *Hermes* 83 (1955): 220–30.

Schille, G. "Erwägungen zur Hohenpriesterlehre des Hebräerbriefes." *Zeitschrift für die neutestamentliche Wissenschaft und die Kunde der älteren Kirche* 46 (1955): 81–109.

Schleiermacher, F. *On Religion: Speeches to Its Cultured Despisers*. Translated by J. Oman. London: Kegan, Paul, Trench, Trubner, 1893.

Scholer, John M. *Proleptic Priests: Priesthood in the Epistle to the Hebrews*. Journal for the Study of the New Testament Supplement Series 49. Sheffield: JSOT Press, 1991.

Schoppe, Christoph. *Plutarchs Interpretation der Ideenlehre Platons*. Münsteraner Beitrage zur klassisschen Philologie 2. Münster: Lit, 1994.

Schröger, F. *Der Verfasser des Hebräerbriefes als Schriftausleger*. Biblische Untersuchungen 4. Regensburg: Pustet, 1968.

Schweitzer, Albert. *Die Mystik des Apostels Paulus*. Tübingen: J. C. B. Mohr, 1930.

Scott, E. F. *The Epistle to the Hebrews*. Edinburgh: Clark, 1923.

Sedley, David. "Philosophical Allegiance in the Greco-Roman World." Pages 97–119 in vol. 1 of *Philosophia Togata: Essays on Philosophy and Roman Society*. Edited by M. Griffin and J. Barnes. 2 vols. Oxford: Clarendon, 1989.

Segal, Charles. *Lucretius on Death and Anxiety*. Princeton: Princeton University Press, 1990.

Selby, G. S. "The Meaning and Function of συνείδησις in Hebrews 9 and 10." *Restoraton Quarterly* 28 (1985–86): 145–54.

Shermer, Michael. *Why People Believe Weird Things*. New York: W. H. Freeman, 1997.

Sihvola, Juha. "Emotional Animals: Do Aristotelian Emotions Require Beliefs?" *Apeiron* 29 (1996): 105–44.

Sihvola, Juha, and Troels Engberg-Pederson, eds. *The Emotions in Hellenistic Philosophy*. New Synthese Historical Library 46. Dordrecht: Kluwer, 1998.

Smith, Barbara Herrnstein. *Contingencies of Value*. Cambridge: Harvard University Press, 1988.

Smith, Jonathan Z. *Drudgery Divine: On the Comparison of Early Christianities and the Religions of Late Antiquity*. Chicago: University of Chicago Press, 1990.

———. "The Temple and the Magician." Pages 172–89 in *Map is Not Territory*. Studies in Judaism in Late Antiquity 23. Leiden: Brill, 1978.

Smith, Morton. "De Superstitione (Moralia 164E–171F)." Pages 1–35 in *Plutarch's Theological Writings and Early Christian Literature* 3. Studia ad corpus hellenisticum Novi Testamenti. Edited by H. D. Betz. Leiden: Brill, 1975.

———. "Superstitio." Pages 349–55 in *SBL Seminar Papers, 1981*. Society of Biblical Literature Seminar Papers 20. Chico, Calif.: Scholars Press, 1981.

Soden, Hermann von. *Books of the New Testament*. Edited by W. D. Morrison. Translated by J. R. Wilkinson. London: Williams and Norgate, 1907.

Solari, J. K. "The Problem of *Metanoia* in the Epistle to the Hebrews." Ph.D. diss., Catholic University of America, 1970.

Sorabji, Richard. *Animal Minds and Human Morals*. London: Duckworth, 1993.

———. "Chrysippus—Posidonius—Seneca: A High-Level Debate on Emotion." Pages 149–70 in *The Emotions in Hellenistic Philosophy*. Edited by J. Sihvola and T. Engberg-Pederson. New Synthese Historical Library 46. Dordrecht: Kluwer, 1998.

———. *Emotion and Peace of Mind*. Oxford: Oxford University Press, 2000.

Soury, G. *La démonologie de Plutarque*. Paris: Les belles lettres, 1942.

Sowers, Sidney G. *The Hermeneutics of Philo and Hebrews*. Basel Studies of Theology 1. Richmond: John Knox, 1965.

Spanneut, Michel. "*Apatheia* ancienne, *apatheia* chrétienne." *ANRW* 36.7:4641–4717. Part 2, *Principat*, 36.7. Edited by H. Temporini and W. Haase. New York: de Gruyter, 1994.

Sparn, Walter. "Aberglaube: II. Kirchengeschichtliche und dogmatisch." Pages 58–59 in vol. 1 of *Religion in Geschichte und Gegenwart*. 4th ed. Edited by H. D. Betz et al. 3 vols. Tübingen: Mohr-Siebeck, 1998– .

Speyer, W. "Zu den Vorwürfen der Heiden gegen die Christen." Jahrbuch für Antike und Christentum 6 (1963): 129–35.

Spicq, Ceslaus. "Alexandrismes dans l'Épître aux Hébreux." *Revue biblique* 58 (1951): 481–502.

———. "L'authenticité du chapitre XIII de l'Épître aux Hébreux." Coniectanea Biblica: New Testament Series 11 (1947): 226–36.

———. *L'Épître aux Hébreux*. 2 vols. Paris: Gabalda, 1952–53.

———. *Theological Lexicon of the New Testament*. Translated and edited by J. D. Ernest. 3 vols. Peabody, Mass.: Hendrickson, 1994.

Spinoza, B. *A Theologico-Political Treatise*. Translated by R. Elwes. New York: Dover, 1951.

Strack, Hermann L., and Paul Billerbeck. *Kommentar zum Neuen Testament aus Talmud und Midrasch*. 6 vols. Munich: Beck, 1922–1961.

Striker, Gisela. "Emotions in Context: Aristotle's Treatment of the Passions in the *Rhetoric* and His Moral Psychology." Pages 286–302 in *Essays on Aristotle's Rhetoric*. Edited by A. O. Rorty. Berkeley: University of California Press, 1996.

Strobel, A. "Die Psalmengrundlage der Gethsemane-Parallele Hebr. 5,7ff." *Zeitschrift für die neutestamentliche Wissenschaft und die Kunde der älteren Kirche* 45 (1954): 252–66.

Swain, Simon. "Plutarch, Plato, Athens and Rome." Pages 165–87 in vol. 2 of *Philosophia Togata: Essays on Philosophy and Roman Society*. Edited by M. Griffin and J. Barnes. 2 vols. Oxford: Clarendon, 1989.

Swetnam, James. "A Suggested Interpretation of Hebrews 9,15–18." *Catholic Biblical Quarterly* 27 (1965): 373–90.

———. "Hebrews 10,30–31: A Suggestion." *Biblica* 75 (1994): 388–94.

――――. *Jesus and Isaac: A Study of the Epistle to the Hebrews in the Light of the Aqedah.* Rome: Biblical Institute Press, 1981.

――――. "The Crux at Hebrews 5,7–8." *Biblica* 81 (2000): 347–61.

Talmon, Shemaryahu. "The 'Comparative Method' in Biblical Interpretation—Principles and Problems." Pages 320–56 in *Congress Volume: Göttingen 1977.* Edited by J. A. Emerton et al. Vetus Testamentum Supplements 29. Leiden: Brill, 1978.

Taylor, Jeremy. *The Rule and Exercises of Holy Living.* 29th ed. London: Longmans, 1815.

Taylor, Vincent. *The Gospel According to St. Mark.* London: Macmillan, 1959.

Tcherikover, Victor. "Jewish Apologetic Literature Reconsidered." *Eos* 48 (1956): 169–93.

Terrien, S. "Fear." Pages 256–60 in vol. 2 of *The Interpreter's Dictionary of the Bible.* Edited by G. A. Buttrick. 4 vols. Nashville: Abingdon, 1962.

Theissen, Gerd. *Untersuchungen zum Hebräerbrief.* Studien zum Neuen Testament 2. Guterslöh: Mohn, 1969.

Thompson, James W. "'That Which Abides': Some Metaphysical Assumptions in the Epistle to the Hebrews." Ph.D. diss., Vanderbilt University, 1974.

――――. *The Beginnings of Christian Philosophy: The Epistle to the Hebrews.* Catholic Biblical Quarterly Monograph Series 13. Washington, D. C.: The Catholic Biblical Association of America, 1981.

Thorson, J. A. "Religion and Anxiety: Which Anxiety? Which Religion?" Pages 147–60 in *Handbook of Religion and Mental Health.* Edited by H. G. Koenig. San Diego: Academic, 1998.

Thurén, Jukka. "Gebet und Gehorsam des Erniedrigten (Hebr. v 7–10 noch einmal)." *Novum Testamentum* 13 (1971): 136–46.

Thüsing, W. "'Milch' und 'feste Speise' (1 Kor 3,1 und Hebr 5,11–6,3): Elementarkatechese und theologische Vertiefung im neutestamentlicher Sicht." *Trier Theologische Zeitschrift* 76 (1967): 233–46, 261–80.

Thyen, H. *Der Stil der jüdisch-hellenistischen Homilie.* Forschungen zur Religion und Literatur des Alten und Neuen Testaments 47. Göttingen: Vandenhoeck & Ruprecht, 1955.

Tongue, D. H. "The Concept of Apostasy in the Epistle to the Hebrews." *Tyndale Bulletin* 5–6 (1960): 19–26.

Trompf, G. W. "The Conception of God in Hebr. 4:12–13." *Studia Theologica* 25 (1971): 123–32.

Trotter, Andrew H., Jr. *Interpreting the Epistle to the Hebrews.* Grand Rapids: Baker, 1997.

Übelacker, W. G. *Der Hebräerbrief als Appell: Untersuchungen zu* exordium, narratio *und* postscriptum *(Hebr 1–2 und 13,22–25).* Stockholm: Almqvist & Wiksell, 1989.

Unnik, W. C. van. "The Christian's Freedom of Speech in the New Testament." *Bulletin of the John Rylands Library* 44 (1962): 466–88.

――――. "Words Come to Life: The Work for the 'Corpus Hellenisticum Novi Testamenti.'" *Novum Testamentum* 13 (1971): 199–216.

Ussher, R. G. *The Characters of Theophrastus.* Rev. ed. London: Bristol Classical, 1993.

Van der Leeuw, Geraardus. *Religion in Essence and Manifestation: A Study in Phenomenology*. Translated by J. E. Turner. 2 vols. New York: Harper & Row, 1963.

Vanhoye, Albert. "L'οὐκουμένη dans l'épître aux Hébreux." *Biblica* 45 (1964): 248–53.

Vermeule, Emily. *Aspects of Death in Early Greek Art and Poetry*. Berkeley: University of California Press, 1979.

Versnel, H. S. "Deisidaimonia." Page 441 in *The Oxford Classical Dictionary*. 3ʳᵈ ed. Edited by S. Hornblower and A. Spawforth. Oxford: Oxford University Press, 1996.

Vivekananda, Swami. *The Complete Works of Swami Vivekananda*. Edited by S. Swananda. 8 vols. Calcutta: Advaita Ashram, 1989.

Vögtle, A. "Das Neue Testament und die Zukunft des Kosmos: Hebr. 12,26f. und das Endschicksal des Kosmos." *Bibel und Leben* 10 (1969): 239–53.

Voltaire. *Philosophical Dictionary*. Translated by. P. Gay. 2 vols. New York: Basic, 1962.

Vorster, Willem S. "*Phobos kai Tromos*: A Greek Idiomatic Expression with a Semitic Background." *Theologia Evangelica* 5 (1972): 39–48.

———. "The Meaning of ΠΑΡΡΗΣΙΑ in the Epistle to the Hebrews." *Neotestamentica* 5 (1971): 51–59.

Wächter, Theodor. *Reinheitsvorschriften im griechischen Kult*. Religionsgeschichtliche Versuche und Vorarbeiten 9.1. Giessen: Töpelmann, 1910.

Walters, James C. "Romans, Jews, and Christians: The Impact of the Romans on Jewish/Christian Relations in First-Century Rome." Pages 175–95 in *Judaism and Christianity in First-Century Rome*. Edited by K. Donfried and P. Richardson. Grand Rapids: Eerdmans, 1998.

Wardman, Alan. *Plutarch's Lives*. Berkeley: University of California Press, 1974.

Watson, Duane. "Rhetorical Criticism of Hebrews and the Catholic Epistles Since 1978." *Currents in Biblical Studies* 5 (1997): 175–207.

Weiss, H.- F. *Der Brief an die Hebräer*. Kritisch-exegetischer Kommentar über das Neue Testament (Meyer Kommentar) 13. Göttingen: Vandenhoeck & Ruprecht, 1991.

Weiss, Johannes. *Die Predigt Jesu vom Reiche Gottes*. Göttingen: Vandenhoeck & Ruprecht, 1892.

Welborn, Laurence L. "On the Date of First Clement." *Biblical Research* 29 (1985): 35–54.

Westbrook, Raymond. "Punishments and Crimes." Pages 546–56 in vol. 5 of *The Anchor Bible Dictionary*. Edited by D. N. Freedman. 6 vols. New York: Doubleday, 1992.

Westcott, B. F. *The Epistle to the Hebrews*. 3d ed. London and New York: Macmillan, 1903.

Wette, W. M. L. de. *Kurzgefasstes exegetisches Handbuch zum Neuen Testament*. 2ⁿᵈ ed. 11 vols. Leipzig: Weidmann, 1846–64.

Wickham, E. C. *The Epistle to the Hebrews*. 2ⁿᵈ ed. London: Methuen, 1922.

Wikgren, Allen. "Patterns of Perfection in the Epistle to the Hebrews." *New Testament Studies* 6 (1959–60): 159–67.

Wilken, Robert L. "Roman Criticism of Christianity: Greek Religion and Christian Faith." Pages 117–34 in *Early Christian Literature and the Classical Intellectual Tradition: In Honorem Robert M. Grant*. Edited by W. R. Schoedel and R. L. Wilken. Paris: Editions Beauchesne, 1979.

——. "The Christians as the Romans (and Greeks) Saw Them." Pages 100–25 in *Jewish and Christian Self-Definition: The Shaping of Christianity in the Second and Third Centuries*. Edited by E. P. Sanders. Vol. 1 of *Jewish and Christian Self-Definition*. Edited by B. F. Meyer and E. P. Sanders. Philadelphia: Fortress, 1980.

——. *The Christians as the Romans Saw Them*. New Haven and London: Yale University Press, 1984.

Williamson, Ronald. "Hebrews 4:15 and the Sinlessness of Jesus." *Expository Times* 86 (1974–75): 4–8.

——. *Philo and the Epistle to the Hebrews*. Arbeiten zur Literatur und Geschichte des hellenistischen Judentums 4. Leiden: Brill, 1970.

——. "Platonism and Hebrews." *Scottish Journal of Theology* 16 (1963): 415–24.

Wilson, S. G. *Related Strangers: Jews and Christians, 70–170 C.E.* Minneapolis: Augsburg-Fortress, 1995.

Windisch, Hans. *Der Hebräerbrief*. 2nd ed. Handkommentar zum Neuen Testament 14. Tübingen: Mohr-Siebeck, 1931.

Wittgenstein, Ludwig. *Culture and Value*. Translated by Peter Winch. London: Blackwell, 1976.

——. *Philosophical Investigations*. 3rd ed. Translated by G. E. M. Anscombe. New York: Macmillan, 1958.

Worley, David R. "God's Faithfulness to the Promise: The Hortatory Use of Commissive Language in Hebrews." Ph.D. diss., Yale University, 1981.

Wrede, Wilhelm. *Das literarische Rätsel des Hebräerbriefes*. Forschungen zur Religion und Literatur des Alten und Neuen Testaments 8. Göttingen: Vandenhoeck & Ruprecht, 1906.

Yarnold, E. J. "ΜΕΤΡΙΟΠΑΘΕΙΝ apud Heb 5,2." *Verbum Domini* 38 (1960): 149–55.

Young, Frances M. *The Use of Sacrificial Ideas in Greek Christian Writers from the New Testament to John Chrysostom*. Cambridge, Mass.: Philadelphia Patristic Foundation, 1979.

Zanker, Paul. *The Power of Images in the Age of Augustus*. Translated by A. Shapiro. Ann Arbor: University of Michigan Press, 1988.

Zenger, Erich. *A God of Vengeance? Understanding the Psalms of Divine Wrath*. Translated by L. M. Maloney. Louisville: Westminster John Knox, 1996.

Ziegler, Konrat. "Plutarchus von Chaironeia." Columns 636–962 in vol. 21.1 of *Paulys Realencyclopädie der classischen Altertumswissenschaft*. Edited by G. Wissowa. Stuttgart: Druckenmüller, 1951.

Zimmerman, Heinrich. *Die Hohepriester-Christologie des Hebräerbriefes*. Paderborn: Bonifacius, 1964.

Index of Modern Authors

Aasgaard, R., 126, 129
Abernetty, G., 85
Adams, J. C., 149
Allen, W., 189
Almqvist, H., 13, 21
Alston, W. P., 58
Andriessen, P., 117, 118, 189, 204
Annas, J., 58, 66, 68, 69, 76, 77
Arnim, H. von, 71
Arnold, E. V., 205
Ashton, J., 20
Askevis-Leherpeux, F., 2
Attridge, H. W., 4, 13, 14, 15, 128, 132, 136, 151, 159, 165, 166, 190, 191, 193, 197, 198, 199, 200, 204, 207, 209, 210, 211, 212, 221
Aune, D. E., 25
Babut, D., 67, 90, 92, 96, 100, 103, 105
Bacon, F., 2
Balch, D. L., 183
Balthasar, H. U. von, 111
Bamberger, B. J., 188
Bammel, E., 137
Bannon, C. J., 126, 134, 145, 137
Bardy, G., 13
Baroja, J. C., 43
Barrett, C. K., 26, 213
Barrow, R. H., 7, 14
Bauckham, R. J., 212
Beaujue, J., 7
Beegle, D. M., 208
Belmont, N., 34
Benko, S., 8
Berardi, E., 86
Berger, A., 170, 174

Berger, P., 107, 112, 127, 147
Berry, E. G., 84
Berthold, F., 114, 208
Betz, H. D., 9, 21, 126, 129
Bianchi, U., 100
Black, C. C., 25
Bodéüs, R., 101
Bolkestein, H., 46
Bolt, M., 112
Bonus, A., 115
Brandenberger, E., 125, 132, 189, 191, 197
Braun, H., 22, 23, 27, 28, 29, 88, 110, 112, 117, 132, 133, 142, 145, 161, 170, 180, 189, 210, 211, 215
Brenk, F. E., 22, 52, 85, 86, 95, 96, 97, 101
Brennan, T., 71
Brinton, A., 60
Brown, R. E., 15
Brox, N., 41
Bruce, F. F., 15, 136, 161, 168, 171, 190, 192, 195, 197, 211
Brueckner, A., 80
Buchanan, G. W., 117, 118, 119, 122, 161, 163, 166, 167, 170, 174, 191, 192, 197, 209
Bulley, A. D., 121
Bultmann, R., 4, 22, 72, 109, 188, 190, 196, 201, 202, 203, 204, 213
Bunyan, J., 179
Burke, E., 1
Burkert, W., 48, 74, 131, 219
Burtness, J. H., 26
Busch, P., 27

Buxton, R., 36
Cairns, D. L., 72
Calderone, S., 7
Calvin, J., 2, 11, 124, 132, 191
Cambier, J., 213
Cantrell, C. H., 112
Carlston, C. E., 179
Casey, J. M., 213
Cerny, L., 112
Champlin, E., 137
Childs, B. S., 170, 172
Conley, T., 63
Cooper, J., 60, 66
Cosby, M. R., 25
Cover, R. C., 150
Cox, C. A., 134, 135
Crook, J. A., 181
Croy, N. C., 25, 122, 178, 179, 182, 185, 200
Cullmann, O., 194
Dahl, N., 146
Deissmann, A., 20
Del Real, C. A., 33
Delitzsch, F. J., 173, 174
Delling, G., 16
Delumeau, J., 110
DeSilva, D. A., 25, 29, 145, 146, 148, 150, 152, 156, 157, 162, 170, 171, 191, 204, 213
Dey, L. K. K., 26, 199
Dill, S., 43
Dillon, J., 15, 16, 54, 57, 85, 92, 97, 105
Dixon, S., 180, 181, 183
Dodds, E. R., 219
Dolfe, K.-G. E., 116
Dörrie, H., 16
Drachmann, A. B., 103
Drews, R., 202
Dunbar, D. G., 124
Dunn, R. F., 112
Dunnill, J., 110, 221
Eagar, A. R., 26
Ehrman, B., 28
Eisenbaum, P., 120, 121, 166, 174
Eliot, T. S., 160

Ellingworth, P., 15, 115, 117, 123, 139, 153, 155, 180, 189, 191, 192, 206, 209, 210
Endo, S., 151
Engberg-Pederson, T., 56, 57, 65, 66, 71, 75
Epley, R. J., 112
Erbse, H., 86, 87
Esler, P. F., 126
Evans, C. F., 193
Eyben, E., 181, 182
Fairhurst, A. M., 26
Fatum, L., 126
Feather, J., 168, 169
Feifel, H., 112
Feld, H., 27
Feldman, F., 80
Ferguson, E., 25, 219, 221
Festugière, A. J., 78, 79
Feuillet, A., 190
Feyerabend, P. K., 35
Filson, F. V., 25, 163
Finn, T. M., 13
Fischer, J. M., 80
Fitzmyer, J. A., 159
Flacelière, R., 85, 86, 89
Ford, J. M., 4
Fortenbaugh, W. W., 46, 58, 59, 60, 61, 63
Frede, D., 63
Frend, W. H. C., 41
Froidefond, C., 57, 86, 92, 100
Fuchs, H., 7
Gamble, J., 26
Gardner, A., 2
Gay, P., 2
Geertz, C., 107
Gill, C., 66
Gladigow, B., 2, 33
Goldhahn-Müller, I., 149, 150
Goldin, J., 175
Gollwitzer, H., 119
Gombrich, E. H., 154
Gordon, R., 42
Gosling, J., 76
Gould, J. B., 70, 75

Grässer, E., 27, 89, 113, 118, 124, 139,
    142, 149, 156, 180, 189, 193
Greard, O., 84, 85
Green, O. H., 80
Grodzynski, D., 7, 37, 39
Gudorf, M., 25, 115, 116
Hadas, M., 54
Haering, T., 26
Hagner, D. A., 15
Hani, J., 103
Harnack, A. von, 4, 109, 189, 190–91
Hartmann, J. J., 84, 104
Hay, D. M., 133
Hegermann, H., 27, 28, 29, 166
Heidegger, M., 111
Helmbold, W. C., 67
Hering, J., 213
Hermann, L., 38
Herrnstein Smith, B., 35
Hershbell, J. P., 55, 96
Hirzel, R., 86
Hodgson, R., 9, 40
Hoelter, J. W., 112
Hofius, O., 25
Hooker, R., 3
Hopkins, K., 98
Horbury, W., 11
Horst, P. W. van der, 16, 25
Hughes, D. D., 101
Hughes, J. J., 136
Hughes, P. E., 212
Hume, D., 1–2
Hurst, L. D., 25, 26, 213
Idziak, J. M., 108
Inwood, B., 66, 68, 69, 70, 73, 74
Irwin, T. H., 65
Izard, C. E., 111
Jaeger, W., 179
Jahoda, G., 2
James, W., 68
Janssen, L., 7, 37, 42
Jarvis, P., 3
Jentsch, W., 185
Jeremias, J., 189, 191, 193, 195
Johnson, L. T., 9, 192
Johnsson, W. G., 222, 223

Jones, C. P., 7, 14, 43, 86
Jones, R. M., 57, 85
Joüon, P., 139
Jülicher, A., 27, 28
Kahoe, R. D., 112
Käsemann, E., 25, 113, 132, 126, 141,
    142,
Kass, L. R., 80
Kerényi, C., 188
Kierkegaard, S., 3, 4, 111
Kippenberg, H., 20
Klaerr, R., 85, 86
Klauck, H.-J., 23, 85, 88, 126, 215, 221
Knuuttila, S., 57, 58
Koester, C. R., 29, 122, 124, 128, 131,
    132, 139, 147, 152, 158, 164, 166,
    170, 171, 189, 193, 197, 200, 204,
    206, 211, 214
Koets, P. J., 5, 7, 43, 44, 51
Kolakowski, L., 35
Kosman, L. A., 64
Kümmel, W. G., 24, 28
Labriolle, P. de, 8
Lampe, P., 15
Lane, W. L., 15, 117, 146, 158, 161,
    167, 180, 189, 191, 196, 207, 209,
    211, 212, 213
Laub, F., 27
Lausberg, M., 38
Lawrence, D. H., 214
Layton, S. C., 140
Le Poidevin, R., 90
Lee, G. A., 188
Leighton, S. R., 61
Lenglet, A., 189, 204
Lescow, T., 190
Lewis, C. S., 36, 108
Lewis, J. P., 211, 212
Lewis, T. W., 158
Lightfoot, N., 189
Lindars, B., 26, 118, 148
Lloyd, A. C., 69
Loader, W. R. G., 124
Löhr, H., 149, 150, 151
Long, A. A., 80
Lorenzmeier, T., 119

Lubac, H. de, 35
Luckmann, T., 127, 147
Lührmann, D., 43
Lyons, W., 62, 76
MacIntyre, A., 36
Mackay, B. S., 12
Macmullen, R., 8, 40, 46
Malherbe, A. J., 21, 27, 126, 131
Malul, M., 17
Manson, W., 27
Marrow, S. B., 139
Martin, D. B., 34–35, 36
Marx, K., 46, 80
März, C.-P., 27
Maurer, C., 189, 191
McCullough, J. C., 14
Medick, H., 134
Meeks, W. A., 10, 25, 127
Meier, J. P., 15
Melbourne, B. L., 193
Meslier, J., 3
Micka, E. F., 110
Mikalson, J. D., 99
Mitchell, A. C., 26, 139, 142
Moellering, H. A., 43, 44, 51, 85, 86, 98, 103, 108
Moffatt, J. A., 26, 27, 28, 29, 114, 115, 148, 151, 161, 165, 170, 173, 184, 207, 211
Monter, W., 33, 84
Montefiore, H., 14, 173
More, H., 1
Muth, R., 43
Nairne, A., 124
Nauck, W., 146
Nelson, L. D., 112
Nestle, W., 8
Neusner, J., 111, 175
Neyrey, J. H., 25
Niebuhr, H. R., 186
Nikiprowetzky, V., 221
Nikolaidis, A. G., 87–88, 96
Nissilä, K., 26, 124
Nock, A. D., 13
Nussbaum, M. C., 56, 58, 63, 65, 69, 70, 77, 78, 80

O'Neil, M. R., 2
Oakesmith, J., 12, 85, 226
Obbink, D., 46, 79
Olbricht, T. H., 122
Opsomer, J., 34, 87
Otto, R., 110–111, 205
Otto, W., 37
Parker, R., 219
Patrick, J. W., 112
Patterson, C. B., 180
Patterson, R., 58
Peake, A. S., 171, 175
Pears, D., 64
Pease, A. S., 37
Pérez Jiménez, A., 87, 106
Petersen, D. L., 129
Peterson, D., 119, 204
Peterson, E., 144, 157
Pfister, O., 109
Pfitzner, V. C., 119
Phillips, C. R., 17
Phillips, D. Z., 33, 88
Pierce, C. A., 147, 222
Pohlenz, M., 66
Pressman, P., 112
Räisänen, H., 85
Ray, R. J., 33
Reasoner, M., 9
Ren Jiyu, 1, 47
Riddle, J., 4, 19
Riesenfeld, H., 169
Riess, E., 43, 48
Riggenbach, E., 25
Rissi, M., 14, 191
Rist, J. M., 68, 69
Roeth, E. M., 27
Rorty, A. O., 60, 61, 63, 64
Rose, L. L., 35
Rosenbaum, S., 82
Russell, B., 3, 109
Russell, D. A., 86
Sabean, D. W., 134
Salevao, I., 11
Saller, R. P., 126, 181, 182
Salzman, M. R., 38, 39
Sanders, E. P., 9, 18–19, 20

Sandmel, S., 17
Sandnes, K. O., 126, 127
Schadewalt, W., 42
Schäfer, K., 126, 127
Schäfer, P., 40
Scheidweiler, F., 190, 191
Schille, G., 125
Schleiermacher, F., 103, 214
Scholer, J. M., 143
Schoppe, C., 100
Schröger, F., 172, 178, 196, 197
Schweitzer, A., 24
Scott, E. F., 27, 28, 29
Sedley, D. N., 13, 80
Segal, C., 78, 81
Selby, G. S., 222
Shermer, M., 2
Sihvola, J., 56, 57, 58, 63, 65, 66, 71, 75
Smith, J. Z., 12, 18, 19–21
Smith, M., 21–22, 37, 55, 84, 86, 88, 104, 215
Soden, H. von, 27, 28
Solari, J. K., 149
Sorabji, R., 60, 63, 69, 75, 77
Soury, G., 85, 108
Spanneut, M., 66, 67, 92
Sparn, W., 33
Speyer, W., 8
Spicq, C., 26, 43, 112, 115, 118, 122, 131, 139, 151, 155, 163, 165, 167, 170, 171, 183, 189, 210, 211, 212
Spinoza, B., 1, 3, 62
Striker, G., 61
Strobel, A., 197
Swain, S., 14, 57
Swetnam, J., 121, 136, 153–54, 189, 191, 194–95, 197–98
Talmon, S., 17
Taylor, C. C. W., 76
Taylor, J., 3
Taylor, V., 196, 205
Terrien, S., 188, 206
Theissen, G., 14
Thompson, J. W., 26, 27, 169, 213, 221
Thorson, J. A., 112

Thurén, J., 133, 191
Thüsing, W., 28
Thyen, H., 25
Tongue, D. H., 149
Trompf, G. W., 125
Übelacker, W. G., 26
Unnik, W. C. van, 16, 17, 139
Ussher, R. G., 45
Van der Leeuw, G., 3, 97, 111
Vanhoye, A., 212
Vermeule, E., 80
Versnel, H. S., 43
Vivekananda, S., 1
Vögtle, A., 211
Voltaire, 2, 3
Vorster, W. S., 208
Wächter, T., 48
Walters, J. C., 10
Wardman, A., 87
Watson, D., 123
Weiss, H.-F., 14, 24, 27, 28, 29, 110, 119, 122, 142, 147, 166, 167, 211
Weiss, J., 24
Welborn, L. L., 14
Westbrook, R., 174
Westcott, B. F., 122, 130, 131, 165 170, 192, 193, 196, 211, 212
Wette, W. M. L. de, 172
Wickham, E. C., 173
Wikgren, A., 204
Wilken, R. L., 8, 9
Williamson, R., 12, 26, 119, 131
Wilson, S. G., 10
Windisch, H., 190, 210
Wittgenstein, L., 3, 33, 154
Worley, D. R., 120, 122, 123, 160
Wrede, W., 163
Yarnold, E. J., 131
Young, F. M., 221
Zanker, P., 41
Zenger, E., 110
Ziegler, K., 14, 56, 85, 86, 90
Zimmermann, H., 124

Index of Ancient Authors

I. Jewish Texts

Aristeas, Epistle of, 221
Artapanus, 168, 171
2 Baruch, 113
Community Rule (1QS), 221
Exodus Rabbah, 175
Ezekiel the Tragedian, 175
4 Ezra, 113, 115, 139, 145, 209
*Hodayot*ᵃ (1QHᵃ), 212
Josephus, 10, 44, 101, 114, 123, 125, 139, 144, 159, 167, 168, 169, 171, 174, 179, 211, 212
Jubilees, 168, 175
Liber antiquitatum biblicaraum (Ps.-Philo), 167
Melchizedek (11Qmelch), 125
Pesher Habakkuk (1QpHab), 159
Philo, 15, 26–27, 50, 111, 114, 125, 131, 139, 141, 144, 150, 154, 159, 164, 167–68, 169, 170, 171, 174, 198–99, 201, 203, 204, 210, 218, 221
Sukkah, 125
Sibylline Oracles, 211, 212
Testament of Issachar, 174
Testament of Judah, 164
Testament of Levi, 113, 164
Testament of Reuben, 144
Testament of Zebulun, 151

II. Christian Texts

Acts of Thomas
Apocalypse of Peter, 212

Athanasius, 44
Augustine, 7, 12, 38, 170
Barnabas, Epistle of, 147, 148, 188
1 Clement, 14–15, 29, 133, 158, 165, 176, 188, 211
2 Clement, 160, 169, 174, 212
Clement of Alexandria, 5, 7, 44, 48, 49, 185
Didache, 164, 188
Diognetus, Epistle to, 11, 120, 133, 169, 223
Eusebius, 7, 44, 46, 168, 171, 176
Gregory of Nyssa, 49
Hermas, 15, 117, 130, 141, 148, 150, 161, 169, 174, 188
Ignatius of Antioch, 148, 157
Irenaeus, 176
John Chrysostom, 44, 166, 175, 193, 194, 211
Justin Martyr, 7, 29, 197
Lactantius, 2, 38, 65
Melchizedek (NHC IX,*1*), 125
Minucius Felix, 38, 212
Origen, 7, 44, 47
Polycarp, 188
Polycarp, Martyrdom of, 148, 203
Tertullian, 7, 41, 160
Theodoret, 12, 44
Theophilus, 212

III. Greek and Roman Texts

Aelian, 44
Aesop, 100
Alciphron, 45

Alexandri historia, 44
Andronicus (Pseudo-), 50, 69, 71
Anonymus Londonensis, 49
Antipater of Tarsus, 48
Apollonius of Tyana, 222
Appian, 48
Aretaeus, 49
Aristides Quintilianus, 49
Aristotle, 43, 46, 56, 57, 60–65, 68, 72,
    76, 77, 82, 83, 91, 92, 93, 104, 114,
    115, 123–124, 128, 139, 142, 146,
    147, 152, 154, 162, 168, 184, 185,
    187, 202, 217
Arius Didymus, 68
Athenaeus, 44, 47, 48
Aulus Gellius, 38, 69
Chrysippus, 49, 55, 66–75, 90, 106,
    162, 199
Cicero, 1, 10, 11, 37–38, 39, 40, 41, 42,
    66, 67, 68, 69, 71, 72, 75, 77, 78,
    82, 94, 121, 126, 131, 132, 161,
    162, 182
Cleanthes, 66, 67, 72, 73
Columella, 38
Cornutus, 50, 74
Democritus, 45, 79, 80
Demosthenes, 96, 143, 157, 159, 183,
    202
Dio Cassius, 40, 157
Dio Chrysostom, 47, 113, 155
Diodorus Siculus, 43–44, 46, 47, 48,
    49, 113, 179, 202
Diogenes Laertius, 45, 47, 48, 49, 50,
    67, 69, 70, 71, 72, 73, 77, 81, 90,
    143, 184, 185, 202, 222
Dionysius of Halicarnassus, 40
Dionysius Scytobrachion, 49
Epictetus, 29, 67, 69, 70, 72, 73, 75,
    113, 114, 121, 139, 145, 162, 163,
    199–201, 202, 210
Epicurus, 29, 56, 75–82, 96–98, 101,
    103, 163, 169
Epimenides, 47
Erotian, 49
Eudoxus, 45
Euripides, 114, 222

Gaius, 137
Galen, 49, 66, 67, 69, 75
Hecataeus, 45
Heliodorus, 44
Hephaestion, 48, 49
Heraclitus, 47, 48
Herodian, 202
Herodotus, 210
Hierocles, 126, 131
Hippocrates, 35, 45, 100
Homer, 93, 99, 102, 134, 151
Horace, 10, 37, 40
Hyperides, 47
Iamblichus, 48
Isocrates, 155, 159
Juvenal, 10, 38
Livy, 38, 39, 40, 41, 42, 46
Lucian, 44, 47, 49, 139, 143, 157, 164,
    221, 222
Lucretius, 78–79, 80–81, 82, 95
Marcellinus, 47
Marcus Aurelius, 48, 66
Maximus of Tyre, 49, 161, 181, 222
Menander, 45
Ovid, 41, 42
Persius, 10
Phalaris, Epistle of, 46
Philodemus, 48, 82, 115
Plato, 29, 35, 57–59, 62, 68, 69, 70, 72,
    76, 82, 83, 90, 92, 93, 95, 96, 98,
    100, 103, 104, 108, 113, 114, 155,
    157, 162, 202, 210, 222
Plautus, 37
Pliny the Elder, 39, 40, 41
Pliny the Younger, 7–8, 12, 37, 38, 39,
    40, 156, 157
Plutarch, 1, 3, 5 11, 12–15, 21–23, 29,
    30, 33–36, 43, 45, 51–54, 55–57,
    67, 75, 82, 84–108, 113–14, 126,
    128–136, 139, 143–45, 147, 156,
    176, 177, 182, 185, 202, 203,
    215–218, 222, 224–226
Plutarch (Pseudo-), 47, 50, 182, 185
Pollux (*Onomasticon*), 48
Polybius, 46–47, 49, 157, 202
Porphyry, 46, 48, 76

Posidonius, 39, 48, 49, 66, 67, 75, 115
Publilius Syrus, 81
Quintilian, 10, 38, 41, 126
Rufus, Q. Curtius, 38, 39
Scholia in Iliadem, 48
Scholia in Odysseam, 49
Scholia in Thucydidem, 47
Seneca the Elder, 182
Seneca the Younger, 7, 29, 38, 40, 41,
    42, 43, 65, 66, 67, 68, 69, 70, 114,
    181, 182, 185, 222
Sextus Empiricus, 46, 56, 75
Silius Italicus, 38
Sopater, 48
Soranus, 47
Statius, 40
Stobaeus, 46, 49, 50, 69
Strabo, 10, 44, 45, 47
Suetonius, 7–8, 15, 37, 39, 40, 156, 223
Tacitus, 7–8, 10, 37, 38, 39, 40, 41, 42,
    156
Teles the Cynic, 49
Theophrastus, 44, 45–46, 88, 91, 94,
    143, 144, 219
Thucydides, 47, 160
Timaeus of Tauromenium, 45
Timolaus, 48
Crito, Titus Statilius, 47
Twelve Tables, 137
Valerius Maximus, 10, 40, 137, 181,
    183
Varro, 38
Velleius, 41
Virgil, 37
Xenophon, 43, 129, 132, 134
Xenophon of Ephesus, 47
Zaleucus of Locri, 46

Index of Biblical Texts

I. Hebrew Bible

Genesis
3:1–19.. 113
4:1–10.. 135
4:5 135
4:9 135
6:5–8... 211
6:8 LXX... 212
9:8–17... 212
14:17–20................................... 125, 216
15:1... 223
25:25–26.. 135
25:29–34.. 135
25:34... 135
27:32... 135
27:41–45.. 135
28:15... 164
45:10 LXX.. 173

Exodus
1:8–22... 167
1:17 LXX... 167
1:21 LXX... 167
2:1–4.. 5
2:2 .... 167, 168
2:11–15.. 5, 170
2:11–12... 170
2:11 LXX... 169
2:14–15 LXX...................................... 170
2:14... 171, 173
3 .... 171, 207
3:1–4:17.. 175
3:14.. 50
4:10... 140

4:19... 175
7:4 153
8:22... 173
9:26... 173
10–14.. 171
10:21–23.. 176
12–14.. 170
12:1–28... 171
12:7... 175
12:13... 175
12:23 LXX.. 175
12:27... 175
12:31–33.. 171
14:8... 176
14:10... 176
14:13... 176
15 176
17:1–7... 141
19:12–13.. 206
19:16–19.. 206
20:18–19.. 206
32 207
32:7–10... 207
32:30–34.. 208

Leviticus
4:1–5:13... 150
7:12... 221
15:31... 201
20:9... 183

Numbers
12:7... 139, 140
14:1–12... 141
14:21–23... 4

15:22–31 150
20:1–13 140
20:1–6 160
20:6–12 207
33:3 176

Deuteronomy
1:37 207
3:26 207
4 210
4:2 50
4:10–14 207
4:11–12 .... 206, 207
4:15–31 207
4:21–22 207
4:23–24 210
4:24 .... 207, 213
4:33 206
5:16 183
5:22–27 208
5:22–25 206
5:23–26 206
5:28 208
9 207
9:3–7 213
9:3 210
9:14 207
9:19 207
9:20 208
17:6 151
19:15 151
20:3 177
21:15–17 .... 135, 183
21:18–21 183
22:22 183
27:16 183
29:24 LXX 174
31:6 .... 148, 164
31:8 .... 148, 164
32 .... 152, 153
32:22 210
32:35 152
32:36 .... 152, 153

Joshua
1:2 140

1:5 148
3:10 209
5:6–7 166
22:24 201

Judges
6:23 223

1 Samuel
15:22 221
18:25 201
18:29 201

2 Samuel
23:67 210
24:14 153

1 Kings
17:17–24 163

2 Kings
4:17–37 163
17:20 211

1 Chronicles
21:13 153

2 Chronicles
29:31 221

Job
1:6–2:6 114
21:30 LXX 160

Psalms
2:7 133
3:6 165
8:4–6 116
14:5 LXX 211
15:8–11 LXX 197
15:8 LXX 211
21:24 LXX 205
21:25 LXX 205
21:26 LXX 205
22 .... 128, 165, 197, 198, 201
22:1 197

22:3 197
22:6 197
22:12 197
22:16 197
22:22 128
22:23 197
22:25 198
23:4 165
27:1–3 165
31 197
33:6 LXX 144
39 197
39:7–9 LXX 195, 222
40 120
40:6–8 221
40:7–9 .... 159, 216
42 197
46:2 165
47:6 211
48:11 209
49:5 165
50:7–23 221
50:14 221
50:23 221
55:4 LXX 165
55:11 LXX 165
58:6 110
61:3 LXX 211
65:9 LXX 211
69 197
78:49–51 175
83 109
94:8 LXX 141
95:7–11 .... 140, 216
95:9–10 213
109 109
109:6 .... 114, 129
110:1 129
110:4 .... 125, 133, 216
111:6 LXX 211
114 197
114:1 197
114:3 197
114:6 197
114:8 197
116 197

117 LXX 165
117:6 LXX 5, 165
120:3 LXX 211
124:1 LXX 211
135:14 152
137 109
137:9 110
139 109

Proverbs
2:8 201
3 183
3:6 183
3:8 184
3:11–12 .... 178, 179
3:11 177
3:17 184
6:23 178
12:1 178
13:18 178
13:24 178
15:10 178
19:18 178
21:3 221
23:13–24 178
28:14 .... 141, 201
30:5 201

Isaiah
1:10–17 221
2:12–22 147
8:12–13 226
8:18 .... 125, 226
24–27 158
26:6 LXX 151
26:11 151
26:19 158
26:20 .... 157, 158
26:21 158
33:11–14 210
40:9 LXX 117
41:8–10 117
41:9 LXX 117
41:10 .... 117, 223
41:13 LXX 117
41:14 LXX 117

43:1 LXX.. 117
43:5 LXX.. 117
44:2... 117
44:8... 117
51:7... 117
54:4... 117
57:11... 201

Jeremiah
2:1–4:4... 179
4:4 210
7:16... 144
7:21–23... 221
10:10... 209
31 146
31:31–34...................... 116, 216, 221
31:34... 146
38:31–34 LXX.................................... 116
38:32 LXX.. 117
49:1–6... 144

Lamentations
1:8 211

Ezekiel
38:19... 210

Hosea
5:15–6:6.. 179
6:6 221

Joel
1:15... 147
3:14... 147

Amos
4:6–12... 179
5:21–24... 221
8:9–14... 147

Jonah
2:9 221

Micah
7:2 201
7:10 LXX.. 151

Nahum
1:7 201

Habakkuk
2:3–4... 158
2:3 158
2:4 .... 158, 159
2:20... 201

Zephaniah
1:14–18... 147

Haggai
2:6 .... 209, 213

Zechariah
2:13... 201
3:1–10.. 114, 129

Malachi
3:16... 201

II. Deuterocanonical Books

1 Esdras
5:62... 199

Tobit
3:3 150

Wisdom of Solomon
1:12–2:24.. 112
1:13–14... 113
2:17–20... 165
2:17... 165
2:18... 116
2:23–24... 113
4:3 180
4:10–15... 145
4:20–5:23.. 113
6:7 159
10:16... 140
11:21... 176
12:12... 176
16:15... 153
17–18... 175

17:1–18:4......................176
17:3–4..........................176
17:6.............................176
17:8.............................201
17:8–15.........................176
17:11............................176
17:12............................176
17:14–15........................176
17:17–18........................176
17:19............................176
18:5–25.........................176
18:14–15........................176
18:17............................176
18:19............................176
18:20–25........................176
18:25............................175

Sirach
2:18.............................153
4:11.............................116
7:29.............................201
11:17............................201
22:22............................201
24:23............................184
40:1–7...........................112
41:1–4...........................112
41:3.............................200
45:17............................123
45:19............................210
51:12............................191

1 Maccabees
2:32–36..........................101
2:42.............................150
3:30.............................201
9:8..............................177

2 Maccabees
3:17.............................210
6:11.............................201
6:18–7:42........................162
6:26.............................153
7:14.............................194
7:31.............................153
8:16.............................200
11:6.............................199

12:22............................210
12:25............................122

3 Maccabees
1:16.............................199
5:7..............................199
5:25.............................199

4 Maccabees
5–18.............................162
8:2..............................122
8:12–9:9.........................150
8:14.............................150
8:25.............................150
8:28.............................150
13:19–22.........................128

III. New Testament

Matthew
1:21.............................192
3:7...............................22
3:11.............................158
4................................195
4:1..............................114
4:3.........................114, 195
4:6..............................195
5:13.............................151
5:17–48..........................223
5:44.............................110
7:13.............................160
8:7..............................133
9:13.............................221
10:26–31.........................154
10:28............................155
10:32–33.........................169
11:3.............................158
19:17............................119
21:9.............................165
21:42............................165
23:33.............................22
23:39............................165
24:37–39.........................203
26:28............................120
26:36–46.........................195
26:53............................195

26:70..169
26:72..169
27:29..198
27:35..198
27:46............................128, 148, 198

Mark
1:27..133
4:41..133
6:52..141
8:31..194
9:9 194
9:12..198
9:31..194
10:5..141
10:18..119
10:34..194
10:45..120
11:9..165
12:10..165
12:11..165
12:18–27..194
14:28..194
14:32–42..195
15:24..198
15:29..198
15:34..128, 198
16:14..141

Luke
1:12–13..223
1:30..223
1:50..188
1:54..117
1:65..223
1:73..128
2:10..223
2:25..203
3:8 128
10:40..148
12:8–9..169
12:13..134
12:58..114
13:35..165
15:11–32..134
17:26–27..203

18:2..188
18:4..188
18:7..198
18:19..119
19:38..158, 165
20:17..165
21:26..154
22:29–46..195
22:42..119
23:16..122
23:34..198
23:35..198

John
1:12..125
1:27..158
3:16..110
4:34..200
5:25–29..113
5:30..200
6:38–40..200
8:46..119
8:53..128
10:11..120
10:15..120
11 163
12:13..165
12:27..191, 195
13:38..169
18:1–11..195
19:24..198
19:30..204

Acts
2:5 203
2:24..197
2:31..148
2:40..192
3:13–14..168
4:11..165
7:2 128
7:20..168
7:24..170
7:32..207
8:2 203
9:31..188

10:35.. 188
16:16–24....................................... 156
17:22....................................... 6, 44, 48
17:32–34.. 8
20:27.. 159
20:35.. 117
22:12.. 203
24:15.. 154
24:26.. 164
25:19... 6, 44

Romans
1:17.. 159
2:5–10... 113
3:18.. 188
4:13–14... 122
4:16–19... 121
4:16....................................... 122, 128
5:5 198
5:6–9.. 120
5:9 192
5:19... 200
6:1 150
7 22
8:3–4.. 120
8:12–17... 128
8:29.. 125
8:35–36.. 23
12:10... 127
12:13... 164
12:19... 152
14–15... 9
16:1–2... 164

1 Corinthians
1:8 147
1:21–25.. 9
2:3 208
3:13.. 147
5:5 .... 113, 147
7:5 114
10:1–5... 130
10:10... 176
15:3.. 120
15:26... 114
16:5–11.. 164

2 Corinthians
1:10... 191
3:14–18... 223
3:14.. 141
4:4–6.. 123
4:9 148
5:10....................................... 113, 188
5:19–21... 120
5:21.. 119
7:1 188
7:15.. 208
10:5.. 133
11:23... 9

Galatians
1:4 120
3:1 22
3:7 128
3:11.. 160
3:13–14... 120
3:15–17... 136
3:18–19... 122
3:19–29... 223
3:26.. 125
3:29....................................... 122, 128
4:3 22
4:6–7.. 125

Ephesians
1:4 160
1:18.. 123
3:9 123
5:3 164
5:21.. 188
6:5 208

Philippians
1:28.. 160
2:5–11... 200
2:12–13... 214
2:12.. 208
3:19.. 160

Colossians
1:15.. 125
3:22.. 188

1 Thessalonians
3:5 114
4:9 127
5:2 147
5:4 147
5:9–10 120

2 Thessalonians
1:7 210
2:2 147

1 Timothy
1:12 212
3:6–7 114
6:2 117

2 Timothy
1:3 212
2:12 169
4:10 148
4:17 198

Philemon
7 212
22 164

Hebrews
1:1–2 226
1:2–3 118
1:2 ..130, 136, 137, 138, 158, 211, 223
1:3–13 14
1:3 .... 122, 144, 220
1:4 136
1:6 .... 125, 137
1:13 .... 129, 151
1:14 .... 117, 131, 136, 138
2:1 182
2:1–4 209
2:3–4 .... 130, 141
2:3 .... 131, 165
2:4 213
2:6–8 116
2:6 116
2:7 131
2:9 ..113, 116, 119, 120, 131, 134, 190
2:10–18 .... 123, 125, 138, 139

2:10 .... 116, 131, 137, 204
2:11 .... 126, 128, 137, 220
2:12 .... 126, 128, 137, 165, 197, 198
2:13 .... 125, 226
2:14–18 .... 117, 118, 215
2:14–16 5
2:14–15 .... 111, 216
2:14 .... 113, 114, 116, 129, 131
2:15 .... 111, 112, 114, 122, 138, 140
2:16–17 193
2:16 .... 115, 116, 117, 128
2:17 ....115, 116, 124, 125, 126, 131,
    137,138, 143, 194
2:18 .... 114, 124, 139, 165, 193
3:1–6 .... 139, 147, 174, 203
3:1 .... 131, 136, 140, 143, 220
3:2 139
3:5 .... 14, 139
3:6 ...110, 139, 140, 141, 142, 146,
    155, 211
3:7–4:13 140
3:7–4:11 .... 160, 213
3:7 .... 130, 216
3:10–11 142
3:11 .... 4, 141
3:12–19 141
3:12–13 143
3:12 .... 28, 130, 141
3:13 .... 141, 142, 147, 216
3:14 .... 131, 136, 140, 141, 142
3:15 .... 130, 141, 216
3:16 141
3:18–19 141
3:18 141
3:19 .... 141, 160
4:1 .... 122, 136,141, 142
4:2 .... 141, 160, 225
4:3 .... 4, 141, 142
4:5–6 141
4:6–11 216
4:6 .... 141, 225
4:7 .... 130, 141
4:9–11 130
4:11 141
4:12–13 .... 143, 144, 176, 217
4:12 124

4:13...................................5, 124, 143
4:14–5:6.................................196
4:14–16.........................124, 143, 146
4:14–15.................................133
4:14.....................................143
4:15....................118, 119, 131, 188
4:16....124, 133, 139, 143, 144, 165,
    212, 213
5:1–3....................................220
5:2 ....131, 150
5:5–10..................................216
5:5–6....................................133
5:6 120
5:7–10..................................203
5:7–8..............................113, 189
5:7 ...5, 31, 119, 188, 189, 190, 191,
    192, 194, 195, 196, 197, 198, 199,
    200, 201, 203, 205, 209, 224
5:8–10..................................133'
5:8–9..............................195, 204
5:8 ....132, 190, 203, 204
5:9 ....131, 132, 133, 138, 169, 203
5:10.....................................196
5:11–14.......................150, 182, 203
5:12–6:1..................................28
5:12.....................................203
5:13.....................................203
5:14................................203, 204
6:1–2.....................................28
6:1 ....28, 204
6:2 ....113, 192, 220
6:4–8....................................178
6:4–6........................130, 148, 149
6:4 123
6:6 129
6:7–8..............113, 160, 211, 224
6:8 211
6:9 131
6:10...............................15, 220
6:11–12..................................182
6:11.....................................211
6:12–15..................................122
6:12...............................136, 184
6:13.....................................136
6:15.....................................136
6:16.....................................129

6:17...........................122, 136, 184
6:18.................................176,211
6:20...............................125, 134
7:1–10:18...............123, 217, 218, 220
7:1–28...................................216
7:1–10...................................137
7:1......................................145
7:3 ....113, 120, 131, 133, 172
7:6 136
7:7 129
7:11.....................................192
7:12...............................133, 223
7:14...............................165, 193
7:15.....................................192
7:16...............................131, 133
7:17.....................................120
7:18.....................................223
7:19...............................133, 211
7:20.....................................120
7:25...........................120, 131, 144
7:26–28..................................119
7:26.....................................220
7:27–28..................................204
7:27...........................11, 148, 220
7:28...............................120, 133
8–10.......................................5
8:1–5.....................................26
8:1......................................122
8:3......................................220
8:4......................................122
8:6 ....122, 134, 136
8:6–9:14.................................136
8:6–13...................................216
8:6–7....................................223
8:8–12..............................146, 221
8:8 ....116, 146, 147
8:9 116
8:10.....................................147
8:12.....................................129
8:13...........................11, 213, 223
9:7 150
9:9 ....118, 144, 220, 222
9:10.....................................223
9:11–14...................................11
9:11......................................26
9:12...........................122, 148, 169

9:13–14 .... 220, 222
9:13 220
9:14 .... 28, 118, 144
9:15–22 133
9:15–17 .... 113, 136, 137, 138
9:15 .... 134, 136, 169, 184
9:17–22 195
9:17 136
9:22 220
9:23–24 26
9:23 .... 220, 221
9:24 134
9:25–28 11
9:26 .... 200, 220, 223
9:27 .... 112, 113, 217
9:28 .... 113, 118, 131, 147, 148, 158
10:1–18 11
10:1–2 .... 220, 222
10:1 .... 26, 133, 220
10:2 .... 118, 144
10:3 129
10:5–10 .... 120, 195, 200, 216, 222
10:5–9 159
10:5 220
10:6 118
10:7 120
10:8 .... 118, 133, 220
10:9 .... 120, 223
10:10 .... 148, 200, 220
10:11 220
10:12–13 129
10:12 .... 122, 123, 220
10:13 151
10:14 220
10:16–17 146
10:17 .... 129, 146, 224
10:19–31 145
10:19–25 .... 145, 149, 150
10:19–22 150
10:19 .... 110, 139, 145, 146, 154
10:21 .... 146, 147, 203
10:22 ... 118, 144, 146, 147, 148, 220, 222
10:23 .... 136, 147, 148, 155
10:24–25 .... 118, 147
10:24 129

10:25 .... 113, 129, 148, 149, 157, 158
10:26–31 ... 130, 148, 149, 152, 154,
    160, 178, 217
10:26–30 211
10:26–27 160
10:26 .... 150, 152, 153, 220
10:27 .... 4, 113, 134, 149, 151, 153, 224
10:28–29 .... 133, 151
10:28 155
10:29–31 154
10:29–30 4
10:29 .... 129, 152, 213, 220
10:30 .... 113, 147, 152, 153, 158
10:31 ...... 4, 29, 109, 149, 153, 154, 214
10:32–39 ... 124, 149, 150, 155, 156,
    166, 175, 182
10:32–34 .... 15, 156, 160, 162, 164
10:32 123
10:34–36 164
10:34–35 160
10:34 .... 154, 155, 161, 164, 169
10:35–36 .... 154, 184
10:35 .... 110, 139, 154, 155, 157
10:36 .... 136, 157, 159, 204
10:37–39 157
10:37–38 158
10:37 157
10:38–39 159
10:38 159
10:39 .... 159, 160
11   .... 121, 173
11:1–40 225
11:1 .... 120, 142, 168
11:3 120
11:4 .... 113, 135
11:5 .... 113, 159
11:6 .... 5, 29, 120, 144, 145, 186, 225
11:7 ... 120, 136, 184, 188, 203, 211,
    212, 224
11:8–10 160
11:8–9 122
11:8 136
11:9 .... 136, 138
11:10 .... 121, 151, 184
11:11 136
11:12–13 122

11:12.....................................113, 121
11:13–16.........................162, 212, 224
11:13.........................113, 122, 131, 136
11:16...122
11:17–19.....................................121
11:17...136
11:18...121
11:19...........................113, 192, 195
11:20...121
11:21–22.....................................121
11:21...113
11:22...121
11:23–31.....................................166
11:23–29.....................................121
11:23–28....................5, 166, 185, 215
11:23....................................166, 170
11:24–26............................168, 173
11:24...169
11:26...121
11:26..............................121, 169, 174
11:27...............170, 171, 172, 173, 174
11:28–29.....................................171
11:28...............................166, 171, 175
11:29...............................113, 166, 176
11:30–31.....................................166
11:31....................................113, 121
11:32–40.....................................224
11:32–38............................121, 156, 161
11:32...4
11:33...136
11:35...............113, 162, 163, 192, 194
11:37.......................................14, 113
11:39–12:2.................................131
11:39–40.....................................122
11:39...............................131, 136, 162
11:40...............................131, 132, 162, 164
12 22
12:1–13..............................132, 170
12:1........................118, 122, 131, 182
12:2..........121, 122, 125, 138, 193, 200
12:3–4...124
12:3...............................121, 129, 182
12:4–11.................................22, 201
12:4........................118, 162, 177, 185
12:5–11....125, 151, 177, 178, 182, 204
12:5–6.............................178, 179, 183

12:5.............................177, 179, 182
12:6...181
12:7–11.....................................181
12:7....................................179, 180
12:8...............................180, 181, 183
12:9....................................129, 182
12:10–11.....................................184
12:10....................................184, 220
12:11...184
12:12–13.....................................131
12:13...183
12:14–15............................136, 220
12:15...213
12:16–17.....................................135
12:16...135
12:17....................................135, 136
12:18–29.....................31, 206, 213
12:18–24.................................5, 208
12:18–21............................207, 209
12:18....................................144, 206
12:19–20.....................................206
12:19...206
12:21...............................206, 207, 208
12:22–24.....................................213
12:22...............................144, 208, 209
12:23–24.....................................209
12:23......................113, 209, 217, 225
12:24...............................134, 135, 208
12:25–29.....................................224
12:25...............................209, 210, 212
12:26–29.....................................212
12:26....................................136, 209
12:27....................................169, 211
12:28–29......4, 111, 154, 188, 206, 209
12:28............5, 160, 188, 210, 212, 213
12:29...............................110, 207, 213
13:1–19.....................................184
13:1–5...5
13:1....................................127, 164
13:2...164
13:3...............................124, 157, 164
13:4......................113, 163, 217, 220
13:5–6.......................................165
13:5....................................125, 164
13:6......5, 124, 156, 163, 164, 165, 215
13:7.....................................15, 165

13:8..148
13:9..213
13:11...118
13:12..193, 220
13:14..122, 169
13:15–16..221
13:16...159
13:17..15, 133
13:18...144
13:20–21...192
13:20........................165, 169, 193
13:21..159, 204
13:24........................14, 15, 220
13:25...213

James
1:2–8...170
1:16–17..144
5:20..191

1 Peter
1:2 133
1:22..127
2:7 165
2:9 160
2:17..188
2:22..119
3:14–15..226
3:18........................119, 120, 148
3:20–21..203
4:5–6...113
4:9 164
5:8 198

2 Peter
1:7 127
2:5 211
3:5–13...212
3:7 ....160, 210
3:10..147
3:12–14..155

1 John
2:2 120
3:5 119
4:10..120

4:16..110
4:17–18..23, 139

3 John
5–8 164

Jude
4 169

Revelation
1:5 125
1:17..223
2:10..114
6:8 114
11:15...198
11:18...188
12:9–10..114
14:6..188
15:4..188
19:5..198
20:13...114

Printed in the United States
15873LVS00003B/55-153